The Politics of Autonomy in L

M000204008

Non-Governmental Public Action

Series Editor: **Jude Howell**, Professor in International Development, London School of Economics and Political Science, UK

Non-governmental public action (NGPA) by and for disadvantaged and marginalised people has become increasingly significant over the past two decades. This new book series is designed to make a fresh and original contribution to the understanding of NGPA. It presents the findings of innovative and policy-relevant research carried out by established and new scholars working in collaboration with researchers across the world. The series is international in scope and includes both theoretical and empirical work.

The series marks a departure from previous studies in this area in at least two important respects. First, it goes beyond a singular focus on developmental NGOs or the voluntary sector to include a range of non-governmental public actors such as advocacy networks, campaigns and coalitions, trade unions, peace groups, rights-based groups, cooperatives and social movements. Second, the series is innovative in stimulating a new approach to international comparative research that promotes comparison of the so-called developing world with the so-called developed world, thereby querying the conceptual utility and relevance of categories such as North and South.

Titles include:

The Politics of Autonomy in Latin America

The Art of Organising Hope

Ana Cecilia Dinerstein
Associate Professor, Department of Social and Policy Sciences, University of Bath, UK

First published 2015 by
PALGRAVE MACMILLAN

Palgrave Macmillan in the UK is an imprint of Macmillan Publishers Limited,
registered in England, company number 785998, of Houndmills, Basingstoke,
Hampshire RG21 6XS.

Palgrave Macmillan in the US is a division of St Martin's Press LLC,
175 Fifth Avenue, New York, NY 10010.

Palgrave Macmillan is the global academic imprint of the above companies
and has companies and representatives throughout the world.

Palgrave® and Macmillan® are registered trademarks in the United States,
the United Kingdom, Europe and other countries

ISBN 978-1-349-32298-5   ISBN 978-1-137-31601-1 (eBook)

DOI 10.1057/9781137316011

A catalogue record for this book is available from the British Library.

Library of Congress Cataloging-in-Publication Data

Dinerstein, Ana C.
    The politics of autonomy in Latin America: the art of organising hope in the
    twenty-first century / Ana Cecilia Dinerstein (associate professor, Department
    of Social and Policy Sciences, University of Bath, UK).
        pages cm

    1. Latin America – Politics and government – 1980–2. Latin America – History –
Autonomy and independence movements. 3. Latin America – Social conditions –
1982–4. Social movements – Latin America. 5. Autonomy (Philosophy) – Latin
America. 6. Indigenous peoples – Latin America – Politics and government. 7. Hope –
Political aspects – Latin America. 8. Hope – Social aspects – Latin America. 9. Political
participation – Latin America. I. Title.

F1414.3.D56 2014
320.09809′04—dc23   2014026513

Transferred to Digital Printing in 2014

To my son Owain Naum, a daydreamer

Contents

List of Illustrations

Figures

Tables

Foreword

There is only one reality. The world as it exists is not true. It is false. It is false because the satisfaction of human needs is merely a sideshow. What counts is the profitable accumulation of some abstract form of wealth, of money that yields more money. What cannot be turned into profit is burned. Failure to make a profit entails great danger. To the vanishing point of death, the life of the class tied to work hangs by the success of turning her human effort into profit as the fundamental condition of achieving wage-based employment. The alternatives are bleak. The class struggle to sustain access to the means of subsistence and maintain labour conditions is relentless. Yesterday's profitable appropriation of some other person's labour buys another Man today, the buyer for the sake of making another profit, the seller in order to make a living. What can the seller of redundant labour power trade in its stead – body and body substances: how many for pornography, how many for prostitution, how many for kidney sales?

Capitalist wealth entails the pauper in its concept. It recognises the pauper as a self-responsible entrepreneur of labour power. In a world of entrepreneurs, enterprise counts and the pauper is thus one who did not employ her labour power well. Human significance vanishes in the form of economic quantities that are measured and calculated with winning intent. Man is the existing untruth in her own social world – at worst, she figures as a metaphysical distraction in the game of economic numbers. At best, she is recognised as the human material of economic quantities – a factor of production, a mere resource, a means for profit. Some say she needs to be paid more and work in better conditions. This is undoubtedly the case. Still its truth is a moment of the false. As an existing untruth, society as economic subject manifests the topsy-turvy world of price and profit in the demand for a just treatment of the mistreated. Time is money and money makes the world go round. In this dazzling world, Man is little more than a time's carcass. Life-time is labour time. The class tied to work struggles for life-time, on the condition that its labour time is competitive on a world-market scale. Failure to achieve this competitive edge over her labouring brothers and sisters reduces this struggle for life-time to a desperate scramble to make ends meet. On the pain of ruin, the existing relations of wealth demands from the Many that they become self-responsible entrepreneurs of their labour power, always eager and ready to adjust to the movement of the economic forces, whatever it takes. Society as the subject of economic forces moves in mysterious ways – for the sake of making a living, it requires the social individuals that comprise society to respond to price signals and adjust to the vagaries of the conditions of trade in labour power. The society of Man manifests itself as the object of a movement of economic things. The real social subject is the economic thing. Political economy captures this well when it says that society as economic subject is regulated by the invisible hand. The invisible is beyond human control. In its secular manifestation, the invisible appears in the form of great economic success for the few or bankruptcy, profitability or insolvency, wage-based access to subsistence or redundancy of labour power. Without warning and at the blink of an eye, the invisible force of capitalist wealth cuts off the supply of the means of subsistence to a whole class of individuals, measured by the rates of unemployment and poverty. The dogma of the false society is that there is no alternative to it, that is, its falsehood is self-righteous.

A critical social theory that explores the meaning of the economic forces and the categories of price and profit is often either rejected as a form of economic reductionism that stands accused of reducing refined social values to economic calculation, or belittled for its alleged analytical blindness that condemns it to perceive of society as an economic derivative. These views contain elements of false truth. The economy really does not have an independent existence. In its entirety, capitalist economy is a perverted form of human social relations. That is, the idea of a social theory beyond the critique of political economy is innately optimistic about the prospects of society. Having freed itself from the fateful economic forces, which movements establish the access to the means of subsistence, sociology becomes a discipline without society. It does not talk about the devil and looks on the bright side. It thus recognises the poverty of nations, if indeed its analytical gaze turns upon it at all, as a miserable market situation, which resolution demands a hegemonic shift in the balance of the contesting social forces to bring in a government that governs for the poor. Sociology without a concept of society does not ask about the social conditions of misery. The experience of misery is entirely alien to it. Misery revolts.

Hegemony is not a critical concept. Its grasp of society is entirely traditional in that it views society as nothing more than a manifestation of the balance of class forces. Its conception of the social forces is purely instrumental. It rejects the hegemony of the capitalist interests, demands the hegemony of the working class, argues for class struggle as the means at shifting the balance of class forces in favour of the working class and leaves the category of 'capital' entirely untouched by thought. What really does it mean to say that the working class has to become hegemonic in capitalism? Is capital really nothing more than some economic means that is corrupted by the capitalist interests? In its practical dimension, the struggle for hegemony amounts to 'ticket thinking'. Such thinking is 'one-dimensional'. It argues in the interests of the dispossessed traders in labour power with a claim to power. That is, instead of stopping to make capitalism, it demands to govern for the sake of a capitalism that works for the workers. The last century was filled with dogmas that have cost us time, suffering and much injustice. It rejected the critique of class society by speaking out for the working class. The critical judgement according to which the being of the productive labourer is a great misfortune was thus turned on its head, leading to the dogma of the productive labourer as an ontological privilege. It, thus, embraced the mad utopia of a rationalised labour economy as the solution to the capitalist question.

The critical concept is governmentality. Society as the economic subject of money that begets more money is hostile to the needs of the social individuals and yet, it is their work. Neither the capitalist nor the banker, nor indeed the worker, can extricate him/herself from the reality in which they live and which asserts itself not only over them but also through them, and by means of them. Society as economic subject prevails through the individuals. Money does not only make the world go round; its possession establishes the connection to the means of life. The struggle for life is a struggle for money – it governs the mentality of bourgeois society and establishes the force of its coined freedom. What a misery! In the face of great social wealth, the dispossessed sellers of labour power struggle for fleeting amounts of money to sustain themselves from one day to the next as the readily available human material for capitalist wealth. Class and struggle are categories of the false society. Its progress has to come to a stop – but how?

Ana Dinerstein's fine book is about this how in the experience of the immense eruption of collective action across Latin America since the end of the last century. Her concerns are entirely removed from the traditional analyses of the so-called pink tide, and its arguments about and for hegemony and the use of state power to achieve a capitalism for the workers. She brings to life the explosion of anger, collective action, attempts at self-government and self-determination of social reproduction – this democracy of the streets, from the assembly to the squares, from the occupied factories to the transformation of the land into a social commons. In distinction to the coined freedom of bourgeois society, this savage democracy demands the satisfaction of human needs and organises social reproduction by its own effort. The pink tide really is the ghost-walking manifestation of this tremendous experimentation in alternative, self-determined forms of social existence. She brings the struggle of social autonomy to the fore as entirely subversive of the existing forces of the wealth of nations and their governmentality of an ordered law of coinage. This struggle cracks the existent respectability of the relations of price and profit; it fissures the synthesis of the false and establishes interstices of alternative practices to social reproduction, in which time is no longer money but rather the satisfaction of human needs. This book goes against the grain. It brings to light what is hidden and establishes the practical meaning of social autonomy in the experienced rage of alter-capitalist experimentation – not to establish a competitor to the capitalist economy of labour but to go beyond it for good.

The *Politics of Autonomy in Latin America* does not look at the bright side. It presents the courage of experienced negation. Its reality is its own uncertainty – it is, says Ana Dinerstein, a social autonomy that does not exist. All that exists is the praxis towards social autonomy that produces the many cracks, interstices, forms of self-government, prefiguring a society aware of itself and thus one that instead of being governed by the movement of abstract economic quantities, governs itself to achieve satisfaction. Dinerstein's journey of alter-capitalist discovery is led by Ernst Bloch's philosophy of hope. In a hopeless world, hope is not powerless. It empowers by cracking the façade of a world that says that there is no alternative. Dinerstein's critical theory of hope is born in the experienced struggle of the great Latin American adventure of rage and self-determination. Nothing is what it seems.

Werner Bonefeld
University of York, UK

Foreword

My *maestro* Raimon Panikkar used to say that a Foreword should be an introductory word about the author, the book and the subject. I declare my admiration for the book and my passion for the subject, and that I only know the author in this way, i.e. through the book and the subject, and through a brief and fascinating correspondence.

As Ana Dinerstein states well in her introduction, autonomy as a form of resistance is not new in Latin America, and it comes from afar. While to label the struggles against colonisation as 'autonomous' would be to colonise the past, these resistances evidently had an autonomic character, in the sense that we give the word today. The struggles of the past were always for the *ejido* – the term, which is derived from *exitus*, designates those common areas shared by peasants, which were located at the outskirts of the Spanish towns in the XVI century. Lacking another term, the Spaniards called *ejidos* the complex and diverse communal regimes encountered on their arrival to the continent. By the end of the eighteenth century, the struggle for the *ejidos* had created what the Spaniards called the 'Indian Republics', i.e. clear forms of self-government and self-determination. Although the indigenous peoples fought for the independence of the *ejidos* and for being able to settle in them, the opposite occurred: they lost everything that they had conquered during the nineteenth century. The Mexican Revolution of 1910 – the first social revolution of the twentieth century – erupted with a call for the 'recovery of the *ejidos*'. Present day struggles of the indigenous peoples belong to that tradition.

During the 1920s the word autonomy acquired a special meaning in Mexico, when it was used to vindicate university autonomy. Autonomy was understood as a special form of sovereignty until 1968. Then, for the first time, a government dared to intervene at a university campus. In neighbourhoods and villages, the term autonomy was employed in another sense, which anticipated the present use of the word. In the 1970s, we used the name 'Analysis, Development and Management' (Análisis, Desarrollo y Gestión, ANADEGES) to designate an independent body that coordinated a group of civil organisations working for farmers, indigenous and urban marginal people. In the 1980s, after listening to what people (whose service we were at) really wanted, we changed the name of the organisation to 'Autonomy, Decentralism and Management' (Autonomía, Decentralismo y Gestión): instead of 'development', people were trying to make their own ways of living and governing to be respected by others. This change was not as significant in the attitudes of ordinary people, as in the perception of those who stood alongside them in the effort to produce social change.

The earthquake of 19 September 1985 in Mexico City led to an explosion of popular initiatives that took everyone by surprise. In search for a word that could describe that social and political novelty, i.e. that social quake, the word *autonomy* emerged together with a renewed notion of *civil society* to designate a new semantic of social transformation.

As this process of transformation from below was taking place in Mexico and elsewhere, another version of autonomy began to circulate in Latin America. Hector Díaz Polanco and Gilberto López y Rivas articulated a Leninist version of autonomy in Mexico, which led to the creation of the Plural National Indigenous Assembly for Autonomy (Asamblea Nacional India y Plural por la Autonomía, ANIPA) in 1995. ANIPA gathered important indigenous organisations, and finally became a political association to participate in the electoral process. This version of autonomy was attractive to the Sandinistas, who were trying to procrastinate the fulfilment of their promise of land distribution and recognition of autonomy made during the war against Somoza. This 'Mexican' formulation of the notion of autonomy that is used in Spain believes that 'self-management' or 'autonomous government' is 'a specific type of governmental order constituted by a system of vertical powers that correspond to the organization of the State' (Díaz Polanco, 1996: 109). Commenting on such regime, when it was established in Nicaragua, a Sumo leader asserted in 1994: 'No doubt it has interesting elements. What we are questioning is whether it can be truly democratic' (Esteva, 2003: 253).

At the beginning of the negotiations between the Zapatistas and the government in 1995, the Zapatistas invited around hundred advisors to Chiapas. At the first meeting in the jungle, Díaz Polanco, one of them stated that autonomy was the most important issue to be negotiated with the government and that, in order to be able to advise the Zapatistas on the matter, it was indispensable to know what their notion of autonomy was. Subcomandante Marcos went on to mention that the Zapatistas applied autonomy practically and daily in their communities, but they knew that theirs was not the only or necessarily the best one. He noted that they had invited the advisors to help formulate one definition that could achieve consensus among the indigenous peoples, for that was the one which was going to be negotiated with the authorities.

The stream led by Díaz Polanco failed to convince the rest of the Zapatistas' advisors, and ANIPA did no better with indigenous peoples. The notion of autonomy that obtained general consensus and was further translated into a limited and provisional fashion in the San Andrés Accords neither contained any element of separatism (does not pursue the creation of an indigenous state) nor did it fit into the design of the nation state either. The autonomic proposal of the indigenous peoples in Mexico has sought to recover the powers and competences that have been taken away from them since the time of the Colony, in order to dispose of their own political and jurisdictional spaces freely, where they can exercise their way of life and government. This notion of autonomy reformulates self-determination as the freedom and capacity to unreservedly take decisions in their own spaces, and to determine, together with other peoples and cultures, ways of living together based on an intercultural dialogue that transcends the totalitarianism of the *logos* and the predominance of one culture, as well as delineate a new horizon of intelligibility in a political design that would no longer be that of the nation state. This notion of autonomy emerged from the indigenous peoples, but may apply to other peoples or social groups, and it is, indeed, what has been taking place. As researched rigorously in this book, with their countless shades and patterns, these two types of autonomy, which negate one another, continue, day after day, to prevail in Latin America.

Ana Cecilia Dinerstein notes, firstly, that since the 1980s there has been a recreation of autonomy by many diverse groups in Latin America, which is simultaneously both a mobilising utopia and an organisational form that prefigures alternatives with political imagination. For her, prefiguration is a 'process of learning hope'. This approach, which guides the entire book, is of enormous importance and enriches substantially the reflection about autonomy. It is a method that effectively shows that there has been an epistemological rupture in reality itself, and that to accept this rupture is vital in order to see and understand what is happening. This is something that cannot be accomplished by those dedicated to conquest or administer the state and want to give autonomy a state form, like Díaz Polanco.

Dinerstein safely escapes both the cul-de-sac that conventional debates about autonomy have reached and the ideological classification of autonomy, particularly in relation to Marxism and Anarchism. This involves recognition of the originality of social practices that are themselves theories, and which are clearly rooted in diverse theoretical traditions and practices but cannot be reduced to them. In relation to the

Zapatistas, for example, instead of attempting to lock them into some contemporary ideological or theoretical classification, there has been increasingly an explicit recognition of the quantity and quality of their innovations. Trying to identify doses of Marxism and Anarchism and other theoretical and ideological currents in their practices is a sterile exercise; in case that a label is required, they are Neo-Zapatistas.

With her idea of prefiguration, Dinerstein radically abandons a position that hangs political initiatives and mobilisations from some kind of Promised Land. This position operates under the principle of a separation between means and ends, which has proved tragic for the left: anything goes, as long as high ideals are maintained, and meanwhile the present is transformed into an always postponed future. The utopian force of autonomy, according to Dinerstein, does not reside in a new formulation of the future but is rooted in the present; it is what is not yet but is already there. While prefiguration can be regarded as a strategy, which involves the separation of means from ends and cannot be detached from its military origin, it also implies the need to give the struggle the shape of its outcome. To Dinerstein, autonomy, a tool for prefiguration, ultimately transcends all demarcations imposed on social reality by the dominant regime. Autonomy is immersed in those demarcations, but cannot be reduced to the logic of power and the patriarchal mentality that determines them.

To present her argument, Dinerstein engages wisely with Ernst Bloch's thought. She separates hope from fantasy or mere desire, finding it instead as a hidden dimension of reality that clearly characterises autonomous movements in Latin America. As it is anticipated in the introduction, by exploring the art of organising the hope by these movements, Dinerstein escapes the dichotomy 'autonomy–the State' and shows the connections between indigenous and non-indigenous autonomous practices. In the process, she points to the limitations of the governments of Argentina, Bolivia, Brazil, Ecuador and Venezuela, which are usually attributed the leading role in the revolutionary fervour of the region. She also dares courageously and perceptively to take her analysis to the abstract terrain of the value form.

An additional merit of the book is the author's good knowledge of history which helps presenting the causes and the conditions under which these movements operate without serious distortions. The theoretical and empirical territory that Dinerstein covers in this book is immense. It is inevitable, therefore, that there are some small inaccuracies or inadequacies. Even the strictest demarcation of the subject demands an examination of complex and diverse realities, in constant transformation, and these perceived from very different theoretical and ideological lenses. A rigorous study of the past and present features of each of the movements that must be taken into account in this book would require such a long time that they would be always fall short and obsolete, in view of the dynamics within which they are all immersed.

Instead of falling into the many temptations that she encountered in the process of writing this book, Dinerstein carefully maintains the thread of her exploration, which is presented as her initial hypothesis and her conclusion, the careful construction of which, in today's tragic moment, amid widespread uncertainty and an increasing despair, is appropriately examined in the book. Hope and surprise appear as the two fundamental pillars of the effort for social transformation. Hope is the essence of popular movements and to retrieve it as a social force has become the condition for survival. By showing autonomy as a form of learning hope, Dinerstein makes sure that her analysis functions as a powerful torch illuminating the present reality. She has made a good decision choosing Latin America as the empirical site for her study of autonomy: it is here that autonomy has been deployed with greatest intensity, creativity and vigour. But by showing autonomy as the art of organising hope, she also reveals that it is a form that already circumscribes social struggles in the twenty-first century world-wide.

Gustavo Esteva
Founder of the Universidad de la Tierra, Oaxaca, Mexico

Acknowledgements

Soy del Sur, como los aires del bandoneón

I started writing this book only four years ago, but the 'production' process began, as one might expect, several centuries ago, or at least this is what it feels like. It is still, as it should be, a resounding unfinished product. The book was written during daydreams, during solitary sleepless nights and during sleep. But the argument came out of copious dialogues, conversations, polemics, by e-mail, and at meetings, workshops, talks, public seminars, and during the production of co-authored working papers, books and articles. This was a remarkable learning process: learning with and about the movements, learning about myself and, above all, learning hope. I am grateful to an awful lot of people who accompanied me in this expedition, but I must be selective.

The book draws mainly from the findings of two research projects funded by the Economic and Social Research Council (UK), Non-Governmental Public Action programme, titled 'The movement of the unemployed in Argentina' and 'Social movements and autonomous organising in Latin America' (RES 155–25–0007). The programme provided an exciting environment for my research and I would like to acknowledge the financial support of the ESRC and thank Professor Jude Howell, the programme director, for her guidance and encouragement during the life of the programme and after. I am indebted to my research team: Daniel Contartese, Melina Deledicque, Luciana Ghiotto and Rodrigo Pascual who were committed to the research projects as much as I was, and their participation in the fieldwork and case study research reports have been crucial to the book. We are all grateful to the movements' activists, interviewees and those who helped us to collect material during different stages of the 'fact finding' between 2005 and 2010, and who have continued to provide us with updated information up until now. Thanks to Luciana Ghiotto for the cover photo.

I have the big-hearted colleagues and friends, both from mine and other institutions, who took the time to read either the whole manuscript or draft chapters and provided invaluable written and/or oral comments: Sarah Amsler, Werner Bonefeld, Laurence Cox, Roger Merino Acuña, Sara Motta, Mike Neary, Daniel Ozarow, Marina Sitrin (with her baby son Camilo), Gregory Schwartz and Graham Taylor. Werner Bonefeld and Gustavo Esteva honoured me with their generous and insightful *Forewords* to my book. Mike Neary and Gustavo Esteva rescued me on time from two moments of confusion with regards to coloniality and capital, and thanks to Marcos and Zapatismo, respectively; both pointed me in the right direction with firm kindness and honesty. And John Holloway, supportive as ever, discussed Chapters 8 and 9 of the manuscript with his Master students attending the seminar 'Esperanza y Crisis' (Hope and Crisis) at the Benemérita Universidad Autónoma de Puebla (BUAP) in June 2014. Therefore many thanks to John, Katerina, Carlos, Yatzel, Blanca, Edelmira, Daniele, Tania, Edith, Sagrario, Fernanda and Byron!

My gratitude also goes to those who joined my presentations at workshops, talks, seminars, symposiums and conferences over the last six years for their inputs have enriched the book from its inception: the ESRC programme workshops 'NGPA in Latin America' (Bradford, 2008); 'NGPA Final Conference' and the 'CINEFOGO Conference', Centre for Civil Society, LSE (London, 2009); the Third Latin American and European Meeting on Organisation Studies, LAEMOS (Buenos Aires, 2010). I acknowledge the support of the British Academy to attend events such as the Historical Materialism Annual Conference (2013); the symposium titled 'A Decade on from the Argentinazo 2001–2011', Institute for the Study of the Americas (London, December 2011); the Annual Conferences of the Society for Latin American Studies SLAS 2012 and 2014; the 'Sociology and Contemporary Global Social Activism' conference convened by St Mary's University College & University of Roehampton (London, 2012); Radical Americas Conference at the Institute for the Americas (London, 2013); and the British Sociological Association Annual Conference (London, 2013).

The whole argument of this book was exposed and scrutinised at four events: the international symposium 'Potential and Limits of the Social and Solidarity Economy' convened by the United Nations Research Institute for Social Development (UNRISD), sponsored by International Labour Organisation (ILO) (Geneva, 2013); the Bloch Symposium at Central Saint Martins, London Graduate School in association with the Centre for Research in Modern European Philosophy and the Centre for Ernst Bloch Studies (London, December 2013); the symposium Prefiguring Democratic Education at the Centre for Educational Research and Development and the Social Science Centre (Lincoln, May 2014); and at the CSE Trans-Pennine Working Group roundtable (Manchester, July 2014). Thank you all for your insightful suggestions.

I am also obliged to my brilliant PhD students, Kate Burrell, Roger Merino Acuña and Frederick Harry Pitts, who 'supervise me' with their ideas and suggestions and to my undergraduate and postgraduate students attending my courses on Political Sociology, Political Sociology of Globalisation, the Politics of Policy in International Context, and Comparative Industrial Relations, for the argument of the book was too often topic of class discussion.

Over the four years, the book manuscript was several times in intensive care. *Muchas gracias* to my friends from Buenos Aires, England and other geographies for being there for me. They are, as Catalan songwriter Joan Manuel Serrat says, 'catch-dreamers, and devoted people who turn up when they know I need them ... for them friendship is first.' And thank you to Professor Ian Butler from the University of Bath who cheered me up with an old joke: 'Willie Rushton used to tell about two people who meet at a dinner party. The first one asks the other what he is up to. The second one answers, "I'm writing a book", to which the first one replies "Neither am I".' My publisher Christina Brian, however, is not laughing! I am infinitely grateful to her and to Ambra Finotello for being sympathetic, helpful and patient beyond words, to Palgrave Macmillan proof readers and editors and to staff who have previously dealt with my book: Alexandra Webster, Liz Blackmore, Renee Takken and Amanda McGrath.

Last but not least, Gregory Schwartz gets my recognition for many years of unconditional support – with IT and Mac, and with life in general. Special thanks – why not? – go to my *koshka* Ella for her company and enchanting purring. The book is wholeheartedly dedicated to my son Owain, a 'young warrior' for being my source of inspiration energy and sense of direction. All the customary disclaimers apply.

List of Abbreviations and Acronyms

AC	Asamblea Constituyente (Constituent Assembly)
ALBA	Alternativa Bolivariana para los Pueblos de Nuestra America (Bolivarian Alternative for the Peoples of Our America)
ANP	Agência Nacional do Petróleo, Gás Natural e Biocombustíveis (Brazilian National Oil Agency)
ARIC	Asociación Regional Independiente de Campesinos (Peasants Independent Regional Association)
AVs	Asambleas Vecinales o de Vecinos (Neighbours' Assemblies)
BPN	Bloque Piquetero Nacional (National Piquetero Block)
CCIR	Comité Clandestino Indígena Revolucionario (Clandestine Indigenous Revolutionary Committee)
CCRI-CG	Comité Clandestino Revolucionario Indígena-Comandancia General
CDAYV	Coordinadora en Defensa del Agua y la Vida (The Network for the Defence of Water and Life)
CEPAL	Comisión Económica para América Latina y el Caribe (Economic Commission for Latin America and the Caribbean)
CGP	Centros de Gestión y Participación (Centres of Management and Participation)
CGT	Confederación General del Trabajo (General Workers Confederation)
CIDOB	Confederación de Pueblos Indígenas del Oriente Boliviano (Confederation of the Indigenous People of the Bolivian East)
CIOAC	Central Independiente de Obreros Agrícolas y Campesinos (Independent Rural and Agricultural Workers Central)
CLDHCN	Comisión de Lavado de Dinero del Honorable Congreso de la Nación (Parliamentary Commission for the Investigation of Money Laundering)
CLOC	Coordinadora Latinamericana de Organizaciones el Campo (Latin American Coordination of Rural Organisations)

CNOOC	Chinese National Offshore Oil Company
CNPC	China National Petroleum Corporation
COB	Central Obrera Boliviana (Bolivian Workers Confederation)
COCOPA	Comisión para la Concordia y la Pacificación (Commission for Agreement and Pacification)
CONADEP	Comisión Nacional sobre la Desaparición de Personas (National Commission for the Disappearance of People)
CONAJUVE	Confederación Nacional de Juntas Vecinales de Bolivia (National Confederation of Neighbours' Council)
CONCLAT	Conferência Nacional das Classes Trabalhadoras (National Congress of the Working Class)
CONTAG	Confederação Nacional de Trabalhadores na Agricultura (National Confederation of Rural Workers)
CPT	Comissao Pastoral da Terra (Land Pastoral Commission)
CSO	Civil Society Organisations
CSUTCB	Confederación Sindical Única de Trabajadores Campesinos de Bolivia (Unified Syndical Confederation of Rural Workers of Bolivia)
CTA	Central de Trabajadores Argentinos (Argentine Workers' Central)
CTDAV	Coordinadora de Trabajadores Desocupados Aníbal Verón (Unemployed Workers' Network Aníbal Verón)
CUT	Central Única de Trabalhadores (Central Workers)
DFI	Direct Foreign Investments
DS	Decolonial School
ECLAC	Economic Commission for Latin America and the Caribbean
ENFF	Escola Nacional Florestan Fernandez (National School Florestan Fernandez)
EZLN	Ejército Zapatista de Liberación Nacional (Zapatista National Liberation Army)
FAO	Food and Agriculture Organization
FaSinPat	Fábrica sin Patrón (Factory without Bosses)
FEJUVE	Federación de Juntas Vecinales (Federation of Neighbours' Councils, El Alto)
FETRAF-SUL Região Sul	Federação dos Trabalhadores na Agricultura Familiar da (Federation of Family Agriculture Movement of the South Region)
FFL-UBA	Facultad de Filosofía y Letras, Universidad de Buenos Aires (Faculty of Philosophy, University of Buenos Aires)

FHC	Fernando Henrique Cardoso
FLN	Fuerza de Liberación Nacional (National Liberation Forces)
FMOEP	Free Market Open Economy Policies
FPDS	Frente Popular Darío Santillán (Popular Front Darío Santillán)
FTAA	Free Trade Agreement of the Americas
FTV	Federación Tierra, Vivienda y Hábitat de La Matanza (Land, Housing and Habitat Federation)
GJM	Global Justice Movement
HIJOS	Hijos por la Identidad y la Justicia contra el Olvido y el Silencio (Children for Identity and Justice against Forgetting and Silence)
ICS	Instituto Chiapas Solidario (Chiapas Solidarity Institute)
ILO	International Labour Organisation
IMF	International Monetary Fund
IMPA	Industrias Metalúrgicas y Plásticas Argentinas (Metallurgical and Plastic Industry of Argentina)
INCRA	Instituto Nacional de Colonização e Reforma Agrária (National Institute for Colonisation and Agrarian Reform)
INMECAFE	Instituto Mexicano de Café (Mexican Coffee Institute)
INRA	Instituto Nacional de Reforma Agraria (National Agrarian-Reform Institute)
IPC	International NGO/CSO Planning Committee for Food Sovereignty
IROS	Imaginary Reconstitution of Society
ISI	Industria Sustitutiva de Importaciones (Import-substitution strategy of industrialisation)
JBG	Juntas de Buen Gobierno (Good Government Councils)
JV	Juntas Vecinales (Neighbourhood Councils)
LC	Ligas Camponesas (Peasant Leagues)
LP	Línea Proletaria (Proletariat Line)
LPP	Ley de Participación Popular (Law of Popular Participation)
LT	Liberation Theology
MAREZ	Municipalidades Autónomas Rebeldes Zapatistas (Zapatistas Autonomous Rebel Municipalities)
MAS-IPSP	Movimiento al Socialismo-Instrumento político por la Soberanía de los Pueblos (Movement for Socialism-Political Instrument for the Sovereignty of the Peoples)

MASTER	Movimento dos Agricultores Sem Terra (The Landless Farmers' Movement)
MDA	Ministério do Desenvolvimento Agrário (Ministry of Agrarian Development)
MDS	Ministerio de Desarrollo Social
MIRA	Movimiento Indígena Revolucionario Antizapatista (Anti-Zapatista Indigenous Revolutionary Movement)
MNER	Movimiento Nacional de Empresas Recuperadas (National Movement of Recovered Enterprises)
MST	Movimento dos Trabalhadores Rurais Sem Terra (Movement of Landless Rural Workers)
MSTA	Movimiento Socialista de los Trabajadores, Argentina (Movement of Socialist Workers, Argentina)
MTD	Movimiento de Trabajadores Desocupados (Movement of Unemployed Workers)
MTL	Movimiento Territorial de Liberación (Liberation Territorial Movement)
MTSS	Ministerio de Trabajo y Seguridad Social
NAFTA	North American Free Trade Agreement
NGO	Non-Governmental Organisation
OM	Open Marxism
OPDDIC	Organización para la Defensa de los Derechos Indígenas y Campesinos (Organisation in Defence of Indigenous and Peasants Rights)
OTB	Organizaciones Territoriales de Base (Grassroots Territorial Organisations)
PAN	Partido Acción Nacional
PC	Partido Comunista (Communist Party)
PCdoB	Partido Comunista do Brazil (Brazilian Communist Party)
PO	Partido Obrero (Workers' Party)
PP	Presupuesto Participativo (Participatory Budget)
PRD	Partido de la Revolución Democrática (Party of the Democratic Revolution)
PRI	Partido Revolucionario Institucional (Institutional Revolutionary Party)
PROCEDE	Programa de Certificación de Ejidos
PT	Partido dos Trabajadores (Workers' Party)
PU	Pacto Unidad (Unity Pact)
QSVT	'¡Que se vayan todos, que no quede ni uno solo!' ('Out with them all! No one should stay!')
SIM	Subcomandante Insurgente Marcos (Insurgent Subcommander Marcos)

SIPAZ	Servicio Internacional por la Paz (International Service for Peace)
SMN	Social Movements Network
SoB	Socialisme ou Barbarie (Socialism or Barbarie)
SOECN	Sindicato Obreros y Empleados Cerámicos de Neuquén (Ceramic Workers Union of Neuquén)
SS	Subaltern Studies
SSG	Subaltern Studies Group
TAZ	Temporary Autonomous Zones
TIPNIS	Territorio Indígena y Parque Nacional Isiboro Secure (Isiboro Secure National Park and Indigenous Territory)
TNCs	Transnational Corporations
UDR	Uniao Democratica Ruralista (Rural Democratic Union)
UN	United Nations
UNASUR	Unions de Naciones de América del Sur (Union of South American Nations)
UNDP	United Nations Development Programme
UOM	Unión Obrera Metalúrgica (Metallurgical Workers Union)
USSR	Union of Soviet Socialist Republics
UTD	Unión de Trabajadores Desocupados de General Mosconi (General Mosconi Unemployed Workers Union)
UWOs	Unemployed Workers' Organisations (Organizaciones de Trabajadores Desocupados)
VC	La Vía Campesina (The Peasants' Way)
WB	World Bank
WC	Washington Consensus
WRC	Workers' Recovered Companies (Empresas recuperadas por sus trabajadores)
WSF	World Social Forum
WST	World-Systems Theory
WTO	World Trade Organization
YASUNI-ITT	Yasuní National Park (Parque Nacional Yasuní)
YPF	Yacimientos Petrolíferos Fiscales (Argentine State-owned Oil Company)

We are not idealists. We know that art alone does not make the revolution.

But we are not fools. We know that revolution is impossible without the art.

Frente Popular Darío Santillán

The same nectar knows how to flourish over and beyond business. This does not depend solely on money that cultivates the seeds of the fruit and lets them grow, for whatever flourishes, sings, and writes in a meaningful way, whatever becomes significant beyond its own way, extends itself into the wide blue yonder beyond what economics has assign it. This is the direction a significant thinker takes in order to move and operate, somebody who subjectively does not at all belong to business.

Ernst Bloch, 1988: 36

1
Embracing the Other Side: An Introduction

Introduction

An explosion of rage and hope irrupted and expanded throughout the Latin American region at the end of the twentieth century. A general sense of injustice felt by millions asserted itself as a series of demonstrations, mobilisations, struggles, strikes, uprisings and upheavals against neoliberal politics and policy. These collective actions undertaken by citizen, popular, labour and indigenous movements embraced 'autonomy' as the tool to resist structural adjustments, and their social, economic and political consequences. These protests and mobilizations soon developed into organizing tools for both to critique capitalism, patriarchal society, coloniality and to explore alternative relations and sociabilities beyond them.

As a form of resistance, autonomous practices, i.e., struggles for self-determination, self-organisation, self-representation, self-management, and indigenous autonomy – are not new. In the region, there is a long-standing tradition embraced by grass-roots and popular movements, inspired in libertarian, autonomist, anarchist and Marxist thinking, combined with liberation theology and indigenous insurgency. Since the 1980s, however, the recreation of autonomy against and beyond neoliberal globalisation by indigenous peoples, the landless, the jobless, low-income and public sector workers and the 'new poor' (middle class) is inextricably connected with hope. 'Autonomy' became both a mobilising utopia and the organisational form of a multifaceted process of prefiguration of alternative realities within contexts of urban and rural vulnerability, hunger, social deprivation and political adversity. The new autonomy is not an ideological project but the everyday territorial and political reality of Latin American people, where radical pedagogies,

1

cooperative work, art and entertainment, care, new forms of defending and revitalising indigenous traditions and customs, environmental awareness and territorialized resistance developed imaginatively into forms of social, political and economic survival. These allow for the experience of realities that lie beyond the contours of the ones delineated by the state, global capital and the law. Hence, autonomy posed new questions to both the ongoing debate about political change in the region and to theoretical understandings of 'autonomy' for radical change, more generally.

The premise of this book is that for the past two decades we are witnessing a turning point in autonomous movement activity that, consequently, requires a shift in our approach to 'autonomy'. By definition, social movements *are* autonomous: they confront power and strive for (radical) social change. The new quality of Latin American movements, therefore, is not that they are unwilling to be trapped into conventional left-wing ideologies and directions and advocate instead independence from political parties and trade unions (Adler Hellman, 1992; Stahler-Sholk et al., 2007; Biekart, 2005). Their key feature is that their autonomous organising is a tool for *prefiguring* alternatives with political imagination.

Prefiguration, I argue, is *a process of learning hope*. Autonomy is the organisational tool of this process. That is, autonomy is a hypothesis of resistance that encompasses the delineation of new horizons beyond the given truth. I offered elsewhere the name 'hope movements' (Dinerstein and Deneulin, 2012) to characterise movements that 'search for a new way of life, which is more conducive to creating an environment where human beings can live in dignity ... human dignity [i]s incompatible with conditions of exploitation and oppression' (Dinerstein and Deneulin, 2012: 589–590). By trial and error ('asking we walk') and by reflecting democratically on the meaning of their collective actions, hope movements confront the state and capital, challenge existing matrices of power and socio-political horizons, fill spaces and/or render alternative forms of cooperative and dignified work, democracy, land, indigenous autonomy, education, relation with nature and politics. These experiences of autonomy in Latin America provide us with the unique opportunity to discuss empirically and theoretically the nature and meaning of autonomy in indigenous and non-indigenous contexts, and to reflect on our epistemological and methodological limitations to grasp and understand these experiences.

The autonomy debate: a deadlock?

The autonomy debate took a sharp turn with the Zapatistas' uprising on 1 January 1994, in Chiapas, Mexico, when indigenous communities politically organised in the Zapatista National Liberation Army (*Ejército Zapatista de Liberación Nacional,* EZLN) stood against neoliberal globalisation in defence of humanity. An unlikely subject, the forgotten indigenous people living in a small place in southeast Mexico, reinvented the language of revolution. The Zapatistas declared war to the Mexican state and defined globalisation as a war against humanity. Soon after the uprising, the EZLN called for an intergalactic encounter in Chiapas (1996) for the people of the world to discuss neoliberalism and humanity with the rebel communities. Other intercontinental meetings through which the Zapatistas weaved its global network followed this.

The Zapatistas' uprising brought back not only a debate about revolution that had been dormant since the collapse of the Soviet Union but also about the role of the state in the revolutionary enterprise among the lefts. This was skilfully captured by John Holloway in his book *Change the World Without Taking Power* (2002a), where he engages with the Zapatistas' experience and their approach to the state to elaborate an innovative proposal. Holloway's argument – infused with many years of elaboration of his Open Marxist critique of capital and the state – is that we can, and should, change the world without taking the power of the state.

The engagement with the Zapatista's struggle has served Holloway to produce a turning point in revolutionary thinking. To Holloway, the Zapatista movement 'moves us decisively beyond the state illusion [that] understands revolution as the winning of state power and the transformation of society through the state' (Holloway, 2002b: 157). 'State illusion' is 'the paradigm that has dominated left-wing thought for at least a century. The state illusion puts the state at the centre of the concept of radical change. The state illusion understands revolution as the winning of state power and the transformation of society through the state' (Holloway, 2002b).

Revolution today, argues Holloway, means precisely the opposite to the traditional formula. It means rejecting state power in favour of developing an anti-power that allows people to invent new worlds. The left's 'notion of capturing positions of power', claims Holloway, 'missed the point that the aim of the revolution is to dissolve relations of power, to create a society based on the mutual recognition of people's dignity' (Holloway, 2002a: 20).

Two antagonistic opinions emerged out of Holloway's groundbreaking proposition: on the one hand, a celebration of autonomy as a tool for radical change. On the other hand, a rejection of this idea for its radical departure from traditional views on the relationship between reform and revolution, the party, the working class and the state. (Dinerstein, 2012:

522, 2005). Those who advocate autonomy as a political strategy in Latin America emphasise – explicitly or implicitly – the significance of grass-roots and communitarian practices direct democracy, anti-bureaucratic forms of self-management, and rejection of the state as the main locus of political of change. Zibechi (2007: 49) postulates that social change and the creation and re-creation of social relations and sociabilities do not necessitate either articulation – centralisation or unification for 'emancipatory social change goes against this type of articulation proposed from the State-academia-parties ... [movements] represent explorations, attempts amidst social struggles'. Gutiérrez Aguilar (2012: 59) claims that 'collective emancipatory action and its profound practice of transforming the social, economic, and political' is a separate trajectory 'from the party struggle for the occupation of government and state'. Escobar points out that 'new social movements are defined more in terms of *change and becoming* than as fixed states, structures and programs' (1992: 44, italics in the original). Sitrin (2006) offers the term *horizontalism* to name new social actions, arrangements and principles of organisations for Argentine autonomous movements. In her discussion on the resurgence and meaning of the left in Latin America, Motta (2006: 899) defends the need to shift our analytic focus from structures of power to the practices at the grass roots for they constitute the bases for left political alternatives.

While they appreciate the significance of grass-roots mobilisation for a broad process of political change, the detractors of autonomy charged it with being a weak political strategy simply because it avoids the 'real' issue: i.e., the state. They draw on a long-standing interpretation of 'autonomy' that associates it with an allegedly ineffective anarchist strategy of rejection of power, in general, and the power of the state, in particular. Boron maintains that the state is 'a pact of classist domination' (Boron, 2001: 180) that cannot be eluded. He claims that 'a new world cannot be constructed ... unless the correlation of forces is radically modified, and very powerful enemies are defeated. The state is precisely the site where the correlation of forces is condensed. It is not the only place, but it is by far the most important one' (Boron, 2005: 37, 2001). The romanticisation of autonomy, claims Katz (2008: 132) has produced a regional imaginary that avoids the discussion about the political struggle that led many governments to appropriate the emancipatory efforts of many movements, so the state cannot be avoided (Katz, 2008: 136). Sader (2008: 18) also disapproves autonomy as a revolutionary strategy: 'the notion of autonomy of the social serves neither the regrouping of mass forces intent on organizing new forms of political action, nor as a way to construct alternative forms of power, but rather as a refusal to confront the issue of power'. Harvey (2010b: 258) contends that 'there is no way that anti-capitalist social order can be constructed without seizing state power, radically transforming, and re-working the constitutional and institutional framework that currently supports private property, the market system and endless capital accumulation'. Interestingly, while they claim to be Marxists, they failed to acknowledge that, as Hudis highlights 'none of Marx's discussions of a post capitalist society in Volume III of *Capital* mentions the state. He instead refers to the control of the elements of production and distribution by *society*. Nor ... does he mention the state in his discussion of post capitalist society in the first chapter of Volume I of *Capital*' (Hudis, 2012: 175). Rather, argues Hudis, 'Marx's conception of a post capitalist society is ... both expansive and visionary [and he] never endorses a given social form as the solution' (Hudis, 2012: 209). Finally, autonomy is regarded as involuntarily serving the neoliberal enterprise thus befitting efforts to reframe policy along the lines of market-oriented liberalism, and the proof is that both neoliberal academics and critical theorists endorse cooperation, participation, horizontality (Roggero, 2010: 359; Žižek, 2008).

Autonomy and the pink tide: sleeping with the enemy?

The arrival of 'the new left in power' (Ellner, 2012) in many Latin American countries led to an 'impasse' in the process of autonomous organising that began with the mobilization against neoliberalism (Colectivo Situaciones, 2012). The emergence of 'twenty-first century socialism' and the strong leadership of Hugo Chávez, Evo Morales and Rafael Correa among others captured the attention of political analysts and the left, thus displacing the politics of autonomy to a second place. The stalemate affected the political debate about autonomy for the previous movements' political centrality was replaced by effervescent discussions about the political strategies and policymaking of new centre-left governments (Reyes, 2012). The 'pink tide' arose expectations for the possibility of new collective – socialist/popular horizons, to be realised through the state. In fact, these governments' took many of the popular movements' demands on board and expanded the rights of indigenous people to articulate an anti-neoliberal, anti-colonial and anti-imperialist discourse and project (Escobar, 2010: 7). With neo-developmentalism (Féliz, 2012; Wylde, 2011), a strategy based on national development led by the nation-state in a global competitive economy – like in Argentina – grass-roots movements were encouraged and supported, financially and politically, by the state. With twenty-first century communitarian socialism (in Venezuela, Bolivia and Ecuador) there has been – in Bolivia and Ecuador – a fundamental change in the form of the state from national to plurinational which requires the recognition and incorporation of indigenous cosmologies into new (pluri)national Constitutions.

The political significance of the shift to the left in the region cannot be overemphasised. Overall, the pink tide's economies are growing faster than during the previous decade, producing a decline of income inequality, improvements in education, social and labour policy, and health-care systems, due to a relatively fairer income distribution. These political experiments clearly reconfigured the geopolitics of the region, particularly in relation to the US and Europe, by opposing their imperialism, accelerating regional integration – for example, the Union of South American Nations (*Unions de Naciones de América del Sur*, UNASUR) – and reinventing the imaginary of the continent called *Nuestramérica* (Our America).

However, the political deliberations about the pink tide, include an enquiry about whether these centre-left governments represent a continuation or rupture of neoliberalism (Morais and Saad-Filho, 2005; Webber, 2012) or not, that is whether they have moved on to a post-neoliberal stage (Grugel and Riggirozzi, 2012). This has been also presented as a question of whether they are leading a reform or a revolution (Webber, 2011b; Regalado, 2009; Moldiz Mercado, 2009; Lievesley, 2009; Prevost, 2012). To be sure, these ways of framing the debate highlight the dilemmas facing the new governments to change the direction of their countries' economies within a dominating neoliberal global economy, but also to what extent these new governments are able to engage with the emancipatory spirit of the movements that facilitated their access to power. However, the focus on the political elites' performance and their ability to undertake the expected radical changes takes us away from the discussion of the process of mobilisation that preceded the arrival in power of these governments. The pink tide's economic policy frequently contradicts their pro-autonomy, anti-neoliberal and bottom-up political discourse, hence disappointing the aspirations of many of the movements in pursuit of indigenous autonomy, agrarian reform, dignified work, democracy and social justice. For example, the increase in Direct Foreign Investments (DFI) has led to the intensification of the commodification and appropriation of natural resources and the expansion of extractive industries by transnational conglomerates that not only make the countries' economies dependent on the former but deeply affect rural livelihoods and indigenous communal life.

Against this background, a new wave of protest and mobilisation emerged around 2006 against the pink tide's political economy pointing to the fundamental contradictions of a project that relies on the state to criticise the coloniality of power and capitalism (Reyes, 2012). Examples of this are abundant. In Ecuador, the incorporation of the *sumak kawsay* (*buen vivir*) indigenous cosmology into a new national constitution required the transformation of the former into a 'development model', which unashamedly disregards the fact that the *sumak kawsay* offers a paradigm of life that is *completely* opposed to 'development' altogether. Indigenous people are mobilising against both the government's natural resource energy and extractivist strategy (Burch, 2012) and the internal colonialism that the state reinforces as it continues 'translating' indigenous paradigms of life into development and implementing multiculturalist policies that maintain a colonial hierarchical structure in place. On several occasions, the government has repressed indigenous movements for upsetting its plans for oil exploration by transnational corporations that work for Petroecuador. In addition to this, in August 2013, we learnt that one of the most original environmental initiatives of the last year, such as the international agreement that protects of Yasuní National Park (*Parque Nacional Yasuní*) and surroundings (Yasuní-ITT), was cancelled (Gudynas, 2013).

President Rousseff has also betrayed her promise of using the country's wealth on behalf of the Brazilian people, that she put forward to defeat her political competitor Supporter of privatisation. In October 2013, the Brazilian National Oil Agency (*Agência Nacional do Petróleo, Gás Natural e Biocombustíveis*, ANP) auctioned a colossal oil field with oil reserves. Transnational companies also got hold of an oceanic oil site that contains circa 12 billion oil barrels. Among the companies who were given the right for exploitation of Libra in a controversial process are Shell, China National Petroleum Corporation (CNPC) and Chinese National Offshore Oil Company (CNOOC) (Honty, 2013). While Transnational conglomerates are gaining terrain in Brazil, the leaders of the Movement of Landless Rural Workers (*Movimento dos Trabalhadores Rurais Sem Terra*, MST) deemed 2013 as the worst year for the agrarian reform in Brazil. (Stédile, 2012; Albuquerque, 2014). Brazil had never undertaken an agrarian reform that could democratise access to the property of the land for poor rural workers. But right now, reflects Stédile, the agribusiness sector has become a hegemonic force within the government, so that rural workers' achievements at the MST's settlements are at a stalemate with regards to making improvements in production. This is a result of speculative practices over agro commodities, which became a form of profit making for *latifundistas* and the rise in the land prices (Stédile, interview by Tavares, 2014).

Arguments against Evo Morales' economic and development policy include accusations of producing the 'bureaucratic stagnation of the Bolivian revolution' (Webber, 2012) and its commitment to neoliberalism. His policies have been praised by the International Monetary Fund (IMF) and the World Bank (WB) (Moldiz Mercado, 2012). The contradictions and inconsistencies between the plurinational state that has given indigenous peoples the right to self-determination and the political economy of 'Andean capitalism' as vice president García Linera named this economic strategy, subordinates the indigenous cosmology of *buen vivir* into the development paradigm.

President Cristina Fernández de Kirchner had to deal with the opposition to fracking in the north and south of Argentina – a country that possesses the third-largest reserve of shale gas in the world, after China and the US. Environmental activists and other non-governmental organisations denounced the government's agreement with Chevron-Texaco. The latter was expelled from operating in Ecuador for its violations to human rights and causing environmental disasters such as river pollution and contamination of indigenous lands. Now, Chevron-Texaco has found a new ally in the Argentine government.

Among the grass roots, there are divisions between those who support the governments and those who feel betrayed. Has autonomous organising only served to defeat neoliberalism? Has it been appropriated by neo-developmentalist and new 'communitarian socialist' politics? Is autonomy only a tool to 'gain terrain within the state that serve to progress into popular conquests' (Thwaites Rey, 2004: 84; see also Petras and Veltmeyer, 2005)? Will autonomy always succumb in the hands of the state? Are the movements 'locked into the position of either supporting or opposing state policy enacted by functionaries who are thought to speak in their names?' (Reyes, 2012: 13). These questions have reanimated the debate about autonomy as a tool for radical change. My contribution to this new enquiry is to problematise the coordinates of the debate and the terms of the questions. Where should we be looking in order to grasp radical change in Latin America today?

Re-examining the problem

In this book, I move away from, and beyond, the historical dichotomous debate among the left that has recently divided scholars and activists for already two decades, between those who regard autonomous organising as a plausible political strategy and those who see it as a well-intentioned and useful form for the mobilisation at the grass roots that eventually would require to take the power of the state in order to receive direction and coordination, and effectively generate radical change. As we have seen, as it is framed, the controversy has reached a stalemate. On the one hand, those who defend the necessity of 'taking the power of the state' picture autonomy as a weak tool to fight against the elites in power and transnational capital. As mentioned above, they charge autonomists with avoiding the 'real problem' and rely on the hypothesis that, at some point, the coordination of all struggles towards the goal of taking the power of the state will occur under the direction of left political parties. Yet, the examples of the pink tide that are often politically vindicated (i.e., Bolivia, Ecuador and Venezuela) are great experiments of 'radical social democracy' (Lievesley and Ludlam, 2009) but far from executing the kind of revolution that the traditional Marxist left has in mind. The use of 'old tools' (Motta, 2009) to judge the politics of autonomy is a symptom of the difficulty of the political left to engage with new visions that might enrich and innovate in their revolutionary projects (Hudis and Anderson, 2002). On the other hand, the anarchist and autonomist view of autonomy has tended to equate autonomy with an 'exodus' (Carlsson and Manning, 2010: 924), or with 'the politics of subtraction' (Žižek, 2008: 405), where autonomy is portrayed as a radical adventure 'outside' or 'parallel' to the realm of state and capital. Generally speaking, autonomy is regarded as a self-contained creative activity, which reorganises and reinvents social relations, but without necessarily putting forward a critique of capital as a form of society. Holloway highlights:

> 'Autonomies' can be seen as self-sufficient units, spaces to which we have escaped, spaces in which we can construct or develop a distinct identity, a difference. In a world based on the negation of autonomy or self-determination, autonomy in a static sense is impossible. Self-determination does not exist: all that exists is the constant drive towards self-determination. (Holloway, 2010b: 910)

To be sure autonomy is above all a creative contradictory practice. The contradictions that crisscrossed autonomy are not just internal to the movements' collective action but relate to the context of production of autonomous practices. Autonomy can be defined as a site 'of the political struggle over what [autonomy] could possibly mean in practice' (Böhm et al., 2010: 27). Autonomy produces 'interstices' (Pikerill and Chatterton, 2006: 8; Wright, 2010: 321; Arditi, 2008: 100) where new practices can be anticipated. Interstices or 'cracks' (Holloway, 2010a) embody both the negation of established practices and the hope for the possibility of the alternative. But these dynamics of autonomy operate within capital, making autonomous practices to be learning processes always at risk to be distorted and integrated into the 'capitalist social synthesis' (Holloway, 2010a). The danger of appropriation is due to the fact that as a social relation, capital is constantly translating autonomy into complementary practices: capital tends to appropriate new forms of commoning in order to preserve itself as a social force (De Angelis, 2010: 957). As argued elsewhere, autonomy endures a tension between rebellion (resistance and world-changing action) and institutionalisation (the incorporation of ideologies and projects into state programs and legislation as officially sanctioned economic, social, cultural and political change) (Böhm et al., 2010; Dinerstein et al., 2013). The (im)possibility of autonomy lies in the (im)possibility of the closeness of the social and of the complete subsumption of human activity into the movement of value producing.

But then another question arises: is autonomous organising a praxis that fluctuates eternally between rebellion and integration? Is there anything else to autonomy than this ongoing contradiction? Do we need to discuss the production of a surplus or 'excess'? Excess has been theorised in several ways by attributing autonomous practices the peculiarity of producing a surplus that is seen as inherent to the social, as a mismatch that results from the impossibility to subsume singularity into the logic of universality or to subordinate doing to abstract labour. I will return to this in the next chapter.

Negation, creation, contradiction and excess are all features of autonomous practices. But most existing theorisations of autonomy have tended to focus on one or two of these dimensions, thus creating a fragmented picture of the autonomous struggle. In other words, with a difference in focus, autonomy is usually understood as *negative* praxis (i.e., rejection of power); or as a force that *creates* new worlds with the political imagination (or both); or as a *contradictory process* marked by the contested relation with, against and beyond the state, capital, the law, policy and as *surplus* activity that cannot be subordinated to power. My argument is that while each of these modes of autonomy are significant in their own way, separately they fall short to account for the complexity of the politics of autonomy in general, and in Latin America in particular.

In addition to this, I have identified a second significant deficiency in present discussions about autonomy. The fondness that anarchists and autonomous Marxist and critical scholar-activists have grown for Latin American movements has led them to produce interpretations of autonomy where the *specificity* of the region and of indigenous autonomy are neglected and/or overlooked. As I discuss in Chapters 2 and 8, I am not simply reproaching the radical left for being Eurocentric, but for not making an effort to understand these differences, even when they are against Eurocentric views on resistance. This unawareness is a handcuff for radical thinkers and activists.

How we understand these differences is important for the autonomy debate. The particular features of the indigenous resistance for example do not simply refer to cultural differences or differences in the historical background or the context of production, but to a differentiated positioning of indigenous peoples vis-à-vis the state, the law and capital. The contribution of indigenous organisations and struggles to the Global Justice Movement (GJM), and the mounting confrontation between rival knowledges from the north and south exposed at the World Social Forum (WSF) (Santos, 2005: xxii) have made these differences apparent and require that we attend to this issue, not by discarding radical theorisations about social change and autonomy produced in the north, but by pointing to the problem of their universalisation (Dikeç, 2010). For example, anarchist activist and writer David Graeber claims that 'we live in the era of anarchism'. He writes:

> [I]t is becoming increasingly clear that the age of revolutions is not over. It's becoming equally clear that the global revolutionary movement in the twenty-first century, will be one that traces its origins less to the tradition of Marxism, or even of socialism narrowly defined, but of anarchism. (Graeber, 2004)

While Graeber's statement appeals to a variety of movements that reject power and encourage democratisation and self-determination, I have two concerns. First, as Chibber suggests, as capital self-expands as a universalising force, this does not mean homogeneisation, that is capital does not only allow but even promotes different 'dynamics of political agency' (Chibber, 2013: 285) not only between the West and the East, but also within the West and the East.[1] I will return to this point in Chapters 2 and 8. Second, and for this reason, the universalisation of any 'ism' can easily become a constraint rather than a liberating idea for autonomous practices in the south. Neka, an activist of the Argentinean unemployed workers organisation MTD Solano explains 'we decided we would not allow ourselves to become any "ist" or "ism". What we're doing is constructing an experience-based practice that speaks for itself' (cited in Sitrin, 2006: 11). Holloway (2010a: 187) highlights that Anarchism is strong in understanding resistance to power and domination, while we can to learn from non orthodox Marxism how human activity is subordinated to abstract labour, value and money

To continue with the example, 'the era of Anarchism' does not inform, say, the predicaments of landless rural workers who joined the MST to struggle for the land against dispossession and the brutal violence of pseudo democratic governments and landowners, and who are producing a synergy between Marxism and liberation theology (LT). In Latin America, the politics of autonomy draw on anarchist and Marxist traditions in higher or lesser degrees which have been amalgamated with own versions of anarchism and other influential currents such as Indigenous Insurgency and LT. In Bolivia, for example, where there was 'like a mutual breeding, a mutual fertilization of thought and an ability to interpret universal doctrine that is basically a European doctrine in Bolivian, Chola and Aymara terms' (Rivera Cusicanqui in Knoll and Rivera Cusicanqui, 2007). The debate about autonomy, therefore, should include a reflection on the specificity of Latin American autonomy and of indigenous and non-indigenous autonomy in order to produce not only a more appropriate understanding of autonomous organising in Latin America but a richer discussion about the politics of autonomy in the north as well.

A third point with regards to the generalisation of autonomy as a universal struggle against or without the state, is that for indigenous people the state has never been either the centre of critique or a tool for emancipation. Indigenous autonomy reflects a praxis based on a cosmology of the world that *excludes* the state *per se*, and regards the political in a completely different way. Indigenous autonomy is not anti-state, but it is against a system of colonisation and oppression that has been and is sustained by the nation state and the law. However, the state is a political tool to attain the legal recognition of autonomous practices that already exist. The Zapatistas (as well as other indigenous peoples in the region) confronted the Mexican government and demanded the legal changes required for the recognition of indigenous self-determination that were agreed in the San Andrés Accords. The self-government councils (*Juntas de Buen Gobierno*, Good Government Councils, JBG) were created after the EZLN's disappointment with the framing of indigenous autonomy as a tool for neoliberal decentralisation, illustrating the predicaments of indigenous peoples in pursuit of autonomy vis-à-vis the state. It is not at all surprising that the Zapatistas did not wish to take the power of the state in 1994. Holloway's proposal to change the world without taking the power of the state is inspired in the Zapatistas' claim that we need to move beyond what the Zapatistas call the 'state illusion' (Holloway,

2002b), but this idea comes from ancestral traditions of the indigenous people and was transformed with political imagination into a new revolutionary proposal that has inspired a disenchanted left. My intention is to emphasise the indigenous element of the Zapatista's rejection of the state and show that, at present, indigenous peoples' *historical* rejection of (yet also engagement with) the state concurs with the revitalisation of autonomy as a strategy of resistance.

Self-determination also means different things to indigenous and non-indigenous collectivities. While for non-indigenous people, autonomy is an 'emancipatory' project, for indigenous people, emancipation is inevitably a *decolonising* project. A decolonising project requires the praxis of autonomous organising that not only rejects the state and capital but also defeats internal colonialism and coloniality: 'there can not be discourse of decolonization, no theory of decolonization, without a decolonizing praxis. Indigenous struggles are mediated by a struggle against oppression, violence and legislation that inform the existing form of internal colonialism' (Rivera Cusicanqui, 2012). As de la Cadena (2010) suggests indigenous politics are not 'ethnic politics' vis-à-vis 'politics'. It is about recognition of alternative forms of politics that correspond to the historical formation of indigeneity and, as such, 'exceeds the notion of politics as usual, that is, an arena populated by rational human beings disputing the power to represent others vis-à-vis the state' (de la Cadena, 2010: 363).

Bearing these three issues in mind, i.e. the fragmented understanding of autonomy, the problems of its universalisation, and the dilemma surrounding the relation with the state I propose an alternative *demarcation* of the problem of autonomy. I reorganise, rephrase and pose the question about autonomy in a different fashion. To that end, by connecting autonomy and hope, I offer a definition of autonomy as *the art of organising hope*. The art of organising hope that entails four simultaneous modes: negation, creation, contradiction and the production of excess. Autonomy and hope are my entry points to a wider discussion about the political significance of autonomy for radical change in historical socio-political, cultural and economic context, and how differences between indigenous and non-indigenous praxis require that we address unsatisfactory categories used to explain contemporary forms of autonomous organising.

Autonomy as a tool for prefiguration

The extraordinary mobilisation of hope in Latin America began to materialise once again after the experience of the 1970s, in the late 1980s when the region became a laboratory for both the neoliberal experiment and experimentations in resistance against it, thus becoming one of the privilege sites for the reinvention of the left (Katz, 2008). Quijano (2009) put it like this:

> It is probably the first time in the history of the colonial matrix of power that we are not only hopeful toward the future, we are also working toward that future, and we are beginning to build that future, we are at this very moment building it. This is not a simple image ... neither is a utopia, in the classical sense of the world. This is happening in the planet and in that sense it is ... a phenomenon that manifests itself as a real tendency of a historical necessity.

There is, then, a process of 'prefiguring' at work. But what is prefiguring? The *Oxford Dictionary* defines 'prefigure' as 'to have particular qualities or features that suggest or indicate in advance something that will happen in the future'. In other words, prefiguring is about anticipating the future that is *not yet* in the present. The term is not new in radical thinking. In his piece 'Soviets in Italy, (Writings from 1919 and 1920)', Antonio Gramsci (1968: 32) discusses how revolutionary signs are being prefigured in the present. To him 'the actual unfolding of the revolutionary proves takes place subterraneous' and 'it is not controllable and documentable: it will be so in the future when the elements that constitute it (the feelings, the desires, the more, the germs of initiative and of habit) are developed and purified'. In the 1960s, Winni Breines used the term 'prefigurative' to portray the novelty of the anarchist politics of the time that rejected hierarchies and power, to which she referred to as 'the new left'. She argued that prefigurative politics 'imposed substantial tasks, the central one being to create and sustain within the live practice of the movement, relationships and political forms that "prefigured" and embodied the desired society' (Breines, 1989: 6).

The need to rethink the meaning of critical social sciences is a significant dimension of the process of prefiguring post capitalist and post development realities. Boaventura de Sousa Santos (2000) calls for a reinvention of sociology which, he argues, is presently undergoing a 'paradigmatic transition', Sociology must undertake the role of inventing 'the maps of social emancipation' and 'the subjectivities able to use them' (Santos, 2000: 380). He argues that this requires both a Sociology of Absences and a Sociology of Emergences:

> I speak of sociologies because my aim is to critically identify the conditions that destroy non-hegemonic and potentially counter-

hegemonic social experience. Through these sociologies, social experience that resists destruction is unconcealed, and the space-time capable of identifying and rendering credible new counter-hegemonic social experiences is opened up. (Santos, 2004: 239)

Santos' Sociology of Absences designates 'an inquiry that aims to explain that what does not exist is, in fact, actively produced as non-existent, that is, as a non-credible alternative to what exists. The objective of the sociology of absences is to transform impossible into possible objects, absent into present objects. The logics and processes through which hegemonic criteria of rationality and efficiency produce non-existence are various' (Santos 2004: 239). Santos suggests five of them: 'the monoculture of knowledge, of linear time, of classification, of the universal and the global, and of the criteria of capitalist productivity and efficiency' (Santos, 2004: 239–240). The Sociology of Absences replaces each of these 'monocultures' with what Santos calls 'ecologies'. The five ecologies that confront the monocultures of capitalist modern society are: the ecology of knowledges, of temporalities, of recognition, of transcale and of productivity, respectively (p. 240). In short, Santos suggests that:

> whereas the goal of the sociology of absences is to identify and valorise social experiences available in the world — although declared non-existent by hegemonic rationality — the sociology of emergences aims to identify and enlarge the signs of possible future experiences, under the guise of tendencies and latencies, that are actively ignored by hegemonic rationality and knowledge. (Santos, 2004: 241)

Santos argues that the Sociology of Emergences is important. It can detect

> 'the tendencies of the future (the Not Yet) upon which it is possible to intervene so as to maximise the probability of hope vis-à-vis the probability of frustration. Such symbolic enlargement is actually a form of sociological imagination with a double aim: on the one hand, to know better the conditions of the possibility of hope; on the other, to define principles of action to promote the fulfilment of those conditions'. (Santos, 2004: 241)

Levitas's work (2013, 2010) is also very significant in this respect. She claims that we need to 'take utopia seriously' and offers a prefigurative method of sociological enquiry that she refers to as 'Imaginary

Reconstitution of Society' (IROS). As a method, IROS would allow sociology to return to its fundamental role in the creation of utopias, -a role that was suppressed in order to become a reputable social science. To her, sociology should be about subjecting the present to critique and imagining human communities that do not yet exist. 'The encounter between sociology and utopia implies reconfiguring sociology itself' (Levitas, 2013: xv). In the same vein, Gibson-Graham (2006) propose to connect with our own desire to change what is wrong, and deploy our abilities to anticipate the future (Gibson-Graham, 2006). Their work takes 'a non space of non-being' (Gibson-Graham, 2006: xxxiii) as a starting point. It is those spaces full of 'absences' that 'have become core elements in our political imaginary' (Gibson-Graham, 2006: xxxiii).

But how can the search for the fulfilment of those absences be organised? What kind of political organising/organisation is required to prefigure better worlds? Should the collective actions directed to radically transform society be at some point institutionalised? Hardt and Negri (2009: 165) argue for the need of political organisation for what they see as 'the multiplicity of singularities that produce and are produced in the biopolitical field of the common [and which] do not spontaneously accomplish exodus and construct their autonomy. Political organization is needed to cross the threshold and generate political events'. Hardt is concerned with the possibility of institutionalisation of social cooperation and the common. But Holloway claims that any proposal based on the creation of institutions (or positive political organisation) reflects an old way of thinking revolution, as the latter 'is always a process of making our own paths' (Hardt and Holloway, 2012). Young and Schwartz (2012: 220), critics of Holloway's anti-organisational, anti-institutional view, argue that prefigurative politics can prevail if strong political organisations and counter-institutions are created and the movements discriminate among dominant institutions when deciding about their engagement with power. While Adler Hellman (2000: 56) also rejects the 'anti-organisational bias of the work of those who are pleased and excited by the spontaneity of isolated grassroots movements', Pickerill and Chatterton explore autonomy 'as a concept comprising different tendencies and trajectories; as a temporal-spatial strategy between and beyond the 'global versus local' axis; as a form of interstitial politics; as a process of resistance and creation; and as a coherent attempt at praxis with its strong sense of prefigurative politics and commitment to the revolution of the everyday' (Pickerill and Chatterton, 2006: 732). They take on board the 'growing critique of movements' failure to suggest, or indeed deliver, workable alternatives stems from autonomous activists' reluctance to build permanent organizations' (Pickerill and Chatterton, 2006: 731).

Neo-anarchist scholar-activists are producing significant knowledge about organisational process of prefigurative politics that have recently emerged such as Occupy and other alter-globalisation movements. They are enquiring as to whether prefiguration and strategy are separate forms of collective action and politics (Sitrin, 2006; Graeber, 2013; Brissette, 2013), whether prefiguration is an effective strategy (Maeckelbergh, 2012: 3) that is fluid in nature (Crass, 2013; Khasnabish and Haiven, 2012), and whether prefigurative politics can prevail (Young and Schwartz, 2012) or bring change on its own (Cornell, 2012). Maeckelbergh (2009: 67) offers a definition of prefiguration based on the rejection of the clear distinction between strategy and prefiguration. To her, prefiguration itself is a strategy in movements collective action: 'alter globalization movements rest upon a practice of social change that take prefiguration as the most strategic means for bringing about the social change they desire' (Maeckelbergh, 2011: 2). She argues that in order for prefiguration to exist there has to be a non-hierarchical and processual form of political participation and organising, through which 'consequentialist' revolutionary strategy, which privileges the end, is eliminated and the focus is on process. She proposes that prefiguration 'as a practice through which movements actors create a conflation of their ends with their means. It is an enactment of the ultimate values of an ideal society within the very means of struggle for that society' (Maeckelbergh, 2012: 2).

I concur that prefiguration *is* the movements' strategy in Latin America and that such strategy is not consequentialist but necessitates to conflate means and ends. As abovementioned, I regard prefiguration as the process of learning hope. This means that utopia cannot reside in the 'future' which is expected to be better as a result of a consequentialist strategy that regards the progression of time as linear. Prefiguration operates on a dimension of reality that is not yet in the present, the latter being an unrealised future. Prefiguration's time is now time (see Holloway, 2010a; Holloway et al., 2009; Bonefeld, 2005). However, I contend that the characterisation of prefiguration as 'the enactment of an ideal society' is too narrow and does not inform the complexity of the politics of autonomy in Latin America. It reduces prefiguration to a self-contained organisational process, and does not tackle the issue of form, embeddedness and struggle that underpin prefiguration. Maeckelbergh argues that 'prefiguration is the ideal strategy for the construction of an alternative world *without* engaging with the state or the capitalist powers, but movements practice must also incorporate a confrontation with these powers, which cannot always be prefigurative' (Maeckelbergh, 2009: 95, my italics). Does this means that the struggles against power (capital and the state) are not part of the process of prefiguration? The account detaches prefiguration from both the political economy and the processes of political struggle that underpin the politics of autonomy. This deficiency surely feeds the argument against the political significance of autonomy for it deprives the autonomous struggle from being the tool for critique. Part of the problem is that while it is true that very few Marxists have explored Marx's idea of alternative to capitalism (see Hudis, 2012) anarchist scholar-activists do not engage with Marx's critique of political economy. As a result, their views on prefiguration have tended to disregard the specific form of a society (capitalist) within which insubordination (as resistance-prefiguration) occurs. Marx's critique of political economy is usually conflated with 'economic determinism' or 'limiting Marx's critique to the economic realm.'

I want to problematise, expand and contextualise the notion of prefiguration by proposing a more complex understanding of the dynamics that intervene in the anticipation of a better world in the present. My argument is threefold. First, in order to be able to speak of prefigurative, autonomy has to be conceived of as a complex collective action that includes the negation of the given; the creation of the alternative; the struggle with, against and beyond the state; the law and capital; and the production of excess. Second, prefiguration is necessarily a *decolonising* process so the *recognition* and discussion of the differences in which the abovementioned four 'modes od autonomy' assert themselves for indigenous and non-indigenous movements is vital to our conversations about autonomy. Third, prefiguration is a practice that is deeply rooted in the process of valorisation of capital.

Prefiguration is criss-crossed by the *tensions* and *contradictions* that inhabit capitalist/colonial social relations; for autonomous practices are embedded in, and shaped by, their past and contemporary backgrounds and context of production and therefore the autonomous struggle triggers struggles *over* the meanings of autonomy – for the state will be always ready to integrate and subordinate autonomy to the dynamics of the value production process. For example, the Piqueteros in Argentina have not just created spaces for the anticipation of dignified work in their neighbourhoods. The demarcation of their territories of hope is a result of their struggle blocking roads and negotiating with the government the management of employment programmes, in a context of criminalisation of poverty and state repression.

From this standpoint, prefiguration is – *ultimately*- about *transcending* the 'parameters of legibility' imposed or made invisible by the capitalist, patriarchal and colonial demarcations of reality, which I refer to as the reality of the value form. And this requires of multiple forms of struggle that simultaneously negate, create, contradict and move beyond what it is. I draw on the term 'parameters of legibility' from Vázquez (2011: 36), who suggests, from a decolonial perspective, that the epistemic violence of modernity 'renders invisible everything that does not fit in the "parameters of legibility" of [its] epistemic territory.' The epistemic territory of modernity, argues Vázquez (2011: 28), 'establishes its field of certainty, its reality, by a movement of incorporation that subdues the multiple, the discontinuous, difference into the realm of presence.' I argue that the state, policy, the law and money, are political, legal and economic mediations that, paraphrasing Vázquez, permanently *demarcate* a reality within which autonomy operates. For the unemployed in neoliberal Argentina 1997, to transcend the parameters of legibility of the state's demarcation (to venture beyond) meant to contest unemployment and engage in a process of naming themselves differently – as Piqueteros (an identity of resistance) and unemployed workers (an identity of work) – and creating concrete utopias of dignified work in their neighbourhoods (Dinerstein, 2014c). This is one example among the one and thousands struggles that populate the Latin American landscape behind the scene at the grass roots.

The state as a mediation: up turning the question

So what about the state? My argument is that the capitalist state is a *mediation* in the process of prefiguration. This is true in both indigenous and non-indigenous struggles for autonomy. As a tool for prefiguration, autonomy is not 'against' the state or 'outside' the state but internal to the social relation of capital. Gibson-Graham (2006: xxx–xxxi) warn us of the dangers of mistaking the practice of theorising the possibility of an alternative 'for a simplistic assertion that we can think of ourselves out of the materiality of capitalism or repressive state practices'. Somehow, strangely, the most critical approaches to capitalism, anarchism and autonomism disconnect themselves from the real struggle that they claim to be involved in. The autonomous struggle is neither outside nor totally absorbed into the capitalist realm. Critique is an internal critique. Autonomy produces a critique of capital as 'anti-value-in-motion' (Dinerstein and Neary, 2002b: 237).

Autonomous organising is *mediated by* the capitalist state –the law and money. This, of course, means very different things for indigenous and non-indigenous, urban and rural movements. In both cases, the state is the most important political organisation translates and integrates autonomous struggles into institutional, legal and political dynamics. The state filters the struggle *over the meaning of autonomy* and displaces it onto struggles over the law, welfare, money, i.e. mediations, in a way that the former appears as a political contention over the *form* of mediations. For example, the struggle against landlessness or for the reinforcement of landlessness on rural workers as a form of profit making manifests itself as a struggle over the legal property of the land or agrarian policy. The process of experiencing another agrarian reform necessitates that the MST actively engages in disputes over the law and policy with the state.

Let me expand further on the notion of mediation. Mediations are not simply *instruments of* regulation, coercion, co-optation, oppression. They are social, political, economic, legal and cultural *forms* of social relations, i.e., form through which capitalist social relations obtain. These forms are 'form processes' (Holloway, 2010: 168). They are not 'established forms but forms in motion. For example, money as a form of mediation can be regarded as 'process of monetisation' (Holloway, 2010: 168) of social relations in the same way that we talk about statisation and legalisation. We can transform the nouns into verbs conjugated in the present continuous tense: monetising, statising, legalising. It is possible then to argue that autonomous organising challenges these form-processes or mediations. Mediations 'intervene' in the appropriation of grassroots autonomous practices by power by legalising them, or monetising them. They form social relations (Holloway, 2010: 168). By so doing they force autonomy to exist in forms that fit the capitalist/patriarchal/colonial demarcation of reality. Mediations are mediations of the capital relation, therefore, they bring about an internal relation of autonomy to capital. What is mediated is a particular –capitalist- form of existence of human activity that in this case is subordinated to the value producing process and, therefore, forced to exist in a *form of being denied* (Gunn, 1987b). That is in an alienated form that is nonetheless experienced as an alienated form.

Mediations are, then, not neutral. They do not represent institution that can be used in one or another. Therefore, their demise without the obliteration of the existence of capitalist exploitation is a chimera. Take the issue of money. Money cannot be simply avoided as in the pursuit of 'life without money' (Nelson and Timmerman, 2011). The de-commodification of life by means of universal income support schemes sponsored by the state (Standing, 2011; Gorz, 1999) will only escape the capital relation falsely: or can the problem of money be resolved with more money? These are what I have called elsewhere a 'bad utopia' (Dinerstein, 2014c). Marx's critique of political economy destroys Adam Smith's belief that money 'is simply an instrument of accounting and exchange that has no substantive economic significance.' (cited by Clarke, 1988: 32). Marx revealed that in capitalist societies money is not simply the means of exchange or an innocent mediation but the concrete expression of value, the substance of which is abstract labour. Neary and Taylor (1998: 13) argue that money is 'a social power rooted in the constitution of social subjectivity: money is 'a supreme social being' (Neary and Taylor, 1998: 13) that shapes subjectivity, fact that has been significantly denied by Sociology (Neary and Taylor, 1998: 13) In this way, money is not 'external necessity' as Mészáros suggests (1970: 91) but the expression of form of existence of labour in capitalist societies.

Gorz, a radical Marxist and advocate of universal basic income support programmes, defines the state as the 'sphere of necessity' (1982: 111), i.e. the heteronomous space where we can locate the management of necessities in order to become autonomous and free. According to Levitas (2001: 462) he believes that:

> 'nation states need to act collectively rather than competitively to limit flows of capital, and to stop colluding in the fiction that globalisation is a natural process. This, however, is simply a transitional demand. The kind of society envisaged by Gorz ... is incompatible with capitalism'.

To discuss Gorz's naïve concept of the state that is beyond the scope of this chapter what I want to argue is that mediations like the state are not external or peripheral to the production of the autonomous subject. We are not 'formally' bounded to them. It should be clear by now that the idea that mediations such as the state or money are neutral tools that can serve to the purpose of advancing radical change, must be discarded. Money, the state, the law, constitute our subjectivity, they are constitutive mediations. Autonomous organising deals with the state, money and the law. This idea will become clearer in my analyses of movements' struggles in part II of the book.

Since mediations are the political, legal, economic, cultural, social 'forms of existence' of the capital relation, or form processes (Holloway, 2010: 168), the term 'mediation inherently contains its own negation' (Bonefeld, 1987: 68). Mediation, argues Gunn (1987a) 'exists as the possibility of demediation and there is no immediacy, not even in revolutions' camp' (Gunn, 1987a: 64) (c.f. immanence). Mediation is apparent in the legislative and institutional changes that have been taken place as result of the mobilisation of the unemployed, the landless, indigenous people in Latin America in recent years. Mediations are clearly transformed as a result of the struggle over the meaning of autonomy. This is an ongoing and unavoidable process. As Bonefeld highlights: 'due to the organisational existence of labour within capital the mediation of the capital-labour relation is permanently driven into crisis-contradiction-de-mediation and further transcendence'. As I show in all cases, but particularly in my discussion about indigenous-popular movements in Bolivia (Chapter 6) 'the presence of labour within capital constantly de-mediates the mediation of capitalism' (Bonefeld, 1987: 68).

The point is not, therefore, to ignore the significance of the state, money and the law for the processes of prefiguration of alternative social relations and sociabilities, but to *change the focus* from the state, the law, policy or the economy to autonomy *without* disengaging with the former and understand the former as part of the prefigurative process. The political and organisational struggle to eliminate the distance between means and ends as a necessary dimension of prefiguration, is mediated by the multiple form-processes that intervene in the maintenance and expansion of the social relation of capital.

What I propose is to invert the terms of the question: *Can we change the world without taking the power of the state* by posing the following question: *How does the capitalist state cope with the radical change brought about by autonomous organising?* While the former question has inspired a first moment in radical thinking directed to remove the category of the state *as pivotal* to revolutionary thinking, my question allows us to move a step further and think about the predicaments of the state, the law and capital to translate autonomy in their own terms. In other words, the latter question enables a discussion of the problems of translation, and for an understanding of translation not as imposition and appropriation but as struggle (Vázquez, 2011: 41). Furthermore, the new question facilitates a movement from translation to *untranslatability*. That is, what are the signs, ideas, horizons, practices, dreams, i.e. elements, that cannot be recuperated and integrated into the logic of the state, the law or capital? The new question indicates a new moment in radical social enquiry as it opens a new space for the exploration of excess.

Autonomy and Ernst Bloch's philosophy:
an elective affinity

The connection between contemporary autonomous organising and the category of hope is intuitive. We feel (know) that autonomous struggles are much more than fighting against power. They are about hope, i.e. about realising something that is *not yet* – by trying, exploring, rehearsing, anticipating different – better – worlds. Without hope, there is no politics. Hope, claims Giroux (2009) rightly, is 'the precondition for individual and social struggle'.

I contend that, there is *an elective affinity* between Latin American movements' autonomous praxis and *the category of hope* that facilitates a conceptualisation of autonomy as *prefigurative*. But this affinity requires to be operationalised in order to allow for the concrete exploration into the processes of prefiguration beyond political rhetoric. The development of my argument that autonomy is a tool for prefiguration for indigenous and non-indigenous movements alike requires that I engage with both Ernst Bloch's philosophy, and the movements' own practices and theorising about their practices. According to my hypothesis, there are multiple significant points of convergence between the two.

Why Bloch? Ernst Bloch (1885–1977) was a German Marxist Jewish philosopher. The world wars, the holocaust, exile and the Soviet period provided the context for his intellectual development. So why is his work relevant for an analysis that uses Latin America as its empirical site? In the three volumes of his masterpiece *The Principle of Hope* (1959) and other works, Bloch presents a philosophical discussion that reflects on the human impulse to explore what is not yet. He argues that the utopian function of hope has historically inspired the creation of architectural, social, medical, political, cultural, literary and musical utopias. By engaging with Bloch's concept of hope, I will not simply argue for hope to always take us back to the question of human emancipation, which is what prefigurative politics are about. What I take from Bloch as the starting point of my journey is that hope is not fantasy or wish but rather the strongest of all human emotions that, when educated, allows us to properly engage with a hidden dimension of reality that inhabits the present one: the not yet. It is hope as the *vision of the 'not yet' reality* and the interaction with this reality that, in my view, characterises present Latin American movements and our desire to explore what this reality might bring.

In Chapter 3, I discuss in depth four main ideas taken from Bloch's philosophy, which, I argue, enable me to elaborate on a new way of understanding the politics of autonomy, in particular in Latin America. First, Bloch understands reality as an open *process*: i.e., the world is unclosed and unfinished. Why is this relevant? Because to Bloch, reality cannot be considered *real if* it does not contain the *not yet* within it. In this respect, the reality of neoliberal *pensamiento único* (singular thought) is unreal: there cannot be only one way of doing and thinking as it was argued with There Is No Alternative (TINA). The *not yet* as the possibility of an alternative is central to both movement's autonomous organising and Bloch's philosophy. If the real is process, then there is a possibility that by negating the given the other reality (inexistent or oppressed) can be experienced. In Chapter 4 how autonomy emerges as a strong force to empower the powerless against the hopelessness created by neoliberal patriarchal and colonial globalisation in the region.

Second, Bloch argues that humans endeavour outwards, beyond, in order to realise what we feel as a lack. Hope moves us forward. Through our anticipatory illuminations we can transform what he refers to as 'the not yet conscious' into concrete – utopian – experiences. This human determination, argues Bloch quite controversially, is not ideological but *anthropological* (i.e., a genuine feature of what makes us human) (Levy, 1997: 181). The concrete utopias created, for example, by workers from occupied factories and recovered enterprises in Argentina are rehearsals of better practices that can be expanded, anticipations of a future that is enacted in the 'darkness' of the present, as Bloch would say. In that sense, they not only challenge the idea that 'it is not possible', for the latter – hopelessness – is the most formidable tool of the powerful, but also provide a direction to hope, as I discuss in Chapter 5.

Third, Bloch's concept of hope is contingent and not confident; it is surrounded by danger, it is vulnerable and it is exposed to disappointment. In Chapter 6, I show how indigenous-popular movements in Bolivia 'struggle' with, against and beyond institutional and political mediations of their autonomous organising (transnational capital, the neoliberal law and the plurinational state). Fourth, Bloch argues that the utopian impulse engages with the reality of the *not yet*. This idea enables me to explore how autonomous organising creates *excess*, and how this excess transcends the given reality towards the anticipation of what is not yet. In Chapter 7, I explore how the MST venture beyond the wire and organise their concrete utopia in the encampments and settlements where hunger is eliminated and anger is channelled into collective dignity and solidarity.

The art of organising hope

Inspired in the movements' collective actions and with the assistance of Bloch's philosophy, I offer a characterisation of autonomy as the art of organising hope. Bloch argues: '[t]he prospect-exploration of What-Is-in-possibility goes towards the horizon, in the sense of unobstructed, unmeasured expanse, in the sense of Possible, which is still unexhausted and unrealized' (Bloch, 1959/1986: 209). Organising hope means a collective pursuit towards the realisation of what does *not yet* exist for each of the movements in question and the concrete anticipation of such unrealised reality in the present. Means and ends come together in the search for something is still unknown but can be, nonetheless, experienced. Lear (2006) notes that the radical nature of hope lies in that it 'is directed towards a future goodness that transcends the current ability to understand what it is. Radical hope anticipates a good for which those who have the hope as yet lack the appropriate concepts with which to understand it' (Lear, 2006: 103; see Dinerstein and Deneulin, 2012: 595). Be it named *a posteriori* as dignified work, self-management, democracy, popular justice, agrarian reform or indigenous self-determination, the *not yet* is the fundamental motivation behind the politics of autonomy in Latin America since the 1980s.

Autonomy, I propose, is not the organisational tool to transform the state but rather the transformation of the latter is a consequence of the movements' autonomous search for what is *not yet*. In order to account for this process, I put *autonomy in the key of hope* (Chapter 3). A reading of autonomy in the key of hope repositions the autonomy debate in two interconnected ways. First, autonomy in the key of hope moves away from the dichotomy 'autonomy and the state' by focusing on the prefigurative potential of autonomous struggles and practices *without* avoiding the problem of the state, which clearly shapes the politics of autonomy. Second, this focus on the prefigurative potential of autonomy allows us to bridge autonomy in the north and south and indigenous and non-indigenous autonomy without universalising classifications or obliterating differences: while the not yet can be filled with very different collective dreams in form and content, diversity is unified by the rejection of the world of capital for human dignity, as it was announced by the Zapatista's uprising twenty years ago.

The name *the art of organising hope*, therefore, problematises existing ahistorical and one-dimensional understandings of autonomy and exposes the shortcomings of universalising conceptualisations of autonomy that do not consider the specificity of the struggle of indigenous-rural-popular movements in Latin America. Organising hope in Latin America is an art that flourishes in extremely adverse contexts. It is the art of using knowledge creatively and politically to weave dreams out of misery, against the odds, amidst brutal state violence, endemic poverty, desperate hunger and social devastation. It means to learn how to engage in the politics of affection and, from there, manage setbacks and endure disheartening circumstances. It is about defying dispossession, governmental mediocrity, and uncertainty about the present and the future. *Organising* in the present continuous tense captures the movement, the process and the open character of autonomous struggles. Organising hope can be seen as 'true criticism in motion' (Tischler, 2008: 171). The art of organising hope is a prefigurative praxis. To Bloch, hope 'revolves around us and does not know where it is going, only we ourselves are the lever and the engine, external, revealed life falters: but the new thought finally breaks out, into the full adventures, into the open, with our defiant premonition, with the tremendous power of our human voice' (Bloch, 1959/1986: 1371). Hope is the ultimate category of struggle.

The book

The rest of the book is organised in three parts. Part I: Theorising Autonomy discusses autonomy theoretically. I identify and consider four modes in which autonomy has been theorised in the past four decades and explore their theoretical meanings, traditions, dimensions and trajectories. I examine the difficulties emerging from their direct application to indigenous autonomies as well as point to fundamental differences between indigenous and non-indigenous autonomies (Chapter 2). I put autonomy in the key of hope and elaborate on each of its modes (Chapter 3): negation, creation, contradiction and the production of excess. The four chapters of Part II: Navigating Autonomy, explore historical and context-specific forms of organising hope empirically. I do not offer a full historical account of the process of emergence and development of the autonomous movements in question, but I engage with their experiences in order to emphasise the four dimensions of the politics of autonomy, one in each chapter. This is a presentational strategy, for the four modes of autonomy are inextricably interlocked. In Chapter 4 (*autonomy as negation*), I examine the factors leading to what I refer to as the 'political construction of hopelessness' during the implementation of savage neoliberal structural reforms in the region. I focus on how the Zapatistas' uprising (1994) initiated a two-fold process of organising negation and restating hope and its implications for the region. In Chapter 5 (*autonomy as creation*), I re-examine the process of autonomous organising that irrupted and expanded in Argentina 2001–2002 and explore the process of shaping concrete utopias by looking at the several urban experiments of democracy, work and justice.

In Chapter 6 (autonomy as *contradiction*), I look into the predicaments of indigenous-popular movements in Bolivia. I focus on the relationship between indigenous popular movement with, against and beyond the state, capital and the law during the period of 2000–2005. I examine four moments of the struggle over the meaning of autonomy with focus on the political translation of indigenous insurgency and cosmologies into the new plurinational state and its contradictions. In Chapter 7 (*autonomy as excess*), I present the experience of the MST and elaborate on the idea that the MST does not only defy the power of the Brazilian state and landowners of *latifundios*, and transnational agribusiness – as well as give voice and facilitate the self-organisation of the landless – but confronts, disputes and transcends the *parameters of legibility* of the capitalist demarcation of reality, by *occupying* the land, *territorialising* their struggles and creating 'territories of hope', or concrete utopia (settlements), where the MST's agrarian dream is concretely fashioned. With this example, I discuss the untranslatability of autonomous organising and the nature of the surplus that cannot be appropriated by the state. In Part III: Rethinking Autonomy, I expose the connection between the value form and the *not yet*. In Chapter 8, I argue that both value and the *not yet* have something in common: they operate in a non-factual reality and they are both *unrealised* materiality. Thus, when the movements venture beyond the given demarcation of reality, value is confronted by hope, hope becoming 'anti-value in motion' (Dinerstein and Neary, 2002b). I also explore how this is different for indigenous autonomy. Finally, in Chapter 9, 'Opening Remarks', I sum up the main ideas presented in the book and suggest that despite crises, austerities and wars, we must regard the present condition as 'living in Blochian times', i.e., a time when utopia can be no longer objected not only in Latin America but in the world.

Part I
Theorising Autonomy

2
Meanings of Autonomy: Trajectories, Modes, Differences

Introduction: autonomy in Latin America

What is 'autonomy'? The concept of autonomy has been historically the subject of enquiry by both scholar and activists alike but it has recently come under acute examination, generating worldwide debates about new social movements, power, politics, the state, policy and radical change. The reason is that for the past two decades the claim and practice of collective autonomy – in pursuit of self-determination, self-management, self-representation and self-government – independently from the state and institutionalised form of labour and party politics, have served new rural and urban movements to revitalised and push forward those legacies of other radical moments of the nineteenth and twentieth centuries. The principle of autonomy has also become a new 'paradigm of resistance' for indigenous movements (Burguete Cal y Mayor, 2010) relatively recently, and has been applied to the defence of self-government, indigenous legality and territoriality against new paradigms domination such as 'multiculturalism' (Burguete Cal y Mayor, 2010: 67). Multiculturalism emerged as a counter-paradigm to control indigenous resistance since the demand from the indigenous for the right to self-affirmation and self-determination together with the right to communal property of the land became part of the international agenda of the UN and other organisations, and new policy frameworks informed by the idea of diversity emerged to integrate this demand into the nation-state policies.

The term autonomy conjures up a multiplicity of resistances. Contemporary (struggles for) 'autonom*ies*' (González, Burguete Cal y Mayor and Ortiz, 2010) bear diverse meanings throughout communities in different contexts (Mattiace, 2003: 187), as they encompass diverse histories, 'trajectories' and 'self-defined collectivities' (Cleaver, 2009: 25). Indigenous and non-indigenous, rural and urban movements, in the North and South have different conceptions and traditions of autonomy.

The indigenous movements' demand for self-determination draws on ancestral practices and experiences against hundreds of years of appropriation and oppression. The claim for autonomy is associated with the indigenous cosmology of *buen vivir*, particularly from those in the Amazon and Andean regions. This covers specific meanings attributed to time, progress, human realisation, and the relationship between sociability, sustainability and nature, embraced by communal practices based on traditions, customs and cosmologies. Here, autonomy is both continuity and innovation (i.e., about the defence of tradition and customs against colonisation, appropriation and oppression) which in no way means the romantic return to the past but a reinterpretation of the past with 'political imagination' (Khasnabish, 2008). For non-indigenous movements, the roots of autonomy originated in the formation of anarchist resistance and mutual societies, cooperatives, Marxism *consejista* during the first decades of the twentieth century, and the work of the French group *Socialism ou Barbarie* (SoB), the Situacionist International at the end of 1950s, and *Autonomia Operaia* and the *Quaderni Rossi* in the 1960s (Albertani, 2009a). The autonomist movement became a political current within the left that embraces anti-authoritarian, libertarian and anti-bureaucratic struggles, particularly in the late 1960s, and during the 1970s mainly in Europe, with resonance in the South.

Leaving aside the disparities between indigenous and non-indigenous understandings of autonomy there are also significant contrasts between autonomous organising in the north and in the south (Ouviña, 2004). While in the North and with urban movements autonomy is associated with the struggle against the state and the abandonment of the idea of the state at the main locus for social emancipation, in the indigenous context, autonomy must be seen as the defence of territorial spaces of indigenous peoples and the recognition of their right to self-government by the state.

While autonomy in the north has been discussed as the anti-politics (Katsiaficas, 2006), as the subaltern vis-à-vis dominant classes and as a model of society (Modonesi, 2009, 2010; Thwaites Rey, 2004), as a temporal spatial strategy and interstitial strategy, and as a process of creation and everyday life revolution (Pickerill and Chatterton, 2006), indigenous struggles are seen as a tool for an insightful critique of modernity/ capitalism, coloniality and the development paradigm (Escobar, 2010; Santos et al., 2008).

Refusal, non-conformity, civil disobedience and the reclaiming of spaces of freedom, democracy and self-determination against global capitalist social injustice in the north do not completely inform autonomous movements in the south, whose collective actions are directly connected to everyday concerns and vital needs usually under conditions of state repression, misery and poverty. Latin American movements have tended to led a 'rebellion from the margins' rather than be part of the mainstream network of social movements. They reject 'politics as usual' (Lazar, 2006: 185) and since they seriously suspect the state, they reject state power in principle, rather than seek to consolidate spaces for negotiation within it like in central democracies. Latin American social movements delivered what it can be seen as community policy (agrarian, labour, social, economic, heath, education) or policy from below which is source of resistance and tool for ameliorating poverty and unemployment. Many of their legitimate activities (like land or factory occupations) are considered illegal by the state. This might be partly explained by the bigger sense of 'distance' of the majority of the Latin American population from the state (Davis, 1999; Lazar and McNeish, 2006).

In Latin America, autonomous practices have been imagined, framed and organised in remarkably creative ways, coping with poverty, tackling the 'absence' of the state policy. This historical extrication was exacerbated by the crisis of the state that has been deeper in Latin America than in Europe –at least until recently (Slater, 1985: 9). Latin American social movements have contested excessive centralisation of decision-making power complemented with administrative inefficiency and the strong influence of informal political actors in the distribution of policy benefits and focus policies (Auyero, 2000), the state's failure to provide adequate services, social security and welfare provision in the context of increasing scepticism about traditional political parties and leaders (Slater, 1985: 8). In addition to this, while it is generally accepted that the (relatively new) indigenous demand for self-affirmation and self-determination (autonomy) must be seen in the light of five hundred years of resistance in defence of indigenous cosmologies, traditions, habits and customs and, against colonial power, the implications of this for a conceptualisation of current forms of indigenous autonomies have not been entirely understood in the non-indigenous world.

The four modes of autonomy

In the following sections, I review different treatments and trajectories of the concept of autonomy. My review is not exhaustive but it is organised around the above-mentioned four modes of the autonomous organising that are usually treated separately in the existing literature on autonomy (see Figure 2.1). I also expose the differences between indigenous and non-indigenous understanding of autonomy and the problems of universalising conceptualisations of autonomy produced in the North to explaining autonomy in Latin America

Negating: refusal to work, negative dialectics and disagreement

Negativity constitutes a key moment in social antagonism, that is, the 'negative, denunciatory moment' (Moylan, 1997: 111) of utopia as the instant of rejection of what it is. Since the 1960s, negativity is regarded as a chief component of autonomous struggles. Refusal to work, one of its forms of expression, materialized as an explicit workers' motto in some sectors of the Italian working class in the 1960s and 1970s. This, according to Cleaver, intended to remind the left that 'the working class has always struggled against work, from the time of primitive accumulation right on through to the present' (in Cleaver and De Angelis, 1993). In Negri's theory of communism refusal to work is an act directed to destroy surplus labour (Negri, 1991: 149). 'Refusal to work' was a form of resistance by *autonomia operaia* within the context of precarious work in Italy in the 1960s. In the late 1990s, the German group Krisis restored

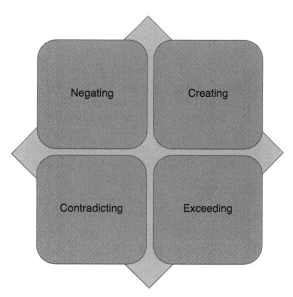

Figure 2.1   The four modes of autonomy

the idea of refusal to work in their 'Manifesto against Work' (Gruppe Krisis, 1999). There, they portray capitalist work as a coercive social principle through which exploitation and patriarchal society exists and call for the abolishment of work altogether. Refusal to work presents itself as an alternative option against both 'socialism imagined either as state-planned economy to alleviate exploitation or as small scale production to remedy alienation' (Weeks, 2011: 101).

But can refusal to work inform autonomy in the present? Lilley and Papadopoulos (2014) argue that in present forms of capitalism (bio-financial) refusal to work has become impossible because that the production of value impregnates every aspect of social life. In this sense, any political 'autonomous' alternative must deal with the contradiction entailed in the embeddedness of autonomous politics.

Holloway points to the contradictions brought about by refusal and negativity, for they inhabit working-class identity. He argues that 'we do not struggle *as* working class, we struggle *against* being working class, and against being classified … there is nothing positive about being members of the working class, about being ordered, commanded, separated from our product and our process of production' (Holloway, 2002c: 36–37, italics in the original). To him, the 'working class' is not constituted but permanently being constituted in a process that is based on the constant and violent separation of object from the subject. It is by engaging with the resistance that inhabits the concept and reality of the working class that we can anticipate not being the working class (Holloway, 2002c: 36–37).

This contradiction of being and not being the working class informs what Holloway and others regard as a current move from identity politics to anti-identitarian politics. It is argued that new forms of mobilisation and resistance *reject identity politics* on behalf of the formation of non-identities of resistance beyond state classifications. Flesher Fominaya (2010: 399) highlights that alter globalisation movements, for example, 'reject ideological purity and fixed identities on principle'. To Seel and Plows, this 'anti-identitarian orientation [constitutes the] "hallmark" of alter globalisation movements' (cited in Fleyer Fominaya, 2010: 399). What this shows is the fluidity in identity formation and the falsehood of *positive* identities, which classify and pigeonhole people as well as close reality and possibilities.

The decision to explain this 'anti-identitarian' mode of autonomous organising has brought Theodor Adorno's negative dialectics into the picture. Despite Adorno's political pessimism, his negative dialectics is argued to engage with the open character of autonomous struggles; that is, an appreciation of the reality as open (Schwartzböck, 2008). How? To Adorno, there is no possibility of closure: 'the negation of the negation would be another identity, a new delusion, a projection of consequential logic – and ultimately of the principle of subjectivity – upon the absolute' (Adorno, 1995: 160). 'Dialectics' in Adorno's words mean 'to break the compulsion to achieve identity, and to break it by means of the energy stored up in that compulsion and congealed in its objectifications' (Adorno, 1995: 157).

Negative dialectics is 'the consistent sense of non-identity, of that which does not fit' (Holloway, 2009a: 13). Matamoros Ponce contends that 'Adorno ... places himself *beyond* the existing path, in the figure of negativity as a constellation of hope, that which is hidden in abnormality and resistance against the hierarchies of value and structuring homogeneity' (Matamoros Ponce, 2009: 201). Negative dialectics means that movements' praxis must be seen as 'practical negativity'. Rather than embrace power or counter-power, negativity – according to Holloway – articulates 'anti-power'. Our 'doing' – which in his critique of capital replaces the category of 'work' and designates what we do, as humans, as people – is anti-identitarian; it is fundamentally *negative*: '[t]he doing of the doers is deprived of social validation: we and our doing become invisible ... The flow of doing becomes an antagonistic process in which the doing of most is denied, in which the doing of most is appropriated by the few' (Holloway, 2002a: 29–30). Doing (autonomy) is the negative movement that resists identity, that defies the forces that permanently transform our creativity and power to do into abstract labour and power over: 'doing changes, negates an existing state of affairs' (Holloway, 2002a: 23). The idea of resistance as practical negativity permits Holloway to make the distinction between negative and positive autonomism. While positive autonomism is classificatory and 'flirts with progressive governments', negative autonomism 'pushes against and beyond all identities, part of the budding and flowering of useful creative-doing. The distinction matters politically' (Holloway, 2009b: 99). Present autonomous resistance struggles are argued to be necessarily anti-identitarian.

The other significant form of conceiving autonomy and negativity is delineated by Rancière's critique of neoliberal democracy. From a radical democracy tradition, Rancière defines politics not as a form of deliberation and consensus but as the *possibility of disagreement*: politics is an 'exception to the principles according to which the gathering of people operates' (Rancière, 2001: Thesis 6). Why is this important for an understanding of the negative mode of autonomy? Rancière defines politics (which is synonymous with democracy and autonomy) as *disagreement*. Politics *breaks* the logic of 'consensus' or the logic of what Rancière calls *la police* (what we normally call politics), which encompass, 'the allocation of ways of doing, ways of being, and ways of saying' (Rancière, 1999: 29) in politics or how things are. Politics entail dissensus *beyond* the conflict between opposed interests or different opinions on an issue. With disagreement, those who do not have a voice within *la police* – disrupt the established order. Events such as the *Caracazo* (1989), the Chiapas uprising (1994) or the popular uprising in Argentina (2001) called into question the foundations of *la police*. Through disagreement, movements opened a discussion about the *meaning of* politics altogether and the possibility of embracing alternative horizons.

Creating: self-instituting of society, self-valorisation and the common

While 'negating' is a key feature of autonomous organising, there is a second equally important and almost inseparable component of autonomous organising: creating. Castoriadis' notion of autonomy -developed throughout the 1950s and 1960s in *Socialisme ou Barbarie* (SoB, 1947) is an example of the emphasis on this dimension of autonomy. Castoriadis articulated a virulent critique of both capitalism and the bureaucracy of the Union of Soviet Socialist Republics (USSR). SoB regarded autonomy and the self-organisation of the proletariat not only as a source of emancipation, but also as a tool to fight against communist parties' and trade unions' bureaucratic power (Blanchard, 2009). SoB's treatment of autonomy was a weapon against state socialism. The group conceptualised socialism as the autonomy of the social, thus innovating the terms of the Marxist debate at the time. SoB described socialism as 'nothing else than the conscious and perpetual activity of the masses' (Chaulieu/ Castoriadis, 1955). In this version of Socialism, the experience of self-determination was crucially important. By referring to the Greek's invention of politics, Castoriadis argues that 'the creation of democracy and philosophy is truly the creation of a *historical movement* in the strong sense' (Castoriadis, 1991: 160–161, italics in the original). The self-interrogation that inhabits autonomy 'has bearing not on "facts" but on the social imaginary significations and their possible grounding. This is a moment of creation, and it ushers in a new type of society and a new type of individuals ... autonomy is a *project*' (Castoriadis, 1991: 165, italics in the original). Autonomy in the wide sense, is a project that illuminates the 'instituting power of society [and] in the narrow sense' is 'the lucid and deliberate activity whose object is the explicit institution of society ... and its working as ... legislation, jurisdiction, government – in view of the *common ends* and the *public endeavours* the society deliberately proposes to itself' (Castoriadis, 1991: 174, italics in the original). Like this, Castoriadis criticises Kant's idea of autonomy as conforming to the law. He proposes that autonomy rather *questions the law* permanently and self-reflexively, individually and collectively. To him, 'autonomy is the reflective activity of a reason creating itself in an endless movement, both as individual and social reason' (Castoriadis, 1991: 164).

Stavrakakis (2007: 57) notes that Castoriadis' focus on creativity finds a close friend in Antonio Negri. Indeed, from a different intellectual tradition, Negri explains the creating mode of autonomy first as working-class self-valorisation and later on as immanence. Amidst the process of autonomous political radicalisation in Italy during the 1970s, the idea of self-valorisation 'inverted' the class perspective by focusing on the development of working-class autonomy as *opposed to* the valorisation of capital. Negri belongs to the branch of Marxism, that Cleaver named as Autonomist Marxism. Negri emphasises 'the positive moments of working class autonomy ... the power of creative affirmation, the power to constitute new practices' (Cleaver, 1992: 129). As articulated by *Operaismo* and *Autonomia* (*Potere Operaio* and *Lotta Continua*), editors of *Quaderni Rossi*, self-valorisation was a process of creation of autonomous spaces not necessarily connected to the labour process (Negri, 1991: 165). *Autonomia Operaia* embraced direct action against institutional forms of labour and politics.

'Self-valorisation' designates 'the ability of workers to define their interests and to struggle for them – to go beyond mere reaction to exploitation, or to self-defined leadership, and to take the offensive in ways that shape the class struggle and define the future' (Cleaver in Cleaver and De Angelis, 1993). Autonomist Marxism provided a general line of reasoning on working-class self-activity and the politics of a diversity of movements and ideas within the Marxist tradition (Cleaver, 2011: 54). The 'inversion' of the class perspective advocated by Tronti (Cleaver, 1992) – centres the analysis on class struggle rather than on capitalist development. Cleaver highlights that the term 'Self-valorisation ... focus[es] attention on the existence of autonomy in the self-development of workers vis-à-vis capital' (Cleaver and De Angelis, 1993) rather than as a derivative of the development of capital. Self-valorisation refocused attention onto the struggle against capital and for new forms of being: it involves 'a process of valorization which is autonomous from capitalist valorization – a self-defining, self-determining process which goes from mere resistance to capitalist valorization to a positive project of self-constitution' (Cleaver, 1992: 129).

To Negri, the year 1968 marked a new phase in the history of class struggle, wherein a decomposition and recomposition of work produced significant changes in the workers' autonomous resistance. Labour was becoming increasingly more abstract, immaterial and intellectual while the industrial form of work was declining, thus giving room to a new form of postindustrial subjectivity. The identity of the 'mass worker' was shifting into the predominance of the 'social worker'. This new class subject was more disperse and its struggles more fragmented as well as expansive. Hence, while Castoriadis 'desires to guarantee at all costs the prospects of a political radical totally unrestrained imagination' and focus on 'creativity and its folding in an immanent space of meaning underlying human life ... Negri ... identifies immanence as the dynamism of life' (Stavrakakis, 2007: 57). In both cases, creativity is seen as a positive and danger-free sphere of life.

More recently, a new generation of autonomist thinkers (and also Negri) renewed the idea of self-valorisation vis-à-vis neoliberal global capital, through the concept of *the common*, where new practices of conviviality and solidarity are emerging. Hardt and Negri define the common by emphasising the productive feature and the harmonic relation of such production with nature, that is, the 'results of social production that are necessary for social interaction and further production, such as knowledges, languages, codes, information, affects and so forth' (Hardt and Negri, 2009: viii). Many of the principles embraced in current social movements such as 'direct democracy, inclusiveness, horizontality' De Angelis claims 'should themselves be seen as constitutive forces of what commons to form and what communities to shape' (De Angelis, 2004: 332–333). De Angelis (2007) argues that 'the commons are forms of *direct* access to social wealth, access that is not mediated by competitive market relations' (De Angelis, 2007, italics in the original). The common indicates that autonomy is a spatial practice (Chatterton, 2010: 901). Pickerill and Chatterton (2006: 720) call these 'autonomous geographies': 'spaces where there is a desire to constitute non-capitalist, collective forms of politics, identity and citizenship. These are created through a combination of resistance and creation, and a questioning and challenging of dominant laws and social norms'.

Holloway (2010) uses the term 'cracks' to represent 'embryonic forms of society', that is 'not a communism but a commonising' (Holloway, 2010: 210). The cracks present not only a spatial rupture but also temporal fissures in domination that challenge capitalist time (Holloway, 2010: 29–30). Esteva (2014) contributes to this 'new thinking an old idea' by arguing for a process of 'commoning' (Esteva, 2014: il55)[1]. He regards social commons as sites for the production of alternative knowledges to the 'institutional production of truth' (Esteva, 2014: il55). Social commons, he suggests, are social relationships, not defined by ownership. Finally commoning is 'realistic' (Esteva, 2014: il55–56): 'Commoning, communism, reclaiming, and regenerating our commons and creating new commons' he argues, 'define the limits of the current era' (Esteva, 2014: il56).

The notion of the common has been also associated to the critique of the development paradigm, for the commons are open spaces for the recovering and creation of forms of knowledge that reject the growth model of development altogether, and reveal the hypocrisy of the alternative development paradigm that, since the 1970s, presents itself as a progressive policy. While embracing and promoting participation from below, alternative development has become a 'buzzword' (Cornwall and Brock, 2005) that facilitates the deradicalisation of the commons and their adaptation to WB-led policy. The commons embrace alternatives *to* development. (Santos and Rodríguez Garavito, 2006; Dinerstein and Deneulin, 2012: 585). Many autonomous endeavours implemented by popular movements in Latin America within the spirit of the social and solidarity economy can be interpreted in this light. Post-development (Esteva and Prakash, 1998; Escobar, 1992, 2010; Santos and Rodríguez Garavito, 2006) regards the commons as attempts to create non-capitalist forms of production and uphold other knowledges (Santos et al., 2008; Escobar, 1992). For post-development critics human flourishing cannot be achieved by improving the management' and 'distribution' of wealth. While WB-led alternative development deepens the 'westernisation of the world', alternatives to development reject it wholly (Latouche, 1993: 161). In this sense, autonomy 'does not call for a "better" way of doing development, not even for "another development"' but a critique that allows to think of alternatives to development for which the role of social movements seems crucial, particularly in creating 'alternative visions of democracy, economy and society' (Escobar, 1992: 22).

Feminist geographers Gibson and Graham coined the term 'community economy' (Gibson-Graham, 2006) to name the politics of possibilities that can shape creatively a post-capitalist society), highlighting that the seeds of a such society are already present within capitalism, that non-capitalist forms of association can be produced today. They claim that there is then no need to 'wait' for a revolution in the traditional sense for 'the making anew political imaginary is under way, or at least a remapping of the political terrain' (Gibson-Graham, 2006: xix; 2005). 'In Take back the Economy', Gibson-Graham (2013) demolish the idea that the economy is something separate from people. They offer a guide to activists as how to recover the 'economy' (taking it back by taking back work, business, the market, property and finance). In the same vein, North (2007, 2010) proposes to create local money to empower communities and contest the power of the financiers, particularly in time of crisis. The local money stays with the community.

Yet, the creative mode of autonomy does not tell us much about the predicaments and difficulties that saying no and create the new bring about to autonomous organising. In general, movements navigate contradictions and struggle to open spaces that foster radical practices. The commons are contradictory spaces that point to the *(im)possibility* of autonomy, that is the (im)possibility of creating life outside capitalism and to the predicaments of the task (Böhm et al., 2010).

Contradicting: autonomy vis-à-vis the system

As argued in the introduction to this book, the analysis of the process of prefiguring alternative realities must include an exploration into the processes of struggle with, against and beyond the state, the law and capital as well as the contradictions within existing forms of insubordination. This multi-faceted struggle is an essential component of prefiguration, rather than constituting another type of struggle. Autonomous practices are embedded in, and shaped by, their past and contemporary backgrounds and context of production so that the state, money and the law mediate autonomy. It follows that prefiguration is not only about the rejection (negation) of the given reality and the creation of new realities. Prefiguration is also about steering through the predicaments produced by capitalist, patriarchal and colonial social relations, and about navigating the challenges of the struggle over the meanings of autonomy – for the state would attempt to integrate, accommodate and subordinate autonomy to the logic of power. In what follows, I explore several approaches to the movement of resistance and integration that underpins autonomous struggles in relation to the 'system'.

Hegemony, counter-hegemony, and the critique of hegemony

Gramsci's thought has returned to the discussion of present forms of autonomous resistance. He challenged the separation between civil society and the state as constructed by liberal democracy and posited the collective action of the subaltern as a counter-hegemonic force within the hegemonic order. Hegemony designates the economic and political control by the dominant class, but also the ability of this class to impose its own views of the world on the subordinate groups, thus becoming the view of society as a whole. To Gramsci, the naturalisation of capitalism as the only possible form of society is not just sustained with state coercion. Hegemony presupposes consent. The revolutionary process, then, requires more than taking the power of the state to succeed. Following Marx's footsteps, within a context of emergence of Fascism, Gramsci argues that civil society is not an uncoerced arena of mutual interaction as it is usually depicted by liberal thinkers, but the sphere of antagonism and conflict. The tension between the role of legitimising capitalist hegemony and forming a new *senso commune,* inhabits civil society. It is from civil society that the elements of a new society will emerge. The first step of the revolutionary enterprise is the anticipation of those elements of a new society within the existing civil society. An intellectual direction by organic intellectuals is required in the 'war of positions' that could articulate a new worldview within the present one that anticipates a future revolution. As Thomas (2009) suggests Gramsci's philosophy of praxis 'was placed in connection with *senso commune* [common sense], beginning with its elements pregnant with a new conception of the world. It aims at an intellectual and moral reform of *senso comune*, thus allowing the subaltern masses to exit from their passivity, to construct a new experience of the world and to become "actors"' (Thomas, 2009: 16). *Subalternity* therefore means that the experience of the subordinated bears a tension between acceptance and incorporation and rejection and autonomisation (Modonesi, 2009: 51).

With Gramsci, the category of 'subaltern' acquired theoretical status for the first time in relation to the problem of subjectivity and subordination within hegemony (Modonesi, 2010: 26). In the 1980s, Eric Stokes and Ranajit Guha formed the Subaltern Studies Group (SSG) to engage with Gramsci's idea of the need for the subaltern to become hegemonic. SSG were critical of existing (Marxist) versions of Indian and South Asian history that had the elites as their protagonists and saw the rebellion of the masses as a *reaction* to their domination. SSG proposed that the 'subaltern domain of politics' deserved its own space for 'developing alternative conceptions of popular consciousness and mobilization in their own right, that is, independent from conventional politics', that accounts for 'new forms of doing politics' (Escobar, 1992: 43). These scholars were not only creating a new field of study but also politically attending to Gramsci's concern with the problem of domination and organisation. Subaltern Studies (SS) articulated a new narrative based on the everyday life experience as well as demonstrations and uprisings of the subordinated. The SSG was both a form of academic knowledge production and a form of acting on the side of the subaltern (Beverley 2001: 49; from the Latin American Subaltern Studies Group, see Rodríguez, 2001). Grosfoguel – who is co-founder of the Decolonial School after a split with the Latin American SSG – contends that despite its significant contribution to the critique of Eurocentrism (i.e., the postcolonial critique), the SSG advocated a Western epistemology that favoured Gramsci and Foucault thus weakening and limiting their critique of Eurocentrism (Grosfoguel, 2008). To Chibber (2013), however, the problem with Subaltern Studies (SS) is of a different kind: he contends that their work 'obscures capitalism', that is, SS cannot explain, or put forward a critique of, global capitalism that they believe do, simply because 'it systematically misrepresents how capitalism works', i.e. particularly by 'accept[ing] a highly romanticized story about power relations in capitalism ... [and] underestimate[ing] capitalism's ability not only to tolerate heterogeneity ... but to actively promote it' (Chibber, 2013: 286–287). As Chibber's book title suggest, the 'spectre of capital' (Chibber, 2013) hunts postcolonial Theory. I will come back to this (see section 'Spot the difference') and discuss the problem in Chapter 8, where I explore the inner connection between autonomy, hope and the value form.

Like the SSG, James Scott theorises the autonomy of the subaltern, but, unlike them he rejects the concept of hegemony altogether and takes issue with ideology. His ethnographic research on the *infrapolitics* of the dominated emphasises the significance of the subaltern's everyday daily experience for an understanding of their resistance to power. Insurgency is a rational process by which the rural masses consciously evaluate their actions. Scott (1990) uses a now-famous citation from an Ethiopian proverb 'When the great lord passes, the wise peasant bows deeply and silently farts' to warn us against the mistake of conceiving domination as a *fait accompli*. To him, there is not hegemony. There are two kinds of transcripts: the public and the hidden, wherein the public transcript 'is not the whole story' (Scott, 1990: 3). The public transcript does not consider the subordinated's opinion so the acquiescence contains a degree of 'performance of deference and consent'. Scott proposes that conformist behaviour is not the result of hegemony – as he thinks Gramsci believed – or the product of false consciousness. It is about an ideological struggle wherein subordinated groups imagine 'the reversal and negation of their domination' (Scott, 1990: 81), but they decide not to act for they have a 'hidden script'.

'Hegemonic' struggles: equivalence, antagonism and (im)possibility

In the mid-1980s, Laclau and Mouffe (1985) offered a distinctive and controversial version of 'hegemony' that implicitly repositioned the discussion of the autonomy of the social field, by recuperating the project of liberal democracy for radical resistance. They tackled the problem of 'appropriation' and recuperation of autonomy by the state. In arguing for the openness of the hegemonic order, they use the term autonomy to designate 'a mode of institution of objectivity: [where] objectivity or the being of things is an effect of hegemonic articulation, and all institution is by nature precarious and incomplete' (Arditi, 2007: 210). To Laclau and Mouffe (1985: 130), there is no possibility of suturation of the social. Society is possible due to the 'logic of equivalence' (Laclau and Mouffe, 1985: 130) that enables fragmented actors to become subjectivity. But, there is also a 'logic of antagonism' at work that disrupts the logic of equivalence and the possibility of some struggles to become hegemonic. This dynamic is contradictory and demonstrates the impossibility of a perfect, social, autonomous arrangement.

The debate about about the '(im)possibility' of autonomy (Böhm et al., 2010; Albertani et al., 2009) was invigorated by the intensification of the process of enclosure and the recuperations of autonomy into the state and capital's domain to which autonomous movements permanently resist in various ways. This has been recently depicted as the 'communism of capital' (Beverungen et al., 2013), a movement towards the 'corruption of autonomy by "free" marketers' (Notes from Nowhere, 2003: 108), or the incorporation of autonomy via 'impersonal market mechanisms' (De Angelis, 2007: 133, 2013). Appropriation does not only control the alternative practices that emerged at the common, but translates them into complementary practices: capital tends to appropriate new forms of commoning in order to preserve itself as a social force, so: 'How can we participate in this commonality without at the same time setting a limit, refusing capital's measure of things and its drive to separate, subsume and co-opt?' (De Angelis, 2010: 957).

Outside hegemony, parallel networks and the logic of affinity: eliminating contradiction

A solution to the problem of appropriation has been to locate autonomy *outside* the dynamic of appropriation. As already mentioned, Bey's (TAZ) (Bey, 2011) suggests that grass-roots politics take place *outside the state*. Radical change would be produced by the 'politics of defection' where utopia is enacted in a particular space/zone (Arditi, 2007: 220). By using the example of the Argentine revolt of December 2001, and without rejecting the theory of hegemony, Arditi claims that there is an outside to hegemony. The argentine uprising was not necessarily 'a sign of disintegration of the hegemony of the nineties in Argentina' (Arditi, 2007: 212). To him, the Argentine revolt shows that there is a 'post-hegemonic outside' that speaks of modes of articulation of an autonomous struggle that not necessarily implies an 'effort to forge a relation of equivalence between them' (Arditi, 2007: 213). This is 'a singularity of and action outside the format of chain of equivalents' that Laclau and Mouffe suggest, that breaks the 'texture of domination' (Arditi, 2007: 217).

Day (2004: 740) concurs that current forms of autonomous resistance are not hegemonic and communicated by a 'chain of equivalents' as Laclau and Mouffe argue, but rather they are articulated by 'the logic of affinity'. The latter emerges 'out of an anarchist tradition of theory and practice which rejects the struggle for hegemony in its dual (Gramscian) nature as domination over others via the state and as "consensual" direction of others via ideological sway over civil society'. Hardt and Negri also explore affinity by offering the concept of 'the multitude' to designate 'the common subject of labor, that is, the real flesh of postmodern production, and at the same time the object from which collective capital tries to make the body of its global development'. In their view, the multitude is a plural subject 'able to act in common and thus rule itself' (Hardt and Negri, 2004: 99–100). But the logic of affinity eliminates the contradictions that materialise during the struggle in and against power, and among different components of the 'multitude'. The multitude appears as an immanent force. To Deleuze and Guattari immanence is 'a plane of non contradiction ... Here, there are no longer any forms or developments of forms; nor are there subjects or the formation of subjects. There is no structure; any more than there is genesis' (Deleuze and Guattari, 1999: 266).

There is no outside: the 'inner connection'

So far, I have discussed the contradictions that populate autonomy by exploring the concept of hegemony and its derivatives – counter-hegemonic, hegemonic, subaltern, anti-hegemonic and outside hegemony. In this section, I present and discuss an alternative view of the contradictions that inhabit insubordination offered by Open Marxism (OM). The OM's critique does not take issue with the concept of hegemony–which it rejects- but with both structuralist and autonomist Marxist conceptions of the capital relation and its implications for an understanding of insubordination. Structuralist Marxist analyses focus on the 'dynamics of capitalism' as a 'system' and to neglect the dimension of class struggle. The approach starts from the 'logic' of capitalist development and its crises that separates structure from class struggle: this entails 'a deterministic conceptualisation of capital in that capital becomes a structure of inescapable lines of development, subordinating social practice to predetermined laws' (Bonefeld et al., 1992 xii). The regrettable outcome of such focus has been that, in their hands, capital becomes the subject, a 'blind subject' (Postone, 1993).

The response of autonomist Marxism to this was to shift in focus from the analysis of 'capitalist development' to that of 'class struggle' (Cleaver, 1992). As already mentioned, Tronti inverted the class perspective to emphasise labour's self-activity and working-class self-valorisation (Negri, 1992). But the critique of the predominance of the *logic* of capital in Marxist analyses by autonomists have created *two subjects* of class struggle that oppose each other: capital and labour. Holloway contends that this is wrong for there is only one subject. The 'real force of Marx's theory of struggle lies not in the reversal of the polarity between capital and labour, but in its dissolution' (Holloway, 1995: 164). To Bonefeld (1994) the fabrication of two entities 'destroys the insight that labour is a constitutive power [for] capital is conceived as a subject in its own right' (Bonefeld, 1994: 44).

The critique of structuralist Marxism requires, therefore, not an inversion of the class perspective from capital to labour but an explanation of the *mode* in which labour exists in and against capital. By separating labour from capital (which allows for the argument for refusal to work and self-valorisation) the autonomist critique of structuralist Marxism cannot explain how human activity is the producer of 'perverted forms' of existence, that is, that labour is against itself in the form of capital (Dinerstein, 2002a). An *inner* rather than external connection between capital and labour must be established. In capitalism, *labour* (human practice) mediates itself and exists in two forms: as labour and as capital (Dinerstein and Neary, 2002b) and becomes dominated by its own objectification, which in turn will also shape the forms of subjectivity. Therefore, labour exists 'in a mode of being denied' (Gunn, 1994; Bonefeld, 1994: 51). This presents a different horizon for the autonomous struggle that emerges from *within* capital, and it is constantly struggling against itself. Autonomy can only be conceived as *a self-contradictory force* embedded within the social relations that labour itself (as a producer and as value-creating activity) creates and mediates (Dinerstein, 2002a).

Excess: extimacy, bio-political exceeding, mismatch and overflowing

I have discussed three modes of autonomous organising that are present in the literature on autonomy and radical change: negativity, creativity and contradiction. In this section, I pose the following question: Is autonomous organising a praxis that oscillates eternally between rebellion and integration or is there anything a surplus produced out of this contradictory swinging movement? Do we need to talk about autonomy and 'excess'?

Following Lacan, Rothenberg (2010: 13) elaborates an innovative thesis to explain how the social is a 'site of excess'. She suggests that the topology of the Möbious band ('with its apparently impossible configuration of two sides that turn out') provides 'a convenient model for understanding how, at every point in the social field, an irreducible excess attends social relations' (Rothenberg, 2010: 12). She offers the term the 'Möbious subject' (Rothenberg, 2010: 12) to solve the problem of understanding social change through either being produced by external causation (i.e., economic forces) or by 'immanent causality' where causes are rendered 'too close to its effects' (Rothenberg, 2010: 30). Her 'extimate causal model' – that draws on Lacan's term 'extimacy' – which describes 'the form of causality peculiar to the subject of the unconscious ... presents the social space as a special unbounded yet finite spatial object' (Rothenberg, 2010: 11). Rothenberg locates her proposal between the two above-mentioned, opposed, 'causal' models: external causation (exemplified by Althuser's structuralist Marxism, in particular), and immanent causation (exemplified by Deleuze's immanence). This approach is tempting but problematic. To deal with my critique fully is beyond the scope of this chapter. My questions are how does the Möbious subject engages with the material process of its own production? What are the dynamics of social change that the Möbious subject is involved in? What constitutes the *substance* of excess produced by extimacy? What are the politics and the political economy of the production of excess?

Unlike Rothenberg, Hardt and Negri resolutely explain the 'excess' produced by social relations of capital by addressing the issue of the measurability of value. In *Commonwealth*, they argue that, in the bio-political context, value cannot be measured for it 'overflows the threshold of political and economic control' (Hardt and Negri, 2009: 317). The 'bio-political exceeding ... overflows the barriers that the tradition of modern political economy built to control labor-power and the production of value' (Hardt and Negri, 2009: 317).

While Hardt and Negri point at the immanent and creative-positive aspect of excess, scholars working at the Universidad Autónoma de Puebla, Mexico (I call them the *Puebla School*) theorise 'excess' by engaging with Adorno's negative dialectics (see previous section on negation). As we have seen, Adorno's negative dialectics points to the way in which the non-identitarian subject rejects the resolution of the dialectic contradiction in a positive synthesis. To Tischler (2009: 103) the *particularity* becomes 'a main critical category' for it 'expresses the surplus of the existing confronted with what is dominant, or the system, a surplus or excess created by social antagonism' (Tischler, 2009: 13).

But what does this mean in terms of autonomy and social change? It means that autonomy is explained, as we have seen, as the rejection of homogeneisation, as non-identity. This is relevant for it reveals that to 'think of radical social change in terms of figures of totality is part of a process of perversion and fetishisation of the idea of revolutionary change' (Tischler, 2009: 109).

Holloway expresses the idea of excess by referring to the *overflowing* that emerges out of the mismatch between doing (our power to do) and abstract labour (Holloway, 2010). There is a continual subordination of human practice (doing) to the value-creation process as the latter self-expands (Dinerstein, 2012), but total subordination is impossible (Holloway, 2010a: 173). To the Free Association, 'moments of excess' connect 'exceptional moments with everyday life': 'our abstract potential always exceeds and tries to escape the conditions of its production ... in the most obvious sense there is an excess in life ... a surplus of collectivity' (Free Association, 2011: 32), that is, an excess produced by solidarity and cooperation. There is, they argue, another type of excess that becomes apparent when 'our "excess of life" explodes' (Free Association, 2011: 32). These are moments of 'subversive energy, freedom and possibility' (Free Association, 2011: 33).

Spot the difference

In this section I expose some of the features of the indigenous struggle for autonomy and point to the problems of universalising conceptualisations of autonomy produced in the north and to characterise non-indigenous resistance. My critique will not address each of the abovementioned theorisations but offers a general discussion about the inadequacy of commonly used approaches and assumptions about resistance in the present.

Identity and the collective

Among anti-globalisation movements there has been a tendency towards non-identitarian politics. My question is to what extent this tendency can be said true in the case of indigenous movements? Indigenous peoples' collective identity is a weapon to negate a reality that oppresses and invisibilises their struggle or in the best case scenario, recognises it in a colonial fashion (i.e. multiculturalism). Some western scholars equate indigenous identity with backwardness. Hardt and Negri (2009), for example, argue against the kind of indigenous resistance that relies on the affirmation of identity for, according to them, it leaves us stuck with 'antimodernity', that is, with the opposition of indigenous struggles to modernity/colonialism. Inspired by their reading of Bonfil Batalla's idea that ethnic identity is not ahistorical or 'foreign to social becoming' (cited in Hardt and Negri 2009: 105), they stand against indigenous fundamentalism, for it is – according to Hardt and Negri, fixed in the past, and if coloniality of power would be defeated, then indigenous people would surely return to their 'authentic' identities. They offer the term 'altermodernity' as an alternative to the binary opposition between modernity-antimodernity.

Although the rejection of any fundamentalism –indigenous or not- is welcome, this way of framing the problem of indigenous identity is misleading for it ignores a simple fact: that indigenous people's defence of memory constitutes their *present* form of resistance, a resistance that brings the 'past' into the future. Aymara people 'are' Aymara. They have not stopped being Aymara or will return to being Aymara in the future. Aymara is a form of being, not an external identity that can be changed or manipulated politically. Identity affirms what they are not allowed to be as a result of coloniality. Are indigenous people 'anti-modern'? For example, the Zapatistas' 'revolutionary we' (*nosotros revolucionario*) (Pascual et al., 2013) affirms Zapata's national revolution, indigenous insurgency and ancestral practices, but to suggest that those who rein-vented revolution for the twenty first century are fixed in the past would be preposterous. For the Zapatistas and other indigenous movements, identity is a form of political resistance against internal colonialism and it is experienced as a point of departure from where to destabilise domi-nant regulatory processes from the state (Mora, 2010: 311) that continue to oppress, render invisible or regulate indigenous cosmologies. The challenge for us is not to find the best classification of indigenous strug-gles as anti modern or altermodern, but to learn what is at stake in the affirmation of identity for organising hope, something I will do in part II of the book.

A note on the Multitude

An appropriate understanding of the meaning of 'being singular plural', paraphrasing Nancy (Nancy, 2000) in the case of indigenous people is crucial for a discussion of autonomy. As will be shown in Chapter 6, the notion of 'the multitude' has been used to characterised the protagonist of the popular struggles (wars) during the period 2000–2005 in Bolivia, which Dunkerley (2007) describes as an 'astonishing acceleration in the pace of mass political activity (Dunkerley, 2007, 137). This process culminated with the election of Evo Morales to power in 2005.

The term multitude is not new. Historians Eric Hobsbawn and George Rudé used it in their analyses of pre industrial England and France. It has been applied in Bolivia to designate the rainbow of networks of indigenous, peasants, labour, movements that mobilised intensely and forcefully connecting the community with the act of rebellion (García Linera, 2008). Scholars from the Bolivian group *La Comuna* –close to Evo Morales, argue that the displacement of the centrality of the working class and its trade unions –what they refer to as the union-form (*la forma sindicato*) allowed for the emergence of the multitude-form (*la forma multitud*). Unlike the *forma sindicato*, the *forma multitud* is not institutionalised. It forms a subject in the euphoria of direct action, without any other affiliation than the need to converge in action against the state sustained by territorial communal associations.

However, when Hardt and Negri go to Bolivia theoretically, as they do in *Commonwealth* (2009), they fail to engage with the indigenous struggle. The multitude, to them, is 'the common subject of labor, that is, the real flesh of postmodern production, and at the same time the object from which collective capital tries to make the body of its global development'. In their view, the multitude is 'not unified but remains plural and multiple [but] is not fragmented, anarchical, or incoherent ... [but] is able to act in common and thus rule itself' (Hardt and Negri, 2004: 99 and 100). My misgivings are not due to Hardt and Negri's lack of 'rigorous classist analysis' (Moyo and Yeros, 2008: 63), but to the following three points. First, as already argued, the multitude is immanent and, consequently, conflicts and contradictions that arise from the struggle of 'the multitude' with, against and beyond the state, capital and the law are simply removed from the analysis. But how can we appreciate like this the difficulties, self-contradictions, dangers, and conflicts that indigenous-popular movements encounter in the process of organising hope in both senses, among different components of the network of resistance and vis-as-vis the state and the law? Second, they ignore that the co-existence of a variety of *worldviews* among which indigenous cosmologies are *predominant* in Bolivia. Indigenous-popular networks of movements do not simply gathered 'a plurality of singularities' together, among which one is indigenous: these networks are composed by indigenous peoples, *campesinos* of indigenous origin and indigenous urban inhabitants of Bolivia mainly. The 'multitude', in fact, contains 'nations' that inhabit Bolivian territory. Third, the application of their version of the multitude to the indigenous struggle for autonomy does not capture what Gutiérrez Aguilar (2005) calls the 'rhythm of the pachakuti', that is a particular form of resistance that produces a singular experience of insubordination guided by a different vision of the world (cosmology) altogether.

Creativity, the Past, the Future and the New

The *creating* mode of autonomy emphasises creativity and self-determination as a form of resistance to the state and capital. For indigenous movements in Latin America, the creation of *alternative realities* is connected with their ancestral practices and therefore rooted in the 'past'. While any form of insubordination draws on traditions of resistance, in this case the new aspirations are *necessarily* filtered by traditions, customs and habits that have been oppressed since time immemorial by colonial powers and capitalist democracies. The beauty of the indigenous struggle for autonomy at present is that while the defence of the 'past' constitutes *a form of resistance* (Aubry, 2003; Ortiz Quintero, 2009), the 'past' is mobilised and articulated with political imagination in a new fashion (Khasnabish, 2008; Hesketh, 2013; Holloway, 2010). While the Zapatistas exercise self-government by engaging with ancestral Mayan traditions, habits and customs, they also claim 'we are united by the imagination, by creativity, by tomorrow' (SIM, 1995, in Ponce de León, 2001: 167).

Note that the word 'past' must be translated as 'memory' (*memoria*), for it refers to *memories* enacted in the present, rather than something that already happened. For many indigenous communities, the past is not behind but ahead. A commentary by one of *The Guardian's* journalists on an ethnographic study of the Aymara people in the Andes in northern Chile shows that 'the Aymara word for past is "nayra", which means sight or front. The word for tomorrow means 'some day behind one's back' (Spinney, 2005: 8). This means that Aymara people do not regard the 'future' ahead -as others do, but as memory in motion, which surely shapes their practices and insurgencies and the role of their ancesters in them. Subcomandante Insurgente Marcos (SIM) captures this wonderfully when he says:

> In our dreams we have seen another world, an honest world, a world decidedly more fair than the one in which we now live ... *this world was not something that came to us from our ancestors. It came from ahead, from the next step we were going to take.* (Ponce de León, 2001: 18; emphasis added)

Furthermore, for indigenous people, physical existence is not the only element of reality. As Vázquez clarifies (2011: 38), for example, *la tierra* (the land) is defended for it is a political responsibility of the indigenous people to protect their ancestors. It is a revolutionary practice that relies on a different conceptualisation of time and being: 'This political responsibility [is] revolutionary vis-à-vis the modern notion of time, in which the present and presence are the sole locus of the real' (Vázquez, 2011: 38). This is the reason why, as Rivera Cusicanqui (2012) highlights, the 'colonial condition' brings many problems to the task of locating indigenous peoples, movements and resistances within the modern world. Cultural postmodernism

> is alien to us as a tactic. There is no *post* or *pre* in this vision of history that is not linear or teleological but rather moves in cycles and spirals and sets out on a course without neglecting to return to the same point. The indigenous world does not conceive of history as linear, the past-future is contained in the present. (Rivera Cusicanqui, 2012)

The defence of existing traditions and practices shows that we are confronted with a different use of history, the future and change (Rivera Cusicanqui, 2012). For this reason, Holloway (2003) provoked an intellectual turmoil among Latin American scholars (mainly ethno-Marxists) when he claimed:

> Spit to history. History, including our history, is a history wherein the struggle against oppression is invaded by the category of the oppressors ... revolutionary thinking means to get rid of the nightmare [of the cult of the past] wake up and discover our responsibilities. Self-determination-communism in other words, as a movement and a objective – is the emancipation with regards to the nightmare of tradition. (Holloway, 2003: 173)

Against this assertion, López y Rivas (2011: 116) argues that history is a decolonising tool for conscientisation and preservation of the collective character of their institutions, cosmologies and the relation among peoples. History assists indigenous people in their reinvention of insurgencies from within a system of exploitation and neglect, i.e. against the *ongoing* process of colonisation and oppression that has asserted itself in different historical forms from colonialism to indigenism and multiculturalism over centuries. Vega Cantor also contends that 'Indigenous peoples of our America ... [celebrate] their struggles, their heroes and leaders, and this does not mean a reactionary cult of the past but a legitimate vindication of something that has been taken away from them, like their own memory' (Vega Cantor, 2004: 187).

Albertani illustrates brilliantly the complexity of questions of tradition, history and change by reminding us to recall John Womack's phrase used at the beginning of his book on Zapata: *'this is the history of some peasants who did not want to change and therefore they made a revolution'* (Albertani, 2011: 32). Without romanticizing indigenous resistance, we must recognise that indigenous autonomy creates new realities by use of political inventiveness, but this entails a demand for the respect of what 'they already have' (Esteva, 2003: 254) (i.e., a demand to incorporate what already exists into a legal juridical system). And, Conway and Singh claim, what already exists is their everyday practices of 'long-standing traditions that have been rendered invisible or unthinkable through the hegemony of Western centric modernity' (Conway and Singh, 2011: 700), by colonial powers. The creation of a 'new' reality in the hands of indigenous movements offers new meanings of the past (past as in 'memory'). *'La historia'*, argues Eduardo Galeano, 'is a prophet who looks back: because of what was, and against what was, it announces what will be' (Galeano, 1971: 8). Bloch would concur: 'mankind is not yet finished; therefore, neither is its past. It continues to affect us under a different sign, in the drive of its questions, in the experiments of its answers' (Bloch, 1976: 8). The Zapatistas' JBG are a great example of this. While the Snails and the JBGs are expression of the Zapatistas' political innovation, the principle of 'command while obeying' is based on Mayan traditions of decision making in the indigenous *ejidos*, an ancestral custom of self-government practice by the Tzeltal, Tzotzil, Ch'ol, Mam, Zoque and Tojolabal peoples in Mexico. So that political imagination is rooted in ancestral practices and those practices are renewed with political imagination. This is a fundamental difference with non-indigenous autonomy.

Real Subsumption and the State

A significant problem in the theorisation of indigenous autonomy is that indigenous people are positioned vis-à-vis the state and the law, and subsumed in capital in very different ways than non-indigenous people. This significant element has been neglected and untheorised by most approaches to autonomy and prefiguration, with the exception of post-colonial theory and in particular SS (see Chibber, 2013) and the decolonial school. It is important, therefore, to discuss how we theorise *this difference in order* to conceptualise the contradictions that emerge from the struggle for indigenous self-determination. To be sure, the difference is not merely related to different historical contexts and cultural backgrounds (Foweraker, 1995: 27). It is rather what Mignolo refers to as 'colonial difference' (Mignolo, 2000), i.e. a difference that emerged from the racial differentiation and hierarchies of the colonial period that persist in the post-colonial period in new forms (Conway and Singh, 2011: 693). Why does this matter for the autonomy debate in the twenty first century?

First, as already mentioned emancipation for indigenous resistance (see Santos, 2007b) needs to be a *decolonising* project. Indigenous autonomy is against a system of colonisation and oppression but paradoxically indigenous movements demand the state the legal and political recognition of their right to self-determination. Aymara politics in Bolivia is characterised by a dual claim for both inclusion into and autonomy from the state) (Gutiérrez Aguilar, 2008). This 'dual intentionality' resulted in the creation of a new form of the capitalist state, the plurinational state, which recognises indigenous nations and their cosmologies (see Chapter 6).

Second, the specific form taken by the subsumption of indigenous peoples in capitalist social relations is different from non-indigenous people and therefore has been a major point of discussion among SS and decolonial school scholars. Their argument – roughly, is that instead of being fully integrated into the labour market, indigenous people have been oppressed and invisibilised (Santos, 2007b). The colonial difference emerged with Western modernity and means that other forms of interaction, politics, sociabilities, etc., that existed in indigenous life were rendered invisible or classified as inferior by the epistemic violence of modernity (Conway and Singh, 2011: 693). In other words, western modernity was instituted on the basis of the oppression of other possible paradigms of life that existed prior to the European conquest of the Americas but have been made invisible by the line traced by 'abyssal thinking' (Santos, 2007b: 1). 'Abyssal thinking', argues Santos, creates 'two realms, the realm of "this side of the line" and the realm of "the other side of the line". The division is such that "the other side of the line" vanishes for its actuality becomes non-existent, it is indeed produced as non-existent. Non-existent means no existing in any relevant or comprehensible way of being' (Santos, 2007b: 1).

But does this mean that indigenous people are not subsumed in capital? In Chapter 8 I resume this discussion and argue that indigenous oppression and invisibilisation presents a particular case of subsumption that I would like to characterise as *real subsumption by exclusion*. By *real subsumption by exclusion* I mean that racial oppression and invisibilisation were *necessary conditions* for the formation of the working-class and the foundation and expansion of capitalist modernity in Latin America. The historical conditions of oppression and invisibilisation became, with the transition from formal to real subsumption, intrinsic to the valorisation of capital. Real subsumption by exclusion delineates a different form of (non)integration of indigenous people into capital, which impacts on their peculiar experience of the contradictory mode of autonomy. Indigenous and non-indigenous autonomy are both *contradictory* vis-à-vis the state, the law and capital, but they are contradictory *in different ways* due to their different position within the subordination of human activity (doing) to abstract labour.

Indigenous cosmologies as surplus

Finally, on the basis of the previous discussion, we can pose the theoretical question: what does 'excess' mean for indigenous resistance? In the literature presented above, excess appears as a mismatch and an overflowing, explained by the impossibility of total subordination of the particularity in the totality, or human doing into abstract labour (value). Although this is also true in the case of indigenous autonomy, there is another element that insinuates a fundamental difference. While in the non indigenous world the form taken by the overflow of human activity that exceed, is *unknown*, the excess produced by the indigenous struggle already exists in their everyday life practices. The Zapatistas' uprising or the Aymara's insurgency stand for the realisation of existing but oppressed and invisibilised indigenous paradigms of life. 'Surplus possibility' (Gibson-Graham, 2006) in this case is deeply connected to indigenous cosmologies that are, and are not *yet*, that is they exist in the mode of being denied. 'Autonomy' argues Esteva (2003) 'is the focal point for a new semantic constellation for social change: a tradition of resistance has been transformed into a project of liberation' (Esteva, 2003: 243). These cosmologies are specific of each language, culture and political context (Gudynas, 2011). But all have

Table 2.1   The four modes of autonomy in non-indigenous and indigenous context

Modes of autonomy	Non-indigenous	Indigenous
Negating	Practical negativity, Non-identitarian politics	Identity as resistance against oppression and invisibilisation
Creating	New practices, horizons and possibilities guided experience and traditions of resistance	Innovative forms of resistance based on ancestral traditions, habits and customs revitalized with political imagination.
Contradicting	Real subsumption	Real Subsumption *by exclusion*
Producing Excess	Impossibility of total subordination. Overflow of human practice (unknown)	Impossibility of total subordination. Existing indigenous cosmologies

been oppressed by colonial powers and *integrated via exclusion* into the world of value-money-capital.

The *buen vivir* cosmology which was first brought to light by the struggles of indigenous and non-indigenous movements and communities in the Amazon and Andean regions. *Buen vivir* in Spanish or *Sumac kawsay* in Quechua, *Suma qamaña* in Aymara, *Tajimat Pujut* in Awajun, contains practical orientations towards production, organization and distribution, as well as collective meanings attributed to time, progress, human realisation and the relationship between sociability, sustainability and nature (see Fatheuer, 2011; Acosta and Martínez, 2009; Huanacuni Mamani, 2010; Gudynas, 2011; Esteva and Prakash, 1997). I will return to this form of excess in Chapter 8. Table 2.1 above, summarises the differences between indigenous and non-indigenous autonomy (4 modes).

Conclusion

Autonomy is a controversial term that designates complex struggles and practices. It has been theorised in several ways over time and within different intellectual traditions in diverse geographical, cultural and political contexts. In this chapter, I draw a sketchy picture of four modes of the praxis and its conceptualization with a twofold aim: first, to expose how different theorisations of autonomy put emphasis on different aspects of the autonomous struggle, according to the political interest of the authors, political and economic conjunctures, intellectual traditions and the willingness to offer a critique and innovate theoretically. In this fragmented picture of the practice of autonomy, some pieces of the puzzle do not match. I suggest that the four dimensions of autonomy as practice and critique interact although disharmoniously in the process of organising hope.

My second goal was to discuss some important aspects of indigenous autonomy that are not informed by certain concepts used in the north and the non-indigenous world. Surely, while indigenous struggles are part of a global struggle for a post development, post patriarchal, post capitalist and post colonial world, the analysis of such struggles cannot rely on concepts that reinforce theoretical and political subordination of the indigenous resistance to the specific forms of radicalization of the north and/or are inadequate to inform both the reality of the indigenous autonomy as it is practiced on daily basis and their paradigms of life that underpin it.

In the next chapter, I translate autonomy *in the key of hope in order* to achieve three things: first, to account for the prefigurative nature of autonomy; second, to overcome the fragmented nature of its theorisation and the separation between the theory and practice of autonomy; third, to bridge indigenous and non indigenous pursuits for autonomy for each of them will attain different forms and attribute diverse meanings to the art of organising hope.

3
Autonomy in the Key of Hope: Understanding Prefiguration

Introduction

The aim of this chapter is to produce an alternative understanding of autonomy that engages with the movements' processes of prefiguration. I offer a definition of autonomy *as the art of organising hope*. I examine the previously mentioned four modes of autonomy through the prism of Ernst Bloch's philosophy. By paraphrasing the language of music, I put autonomy *in the key of hope*. This means that, as a 'composer', I use hope as my basic material. If I make use of other concepts, notions and ideas, I will point to the way they are modified by the category of hope. A reading of autonomy in the key of hope repositions the debate about autonomy in three ways. First, it moves away from the dichotomy 'autonomy vs the state' by revealing the prefigurative nature of autonomy *without* avoiding the problem of the state and capital; second, it overcomes the fragmented understanding of autonomy; third, it bridges indigenous and non-indigenous autonomous practices.

Finding inspiration in Ernst Bloch: humanist Marxism, utopia and agency

Ernst Bloch is considered a 'Humanist Marxist' (Geoghegan, 1996; Dussel, 2013). Bloch framed class struggle as a struggle against 'deshumanisation' and for the realisation of humanity: 'Marxism in general is absolutely nothing but the struggle against the deshumanization which culminates in capitalism until it is completely cancelled' (Bloch, 1959/1986: 1358). Bloch looks at humanity in a singular way, that is, by placing the *not yet* at its centre. Humanity is unfinished, it is a possibility: 'a challenge to become, not []a given, and this means that no actual assumption concerning the content of being can be made ... Humanity', he indicates, 'does not have possession of itself simply as it is. Rather it "is something that has yet to be discovered" (Traces, 18)' (Daly, 2013: 172). This 'discovery', however, is not contemplative or passive. Bloch regards Marx's humanitarianism as real struggle and not as an abstract concept: 'Marxism is essentially only this struggle against the deshumanization which reaches its acme in capitalism' (Bloch, 1971: 21).

Bloch's Marxism, as shown below, is prefigurative, for he engages with Marx's inspiring yet not shaped, ideas about alternatives to capitalism. This is a dimension of Marx's work that remains almost unexplored, with some exceptions. Bloch embraces Marx's writings in so far as, 'serve as a kind of midwife of the new society ... [for Marx] ... does not give birth to the idea of socialism or communism: he elicits it from the movement of capitalism itself' (Hudis, 2012: 212). Bloch's concept of hope is a force that drives us in that direction but not in a linear way. Bloch was interested in finding out 'why people are attracted to something which is not yet there' and suggests that the human urge to navigate the unknown and engage with the *not yet* reality by means of anticipating concrete utopias is anthropological, that is, 'an inseparable part of human consciousness ... the true roots to utopia have to be looked for not in the social tier but in the anthropological' (Levy, 1997: 181).

Bloch's emphasis on humanity as struggle made his philosophy appealing for religious revolutionary thinkers like Gustavo Gutiérrez, the creator of LT, a branch of the Catholic Church that has widely influenced Latin American radical, grass-roots politics since the 1960s. Bloch's philosophy offered an – unlikely – synthesis between Marxism and religion and empowered radical priests, for it removes 'the traditional God of Christianity and insist[s] on the power of future possibilities that humanity has yet to know' (Moylan, 1997: 97). But Bloch was not a religious man. Following Löwy, Bloch, like many Latin American radicals, distinguishes the 'theocratic religion of the official churches, opium of the people, a mystifying apparatus at the service of the powerful' from 'the underground, subversive and heretical religion' in a way that refuses to see religion 'uniquely as a "cloak" of class interests' (Löwy, 1988: 8). As a 'religious atheist', Bloch regarded religion as 'one of the most significant forms of utopian consciousness, one of the richest expressions of the Hope Principle' (Löwy, 1988: 8). In Bloch's thinking, Marxism and religion engage in a dialogue that inspired Gutiérrez. He took up the idea that 'the hoped-for salvation of humanity comes about not in the historical incarnation of hope represented in the activities of Jesus and a community of believers but, rather, in a transcendent future which makes the promise available to a receptive humanity' (Moylan, 1997: 101). In his writings, Father Gutiérrez describes Bloch's Principle of Hope 'as an activity which "subverts the existing order"' (Moylan, 1997: 103). What Gutiérrez appreciated in Bloch's philosophy was 'the area of possibilities of potential being' in a way that 'allows us to plan history in revolutionary terms' (Moylan, 1997: 103).

Bloch's philosophy also appeals to those who aim to escape the caricatures of ready made Marxist utopia and wish to rephrase resistance, antagonism and revolution today. Bloch has influenced the critique of 'close' Marxism produced by Open Marxists since the late 1980s (Bonefeld et al., 1992a, 1992b, 1995) and further analyses of present forms of resistance and emancipation (Holloway, 2010a), political imagination (Khasnabish, 2008), radical pedagogies (Giroux and MacLaren, 1997; Motta, 2014; Motta and Cole, 2013), the innovation of sociology (Santos, 2004; Levitas 2013) and alternatives to capitalist work (Weeks, 2011; Levitas, 2001). The term *hope* has been also used *blochianly* without reference to Bloch to describe prefigurative features of grass-roots movements (Zibechi, 2007, 2012; Stengers and Zournazi, 2002); the emergence of 'community economies' (Gibson-Graham, 2006) and alternatives to development (Earle and Simonelli, 2005; Esteva and Prakash, 1997). All produced accounts of movements' political inspiration, attitudes and collective actions that defy impossibility.

I contend that hope is a category that corresponds to the movements' present call for prefiguration. Hope offers a *reciprocity* 'between the categories of theory (which interrogate practice) and the categories of practice (which constitute the framework for critique)' (Bonefeld et al., 1992a: xi). It is a category able to conceptualise the 'openness of society' (Holloway, 1993: 76). The *not yet* occupies a significant place in the politics of Latin America.

The term hope was reintroduced by the Zapatista movement in 1994, and travelled around the world to resonate in the global justice movement and other movements' discourses. Bloch's ideas materialised in a different time, a time when it was urgent to reflect on the dangers surrounding hope (War and Nazism) and to make connections between past-present and future possibilities. As a *category of struggle*, hope transcends Bloch's own limitations, geographical demarcation, and political constrains and allows for the understanding of present forms of utopia within specific material conditions that surround processes of prefiguring. This includes indigenous struggles. As Rivera Cusicanqui put it aptly, 'the project of indigenous modernity can emerge from the present in a spiral whose movement is a continuous feedback from the past to the future – a "principle of hope" or "anticipatory consciousness" – that both discerns and realizes decolonization at the same time' (Rivera Cusicanqui, 2012: 96). Bloch's philosophy contests a narrow conceptualisation of reality simply associated with facts, that are produced as part of the reality that movements want to criticise. I contend that it is not enough to continue discussing the power of resistance vis-à-vis the state and capital without questioning the parameters of legibility of the colonial/patriarchal/capitalist *realities*. We must discuss how we define the contours of reality.

Deciphering autonomy in the key of hope

My working definition of autonomy as the *art of organising hope* comprises four modes of the autonomous praxis: negating, creating, contradicting and excess. In the key of hope, *negating* is deciphered as a rejection of the given – capitalist, patriarchal and colonial – realities. This requires an approach that accounts for collective actions beyond factual reality. The *creating* mode of autonomy anticipates the future by *modelling concrete utopias* (i.e., invents new practices, relations, sociabilities and horizons or pushes forward and organises customs, habits and traditions that already exist in a new light). The *contradicting* mode of autonomy is about navigating and resisting the danger of appropriation and translation of autonomy into the grammar of power and the necessity of *disappointment*. Finally, *excess* is informed by the category of the *not yet* (i.e., it is related to the search towards the realisation of a *an* unrealised reality that can be invented or rendered visible by anticipating it in different contexts). The art of organising hope is about playing the four modes *al unison* in the key of hope (see Figure 3.1).

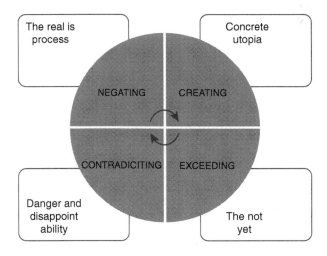

Figure 3.1   Autonomy in the key of hope

Negating: The real is process

In the previous chapter, I discussed the significance of 'negativity' in activist and scholarly writings about resistance, in general, and autonomy, in particular. The rediscovery of Adorno's work (see Holloway et al., 2009) and the revitalisation and discussion of Rancière's notion of disagreement (Arditi, 2007, 2008, 2011; Bowman and Stamp, 2011) are two examples of this tendency. I also pointed to the interesting paradox that, in the indigenous case, the rejection of the given order (negativity) is achieved and develops through an affirmation of indigenous identity as resistance. Affirmation of identity is a true revolutionary act against power.

Bloch does not discuss negativity directly, but (his) philosophy begins with the idea that a world that is wrong must be rejected. Negativity is inextricably connected to the possibility to anticipate a new or oppressed reality that is latent in the present. In Bloch's words 'the Not with which everything starts up and begins, around which every Something is still built' (Bloch, 1959/1986: 307) is undefined and empty, but contains already within it the *not yet*. It is very difficult to disentangle negation and creation, for negation makes possible to engage in the new that is already on its way, or is going to be released from its oppression.

'Hope' is not synonymous with 'wish', confidence or optimism in a better future but a principle based on an understanding of reality as an open *process* in an unclosed and unfinished world. The *not yet* is not an illusion or a fantasy: It is an unrealised *materiality* that is latent in the present reality (Dinerstein and Deneulin, 2012: 594). The *not yet* is central to human action. In other words, Bloch, as Mittleman highlights, puts at the centre of his philosophy a 'category of that which does not yet exist as if it were an attractive force' (Mittleman, 2009: 188).

To Bloch, facts are 'simply processes, i.e. dynamic relationships in which the Become has not completely triumphed' (Bloch, 1959/1986: 196–197). The negation of the present reality, be it landlessness or unemployment, rejects the 'objectivity of verified facts' and contests the meaning of reality itself. As the art of organising hope, autonomy questions the given reality. The real possibility of articulating collective dreams of, say, dignified work lies in the conviction that 'the Real is process ... the widely ramified mediation between present, unfinished past and above all: possible future' (Bloch, 1959/1986: 196–197). In other words, 'the present "boundary condition" ... is never a closed door. It is an open threshold – a threshold of potential' (Massumi in Massumi and Zournazi, 2002: 212). Without challenging the given demarcation of what is real and what is not, what exists and what does not, there cannot be true openness. The given reality, i.e. a reality that is not challenged, is not 'objective' but, rather, it is the result of a process of objectifica-*tion*, the partial outcomes of which are presented as objective. As Tischler highlights, 'objectivity is class struggle' (Tischler, 2009: 116). Negation challenges the 'codification of the possible' (Arditi, 2011: 292) and opens a space for the end of such codification. Bloch proposes that we need a different concept of reality: 'a different one to that of positivism to which the idea of process is alien ... Sometimes the ossified concept of reality even penetrated Marxism and consequently made it schematic' (Bloch, 1959/1986: 196).

Anyone would agree with the statement: 'No thing could be altered in accordance with wishes if the world were closed, full of fixed, even perfected facts' (Bloch 1959/1986: 196). It is common sense. In Bloch's thought, however, it means that a reality that does not shelter a dimension of the *not yet* within it (as in, unknown future possibilities that lurk in the present reality in the form of latency) *cannot* be called real (Dinerstein, 2013a). The *not yet* that inhabits the real is not unreal but *unrealised*. It exists as a dimension of reality that, as Bloch claims, does not 'correspond to the facts'. Facts are constructed and demarcated in a way that silences the utopian function of hope.

Capitalist reality is an ongoing process of struggle for the construction of its own reality which subsequently becomes naturalized as a human reality. Fisher proposes that 'one strategy against capitalist realism could involve invoking the Real(s) underlying the reality that capitalism presents to us' (Fisher, 2009: 18). This would disclose or render visible another politics that exists beyond the parameters of legibility demarcated by the institutional politics. Another reality imperfect, incomplete and undecipherable yet desired is lurking underneath the surface of the topsy-turvy world of capital.

The Zapatista uprising was both an act of refusal and an act of hope that 'announced the beginning of an epoch' (Albertani, 2009b: 503). As we will see in the next chapter, they proposed an elaborated interpretation of neoliberal globalisation in the key of hope that depicted neoliberal globalisation as anti-human, as an attack on humanity. The Zapatistas rejected the 'lie' that hope and dignity were defeated and called for the internationalisation of hope from the Caracol *La Realidad* (which is not called like that for nothing). The same act of negation was present in the land occupations in Brazil (1979–1984), the disorganised form of the Caracazo (1989), the Argentine uprising of December 2001 and the struggles in La Paz in October 2013, among many others.

Creating: concrete utopia as praxis

In the key of hope, the second mode of autonomous organising (i.e., creating) takes the form of *concrete utopia*. As we have seen, the creative power of autonomy transpires in most theories about autonomy. Be it constituent power, self-valorisation, the common or the openness of the crack, autonomy is regarded *per se* as an instrument of collective creation and political imagination. 'Creativity' in the indigenous case is the use of political imagination to articulate both ancestral traditions and new horizons in the present context.

Bloch argues that the utopian function of hope makes humans strive for something else – outwards, beyond, recognising their lack and the will to realise that lack. Hope is an expectant emotion that drives humans to engage in utopian thinking and actions. We can experience anticipatory illuminations that facilitate the action towards the anticipation of our dreams. Anticipatory illuminations transform what Bloch calls 'the not yet conscious' into a concrete experience. Human beings have the capacity to dream and anticipate our dreams in concrete utopias: we can prefigure better future worlds in the present. And this drive is not external or ideological but a genuine feature of what makes us human.

Concrete utopias are not abstract utopias. They are praxis. Concrete utopias are 'stepping stones of what the human individual and the world could become' (suggests Zipes, 1988: xxvii). Bronner observes that 'Utopia in Bloch's philosophy is no longer "nowhere", as an Other to real history. It is a constituent element of all human activity and, simultaneously, historical, the question becomes how to articulate and realize the hopes unconsciously shared by humanity' (Bronner, 1997: 166). In Chapter 5 I show that the concrete utopias that emerged out of the Argentine popular insurrection of 2001 (self-management, dignified and cooperative work, justice, democracy) expose the incompleteness and shortcomings of the present and anticipated alternative – better – futures.

The anticipatory consciousness of the *not yet*, develops during daydreaming. Daydreaming moves us forwards.

> The content of a daydream is not, like that of the night-dream, a journey back into repressed experiences and their associations [à la Freud]. It is concerned with an as far as possible unrestricted journey forward, so that instead of reconstituting that which is no longer conscious, the images of that which is not yet can be fantasised into life and into the world. (Bloch, 1970: 86–87)

Concrete utopias are acts of *collective daydreaming* in permanent construction through autonomous struggles. When the workers of the Brukman factory gathered in the evening of 18 December 2001 and evaluated what to do for their boss was gone but had left the lights on in his office to deceive the workers. They began intuitively to consider the possibility of not leaving the factory which turned out to be an 'occupation' of the factory. They followed their heart and their fear soon became the hope for self-management: although uncertainty prevailed, hope made the space breathable again. They began to organise themselves, collectively within and outside the factory. Bloch's concept of concrete utopia informs the process through which movements delineate territories and democrate realities– in this case, by workers, neighbours, the unemployed, pensioners, human rights movements, the new poor – in Argentina 2001–2002.

Bloch criticised utopian thought that was not transformative, that is, that was not anticipatory (Levitas, 2008: 43). He insistently points to the fundamental difference between abstract and concrete utopia. In the historical sense, abstract utopias are created 'before the emergence of the revolutionary proletariat' or 'subsequent utopianism, which is ... detached from the progressive proletarian movement' (Geoghegan, 1996: 38). In the critical sense, abstract utopias perform as collective imaginations that will be realised in the future, when the expected conditions arise, or following the party's plan. Instead, concrete utopia is a collective act of venturing beyond, here and now. Levitas indicates that Bloch's idea of concrete utopia 'is not simply a "correct" version of utopia, but a praxis-oriented category' (Levitas, 1997: 70). Concrete utopia is *praxis* (Geoghegan, 1996: 38): 'The only seemingly paradoxical concept of concrete utopia would be appropriate here' –argues Bloch -, 'that is, of an anticipatory kind which by no means coincides with abstract utopia dreaminess, nor is directed by the immaturity of merely abstract utopian socialism' (Bloch, 1959/1986: 146). Bloch follows Marx in his reflection of the defeat of the Paris Commune, Marx writes: 'The working class did not expect miracles from the Commune. They have no ready-made utopias to introduce *par décret du people* ... They have no ideals to realize, but to set free the elements of the new society with which old collapsing bourgeois society itself is pregnant' (Marx, 1871).

Abstract utopias lack adequate mediation. Bloch writes: 'Utopians all too frequently had to construct the outlines of a brave new world out of their own hearts and heads – or, as Engels says: "For the basic plan of their new edifice they could only appeal to reason, just because they could not as yet appeal to contemporary history"' (Bloch, 1970: 90).

Instead, the concrete utopia is a *process at work* that involves 'no transcendence' (Bloch, 1971: 41). The contention between neighbours of the popular assemblies and the political parties of the left in Buenos Aires 2002 (see Chapter 5) illustrates the difference between the two kinds of utopia. While the latter desired to impose a revolutionary action plan onto an assembly of neighbours who rejected to be classified by class or ideology, the former had thrown themselves into the unknown and exciting process of reinventing democracy.

The absence of 'facts' to explain a situation does not limit the possibility of conceiving of concrete utopia. The opposite is actually the case: concrete utopias make apparent how constraining is the reality represented by 'facts'. There is much more than facts. And we struggle to grasp this much more that there exist beyond facts. Hope anticipates something that we cannot yet explain (see Dinerstein and Deneulin, 2012; Lear, 2006). As Esteva contends, 'the accusation of "unrealisable utopia" to autonomous movements and the demand that they should make explicit what is the alternative they are fighting for is wrong: 'transformative action', he says, 'does not require a future vision of society as a whole ... it can be seen as an horizon or perspective of the rainbow type: like it, it has brilliant colours and is always unreachable [as argued by Foucault] (Foucault, 1979)' (Esteva, 2011: 136).

In the case of indigenous autonomy, the creative mode responds to the possibility of ending colonial oppression and receive fully recognition of their practices. [1]The realisation of autonomy requires of a process of struggle that is full of surprises. A young member of the Zapatista movement makes a similar point when he describes how the creation of the JBG came about: 'we did not know how were we going to achieve this, but now we are already seeing it ... We did not imagine that we were going to form the Autonomous Councils and that we were going to have *Juntas de Buen Gobierno*' (cited in Cerda García, 2011: 9).

But if there is no 'plan', then how is praxis guided? Bloch proposes that praxis is guided by 'educated hope' (*docta spes*), which mediates between reason and passion. To Bloch, 'It is a question of learning hope ... . The work of this emotion requires people who throw themselves actively into what is becoming to which they themselves belong ... ' (Bloch, 1959/1996: 3). It is not fortuitous that a key feature of autonomous movements in Latin America has been the development of their own pedagogies and knowledges. The MST's pedagogical enterprise is inspired in Paolo Freire's 'language of hope and utopian vision' (Giroux and MacLaren, 1997: 147). Freire's utopian praxis, as Giroux and MacLaren highlight, is critical of utopianism. He 'insists that education must always speak to the "annunciation of a new reality" which becomes not only a temporary "concrete reality" but a "permanent cultural revolution"' (Giroux and MacLaren, 1997: 149).

It is important to differentiate concrete from the real utopias that are discussed in many writings of the left at present (see Levitas, 2008: 44). Wright (2010, 2013) uses the term 'real utopias' to describe how new movements envision new worlds and can transform capitalism. Wright advises that the steps to follow are, first, to produce a critique of capitalism; then, to imagine the feasible alternatives to the capitalist way of organising society, and to theorise social transformation. The key word here is not utopia but 'real'. Wright himself suggests that the expression 'real utopia' 'is meant to be a provocation, for "utopia" and "real" do not comfortably go together ... Utopia is ... both a nowhere place and a good place. It is a fantasy of a perfect world that fully embodies our moral ideas' (Wright, 2013: 3).

The idea of 'real utopia' in Wrights' terms emphasises 'the tension that exists between dreams and practice: utopia', he argues, 'implies developing visions of alternatives to dominant institutions that embody our deepest aspirations' (Wright, 2013: 30). To Wright 'real' means 'proposing alternatives attentive to the problems of unintended consequences, self-destructive dynamics, and difficult dilemmas of normative trade-offs' (Wright, 2013: 3). Is this proposal as provocative as Wright suggests? Probably not, since Wright uses the term 'real' as synonymous with feasible: 'alternatives can be evaluated in terms of their *desirability*, their *viability* and their *achievability*. If you worry about desirability and ignore viability or achievability, then you are just a plain utopian. Exploration of real utopias requires understanding of these other two dimensions' (Wright, 2013: 8).

Bloch's notion of utopia is radically different. He is not concerned with the 'feasibility' of utopia, or the moral principles that should guide them, but he problematises the concept of the 'real' associated to utopia. To Bloch, utopia must be concrete (as opposed to abstract and idealist) but this does not mean real as in feasible and viable. In this respect, Wright's real utopia corresponds to the realm of the given 'objective' conditions that surround utopia, something that is possible or that cannot be discarded, viable, although it might not be obvious in the present and therefore the creation of viable alternatives requires utopian vision and political imagination by political actors informed by a 'theory of transformation' (Wright, 2013: 3). The main idea is the institutionalisation of these alternatives towards the realisation of better societies. Participatory budget, for example, is an example of Wright's real utopias. While Wright proposes to make utopias real (Wright, 2010: 366) for real utopias can contribute to the process of 'eroding of capitalism', [2] Bloch suggests that real possibility lurks in any reality as the not yet that can be anticipated in the present. Anticipated does not mean created and institutionalised. Real possibility, to Bloch, is not necessarily objective or viable possibility: The distinction between 'objectively possible' and 'really possible' is crucial for an understanding of the prefigurative potential of autonomy:

> *Objectively* possible is everything whose entry, on the basis of a mere partial-cognition of its existing conditions, is scientifically to be expected, or at least cannot be discounted. Whereas *really* possible is everything whose conditions in the sphere of the *object itself* are not yet fully assembled; whether because they are still maturing, or above all because new conditions – though mediated by existing ones – arise for the entry of the real. (Bloch, 1959/1986: 196–197)

Unlike 'real utopias', *concrete utopias* belong to the realm of the really possible. Bloch is adamant:

> Real possibility ... is the categorical In-Front-of-Itself of material movement considered as a process: it is the specific regional character of reality itself, on the Front of its occurrence. How else could we explain the future-laden properties of matter? *There is no true realism without the true dimension of this openness.* (Bloch, 1959/1986: 237–238, my italics)

Hence, while real utopia operates within the given reality but aims to transform it, *concrete utopia radically challenges the demarcation of the given reality* and operates within the space that is not yet, with no expectations or having decided a priori the principles to would guide it. Concrete utopia has a great component of intuition and affective politics. It does not criticise society or represents a critique of society: *it is itself critique.*

Contradiction, danger and disappointability

So far, I engaged with Bloch's idea of the 'real is process' to account for the process of negation of the given reality that underpins autonomous organising, and the notion of 'concrete utopia' to theorise the creative mode of autonomy. But organising hope is an uncertain and contradictory process. To Bloch, hope is not a contemplative and naïve attitude but signals struggle. Hope is not confident; it is chance and contingency, it is surrounded by danger. As Daly highlights, 'every illuminated moment is in danger of being captured by the dull, the fraudulent, the constricting, or diverting, if not the cunning, embittered, or spiteful' (Daly, 2013: 165–166). The journey is uncertain for 'hope involves danger and fundamental insecurity ... at its most difficult, it approaches and resides in a zero-point of emptiness and darkness. But this is the place where fear creates yearning and longing, against which the darkness most obscures and depreciates' (Daly, 2013: 195–196).

As mentioned in Chapter 2, autonomy is always at risk of being integrated into the logic of capital and the state and the new forms of the coloniality of power such as the policy of multiculturalism. In the key of hope, the contradictory mode of autonomy entails disappointment.

> Bloch pursues a sense of an uncertainty sufficient to open paths for the realization of possibility and a 'still nameless future' via what he refers to as 'sigillary signs – symbols that remain unfulfilled and yet encapsulate a desired image of what might be, and this involves ... a problematic starting point. (Daly, 2013: 165–166)

The movements' predicament between rebellion and integration (see Dinerstein et al., 2013), and between oppression and self-determination, is also a dilemma of Bloch's utopian politics and method. Moylan (1997) illuminates the predicament that lives at the heart of Bloch's philosophy:

> Although a long-range vision enables humanity to move beyond the darkness of the lived moment, unless that vision includes an *immediate critique* of the ideological appropriation of the 'utopian' achievements along the way, the vision itself can betray the very process which are meant to lead toward it ... unless the negative, denunciatory moment and the positive, annunciatory moment are both employed so that each challenges the limitations of the other – the utopian method will fail through a[n] acceptance of the provisional 'success' valorized by short-sighted ideology. (Moylan, 1997: 110–111)

Autonomy is threatened by *translation* not only from the state and capital, but from abstract utopians and other collectivities and organizations. I use the term 'translation' to refer to the processes, mechanisms and dynamics through which autonomous organising is integrated into the logic of power, and through which what does not fit into this demarcation is invisibilised or politically obliterated. The translation of autonomous organising into the logic of power has been instrumental to the construction of hopelessness and the destruction of hope in Latin America, during the neoliberal period.

But translation is itself a process of struggle. During moments like in those Chiapas (January 1994), Buenos Aires (December 2001) and La Paz (October 2013), when the distance between subjectivity and objectivity seems to vanish. Since capitalist mediations are exposed to class struggle, therefore, they are prone to enter into crisis and produced moments of de-mediation (Gunn, 1987a; Bonefeld, 1987). De-mediation is an instance of de-fetishisation of the capitalist mediation (the law, the state, money, institutionalised forms of resistance based on the state-form) produced by class struggle. The space for autonomy opens up, and appropriation seems impossible. Collective action becomes 'collective ecstasy' (Dinerstein, 2005b). Yet, Bloch highlights that while at this point it seems that 'utopia cannot go any further', moments of 'Becomeness' are unreachable: 'As is unfortunately only too evident, what is intendable as such presence, as such manifested identity does not yet lie anywhere in a Becomeness, but it lies irrefutably in the intention towards it, in the intention which is never demolished' (Bloch, 1959/1986: 315–316). This unresolved contradiction touches on the impossibility of achieving the *not yet*, but we do not know. Disappointment is not something that has to be avoided but is a necessity of the process. In Chapter 6, I explore the process of re-translation of the period 2000–2005 into the logic of the plurinational state created in 2009 under the Morales administration, that marked a new chapter for indigenous-popular movements in Bolivia. The formation of the plurinational state (an achievement for indigenous movements) began a new process of translation of autonomy into the state. Autonomy requires that the hope it brings *must be disappointable*. Bloch discussed this in his inaugural lecture entitled 'Can Hope be Disappointed?' at the University of Tübingen in 1961: 'Hope must be unconditionally disappointable ... because it is open in a forward direction, in a future-oriented direction' (Bloch, 1998: 340). Bloch reminds us that

> Hope is not confidence. If it could not be disappointable, it would not be hope. That is part of it. Otherwise, it would be cast in a picture. It would let itself be bargained down. It would capitulate and say, that is what I had hoped for. Thus, hope is critical and can be disappointed. However, hope still nails a flag on the mast, even in decline, in that the decline is not accepted, even when this decline is still very

strong. ... Hope is surrounded by dangers, and it is the consciousness of danger and at the same time the determined negation of
that which continually makes the opposite of the hoped-for object
possible. (Bloch, 1988: 16–17)

This points to the complexity and contradictory nature of hope.
Ironically, to Bloch 'the hope that is disappointable is the hope that
cannot be fully annihilated. By the same token, hope as confidence or
calculating certainty is hope that can' (Richter, 2006: 52).

Excess: Encountering the not yet

In the section on excess (Chapter 2), I posed the question of whether
there is any way out of the movement 'rebellion and integration'. I
explore this question by putting excess in the key of hope, that is, in
the *not yet* mode that speaks of an unrealised or an existing- oppressed
reality. Bloch argues that the 'not yet' constitutes an essential component of the present. The Real, 'is that *which does not yet exist, which is
in quest of itself in the core of things and which is awaiting its genesis in the
trend latency of the process'* (Bloch, 1971: 41, italics in the original).

Hope possesses a utopian function that helps us to engage with the
reality of the *not yet*. The utopian impulse transcends the given reality
towards the anticipation of what is not. The rebel communities of
Chiapas envisioned another reality that was *not yet* realised – based on
their *lack*, a lack that was latent within their present reality, ready to
be enacted. Hope drove the six founding members of the MST 'beyond
the wire' (see Chapter 7). The MST did not only challenge the power of
landowners and the state but also questioned their demarcation of what
was *possible* and what was not. What is *possible* does not depend on
the objective probability of changing things. The struggles of the landless in Brazil did not have an objective possibility of success. Rather the
opposite. Yet, they have a real possibility of success for the latter –whatever it means for them- could not be discarded a priori. Indeed, "Real
Possibility" is in the end always 'possible' (Levy, 1997: 176–177).

'Possibility' is a key concept in Bloch's thought for hope, as Bronner
(1997) highlights,

> expresses the vision, or the foresight, of the possibility to realize
> something which is not yet anywhere ... what is ruled a priori is
> impossible; it cannot even become an object of hope, and will never
> become a utopia ... he characterises the utopian future as 'dawn
> forwards' ... The singular characteristics are not yet because the sun

which radiates its light on everything has not yet rise; it is still dawn, but no longer dark ... hope is not merely a projection of reason, a 'mental creation' of human thought, but an expression of what is really possible. (Bronner, 1997: 177)

Workers recovered companies (WRCs) are part of everyday life in today's Argentina. But it was not always like this. As I will discuss in Chapter 5 it was not 'feasible' that workers could occupy the factories illegally under a neoliberal government of the 1990s. The occupation was an act of hope and dignity, based on the 'lack' that threw workers on the verge of becoming unemployed into an uncertain but necessary and dignifying journey, with no direction yet. It was not plausible or expected for indigenous-popular movements in Bolivia to organise in the Network for the Defence of Water and Life (*Coordinadora en Defence del Agua y la Vida*, CDAYV) and succeed in defeating the process of privatisation of water by the company, Aguas del Tunari. It is only *a posteriori* that we can ask or argue that these actions were plausible. There were no 'objective' conditions. These were, however, 'anticipatory illuminations' that provided a far-reaching vision to enlighten – paraphrasing Bloch, the 'darkness of the lived present' and triggered a process of prefiguration. What is possible depends then on the capacity to transcend the distinction between what is possible and impossible, and to engage with latent alternatives that inhabit the present 'open' reality. Intuition, emotion and reasoning must come together in order to act upon what feels right.

Bloch's argument is that 'only in the light of the not yet, the darkness of the now is redeemed, the cloud of unknowing dispersed. The future lends the present its sense' (Mittleman, 2009: 188). However, the *not yet* is not something that will happen later on, in the future, or as Bloch claims, 'something expected according to its "disposition" in reduced form, as if *encapsulated*'. This is to Bloch a 'backward interpretation of Not-Yet [that] would suppress or fail to understand precisely the dialectical leap into the New' (Bloch, 1959/1986: 1373). The *not yet* alters the linearity of time and its temporalities. When Bloch speaks of the 'future', he is referring to an unresolved form of the present. By distinguishing three dimensions of human temporality, Bloch offers 'a dialectical analysis of the *past* which illuminates the *present* and can direct us to a better *future* [so that] unrealised potentialities are latent in the present, and the signs of foreshadowing that indicate the tendency of the direction and movements of the present into the future' (Kellner, 1997: 81).

The *not yet* is inextricably related to the category of the *Novum*, a different way of seeing temporality: 'it is through the *Novum* that we orient ourselves and reshape the inconstruable question about the nature of human existence in concrete ways so that we can see more clearly the direction of utopia' (Zipes, 1988: xxxvii). The act of venturing beyond is inclined to the Novum. Possibility appeared in front of MST's founders as an opening outwards and forward, bursting from the contours of the demarcated reality. The sequence was not positivistically scientific: I explore possibilities – if it is possible, plausible, doable, then I launch myself into the realisation of the plan. The sequence was: the given reality is unbearable and inhuman (landlessness means hunger and potential illness and death), there has to be another way, I feel this emotion and begin to lose fear. We learn what is wrong, we have experience, we know, we can educate our hope further, we are driven by the utopian function of hope, and we can anticipate another *possibility* that is not objectively possible but really possible, for we are humans and there has to be a way of not dying of hunger in a world of plenty. We need to organise hope. It is not easy. And there would be suffering. But we will demarcate a new territory of hope, a settlement where we can stop not only being hungry first and foremost, but also become dignified and self-confident: a peasant-led agrarian reform. Hope, then, 'expresses the vision of the possibility to realize something which is not yet anywhere ... [this] nowhere ... can be reached *in potential.*

As the art of organising hope, autonomy engages with real possibility rather than probability. 'If we follow probability there is no hope, just a calculated anticipation authorised by the world as it is. But to "think" is to create possibility against probability' (Stengers in Stengers and Zournazi, 2002: 245). Like Bloch, Stengers argues that '*possibility* cannot be calculated *a priori* because it implies the fact that the very description of the system itself can change. And you cannot calculate that' (Stengers and Zournazi, 2002: 246). The lack of correspondence between probability and possibility points to the existence of excess that does not yet exist. In the case of the indigenous struggle the lack of correspondence is mediated by the colonial oppression of another paradigm of life that does exists in a mode of being denied. Bloch explains 'outflow' as something that emerges between the darkness of the now and the openness of the *not yet*: the source is characterised by the *darkness of the Now,* in which realization rises, the outflow by the *openness of the object-based background*, towards which hope goes' (Bloch, 1959/1986: 288–289).

Table 3.1 summarises the elements of autonomy in the key of hope.

Table 3.1   Autonomy in the key of hope in non-indigenous and indigenous context

Modes of autonomy	Autonomy in the key of hope	Non-indigenous autonomy	Indigenous autonomy
Negating	The real is process	Non identitarian politics and negative praxis. Disagreement Anti-capitalist/anti-patriarchal	Affirmation of identity as form of resistance. Rejection of coloniality, capitalism and development;
Creating	Shaping concrete utopias	Rupture and invention of new practices related to work, democracy, justice, land, environment	Innovation and political imagination with a defense of traditions, habits and customs; autonomy de facto
Contradicting	Danger and Disappoint-ability	Real subsumption and struggle over the meaning of autonomy; conflict with, against and beyond the state, capital and the law; and with, against and beyond other forms of resistance	Subsumption by exclusion. Dual intentionality: demand for inclusion into the nation-state and for recognition of autonomy (that already exists)
Excess	Not yet	Dignified work, true democracy, peasant-led agrarian reform, food sovereignty, popular justice, alternative economies	Indigenous autonomy; realisation of indigenous cosmologies such as *buen vivir*

Conclusion

In this chapter, I examined four modes of autonomy through the prism of Ernst Bloch's philosophy. By paraphrasing the language of music, I played autonomy *in the key of hope*. I decoded negation, creation, contradiction and excess into Bloch's concepts of the real as process, concrete utopia, disappointment and the *not yet*. My performance in the key of hope highlighted the prefigurative nature of autonomy and, by exploring the principle of hope, I repositioned the debate about autonomy. I presented autonomy as a contradictory struggle that produce an excess that can not only be heard in the key of hope, and which is different in form and content in indigenous and non-indigenous contexts. The four chapters of Part II offer an empirical journey with four movements informed by their own experience of organising hope.

Part II
Navigating Autonomy

4

Organising Negation: Neoliberal Hopelessness, Insurgent Hope (Mexico)

Introduction: neoliberal globalisation and Latin America

During the 1980s and 1990s, Latin America became the privileged site for both neoliberal experimentation and the emergence of laboratories of resistance against and beyond it, in the jungle, the forest, the neighbourhoods, the settlement, the outskirts, the city: a 'laboring laboratory *possibilis salutis*' (Bloch, 1977: 389). Recent studies of Latin American social movements frame this period as one of intense 'opposition to' neoliberalism (Deere and Royce, 2009; Sader and Gentili, 2003; Boron et al., 1999; Burdick et al., 2009; De Almeida and Ruiz Sánchez, 2000; Grugel and Riggirozzi, 2012; Roberts, 2009; Veltmeyer et al., 1997). Indeed, opposition, i.e. the demunciatory moment was initially reflected in a wave of citizens' protests motivated by different reasons, which led to the departure of nine presidents ahead of time: in Brazil in 1992, in Venezuela and Guatemala in 1993, in Ecuador in 1997 and 2000, in Paraguay in 1999, in Peru in 2000 and twice in Argentina in December 2001 (Ollier, 2003: 170), followed by process of movement formation led by the landless, anti-labour bureaucracy and local trade unions, the unemployed and the urban poor.

Structural adjustments went far. Encouraged by the Washington Consensus (WC) stabilisation packages were promoted in the region by neo-populist governments and neoliberal economists united by an 'unexpected affinity' (Weyland, 1996: 3). They agreed that stability was a precondition for economic growth. During the 1980s and mainly the 1990s, Latin America was immersed into 'neoliberalism'. First implemented by right-wing political military and civilian elites like Pinochet in Chile and Fujimori in Peru, and later on adopted by leaders of nationalist ideologies like *Partido Revolucionario Institucional* (Institutional

Revolutionary Party, PRI) in Mexico, Peronism in Argentina and the National Revolutionary movement in Bolivia, neoliberal policy also gained adepts among social democrats such as the Chilean Socialist Party, Democratic Action in Venezuela and Social Democratic Party in Brazil (Sader, 2008: 7). The WC imposed the view that instability and lack of growth were both rooted in the ill-conceived import-substitution strategy of industrialisation (ISI) adopted by most populist governments after world war II (Fanelli et al., 1994: 102). Both statism and economic populism were to blame for these failures (Boron, 1993: 62–63).

Accordingly, the 'Free Market Open Economy Policies' (FMOEP) (Richards, 1997) were applied throughout the region under the supervision of the IMF, with little consideration of the differences among the countries. Homogeneity does not mean that the implementation and the outcomes were similar for governments had to confront challenges and resistance of different kinds within different contexts and historical backgrounds. This led, for example, to the increase of the amount social expenditure per capita in Mexico, Chile and Bolivia, and less in Venezuela and Brazil (Veltmeyer, 2004). While policy must be analysed separately from the homogeneous discourse that promoted market-led policy (Veltmeyer, 2004): all reforms responded to the WC requirement of fiscal discipline and the reduction of public expenditures, deregulation and the opening of the economy to capital investments, privatisation and an efficient private sector (Tedesco, 1999).

Most assessments of neoliberal policy in Latin America point at the failure of the reforms in connecting stability with growth. The form of stabilisation promoted by the WC restricted economic growth and increased existing social and economic acute problems, such as poverty and lack of social security, as well as created new ones, such as mass unemployment (Huber and Solt, 2004), thus proceeding 'beyond the point of no return' (Munck, 1994: 91). Scholars point to the lack of social safety nets as part of economic reforms and democratic mechanisms in shaping economic and policy reforms (Huber and Solt, 2004: 159) and use the term 'high social costs' to characterise the impact of the reforms upon society (Tavares Ribeiro Soares, 2001; López Maya and Lander, 2001; Sader, 2001; Sader and Gentili, 2003; Boron, 2003).

The demise of the import-substitution model of development, the subsequent shift to economic programmes based on agro exportation and the transnationalisation of internal markets as required by the advanced capitalist countries in the North repositioned Latin American economies within the new global economy. The destruction of national industry became the engine of growth, with the privatisation of state assets and state-owned companies, the re-regulation of labour markets by means of their deregulation, flexibilisation of labour, and financialisation. It is acknowledged that these quickly implemented changes were aimed at sending the correct signals to the main centres of power in order to obtain financial provision that would help to produce the mandatory changes.

In Argentina, the attempt to return to the agro-export model, accompanied by speculative financial practices from 1976 to 1982 marked the beginning of the process of 'social disarticulation' (Teubal, 2000: 461) by means of the destruction of real wages and the transference of resources to concentrated and transnational economic groups, leading to increasing social exclusion. Advocates of this 'shock strategy' (Calcagno, 2001: 76), like those in Chile under the Pinochet's dictatorship (see Haworth and Roddick, 1981), also embraced 'market fundamentalism' (Boron et al., 1999: 234) as a tool to reorganise the economy, social relations and the social structure. Advisors explicitly recognised that the *ajustes salvajes* (savage adjustments) would produce human casualties and social injuries such as mass unemployment, more poverty, and loss of human and labour rights (all called 'social costs'). Yet international experts reassured governments that this would not last long for the economy would recover after the radical changes were thoroughly implemented, thus favouring everyone. As Weyland highlights, 'like surgery, market-oriented reforms promise sustained benefits, in the long run at the price of considerable pain in the short run' (Weyland, 1996: 18). International agencies such as the United Nations Development Programme (UNDP) facilitated the implementation of local and national special benefits and focused social programmes of poverty reduction and basic health care for the poor as a way of counteracting the social effects of the brutal adjustments.

Latin American scholars and Latinamericanists elsewhere produced invaluable critical and well-documented analyses of the neoliberal transformation in the region in general and per country (Sader, 2001; Smith et al., 1994a; 1994b; Sader and Gentili, 2003; Boron et al., 1999). I offer here an interpretation of the neoliberal period that characterizes it for the formation of an *imaginary of hopelessness* in the region. Social *imaginaries* are not ideologies, myths or illusions but material dimensions of social practices. They are not just 'external' ideas to be 'internalised' by the subjects involved, but they are *constitutive* of our way of existing and resisting, and of understandings of reality. My argument is that a key feature of neoliberal globalisation with regards to other forms of capitalism is the *political construction of hopelessness*. This means the systematic use of fear and frustration *as the means for* economic and social transformation to proceed.

The social imaginary of hopelessness was formed as the neoliberal *paquetes de medidas* began to produce all-encompassing material changes that worsened and degraded individual, collective and social lives, and generated excruciating working and living conditions plagued with uncertainties, fears, unhappiness, violence and exclusions. By being elevated to the *only possible way to go*, the neoliberal way delineated the contours of a new *reality* within which democracy would operate. 'Neo-liberal utopia' highlights Bourdieu (1998: 94) 'manages to see itself as the scientific description of reality', the close reality of the *pensamiento único*. Subcomandante Insurgente Marcos (SIM) called it 'the inevitable':

> 'The inevitable' has a name today: fragmented globalization ... the end of history, the omnipresence and omnipotence of money, the substitution of politics for police, the present as the only possible future, rationalization of social inequality, justification of super-exploitation of human beings and natural resources, racism, intolerance, war. (cited in Carlsen, 2006)

'The inevitable' relies on the political construction of hopelessness, that is, the articulation of a cynical political narrative and policy discourses that do not simply cut short political possibilities but *celebrate the lack of alternatives* as 'doing well', thus forcing millions of Latin Americans to conform to the 'neoliberal reality of our time'. In the process, the experience of dispossession, injustice and exploitation was matched with a discourse that not only accepted human 'sacrifice' and 'pain' but reified it as the best tool for economy's improvement. As it happens in Europe at the time of writing (August 2014), unlike other forms of capitalism, neoliberalism rested on both the production of an unbearable present without a real promise of a better future in the horizon and the discursive justification of this as the best option. My interpretation of neoliberal globalisation as the political construction of hopelessness facilitates a better understanding both of the current forms of accumulation of capital ('by dispossession') (Harvey, 2005) and the new autonomous struggles that emerged within and against it to organise hope. The political construction of hopelessness was an active process of demarcating and coding reality in a way that the neoliberal truth became *the* truth.

Constructing hopelessness

There are several factors that contributed to both the construction of hopelessness and the emergence and expansion of the process of organising negation and hope in the late 1980s and 1990s in Latin America. These factors, policies and political dynamics constitute the material foundations that underpin the struggle over the meaning of autonomy during the late 1980s up until the 2000s. I am not arguing that neoliberal globalisation is the *cause* of the revitalisation of autonomous organising in Latin America or that autonomous movements *reacted to* neoliberal globalisation. My argument is that there is rather an 'elective affinity' *à la* Weber between both, that is, a reciprocal-yet-antagonistic connection between them that is revealed in the way in which neoliberalism touches subjectivity, thus becoming a key factor (although not the only one) for both the decomposition of the old protagonists and the formation of new subjects of resistance. Examples of these are the emergence of new indigenous-popular movements in Bolivia after the decomposition of the Bolivian Workers Confederation (*Central Obrera Boliviana*, COB) (an outcome of the neoliberal reforms) or of the Movement of Unemployed Workers (*Movimiento de Trabajadores Desocupados*, MTD) in Argentina (the product of mass unemployment there), or of the EZLN (the outcome of years of oppression and exclusion of indigenous communities accelerated by the modification of Art 27 of the Mexican National Constitution that put indigenous land on sale), or of the MST (when its funders started taking the land, inspired in a dream, and began to realise in extreme poverty and danger, against the odds).

Uprooting revolutionary dreams: dictatorial regimes and the crisis of the left

The defeat of armed revolutionary projects that, at the time, enjoyed popular support was essential to the imposition of the neoliberal doctrine and policies in the region. Guerrilla movements that embraced a variety of revolutionary traditions became a fetter to the circulation and expansion of capital. The freeing of capital as a result of the end of the political regulation of global money through the Bretton Woods Agreement in 1971 led to a growing pressure from US banks and the United States government onto Latin American administrations to open national economies up and embrace market reforms, to allow mainly privatisation and free trade to proceed. This strategy clashed not only with a high level of political mobilisation and resistance to any neoliberal policy but with a variety of revolutionary projects in the making led by a new young vanguard, the New Left.

Capital's pressure to reduce the barriers to its expansion under these conditions led to an 'era of military coups' (Sader, 2008: 6) and a process of militarisation, both supervised by the US. In the Southern Cone, the military regimes brutally disarmed guerrilla and popular movements by means of imprisonment and torture in detention camps, forced disappearance without knowing the crime committed and the fate of the bodies of victims, mass execution by firing squad, death flights, and the handing over in unlawful adoption of children born in captivity or captured with their parents in military operations, appropriation of the victim's and family's material possessions, legalised prisoners in prisons of extreme security, exile in other Latin American (e.g., Mexico, Venezuela) or European countries, and domestic exile, with the loss of elementary rights. (See CONADEP, 1986). Horror and terror produced by the physical and spiritual annihilation of a generation of left, trade union and social movement leaders and activists, paved the way for the implementation of drastic economic reforms leading to financial speculation and the use of state's subsidies and expenditures to produce quick profit and undertake further transformations in the labour and financial markets.

Rather than an *anomaly* or 'state of exception', dictatorial regimes in Latin America became 'a paradigm of government' (Agamben, 2005: 1) for a decade. By *disappearing* the opposition and spreading fear and uncertainty to the whole social field by means of state terrorism, dictatorial regimes did the 'dirty job' (De Oliveria, 2004: 113) of eradicating the revolutionary dream, creating hopelessness, while laying out the foundations for the realization of the neoliberal paradise.

The annihilation of the revolutionary projects paved the way to the renewal of the social democratic/populist) promise. After terror, democracy became a mobilizing utopia. The revolutionary utopia remained an abstract project, disparaged by the critique of the Union of Soviet Socialist Republics (USSR) state socialism, the defeat of the revolutionary movements of the region and the emergence, expansion and relative consensus achieved by the *pensamiento único* that endorsed market fundamentalism. In this moment of retreat, communism, emancipation, socialism and utopia were trivialized. The discussion of alternative possibilities was cancelled until further notice. The concern was how to lead the transition to democracy, to re-establish a democratic regime. Critique took the form of a critique of authoritarianism. But transition to democracy was not a problem of political engineering but of class struggle. Transition to democracy meant opposed things to social, human and labour movement, and to international financial institutions and banks. Whereas the former strove for the realisation of postponed demands and the further democratisation of society and the state, the latter commanded the implementation of IMF stabilisation plans that would offer a platform for the neoliberal transformation of the economy and the expansion of international capital in the region. During the 1980s social mobilisation and political struggles made apparent the most vital contradiction of the process of transition to democracy in Latin America: that the recognition of popular demands that had emerged as a result of the authoritarian period and the policies implemented to satisfy them –which were considered fundamental to the consolidation of democracy, became the obstacle to democratic consolidation. In Argentina, the transition to democracy ended with the resignation of president Alfonsin before completing his term in office, forced by new military uprisings, the pressure of human rights militants, hyperinflation and the international creditors allied with the Peronist Party, whose elected candidate was Carlos Menem. President Menem's pragmatic and messianic approach to policies 'solved' the main dilemma of the Alfonsín administration quickly by officially declaring that democracy was formally 'consolidated'. His task was to stabilise the economy. This meant a transition from the illegal terrorism of money to the legalisation of the terrorism of money in the form of 'stability'.

Indebtedness

Debt also contributed greatly to the political construction of hopelessness under neoliberal regimes. As Lazzarato (2012: 23–25) highlights 'debt creation ... has been conceived and programmed as the strategic heart of neoliberal politics'. The indebtedness of the Latin American economies and their people was intrinsic to the recomposition of global capital through the global movement of money, and not a consequence of it. The 1970s and early 1980s was a period of debt-led (and inflationary) growth as the flow of capital travelled south to be offered as international loans, fostering an unprecedented external debt for most of the countries, which reached a critical point in 1982. As Marazzi highlights, 'the total amount of credit required by the poorer countries has been calculated at $40 billion in 1976, while about 50 per cent of the profits of the major US banks now come from loans to these same countries – a situation which makes it unlikely that moratoria will be widely permitted' (Marazzi, 1996: 86).

The degree of indebtedness of Latin American economies can be observed by looking at the relation between external debts and exports during the 1970s: following Schatan (1998: 25–29), whereas in 1977 the payments for the external debt represented 191 per cent of exports, in 1985 they represented 330 per cent of it. The debt grew 34 per cent from 1990 to 1995, with the weight of the debt carried by only a few countries: Mexico, where the debt grew by 33 per cent; Argentina, where the debt grew by 44 per cent; Peru, where the debt grew by 50 per cent; Chile, where the debt grew by 33 per cent; and Venezuela, where the debt grew by eight per cent.

The absence of any kind of democratic control over expenditure and credit *created* an external debt by means of a dynamic involving international private capital, IMF, WB and the national bourgeoisie and landed classes led by the Chicago think tanks (Ferrer in Teubal, 1986: 23). The creation of the external debt is explained by the expansion of private international business by means of the creation of the market in Eurodollars and the consequent availability of credit on a global scale: 'foreign credit was resurrected in unlimited supply' (Canitrot, 1994: 79). This was accompanied by the facilities and pressure that the governments of powerful countries put on the Latin American ones. For instance, the main nine international banks lend to Latin American countries an amount equal to 135 per cent of their capital (Teubal, 1986: 23). The external debt acted as a form of escape recession in the US, supported by the IMF. The profitability regarding international transactions of the first ten multinational banks of the US grew by more than 33 per cent per year between 1970 and 1977. The profit made by those banks as part of general profit grew from 17.5 per cent in 1970 to 52.5 per cent in 1975, the year of recession in the US (Moffitt in Schatan, 1998: 37).

The three main forms in which the external debt was created by the debtor countries in Latin America were the flight of capital and illicit transactions, superfluous spending and the expenditure in the weapons industry (Schatan, 1998: 50). In Argentina, during the 1970s, capital's flight was a form of obtaining quick profit. The essential component of the external debt was 28 billion dollars of *capital fugado* (escaped capital) (Minsburg, 1987: 102). Capital flight during 1979–1981 – which amounted to US$16.2 billion – was around 23 per cent of Argentina's GDP' (Tedesco, 1999: 45). The amount of *capital fugado* between 1979 and 1983 was 63 billion dollars, of which 12 billion dollars were from Argentina (Schatan, 1998: 51). 'Between July and November 1976 the [A]rgentine government deposited in the Chase Manhattan Bank of New York more than monthly 22 million dollars' (Schatan, 1998: 53). Whilst in December 1976, the external debt – private and public – was 8.279 billion dollars, in 1983 it had reached 47.234 billion dollars and 90 per cent of this figure corresponded to financial debt (Minsburg, 1987: 100).

The external debt was also produced by several mechanisms used by the government to fund military and repression costs, such as detention and torture camps, gigantic public works and events to build up popularity such as the 1978 Football World Cup (Argentina). Finally, there was a growth in expenditure in the weapons industry: between 1977 and 1980, only four countries (Argentina, Brazil, Chile and Peru) imported almost 3 billion dollars in weapons (Schatan, 1998: 63).

With the recognition by international creditors of what they called the 'excessive indebtedness', debtor countries tried to build a front so as to find common solutions to the debt crisis. In the *Consenso de Cartagena* (May 1984), four Latin American presidents – Raúl Alfonsín from Argentina, João Figueiredo from Brazil, Belisario Betancur Cuartas from Colombia and Miguel de la Madrid Hurtado from Mexico, issued a joint declaration with regards to the international economic circumstances that affected the region, in particular their external debts, and established mechanisms of consultation and decision making (see O'Connell, 1988). The *Consenso de Cartagena* was followed by the creation of a debtor's club (after the 1985 Montevideo Declaration). The debtors' joint action, however, failed vis-à-vis Paris Club's unified strategy which imposed individual negotiations on the indebted countries (Drimer, 1990: 40).

Argentina provides also a template of how debt can become a burden for new democratic governments. When credit was cut off in 1982 the reduction of private debt was achieved by means of a financial reform and the Central Bank subsidies in the form of debt swaps. This not only helped the private sector to cancel its external liabilities at a subsidised price (Tedesco, 1999) but *nationalised* the private debt for 'the Central Bank assumed the private dollar debt and became creditor of local debtor firms in domestic currency' (Canitrot, 1994: 80). The public sector took responsibility for 52.3 per cent of the external debt in 1979 and that rate increased to 62.2 per cent in 1982. This liability would ceaselessly grow as a snowball up to December 2001. While it served to the accumulation of capital, the external debt was mainly the 'Trojan horse of neoliberalism' (Schatan, 1998: 17) for debt relief came with the obligation to swallow the 'poison pill of neoliberal institutional reforms' (Harvey, 2007: 73–75). New credit was offered to help the region to face the interests of the external debt and fulfil a plan called 'structural adjustment with economic growth'. The solution to 'the lost decade' of endless negotiations around the debt crisis and the level of indebtedness of the Latin American economies was (ironically) the implementation of structural reforms leading to more indebtedness and hopelessness.

Democracy

As above-mentioned, at the time of the Mexican debt crisis of 1982, many South American countries were facing the transition to democracy. The direction of such transitions was marked by debt because new administrations, like Roldós in Ecuador, Belaúnde Terry in Peru, Siles Suazo in Bolivia, Alfonsín in Argentina and Sanguinetti in Uruguay, fell trapped between two antagonistic demands: for the recognition and attainments of brutally repressed and postponed demands, particularly with regards to poverty, wages and the violation of human rights during the dictatorships (see Calderón, 1986) and the requests from the government of the United States, banks and the IMF pressure to achieve stability and service the external debt.

However, pluralist-politicist analyses that prevailed at the time regarded the problem of the democratisation of Latin American political regimes mainly as an issue of political engineering and governability (O'Donnell et al., 1986). Political parties were seen as key actors of the 'political process' so that other social conflict and mobilisation demanding policy changes were circumvented in favour of analyses of institutional mechanisms guaranteeing stability (Dinerstein and Ferrero, 2012). Although scholars, many of whom were government advisors, acknowledged the significance of the debt crisis and economic constraints for the process of consolidation of democracy, they argued for the autonomy of the political and the possibility that a consolidated democracy could coexist with poverty and social exclusion. They were guided by the notion of 'governability' imposed by the Trilateral Commission in the 1970s. Democracy was defined as the 'explicit set of structures and procedures established *a priori*'. 'Consolidation' was then the routinisation of procedures and the re-creation of a democratic political culture.

It was argued that the democratisation of the political regime that was politically inclusive was occurring simultaneously with a process of economic modernisation of the state that was tending to produce social exclusion. To Smith and Acuña this meant that Latin America experienced the consolidation of a weak form of democracy, which took place '*in spite of* the economic reality confronted by these societies' (Smith and Acuña, 1994: 21, my italics). Being exceedingly concerned with the classification of military regime and transition types and the problem of institutional change, these accounts failed to grasp that the process of consolidation of democracy was embedded in deep transformations in the economy and that new 'consolidated' democracies risked becoming essential to the legitimisation of neoliberal reforms, which undermined democracy. Harvey correctly explains that this legitimation was accomplished by the construction of a common sense that articulated consent on the need to reform and stabilize the economies: 'powerful ideological influences circulated through the corporations, the media, and the numerous institutions that constitute civil society – such as the universities, schools, churches and professional associations' (Harvey, 2007: 39). This does not mean that everyone agreed with the policy but that the neoliberal option appeared as the *only one available* after ruthless dictatorships and the economic instability that has always threatened democracy in the region. Any demand by mobilised citizens, human rights activists and trade unions was measured with the rod of stability and commonly censured as either impossible to be fulfilled or as 'destabilising stability' (Dinerstein, 1999). Stability relied on the individual fear of not being able to satisfy those postponed needs. As Deleuze and Guattari (1999 28) highlight 'the deliberate creation of lack as a function of the market economy is the art of a dominant class.'

When common sense failed, hyperinflation episodes induced by corporations and economic elites performed as a disciplinary tool. *Market coups* (Canitrot, 1994) (like in Argentina, Bolivia, Brazil, Chile and Peru) disclosed the violence of money-capital. Hyperinflation dramatically results in both monetary speculation and poverty. It reveals that money is not the efficient means of exchange but the means of creating hopelessness. The fear of hyperinflation paved the way to the reluctant or full acceptance of neoliberal policies that guaranteed to stabilise the economy, achieve economic growth and 'competitiveness'. As Weyland highlights 'while neoliberal policies impose initial losses to many sectors of society, these costs pale in light of the imminent catastrophe of full-scale hyperinflation that market-oriented adjustment helps avert' (Weyland, 1996: 17).

Money as command and dispossession

Connected to the previous three factors, there is a fourth dynamic that contributed to the social construction of hopelessness: the intensification of the command of money over society. The breakdown of the Bretton Woods international agreement in 1971 ended the dollar convertibility and the monetary regulation by national states. New currencies emerged as international standards of 'quality' with the consequent new territorialisation around regional cooperation (Bonefeld and Holloway, 1996: 5–6; Clarke, 1988). Debt crises and crashes followed thereafter. The breakdown of Bretton Woods' system 'developed through the debtor crisis of the 1980s, the crash of 1987 and the recession of the early 1990s ... emphasised since the fall of the Berlin Wall in 1989 (Bonefeld and Holloway, 1996: 6). The global 'terrorism of money' (Marazzi, 1996; Fuchs and Vélez, 2001) fostered instability. The previous fixed exchange rates allowed national currencies to be strong but, at the same time, it produced severe problems in the balance of payments. Now, the focus was put on monetary management and this placed the central bankers at the centre of the stage. It was the emergence of what is called 'monetarism' or the concern about the flow of money in the system instead of fiscal concerns (Keynesianism) (Clarke, 1988). The conversion of capital into money, that is, 'over-accumulation of capital' meant a 'detachment' of money from the basis of its own existence. (Holloway, 1994: 40)

What matters for our concern here is that while first facilitating the creation of the external debt, over-accumulated capital put pressure onto the Latin American governments via international financial institutions to penetrate their country's economies, invest and profit. As already mentioned, dictatorial regimes and neoliberal structural reforms in Latin America cannot be understood properly without considering the role that over-accumulated capital in the North played in it. This facilitated the expansion of 'accumulation by dispossession'. Financialisation is a key element of accumulation by dispossession for it allows few transnational corporations to mobilise investments throughout the world and to obtain benefit from the different exchange rates via financial speculation. Financialisation has disciplinary faculties over society and the state. As Harvey argues 'the way of financialisation that occurred after the mid-1970s has been spectacular for its "predatory style" connected to dispossessions of all kinds of assets' (Harvey, 2010a: 245).

In Argentina, money laundering was utilised to promote the successful circulation and reproduction of money capital in the North. An enquiry led by the Parliamentary Commission for the Investigation of Money Laundering (*Comisión de Lavado de Dinero del Honorable Congreso de la Nación*, CLDHCN) in August 2001 revealed hidden devices set in place for the debt equity swap system, the role of newly created offshore companies, the different *modus operandi* between national, foreign and offshore companies, the mechanisms leading to the emptying of the financial system as well as the existence of clandestine circuits of money, bribes, money laundering from bribes and traffic of drugs, the constitution of companies abroad, and the link between the external debt and the flight of capital (CLDHCN, 2001, 2002;). Particularly interesting are the mechanisms set up for money laundering between national banks and offshore companies – a *parallel* financial system within which the state regulations under parliamentary control were systematically bypassed and replaced, with the connivance of high-level public sector managers, by new rules. This form of reproduction and circulation of capital and profit making, linked with offshore banking and companies would not have been possible without an 'internal' political dynamic, which supported and reproduced the circuit of easy profit making which initially involved high levels of the political elites in power, local and foreign banks, and national economic groups such as Citibank, Banca

Nazionale del Lavoro, Bank Boston, etc. (see CLDHCN, 2002; see also Llorens and Cafiero, 2001 and 2002).

Privatisation and decentralisation became the two chief issues of the programme supervised by the WB, which intervened directly in its implementation (Fuchs, 1993: 147). Selling the family jewellery was argued to be the best way to reduce debt and make public services more efficient. In the government's rhetoric, the improvement of the quality of public services, the promotion of economic efficiency, and the democratisation and generation of new investments in key areas like education were the priorities. The marketing of state-owned companies, some of them being gold mines, offered governments the possibility to achieve a quick reduction of the external debt by means of debt-equity swaps (Fuchs, 1993). In order to attract capital, governments prepared the terrain by doing a quick job, which included the deterioration of the quality of service provided (Basualdo and Azpiazu, 2002), mismanagement, propaganda against trade unions, increase in the service tariffs and lack of investment. Once in motion, the process of privatisation reconciled 'domestic' and 'external' interests as well as obtained political support from the capitalist class for further reforms (Basualdo and Azpiazu, 2002; Thwaites Rey, 2001; 2003). The process of privatisation allowed a fast recomposition and regrouping of the capitalist class in each country, permitting the formation of a 'business community' and sanctioning the high concentration of capital in few hands (Basualdo and Azpiazu, 2002).

These companies consolidated as oligopolies in the areas of energy (water, electricity, gas and oil, water) transport and iron and steel industries, thus transforming the economic and financial performance of the country. The 'privatisation crusade' (Boron et al., 1999: 62) was strategic to the accumulation by dispossession in two ways: on the one hand, the privatisation of public assets and state-owned companies was a good choice for external creditors, local and foreign investors and also the governments, which were under pressure from foreign creditors trying to collect debt payment in arrears and therefore wanted to re-establish the state's cash flow and put the foreign accounts in order (Gerchunoff, 1993: 18–19). On the other hand, the privatisation of hydrocarbons and water (see Spronk and Webber, 2008) provided direct sources for investment and profit making.

Workers experienced the privatisation of state-owned companies as an intense physical and emotional distress. The workplace became a battlefield where workers felt 'knocked out ... injured ... we have been shocked in many respects and in many forms' (Employee, Gas del Estado, Buenos

Aires, 1996). Privatisation restructured and moved workers around; put pressured for the so-called 'voluntary redundancy'; transferred workers to other sectors of the city, other cities or other companies (contracting out); and dismantled the companies' provision of welfare and social benefits (e.g., children's recreation park, holidays, accommodation facilities). These changes impacted dramatically on everyday private and social life, bringing a sense of loss within and outside the enterprise, since privatisation involved workers and their families' lives, culture and traditions as well as labour relations and forms of trade unionism.

Demolishing the world of work: the virtual disappearance of labour

Capitalist domination, argues Bonnet, is exercised in contemporary capitalism, as the 'command of money-capital that, through its movement, sanctions the conditions of exploitation and domination of labour' (Bonnet, 2002: 124). The celebration of the rule of money by the state as *the* growth strategy requires as its counterpart what I call the 'virtual disappearance' of labour. While physical 'disappearance' is the ultimate political weapon of state terrorism, *virtual disappearance* is the most sophisticated weapon of market fundamentalism. By *virtual disappearance* of labour I mean the de-recognition of the state's role in the reproduction of labour and the subsequent depoliticisation and invisibilisation of significant sectors of the labour force. This allows for the legitimisation of what is presented as 'exclusion' leading to impoverishment, landlessness, unemployment and casualisation of labour, to which the state attends via focused policy which, in turn, produces more public indebtedness. In both cases, physical (assassination) and virtual (unemployment) disappearance, the *disappeared* are non-existent beings – as defined by General Videla from one of the Argentine military *juntas*. He claimed in 1979 that the disappeared: '*is not*, that is it is neither dead nor alive, does not have entity at all' (*La República perdida II*, 1986).

The 'dismantling of the world of work' (Boltanski and Chiapello, 2006 217) was the kernel of the neoliberal reforms and was arguably experienced as an *assault* on labour. There is an extensive literature on this, with focus on the transformation of industrial relations, the regional effects of privatisation, the economic adjustment on the labour market and forms of employment in a context of social exclusion and poverty, and the crisis of trade unions (Zapata, 2004; De la Garza Toledo, 2005). Structural reforms reduced the portion of wage labour that contributed to social security from 67 per cent in 1990 to 60 per cent in 1998, having Uruguay and Peru with 79 per cent and 43 per cent, respectively. Wages were reduced 28 per cent in the 1990s and the decrease was spectacular in El Salvador, Mexico and Peru. There was an increase and common use of temporary contracts and casualisation of work. In Argentina, towards 1997, 35 per cent of the wage labourers were working in these conditions, with 30 per cent in Chile, 39 per cent in Colombia and 74 per cent in Peru (Salas, 2000: 191). Due to the instability and low wage levels, the number of people at work increased and there was a feminisation of the labour force in general (Salas, 2000: 190; Munck, 2000). Workers were the main bearers of the social debt of structural adjustments for 'in the course of 1980, the minimum wage in Latin America declined by a quarter and average earnings in the informal sector fell by 42 per cent [PREALC, 1991: 35]' (Munck, 1994: 91) with an increasing flexibilisation of labour.

Despite that more people have become part of the labour force, the structural reforms produced unprecedented levels of unemployment: in Chile, unemployment jumped from five per cent of the labour force in 1970 to 16.7 per cent in 1980 (Haworth and Roddick, 1981: 54); in Argentina, unemployment rose from six per cent in 1991 to 18.5 per cent in 1995. In the capital city and Greater Buenos Aires (where half of the unemployed are concentrated) the rate of unemployment went up to 20.2 per cent in May 1995. But the main problem was not *just* unemployment but the explosive combination of unemployment with underemployment, affecting around 7 million out of 13 million workers. In July 2000, the rate of unemployment reached 15.4 per cent and it is estimated to reach 17.1 per cent in 2003 (Dinerstein, 2001).

The reform of the state transformed the relation between nation-state and labour. In Latin America, (quasi)Keynesian policies and ISI led to the *recognition* of the centrality of the working class in the reproduction of the Keynesian virtuous circle of production-consumption-profit-investment-production, legitimised by the social democratic/populist pact. Keynesianism means that the state 'organises' the inherent contradiction of capitalism at a national level in a particular way, without solving it. In the late 1960s and early 1970s, the neo-Keynesian 'pattern of the containment of the power of labour' (Holloway, 1996) collapsed. To Cleaver (1996: 141), 'in the era of Keynesianism state money played a fundamental role in the capitalist management of class relations at both the national and international levels'. He highlights that 'with the cycle of working class struggle that brought that era to an end' led to crisis of the Keynesian monetary control and the emergence of new approaches and more repressive uses of money. As we know, monetarist policies rejected 'the political commitment to full employment in favour of the subordination of social-relations to so-called market freedom' (Bonefeld et al., 1995: 52) above all because 'the increased mobility of capital undermined working class resistance to the reorganisation of the labour process' (Clarke, 1988: 320).

Trade unions were affected by the neoliberal transformation, as they were overwhelmed by both the neoliberal attack on workers and trade unions rights and by the collective action of new social movements (De la Garza Toledo, 2005: 17). Strategic orientations were influenced by specific political configurations in each country. Zapata (2004: 3) suggests that the crisis of trade unionism in Latin America is a product of changes in the traditional sources of power for trade unions in the region: the control of the labour process and their access to political power and the state. The control of the labour process was affected by the demise of the import-substitution model and the consequent priva- tisation and transnationalisation of the internal market. The access to political power and the state was affected by the transition from democ- racy to dictatorial regimes, with the implications of the state violence on labour and labour activism, and the further process of political change that transitions to democracy under neoliberal adjustment process brought about. In this vein, Munck (1994) points to the high impact of structural adjustment on the social pact (*concertación social*) particularly during transition to democracy in the Southern Cone.

Poverty and the maiming of the social fabric

In addition to the virtual disappearance of labour, during the 1980s and the 1990s the entire Latin America continent was transformed into 'an enormous factory of poverty (Boron, 1995: 4). What was initially inter- preted as income poverty was soon materialised as structural poverty, which was particularly significant in those countries that had a signifi- cant middle class. The Economic Commission for Latin America and the Caribbean (*Comisión Económica para América Latina y el Caribe*, CEPAL) suggests that Latin America has the highest rates of inequality in the world, which increased in the late 1990s and beginning of the 2000s (De Oliveira, 2004: 111). While Mexico and Brazil remained more or less stable, Argentina and Uruguay suffered a significant social polarisation. Tensions among workers and within trade unions were exacerbated by unemployment and the casualisation of work, which gave protagonism to social actors other than the organised working class (De Oliveira, 2004: 112). Schatan (1998: 123) points to the substantial increase in poverty rates in urban areas due to the migration from countryside to big urban conglomerates, which meant the 'urbanisation of rural misery', for poor urban population doubled between 1980 and 1994 as a result of the structural adjustment policies post-debt (Schatan, 1998: 124). The impact of structural adjustment in Latin America goes beyond the economic arena 'to affect the very fabric of social relations' (Munck, 1994: 90).

The use of state violence for policy implementation

The end of military regimes in the region and the replacement of physical disappearance by virtual disappearance of labour did not end repression and physical annihilation of the opponent by power, although it was clearly reduced. State violence is always a resource to be used with the aim of maintaining the conditions created by policy. While state violence is a permanent feature of capitalism, during the neoliberal reforms the latter became a tool to silence activists, protestors and entire communities' resistance to inhuman policy. Neoliberalism is inherently authoritarian for it cannot survive in a truly democratic political environment. In Latin America, neoliberal reforms were (are) what González Casanova (2002) refers to as 'war neoliberalism', that is, the reconstruction of systemic governability by means of the military control of society (Seoane et al., 2009: 23). Particularly during the neoliberal period, development policy was conducted through oppressive and repressive forms of social control that praise 'citizen participation' and 'empowerment' as tools for the attainment of 'internal order'. Public policy promoted reforms that tended to reinforce the punitive capacity of the state and criminalise social protest and social movements' actions, particularly the urban poor, with the revival of the idea of the 'dangerous classes' (Seoane et al., 2009: 23). The *Sacudón* or *Caracazo* was the first officially acknowledged act of 'police excess' against anti-neoliberal protesters. The unprecedented use of state violence in Venezuela in February 1989 led to around 300 deaths of mainly poor people. This is comparable with the repression exercised during the dictatorial period in other countries of the Southern Cone (Martínez, 2008; López Maya, 2003).

A more subterranean and ubiquitous repression is always at work. Massacres and assassinations of mobilised people are not uncommon and usually go unprocessed. They are not 'police or military excesses' but one of the strategies of intimidation to create fear and hopelessness utilised by the governments to implement and sustain unpopular and unjust policies. In Chiapas, while the San Andrés Accords between the government and the Zapatista movement were taking place, the Zedillo administration opted for massacre. The Acteal massacre (1997) of 45 people (many of them women and children) (see Ceceña 2001b) was a governmental tool for negotiation wth the Zapatistas by means of intimidation. In Brazil, the massacres of Corumbiara (Rondônia) in 1995 and in Eldorado dos Carajás (Pará) in 1996, where 19 MST members were killed and 69 others were severely injured, were directed against young and courageous rural workers and were significant to the implementation of 'social democratic' repressive policy of President Cardoso. Eldorado dos Carajás massacre, was the 'largest criminal case ever brought to trial in Brazil, with over 150 defendants, all military policemen[, i]n contrast with the massacre in Corumbiara' which surprised Brazilians and the international community about rural violence (Issa, 2007: 124).

During the battle of Buenos Aires in December 2001, the state responded to social mobilization with ruthless repression leading to the death of more than 30 people while hundreds were injured. In June 2002, two young, unemployed activists from the Unemployed Workers' Network Aníbal Verón (*Coordinadora de Trabajodores Desocupados Aníbal Verón*, CTDAV), Maximiliano Kosteki and Darío Santillán, were assassinated by the Greater Buenos Aires police during a protest (roadblock). During the process of mobilisation that took place between 2000 and 2005, in particular the water and oil wars, and the defence of coca plantations in Bolivia, many were injured and killed. And so on.

Commodification and privatisation of indigenous lands and rural landlessness

Finally, the commodification and privatisation of indigenous and rural workers' communal land features as my last component of my puzzle of the political construction of hopelessness. Following Harvey, crucial to the process of accumulation by dispossession is the expulsion of peasants from their lands, 'the suppression of rights to the commons; commodification of labor power and the suppression of alternative (indigenous) forms of production and consumption; colonial, neo-colonial, and imperial processes of appropriation of assets (including natural resources)' (Harvey, 2005: 159).

Latin American peasants are the poorest among populations, with the worst health, education, life expectancy and political participation indicators. They are usually involved in violent conflict around the land (Arruda Sampaio, 2005: 17–20). Rural workers and families played a important role in the struggle for the land and agrarian reform against neoliberal structural adjustments. Latin American peasants, argues Arruda Sampaio (2005: 19), are now aware of the exploitation they have suffered for centuries and are determined to end it.

Table 4.1   Elective affinity: neoliberal hopelessness and insurgent hope

Neoliberal hopelessness	Insurgent hope
Obliteration of revolutionary dreams	New revolutionary dreams
Indebtedness	Critique of money
Undemocratic/restricted democracy	Horizontal and direct democracy, pursuit of popular justice, indigenous autonomy
Money as command and dispossession	People before profit, non profitable and solidarity collective actions
The virtual disappearance of labour	Dignified forms of work, production and cooperation
Poverty and the damaging of the social fabric	Policy from below, creation of cooperatives at the grass roots, the common, autonomous practices in indigenous communities; *buen vivir*
The use of legitimate state violence for policy implementation	Affective politics
Commodification and privatisation of indigenous lands and rural landlessness	Indigenous autonomy, land occupation and peasant-led agrarian reform, food sovereignty

This is the 'recognition that dispossession maybe a necessary precursor to more positive' (Harvey, 2010a: 250). The increase and expansion of land conflict led to a 'more concerted form of rural social mobilization' (Bebbington, 2007: 807). This new wave of struggles was peasant-based but also peasant-led, articulating action with indigenous communities for 'land, territorial autonomy, and freedom and democracy' (Veltmeyer, 2007: 124).

Neoliberal globalisation enabled the creation of 'sacrificial zones' (Di Risio et al., 2012) where over-accumulated capital from the North is being invested in extractive industries and agribusiness, thus intensifying the subjugation of indigenous and rural workers to the rules of transnational corporations. Extractive industry, energy and agro policies in Latin America are devastating rural livelihoods and indigenous communal property and life on behalf of transnational corporations. As Choudry et al. suggest, WB- and IMF-led structural-adjustment programmes of the past 30 years in the global South are expression of neocolonialism, that is, a 'debt-driven model of colonialism imposed on the South through structural adjustment connected to the "repauperization of the North"' (Choudry et al., 2013: 70). Table 4.1 presents a summary of the elective affinity between the political construction of hopelessness and the emergence of insurgent hope.

Chiapas: a land of hopelessness and dreams

In the previous section I argued that the political construction of hopelessness was a key feature of neoliberalism in the region. In this section I explore the emergence of hope by learning from the Zapatistas' revolutionary experience in Chiapas, an incredible remote and beautiful place, which until 1 January 1994, was the embodiment of neoliberal hopelessness. At the time the Mexican left was in a bad state following the fall of the USSR in 1991, the crisis of *Sandinismo* in 1990, the expansion of the 'anti-communist euphoria'. Although Mexico never experienced a military coup like other countries of South America, the reign of the PRI for 71 years meant the lack of democratic political competition and alternation in power, but also decades of corruption and electoral fraud. In August 1982, the Mexican government declared that it could no longer serve its debt and triggered a crisis that affected most of Latin American countries and facilitated the intervention of the IMF in domestic finances – providing loans and control mechanisms – thus marking the beginning of a new epoch in Latin America's subordination to international financial institutions and the US multinational banks (Richards, 1997: 22–23). In the 1990s, the PRI led a fast and deep structural adjustment in Mexico (as fast as in Argentina), which affected the Chiapas communities directly. The above-mentioned process of privatisation of state-owned assets, liberalisation of trade and deregulation of financial and labour markets was the necessary consequence of the desperate need to repay a debt that has been created as a strategy of neoliberal politics (Lazzarato, 2012) for indebtness from now onwards would frame the political, cultural and social conversations about the future, a future that was now mortgaged. Money and its crisis were now the form of command over Mexican society. The new form of accumulation brought about by neoliberal globalisation (i.e., accumulation by dispossession) led to an intensification of the commodification of land and natural resources, extractivism and displacement, and expulsion and exclusion of rural workers and indigenous peoples as part of an ongoing process of primitive accumulation (Harvey, 2005; Bonefeld, 2008; De Angelis, 2008) that is creating a world that has no room for them.

The impact of the liberalisation of trade, investment and privatisation in Mexico included the privatisation of basic services and privatisation of the forms of farming and communal use of the land conquered with the Mexican Revolution at the beginning of the twentieth century. The neoliberal restructuring, like in other countries, intended to shift from the import-substitution model to an agro-export model to which the *ejidos* (indigenous land) became new territories for the expansion of capital (Hesketh, 2013: 73). The signing of the North American Free Trade Agreement (NAFTA) by Mexico supported by a discourse that regurgitated the benefits of being part of the regional block of power (i.e. member of the first world), gave –following Carlsen (2006) 'unprecedented privileges to transnational corporations, the stage was set for decades of corrupt control and "development" marked by a sharply unequal distribution of wealth and power and loss of national sovereignty' (Carlsen, 2006).

Zapata's Plan of Ayala of 22 November 1911 and the agrarian law of October 1915 had nationalised the land and called 'for peasants to immediately reclaim lands themselves and to defend them by force of arms, without the need for approval by any higher authority' and reinforced indigenous people's rights to the land to cover their needs and the needs of their families, respectively (Khasnabish, 2008: 95). In Zapata's revolution, the land was inalienably for the people who work and live from and in it. The *ejidos* were created after the (first) Zapatista revolution of 1910–1917 to respond to peasant unrest and under President Cardenas, ejidal land increased from 13 per cent of cropland in 1930 to 47 per cent in 1940 (Hesketh, 2013: 73). The new reform of Article 27 of the National Constitution that freed indigenous *ejidos* for trade and investments (after a long process of privatisation of them) reversed the revolutionary change led by Zapata at the beginning of the twentieth century.

NAFTA also forced even more the reorientation of strategic resources like oil and the development of the Maquiladora industry to conform to the US demands made to the Mexican government as a precondition to enter the international agreement (Ceceña, 2001a). NAFTA demanded the abolition of the Mexican Coffee Institute (*Instituto Mexicano de Café*, INMECAFE), which led to the dramatic fall in the price of coffee and obliterated the possibility for Chiapanecos indigenous peasants to sell coffee and corn. Policy was implemented by the indiscriminate use of state violence by Chiapas Governor Patrocinio González (1988–1993) against indigenous people who stood against these policies and were not happy with the Independent Rural and Agricultural Workers Central (*Central Independiente de Obreros Agrícolas y Campesinos*, CIOAC) and the Peasants Independent Regional Association (*Asociación Regional Independiente de Campesinos*, ARIC), encouraging more indigenous people to join the Zapatista movement (Almeyra and Thibaut, 2006).

Poverty is a horrifying fact in Chiapas, a region that possesses the highest mortality rate in the country due to the permanent draining (*desague*) of resources by big business and governmental neglect. Subcomandante Insurgente Marcos describes how, as soon as you enter Chiapas, you realise the misery that neoliberal global capital causes:

> Chiapas loses blood through many veins: through oil and gas ducts, electric lines, railways; through bank accounts, trucks, vans, boats, and planes; through clandestine paths, gaps, and forest trails. This land continues to pay tribute to the imperialist: petroleum, electricity, cattle, money, coffee, banana, honey, corn, cacao, tobacco, sugar, soy, melon, sorghum, mamey, mango, tamarind, avocado, and Chiapaneco blood all flow as a result of the thousand teeth sunk into the throat of the Mexican Southeast. (SIM, 2001: 22–23)

Ceceña and Barreda (1998: 39) endorse this view and point to the strategic role of Chiapas for the global economic restructuring and to the significant capitalist contradictions that there exist in Chiapas: while an abundance of natural resources makes it one of the 'world's paradises' and brings 'unparalleled conditions for the development of life', this makes Chiapas, paradoxically, 'one of the most inhospitable environments for human life' (Ceceña and Barreda, 1998: 56). As SIM explains,

> Chiapas is rich in plant varieties, mammals species, reptiles and amphibians, bird species, freshwater fish, butterflies species, rainfalls. But [continues Marcos] its greatest wealth is the 3.5 million people of Chiapas, two-thirds of whom live and die in rural communities. Half of them don't half potable water, and two-thirds have no sewage service ... Communication in Chiapas is a grotesque joke for a state that produces petroleum, electricity, coffee, wood and cattle for the hungry beast. (SIM cited in Ponce de León, 2001: 24)

Enough is enough! The Zapatistas say NO to the *inevitable* with dignity

Enough is enough! (*¡Ya Basta!*) These words powerfully resonated in the mountains of the south-east of Mexico in January 1994 when quiet indigenous people made themselves heard. The Zapatistas' uprising was both an act of refusal and an act of hope. At the time, the Zapatistas' *¡Ya Basta!* captured a regional feeling of exhaustion and anger that had not yet materialised, but when it did, it transformed Latin America into a laboratory of organising hope. The Zapatistas' global appeal to refuse the reality of neoliberal globalisation came from the poorest and most forgotten people in Mexico and probably the world: the indigenous people of Chiapas.

The nature of their plea and the place from where it was heard and made known have a significant impact on the way we understand autonomy. With *¡Ya Basta!*, there were multiple ruptures and resonances. *¡Ya Basta!* announced the *not yet*, a struggle informed by the principle of hope. 'The No' argues Bloch, 'lies in origin as the still empty, undefined, undecided, as the start of the beginning ... it presupposes exertions, long erupted processes ... The Not is of course emptiness, but at the same time, the drive to break out of it' (Bloch, 1959/1986: 306). The 'No' entailed in the Zapatistas' *¡Ya Basta!* triggered a process of articulation of the multiple dimensions of a new politics of hope in Chiapas, Latin America and the world.

During the 1980s and 1990s, the neoliberal 'facts' had begun to be seriously challenged. The violence of market-led policies (privatisation, breakdown of institutions, regressive income distribution, unemployment, poverty) had created, as Biekart (2005: 2) indicates, a 'time-bomb that only needed to spark off'. *Hope as negation*, courage and imagination burst out against impossibility, leading to two decades of intense mobilisation around the issues that constituted the core of the neoliberal reforms: commodification of land and landlessness, joblessness, poverty and deprivation, dispossession, repression, unemployment, deregulation, lack of democracy. The possibility of reinventing reality lies in understanding the real as process rather than as the closed system portrayed by neoliberal crusaders. New movements contested the closeness of the neoliberal truth. At this stage in the development of autonomy as prefiguration, movements engaged in organizing the rejection of the project of dystopia (Dinerstein and Neary, 2002a) that celebrated the end of social dreams. The 'scream of No', claims Holloway, '[broke] the sheet of ice covering a dark lake of possibility' (Holloway, 2010a: 17). Autonomy became the tool for organising negation. This revolution represents the crisis of neoliberalism. The latter cannot be explained by looking at institutional or economic spheres: it is ultimately a crisis of subjectivity. The movements' negation of the capitalist reality in its neoliberal form contested, as Melucci (1988: 248) put it, the 'dominant codes upon which social relations are founded' or, what Arditi (2007: 91) refers to as the 'realist coding of the possible.' To challenge the neoliberal 'coding', i.e. hopelessness has been an essential dimension of the negative mode of the process of autonomous prefiguration.

To be sure, the Zapatistas' uprising was not a 'reaction' to neoliberal policies but the highpoint of a revolutionary organising that was taking place in Chiapas since the early 1980s. SIM's description of the seven stages in the history of the EZLN (Muñoz Ramírez, 2008: 20) from the early 1980s up until 1994, shows that the EZLN progressed from being a minuscule guerrilla foco into a revolutionary movement of a new type that challenged revolutionary traditions based on class, exploitation and state power. The stages involved the selection of the National Liberation Forces (*Fuerza de Liberación Nacional*, FLN), the creation of the EZLN, the learning process of how to survive in the jungle, contact of EZLN with the insurgent indigenous from local communities, expansion, communities preparing for war and combat preparation before the uprising (Khasnabish, 2008: 71–72).

Zapatismo combined political, religious and ideological influences. First, Zapatismo represents Maya traditions of Tzeltal, Tzotzil, Ch'ol, Mam, Zoque and Tojolabal peoples, particularly with regards to customs of decision-making processes in the *ejidos* (command while obeying). Second, in Chiapas, religion and politics interact actively (Ghiotto and Pascual, 2008). LT Priest Samuel Ruíz from San Cristóbal de las Casas Catholic Church was a key figure in the organisation of the *First Indigenous Congress Fray Bartolomé de las Casas* that took place in Chiapas in 1974. Ruiz connected religion with Maoist principles through his contacts with the guerrilla foco Proletariat Line (*Línea Proletaria*, LP). The role of the church in the uprising was significant. The local catholic church of San Cristóbal de las Casas actively worked for the *concientización* of indigenous people about the reasons for their poverty. The church facilitated self-organisation of the Ecclesiastic Base Communities (*Comunidades Eclesiales de Base*), thus creating a new political and religious culture (Matamoros Ponce, 2005). The third set of currents that converged in Zapatismo are Marxist Guevarist and Maoist ones. In 1980, LP broke the agreement with Father Ruiz, and he moved on to another guerrilla movement of Guevarist ideas, the FLN, which would later become part of the EZLN. An army created in 1991 recruited thousands of militants. The military work led by EZLN was intertwined with deep social work in the communities (Ghiotto and Pascual, 2008). At the Lacandona Jungle, the arrival of students, who were escaping political persecution and civil war, and were survivors of the Tlatelolco massacre of 1968 and exiles of the Guatemala civil war, transformed the jungle into an ideal setting (Henck, 2007: 57) for the development of a revolutionary cell – a place forgotten in the world, which up to the end of the 1980s was state-free (see Colectivo Situaciones, 2005). In the jungle, the six revolutionaries that arrived in Chiapas with the aim to create a guerrilla foco in November 1983 learnt how to survive and interact with the Chiapas indigenous communities. In the process, their 'squared' Marxist ideology to become something else (Esteva, 2005): 'Zapatismo was born out of this inter-cultural dialogue and, little by little, was rooted in hundreds of communities' (Esteva, 2005: 9). Marcos explains:

> We thought it was the same to talk with the proletariat, with a peasant, with a worker, or with a student ... And instead we found ourselves in a new world with regard to which we had no answer ... It is very difficult when you have a theoretical framework that seems to explain all of society and you get to a place and find out that your frame doesn't explain anything ... We really suffered a process of re-education, of remodeling ... It was as if all the elements we had – Marxism, Leninism, socialism, urban culture ... became dismantled. They disarmed us and then armed us again, but this time in a much different form. (Marcos in Le Bot, 1997: 148–151, translated by Walsh, 2012: 15)

The EZLN declared war on the Mexican state on 1 January 1994. The main intention was not to seize the power of the state but, in the best indigenous tradition, to reject it and disclose a new revolutionary grammar and praxis that appealed to the world from the *comunidades autónomas rebeldes* of Chiapas. At the international First Encounter for Humanity and Against Neoliberalism (1996), people from all over the world gathered in Chiapas to reflect collectively on the different forms in which people are subordinated to the logic and the command of money-capital and what would it mean to live with dignity: 'we are united by a world order that destroyed nations and cultures. Today, Money – the great international criminal – has a name that reflects the incapacity of Power to create new things. Today we suffer a new world war, a war against all peoples, against humanity ... It is an international war' (SIM, 1995 in Ponce de León, 2001: 167). The Second Encounter for Humanity and Against Neoliberalism this time held in Spain (De Angelis, 1998: 138) continued discussing the main Zapatistas' demands and the form and content of the neoliberal threat to humanity.

The Zapatistas' demanded *democracy*, *liberty* and *justice*. As Cunninghame and Ballesteros Corona highlight, these three essential demands are preconditions to the fulfilment of the 13 demands that the Zapatistas put forward as a result of a self-organised referendum in August 1995: 'land, work, food, health, housing, education, independence, democracy, justice, freedom, culture, access to information, and peace' (Cunninghame and Ballesteros Corona, 1998: 17). Democracy means a transition to parliamentary democracy free from 'fraud and intimidation' and the encouragement of participation of civil society at various levels. As for liberty, the Zapatistas mean autonomy and self-determination for indigenous peoples in Chiapas within the Mexican territory (right to self-organisation, defence of customs and habits, self-government). Finally, justice means 'synonymous with dignity and respect for indigenous cultures and ways of life', indeed, for 'all differences within Mexico' (Cunninghame and Ballesteros Corona, 1998: 17).

The Zapatistas' 'revolution of dignity' (Holloway and Peláez, 1998) overshadowed traditional Marxists' concerns with class, exploitation and power. Dignity was proposed to be the essential value for the revolutionary movement. This made the dialogue between the Zapatistas and the left difficult for Zapatismo challenged the assumptions of a left in crisis by articulating another revolutionary praxis. Dignity is *not simply an ideal* to guide the struggle of the working class for social reforms or for a future socialist revolution. Dignity is a project with wider political dimensions.

Restating hope

In their First Declaration of La Realidad, the Zapatistas delivered a clear message from Chiapas to the world:

> A new world war is waged, but now against the entire humanity. As in all world wars, what is being sought is a new distribution of the world. By the name of 'globalisation' they call this modern war, which assassinates and forgets. The new distribution of the world consists in concentrating power in power and misery in misery. (SIM, 1996a)

This is a new 'war for the conquest of territory' that excludes the majority of the world, which power calls 'minorities' (immigrants, people of colour, women, youth, indigenous, peasants, workers) (SIM, 1996). In June 1997, from the mountains of the Mexican southeast, SIM (2001) exposed the seven pieces of the neoliberal 'global jigsaw puzzle': the concentration of wealth and the distribution of poverty; the globalisation of exploitation (with migration being the errant nightmare); financial globalisation; the globalisation of corruption and crime; legitimate violence on behalf of an illegitimate power; mega politics; and the seventh piece is the existence of new pockets of resistance. The pieces, he argued, do not fit. He concluded that we need

> a world where many worlds fit, where all worlds fit ... Resistance against neoliberalism does not only exist in the mountains of south-east Mexico. In other parts of Mexico, in Latin America, in the United States and Canada, in Europe, which belongs to the Treaty of Maastricht, in Africa, in Asia, in Oceania, the pockets of resistance multiply. Each one of them has its own history, its differences, its equalities, its demands, its struggles, its accomplishments ... If humanity still has hope of survival, of being better, that hope is in the pockets formed by the excluded ones, the leftovers, the ones who are disposable. (SIM, 2001)

In the Zapatistas' declarations, communiqués and documents, *hope* is portrayed as the opposite of globalisation and as a rejection of conformity and defeat. In the First Declaration, the Zapatistas assert: 'A new lie is sold to us as history. The lie about the defeat of hope, the lie about the defeat of dignity, the lie about the defeat of humanity'. They propose:

> Against the international terror representing neoliberalism, we must raise the international of hope. Hope above borders, languages, colors, cultures, sexes, strategies and thoughts, of all who prefer humanity alive. The international of hope (SIM, 1996a).

This characterisation is replicated in the subsequent Zapatistas' documents and resonates in many manifestos and documents written by other Latin American or other movements of the world.

Autonomy *de facto*: an enlivened utopia

The creation of the JBG in 2003 – a 'territorial response to the Mexican policy of dispossession' (Hesketh, 2013: 79) – originated in the struggle with and against the Mexican government for its lack of compliance of the San Andrés Accords. The five previous EZLN's territories called '*Aguascalientes*' where the Clandestine Indigenous Revolutionary Committee (*Comité Clandestino Indígena Revolucionario*, CCIR) operated, were reorganised into five 'caracoles' (snails) and their JBGs. These forms of self-government resulted from the disappointment with the government's betrayal to the indigenous of Chiapas. The San Andrés Accords signed between the Zapatistas and the Mexican government in 1996 after the ceasefire, with mediation from the Commission for Agreement and Pacification (*Comisión para la Concordia y la Pacificación*, COCOPA), had established that the government was going to undertake the reform of the National Constitution to allow the recognition of the indigenous people's right to autonomy and the guarantee of self-government and collective production. The COCOPA provided protection to the rebels, ensured a peaceful process of negotiation and opened a path for the potential creation of a *plurinacional* state in Mexico (González Casanova, 2001). But, instead of the right to self-determination, President Zedillo gave the Zapatistas a warning: he used assassination *as a tool for policy implementation* against indigenous people of Chiapas, to those who were already dying for lack of health care, food and drinkable water, who suffered the highest mortality rate in Mexico. The massacre of Acteal not only contradicted the government's willingness to negotiate but showed the government's incapacity to deal with indigenous resistance democratically.

During the years that followed the Acteal massacre, the Zapatistas mobilised, demanding the implementation of the San Andrés Accords. The Zapatistas' 37-day March for Indigenous Dignity began on 24 February 2001, passed through 12 Mexican states, gathering people in 77 public acts, and ended in Zócalo, city centre of México, DF (Ceceña, 2001: 10). But the hope brought about by the end of 71 years of rule of the PRI, which gave rise to the election of President Vincente Fox from an opposing party, soon vanished.

When the Constitution reform of 2001 was put into practice by the Mexican government it became apparent that the law accredited the right to self-government to indigenous communities in political and administrative form of *free municipality*. This administrative figure was not new. The problem with it was that rather than recognizing indigenous autonomy, it only recognized indigenous people as subjects of state policy. Thus, the law also specified what kind of indigenous authorities were legally recognised by law and how they should be elected – by free and secret ballot. The legislation transformed indigenous autonomy into a form of local (liberal) democracy (see Burguete Cal y Mayor, 2004).

The Zapatistas rejected this insufficient and misleading 'translation' of indigenous autonomy by the law. Like this argues Marcos, 'the communities [would] not be capable of deciding within their own territories, nor will be able to design their own plans that have to do with ethno development in which communities get to decide' (SIM, 2003 cited by Otero, 2004: 229). Genuinely disillusioned, the Zapatistas took time to reflect on the outcome of their struggle. After two years of using 'silence as a strategy' (Muñoz Ramirez, 2008: 292; Esteva, 2005: 22), the

EZLN began a process of demilitarisation of the movement towards the strengthening of its civil component (i.e., the autonomous communities) to create their own governmental bodies. Since the formation of the JBGs, the EZLN retreated from its political role in the construction of the Zapatista autonomy. As SIM and the Zapatistas (2006: 79) explain, the EZLN was excessively involved in communal decisions and that was regarded as undemocratic. After the demilitarisation, the EZLN has a role that accompanies the democratic processes and safeguards the JBGs.

The JBGs are concrete utopias for the indigenous communities of Chiapas. Each Snail delineates territories of hope for the realisation of a reality of 'deep Mexico', a not yet reality, awaiting to be anticipated, within the reality of 'imaginary Mexico', as Bonfil Batalla (1987) called these two coexistent worlds on Mexican soil.

Predictably, the Zapatistas' 'lived utopia' (Mattiace, 2003: 187) triggered further attempts to appropriate and translate indigenous autonomy into the coding of neoliberal governance. Governmental strategies changed. Between 1996 and 1997, after the San Andrés peace treaty was signed, state violence had increased in Chiapas, coinciding with the exponential growth of support for the Zapatista movement. From 2000 to 2006, under President Fox, there were some retreatments of military bases and camps,, migrations and police controls in Chiapas. But it was the shift in the EZLN's strategy (demilitarisation) which put indigenous autonomy at the centre of the political debates – particularly since 2006 when the Sixth Declaration of the Lacandon Jungle was made public – and the government's strategies shifted from disarming the EZLN to disarming the communitarian power of the Zapatistas autonomous rebel communities. In the Sixth Declaration, the Zapatistas assessed their revolution thus far and discussed what they wanted to do and how they were 'going to do it'; that is, their plan to expand through the 'other campaign' (that anticipated the 2006 presidential campaign) to 'link non partisan anticapitalist national liberation struggles around the country' (Mora, 2007: 64). The 'other campaign' became the tool for both the creation of a space among and for those who struggle 'against neoliberalism and for humanity' like the Zapatistas (Subcomandante Insurgente Marcos and the Zapatistas, 2006: 131), without the Zapatistas' hegemony and without disputes over the support to the Party of the Democratic Revolution (*Partido de la Revolución Democrática*, PRD).

On the one hand, the government of Chiapas moved on to a more flexible approach. Direct military action was replaced by a low-intensity war, with a more subtle police and paramilitary control of the communities, which was justified as the government's war against drug trafficking. Direct repression was replaced with a strategy that aimed to influence public opinion by manipulating information, making alliances with political forces and networking with civil society actors (Hidalgo Domínguez, 2006). Paramilitary organisations became non-governmental organisations (NGOs) and began to promote the formation of cooperatives and facilitating the access to the deeds to indigenous land, thus taking on board a key issue for the Zapatistas communities (i.e., the land) and competing with the 'illegal' land distribution undertaken by the EZLN via its revolutionary agrarian reform (Ghiotto and Pascual, 2008). For example, in order to dispute the Zapatistas' support, the Organisation in Defence of Indigenous and Peasants Rights (*Organización para la Defensa de los Derechos Indígenas y Campesinos*, OPDDIC) and the former Anti-Zapatista Indigenous Revolutionary Movement (*Movimiento Indígena Revolucionario Antizapatista*, MIRA) organised productive collective projects among the Chiapanecos, which are subsidised by political parties (CIEPAC in Pascual et al., 2013). On the other hand, while the low-intensity repression and military surveillance of the Chiapas region remains in place, a series of (counter-insurgent) policies also launched and were implemented between 2006 and 2008.

The 'domestication of dissident claims' by means of the state's 'co-responsibility' with the affected population (Mora, 2007: 67–68) is key to the neoliberal governance. In this case, the policy was oriented to channel citizens' demands; to reorganise geographically the population of Chiapas; and to provide public services to the Chiapas territory.

The creation of the Chiapas Solidarity Institute (*Instituto Chiapas Solidario*, ICS) aimed at organising 'civil society' through the state 'democratic planning' in order to open institutional channels for participation to solve the crisis of democratic representation in Chiapas. The Zapatistas interpret 'democratic planning' as an attempt to institutionalise governance in Chiapas. ICS mediates between the Chiapanecos and the state, and competes directly with the Zapatistas' self-government. The programme 'Sustainable Rural Cities' was launched to fight against 'exclusion via dispersion' of the population who enjoy few or no basic services. The programme promised to relocate and reorganise the population as the means for development in eight new cities to maximise service provision following the WB's recommendations written in its 'New Economic Geography' report. To the Zapatistas, this regional development strategy matches the WB's *Plan Puebla-Panamá* (and the trade agreement called *Proyecto Mesoamérica*, a version of the former) that intends to amalgamate a dense tangle of interests related to oil, gas and petrochemical, biodiversity, mines, construction and transport (railways and motorways), and airports and telecommunications, all of which aspire to clear the legal and political obstacles to the exploitation of resources from southeast Mexico to Panama, some of them involving indigenous lands (Alvarez Béjar, 2001: 127; Cortez Ruiz, 2004). Although the Chiapas government increased the portion of the budget dedicated to implementing development policy that responds to community needs, and there have been efforts to address indigenous poverty in Chiapas, the geographical reorganisation of the population meant to vacate land for commercial, tourist and natural resources exploitation by private investors (CIEPAC, August 2008) (Pascual et al., 2013). While the 'Sustainable Rural Cities' programme benefited the companies that participate in the urban construction, it affected negatively on the Chiapas communities who believe the programme 'alienates the people from their land, thus making the land available to large multinational corporations who focus on "cheap labour", destroying ancient farming practices, imposing community development models and forcing the population into the financial circle of capitalism' (Ilel, 2011). The Zapatistas resisted.

On their twentieth anniversary, the Zapatistas celebrated inwardly rather than making loud political statements (Carlsen, 2014). They celebrated the EZLN's birthday with the many students attending *La Escuelita* (Little School), a wonderful way of connecting and explaining to the world who are the Zapatistas and how they understand the world.

Conclusion

Among the four movements discussed in this book, the Zapatista movement stands out as the ambassador of autonomy and the translator of indigenous experiences for a non-indigenous world of insubordination. Their unprecedented and compelling grammar of revolution is bridging indigenous and non-indigenous worlds of resistance. Both the Zapatistas' depiction of neoliberal globalisation as a 'war against humanity' and their call for the formation of the 'international of hope' reverberate in the region and elsewhere. Surely, neo-Zapatismo connects the local and the global in a way that has led to the formation of a 'new internationalism' (De Angelis, 2000; Khasnabish, 2008; Cunnighame, 2010; Olesen, 2005; Cleaver, 2009b; Gautney, 2010).

The Zapatistas' critique transcends the critique of neoliberal globalisation (capitalism) to offer a critique of political economy, that is a critique of value-money as an impossible form of human society (Dinerstein and Neary, 2002b). This critique of capital, in the hands of the Zapatistas, advocates the plurality of resistance without hierarchies, unified in human dignity. The Zapatistas' uprising was not an ideological upheaval but an act of hope against a multiplicity of oppressions, which changed the course of neoliberal globalisation and the way the non-indigenous world understands indigenous oppression. An 'experience of hope' by 'an army of dreamers' (Marcos in Lorenzano, 1998: 157) that resonated in other movements that reintroduced hope in politics (Dinerstein and Deneulin, 2012) through 'intergalactic' resistances. This was possible because, at the time of the uprising, Latin America was not 'depoliticised', but rather, its resistances were latent and *invisibilised* by neoliberal propaganda and state repression. The left was in crisis and required of a new anticipatory illumination that could transform fear into hope.

Neoliberalism in Latin America could not find the basis for its stabilisation. But the reason for this does not lie, as Sader (2001) suggests, in mistaken policy, institutional weakness, or wrong alliances between economic and political elites, but in the limits imposed by acts of negation and hope. A series of 'enough is enough!' events followed the Zapatistas' uprising. Events, as Rothenberg suggests, bring 'something new into the world that changes the determinants and significance of the very terms by which we had previously comprehended the situation' (Rothenberg, 2010: 156). In essence, the social construction of hopelessness also constituted the key for the re-emergence of *hope* throughout the region and lay the foundations for autonomy to become a mobilising utopia. The protagonists of these new struggles were not the traditional political left or trade unions but movements of the dispossessed. They rejected the sacrificial tone of neoliberal globalisation and began to *organise hope* in various forms. SIM (1992, in Ponce de León, 2001: 32) highlights that

> not everyone who hears the voices of hopelessness and conformity are carried away by hopelessness. There are millions of people who continue without hearing the voices of the powerful and the indifferent. They can't hear; they are deafened by the crying and blood that death and poverty are shouting in their ears. But when there is a moment of rest, they hear another voice.

The Zapatistas stood against the cold-bloodedness and the dreamless character of neoliberal global capitalism. In this 'dreamlessness in regard to the future' as Bloch insinuates 'there is fear, not hope; and instead of an understanding of the future as the greater dimension of the present ... there is only an anti-climax' (Bloch, 1971: 32–33). While autonomy is not a 'single' project in Chiapas and the interpretations of what this means differ for different communities in different contexts (Mattiace, 2003: 187), the Zapatistas' rebel communities successfully articulated in one word what characterises the autonomies practiced in Chiapas: Hope. As Esteva (2005: 25) highlights, 'the Zapatistas have brought prosperity to the communities in the original sense of the term: from latin pro spere, i.e. according to hope. In tzeltal wisdom means "to have strength in your heart to wait"'. To wait in spanish is ESPERAR, and hope is ESPERANZA. According to Lummis (1996: 11 cited in Esteva 1999: 174) 'radical hope is the essence of popular movements' and 'the conviction that something is worthy regardless the result' (Esteva, 2005: 25).The Zapatistas stood with and for dignity and their struggle resonated and reverberated throughout Mexico and the world.

5

Shaping Concrete Utopia: Urban Experiments (Argentina)

Introduction: money, crisis and absences

All of them out! Much has been written about the Argentine financial crisis and the popular insurrection of December 2001, and their legacies. But today the slogan of the popular insurrection of December 2001, i.e. *'¡Que se vayan tod@s!'* (referred to as 'QSVT' now onwards) sounds like a beautiful melody that brings nostalgia. Just before the new default of the external debt in 2014 as a result of the pressure from the so called 'vulture funds' the country's economy was stable and the GDP growing. Back to normal the political debate refocused on institutional politics after a period when society had been at the centre of politics. Like in the old times, with the arrival of a new Peronist government to power, society became divided into pro (Kirchneristas) and against (anti-Kirchneristas). Yet, the negation voiced in the event that reverted hopelessness in Argentina remains lurking, indescribable, still unanswered: 'the desiderium, the only honest attribute of all men, is unexplored' (Bloch, 1959/1986: 5).

In this chapter, I draw on the events of December 2001–2002 as my empirical site for a discussion of the creating mode of the autonomous organising that, in this case, occurred within a particular conjuncture of crisis. This is a dimension of autonomous organising that demarcates new territories of hope and crafts other realities beyond present the parameters of legibility established by the state and the capitalist powers. Argentina's experiments horizontal democracy, dignified work and popular justice that were realised by neighbourhood assemblies, unemployed workers' organisations (Piqueter@s), the movement of factory occupations and the new expressions of the human rights movement – for example, Children for Identity and Justice against

Forgetting and Silence (*Hijos por la Identidad y la Justicia contra el Olvido y el Silencio*, HIJOS) – during the immediate period that followed the crisis have been explored in detail. I offer a transcription of some of the abovementioned experiences into the key of hope. I refer to them as concrete (social) utopias and reflect on the nature of political change in Argentina 2001.

Background: *¡QSVT!*

The popular insurrection in December 2001 in Buenos Aires and other cities of Argentina took place amidst the most phenomenal financial collapse that shocked the world. Governmental measures to avoid default of 132 billion debt repayments and devaluation failed vis-à-vis the interest of financial institutions and international banks to sink the argentine economy, backed up by the IMF, whose decision to deny a new loan to the country triggered the collapse. However, the failure of its poster child to pass the last test put the IMF under scrutiny and criticism. The financial collapse of December 2001 marked a turning point in Argentina's politics and economy. Social mobilisation forced the resignation of national authorities. Argentineans said *enough!* Direct and radical forms of action rejected the representative and institutional politics.

A long-standing process of mobilisation of different subjects of struggle from human right activists to workers, the unemployed, citizens, impoverished middle classes, etc., materialised in a singular event that negated the reality of austerity. The Argentinazo's anti-institutional ethos was moment of disagreement (Rancière, 1999) not just against specific neoliberal policy or corruption, but against *what politics was about*, how things were done. As the embodiment of hopelessness, the powerful social imaginary constructed on the basis of austerity and repression (i.e., stability) collapsed. The re-politicisation of the social field and the collective engagement in political activity became the means for the rejection of institutional, hierarchical, mediated and abstract politics, on behalf of direct democraticparticipation, with the intention of redefining the meaning of the political altogether.

While the financial clearly played a significant role in the production of overall crisis, the latter was deeper than that. In December 2001, money as a mediation was exposed and crisis touched subjectivity: 'the crisis' could no longer be identified as financial, economic, social or political. Insubordination could no longer be identified as labour, social or political. The crisis of capital in its money form allowed for an intense moment of de mediation of the capitalist social relations. This fleeting moment of demediation made apparent the violence of neoliberal stability (Dinerstein, 1999; 2001; 2002b) and opened up a space for the reinvention of the concrete practices, ideas, horizons. December 2001 did both: put a limit to the madness of capital and expressed the incommensurable force of human praxis: 'the December insurrection put forward a radical critique and led to a progressive reconciliation of people with politics *which asserted itself as anti-politics.*' (Dinerstein, 2003b: 9).

Bloch uses the term 'concrete utopia' to describe medical, geographical, architectural, technological, artistic and social utopias he sees the latter as forms of venturing into the 'critical awareness of elaborated anticipating' (Bloch, 1959/1986: 5). Here, I adopted the term to characterise 'the dreams of living together in a better way' (Bloch, 1959/1986: 479). These are praxis-oriented searches into the *not yet,* the seeds of which exist within the present reality in a latent form. I exposed here how an autonomously mobilised society *shapes absences.* Shaping absences is a process of discovering the lack and acting on it collectively, thus anticipating here and now what could be in the future:

> Concrete utopia is therefore concerned to understand the dream of its object exactly, a dream which lies in the historical tendency itself. As a utopia mediated with process, it is concern to deliver the forms and contents, which have already developed in the womb of present society. Utopia in this no longer abstract sense is thus the same as realistic anticipation of what is good; which must have become clear. (Bloch, 1959/1986: 623)

QSVT put hope before politics and negated the reality of the violence of stability. QSVT was 'expressed in the subjunctive – the tense of desire, of longing, craving, searching, hoping' (Dinerstein, 2014b: 374). Clearly, negativity persists in the creative exploration of the alternative. Negativity evolves into 'a yes that is anchored in the no of the *gestus* of the action of dignity as a mode of life against death', as Matamoros Ponce (2009: 201) suggests. The act of negation unlocks and unravels the 'impetus and a sense of being broken off, a brooding quality and an anticipation of Not-Yet-Become' (Bloch, 1959/1986: 11–12) that underpins the realisation of concrete utopia. The articulation of concrete utopia in Argentina 2002 did not go smoothly. My discussion includes dilemmas and conflicts that autonomous organising confronted in the process of anticipating new realities particularly vis-à-vis the capitalist powers, mainly the state but also with and against other forms of resistance.

Reinventing the agora

While political scientists, the media and politicians framed the popular insurrection of December 2001 as 'a crisis of democracy', those deliberating in the neighbours' assemblies (*Asambleas Vecinales o de Vecinos,* AVs) experienced it as the return of democracy. This is not paradoxical for QSVT rendered visible the massive questioning of representational democracy (crisis) and facilitated 'the time of democratisation' (Jelin, 1986). The hatred towards the political class was naturally accompanied by horizontalism (Sitrin, 2006). Democracy stood against democracy (Rancière, 2011b). The reinvention of democracy 'beyond the liberal cannon' (Santos and Avritzer, 2007) was regarded as an essential condition for the prefiguration of a democratic world.

The AVs emerged out of the pot-banging protests (*cacerolazos*) that expressed peoples' anger during and after the demise of Fernando de la Rua's government, and they expanded during 2002 and 2003. They brought a history of autonomous grass-roots resistance to the present. Pablo Solana, an activist of the MTD Lanús (Solana, 2011: 47) points to the continuities and reconfigurations of 2001. The *dinámica asamblearia* (assembly dynamic) adopted by the QSVT movements was not new, but the political conjuncture of December 2001 actualised mass popular practices and principles of revolutionary traditions that had been abandoned after the failure of the various revolutionary projects of the 1970s, and they were reintroduced by the movement of the unemployed in the neighbourhoods of Greater Buenos Aires.

The AVs shaped – temporality and contingently – the collective dream of democratic praxis that self-interrogates and questions, as Castoriadis suggests, the laws that govern society. This self-interrogation did not assert itself as a debate about form and substance of democracy, like in the 1980s during the transition to democracy, but enquired about the possibility of realising unrealised forms of democracy. The AVs contested abstract democracy. What do I mean by 'abstract democracy'? Žižek highlights that modernity makes the abstraction of the citizen the epitome of equality when, in fact, the abstraction is a decisive act of violence: 'there is in the very notion of democracy no place for the fullness of concrete human content, for the genuineness of community links: democracy is a formal link of abstract individuals' (Žižek, 2000 163). The *vecino* (neighbour) replaced the citizen and named a concrete identity of the democratic citizen that rejects an identity given by others (Arditi, 2011: 297). The 'citizens prefer to be called "*vecinos*" for they refused to use – sometimes to the point of exasperation – the old forms of naming political actors and relations' (Feijóo and Oroño, 2002: 30).

The AVs developed quickly into forums for collective practice of democracy and social justice *beyond* the state. *Vecinos* described being in the streets with others, in the hot evenings of January 2002, chatting and discussing, organising and contributing with their knowledge, it was about to having something to give: 'it was really touching to see people at midnight sitting on the sidewalk, in the streets, the squares, conversing. That tells us about something new, good, something fantastic' (Asambleísta Villa Pueyrredón, Meeting at the Faculty of Philosophy, University of Buenos Aires (FFL, UBA, 24.5.02, Buenos Aires). Their experience resonates with Lummis' description of radical democracy, which 'envisions the people gathered in the public space, with neither the great paternal Leviathan nor the great maternal society standing over them, but only the empty sky – the people making the power of the Leviathan their own again, free to speak, to choose, to act' (cited by Esteva, 1999: 155). The collective experience in the AVs was enjoyable and exciting but not idealistic or romantic. It dealt with fear and crisis-ridden uncertainty.

In the *vecinos'* democratic utopia, delegation was reduced to a minimum and issues proposed were discussed openly and lengthily. Within this permanent deliberative state the *asambleas* challenged the hierarchical and corporatist political rationality. The new, engagement with autonomous politics was facilitated by the dejection with representational politics: 'it was the fact of not feeling represented by anyone and of wanting to change the customs' ... we have moved away from the place of mere passive spectators of an alien reality, this is the first step for any kind of new political project (Hauser, 2003a). *Vecinos* saw the *asambleas* as contributing to a process of deconstruction of the given reality by creating aternative practices. For this objective, *horizontality* (Sitrin, 2006) was seen as a marvellous tool: the *asambleas* defined where they want to go but not in a programmatic manner (Hauser, 2003a).

The personal abilities and experience of the *vecinos* were put at the service of the everyday life of the commons. The AVs became *nodes* of solidarity action. 'The asamblea is a body that thinks by doing' (Mattini, 2002: 54). The results of a poll among *vecinos* participating in the Centenario Park weekly inter-neighbourhood assembly (*asamblea inter-barrial*, henceforth *interbarrial*) showed that the issues taken on board by the AVs (as demonstrated in the formation of ad hoc working groups around those issues) were inextricably connected with the material reality of economic and political oppression and exclusion.

Venturing into the democratic utopia was challenging. First, the organisational dynamics *within* the *asamblea* in particular the balance between consensus and dissensus was not easy to achieve. In times of frantic politics, understanding, patience, listening and respect became the 'musts' of the AVs: 'Those who are politically "anxious" do not understand that the pace of the asamblea, its rhythm, is different from theirs' (*Asambleísta*, Plaza Irlanda, FFL, UBA, 24.5.02). The idea was to practice dissent: 'the only predictable result is the emergence of a subject with thousand eyes and two hundred ways of thinking: that is the asamblea' (*Asambleísta*, Caballito, FFL, UBA, 24.5.02). Coordination among *asambleas* was achieved by several instances of horizontal interaction. In the city of Buenos Aires, the *vecinos* created an inter-zone assembly that gathered different *asambleas* of the same zone of the city and the *interbarrial* that met on Sundays in Centenario Park to coordinate action among *asambleas*.

Connected to the first, the second challenge was the relation between the AVs and political activists from traditional left parties. Enthused by the abstract utopia of a future revolution, wherein the AVs were seen in some cases as the tools for the maturation of the consciousness of the masses, left political militants became a problem for the *asambleas*.[1] While the left militants' analysis of the socio-economic and political conjuncture were appreciated by the *vecinos*, the latter scorned the former's intention to appropriate the spaces created by the AVs and subsume the AVs into the logic of the various revolutionary parties for their political goals. For example, it was argued at the time that the 'Argentinazo' had opened the possibility for a revolutionary way out of the crisis. The struggle over power was seen as 'objectively set' and 'the bridge between the current workers' consciousness and their class consciousness could be developed as a consequence of the crisis of power ... the necessary time required for the maturity of the masses presupposed also a maturation of the international crisis and the revolutionary development of Latin America' (Altamira, 2002: 322). The role of the party was presented as crucial to move on to a revolutionary situation. Militants encouraged debates and promoted slogans, which did not reflect the spirit or the aims of the AVs. The *vecinos* experienced this attitude as sectarian, elitis, factionalist and manipulative and therefore as a deterrent for the emergence of alternative political practices.

A fist fight between militants from different parties of the left over the organisation of the celebration of 1 May, during the Sunday *interbarrial* triggered the decision to shift from one vote per person to 'one assembly, one vote' and to give mandate to one representative per assembly to the *interbarrial*, in order to prevent political militants from appropriating the *interbarrial* assembly by faking their participation in a particular assembly and winning the vote. Decisions relayed back to the neighbourhood and returned the following Sunday to the interbarrial. *Asamblea Liniers* called 'all political and social organisations to give up their sectarian practices in order to become part of the *asambleario* process without producing ruptures which only favour the government and our enemies' (Declaration of the Liniers Popular Assembly, 27.4.02, pamphlet).

The third challenge was the relation of the *asambleas* with the city's government. The Centres of Management and Participation (*Centros de Gestión y Participación*, CGPs) of the city of Buenos Aires are micro bodies that decentralise some governmental functions to a lower level of management and supposedly estimulates interaction between local policy makers and the city inhabitants. The efforts of the CGPs to integrate (and deactivate) the AVs fostered intense debates among *asambleistas*. Should the *asambleas* be institutionally incorporated into the CGPs? Was it possible to resist co-optation? The response to the CGPs attempts at coopting the vecinos varied. In general, the *asambleas* rejected political manipulation but some did engaged with the governmental proposal, depending on the social constitution of the *asamblea*, the personal experience of the participants with the government of the city, etc. A great example of the open opposition to the CGPs is provided by the *asamblea* Lacroze y Zapiola. In a written declaration approved on 27 March 2002, the *asamblea* revealed the difficult relationship between *vecinos* and the CGPs in the neighbourhood of Colegiales. The *vecinos* established some guiding principles as to how to relate to the CGP: the declaration made apparent that the resolutions approved by the *asambleas* were not taken into account by the government of the city of Buenos Aires. Instead, the CGP had become a tool to co-opt *vecinos* into the Participatory Budget (*Presupuesto Participativo*, PP).

As Rodgers (2010) highlights, in Buenos Aires democratization via PPP was only contingent. The *vecinos* considered the CGPs as illegitimate, unconstitutional and illegal body; and the authority of the CGPs for being a double-standard bodies (i.e., they argued that the participation of the neighbours was crucial for the governance of the city while the CGPs used coercive traditional forms of political power to control the vecinos). They demanded that the CGPs, as the administrative and political bodies of the commune of Buenos Aires, should subordinate themselves to the needs and proposals of the AVs. The Declaration of the Asamblea Colegiales ended with the motto: 'All of them out! Democracy must remain! Justice must come!' (*'Que se vayan tod@s!, Que se quede la democracia! Que venga la Justicia!*).

The call for April 2003 general elections by the Duhalde administration presented a dilemma for the neighbourhood *asambleas*. To vote or not to vote. Between January 2002 and March 2003 there was intense debate with regard to this matter. By March, the *asambleas* unanimously refused to participate in the elections and planned to boycott them by means of civil disobedience, demonstrations, pamphlets, graffiti, pot banging, organising a large popular assembly and ballot papers with 'QSVT' written on them, used as spoiled ballots (Hauser, 2003b). See below a draft of an anonymous pamphlet prepared to repudiate elections:

> *Quieren Sitiarnos, Volvernos Temerosos/ They Want to Siege us, to Frighten Us*
> *Que Silenciosamente Votemos Tiranos /That We Silently Vote for Tyrants*
> *Quieren Saciar Voracidades Tremendas/ They Want to Satisfied their tremendous voracities*
> *Que Siniestramente Vendamos Todo/That We Sell Everything, Disturbingly*
> *Quieren, Sátrapas Vomitivos, Tramoyas/They Want –Satraps, Disgusting People, Delinquents*
> *Quemar Sonrisas, Voluntades, Talentos/Burn Smiles, Wills, Talents*
> *Quienes Sufrimos Variadas Tristezas/Those of us who Suffered Many Sorrows*
> *Queremos Sonreir, Verdaderamente, Todos/We Want to Smile, Truly, All of Us*
> *Quienes Salimos, Valientes, Tenaces/Those of us Who Came Out, Courageously/with Tenacity*
> *Queremos Sacarlos, Vapuleralos, Tirarlos/We Want to Take them Out/Trash Them/Throw them Out*
> *Quienes Siempre Vivimos Trinando/Those of us who Live Chirping*
> *Queremos Silbar, Vibrar, Tararear/We Want to Whistle, Vibrate, Hum*
> *QUE SE VAYAN TOD@S/ALL OF THEM OUT*
> *QUE SE VAYAN TOD@S/ALL OF THEM OUT*

The *vecinos* who opposed elections argue that:

> Elections have the purpose of achieving a sort of 'All of them "in"!' We don't have a choice, except different variations of the same regime ...

> Once again, democracy invites us to vote in elections which while it is presented as the great solution for the poor it will repeat the usual politics of misery and hunger ... we need to unite to vote together for QSVT!

> We reject not only what is being imposed upon us but we want to develop new forms of organisation that discuss how to deepen our action towards the realisation of QSVT in order to develop another

kind of society ... We are organising an active rejection of the elections because we want to develop a wider and direct form of democracy ... we reject this trap. (From pamphlets and several *asambleas*
websites, cited by Hauser, 2003b)

These quotations capture the atmosphere of disappointment with representational politics in 2003. However, the winner in the second round
of the presidential election in May was not the spoiled ballot by radical
citizens but Duhalde's candidate, the Peronist governor of Santa Cruz,
Néstor Kirchner.

The disillusion with representational politics was not reflected
in spoiled ballots. The official figures showed that 80 per cent of the
electorate voted in the election, primarily to prevent former president
Menem from returning to power. The tricky logic of the system of electoral representation imposed the false choice of Menem or Duhalde
to the electorate. More than 60 per cent of the voters chose a political
option that did not entail radical changes. This is explained to some
extent by the fact that the spoiled ballot would have given advantage
to the minority (in this case Menem), as the only votes which count
are those for a stated candidate. Between Menem's continuation with
neoliberal policies and Néstor Kirchner's populist reformism, the latter
was the less harmful option.[2] The vote on 27 April was essentially against
Menem's neoliberalism. The election of President Kirchner brought
Menemist Peronism to an end and a renewed centre-left Peronism to
power. Just as clearly, this did not mean the realisation of QSVT.

The appointment of President Kirchner changed the social mood as
institutional politics and the state recovered credibility. Populist senti-
ments were re-energised as some of the new policies took on board of
the demands put forward by QSVT and the movements that followed
it. Kirchner distanced himself from Duhalde by locating the search for
urgent solution to social needs as a priority in the political agenda,
which consequently lowered the demand from IMF and the international financial community to a place.

The asambleas' democratisation of democracy (Santos and Avritzer,
2007) still resonates in the streets of Buenos Aires. The asambleista
movement put forward a critique of representative 'abstract' democracy and was a learning experience of non-representational forms of
politics and social intervention. After 2003, the AVs decreased in their
capacity to mobilise but continue to be committed to communal work.
They embraced the solidarity economy (Hauser, 2003c), and began
to be involved in delivering of 'social policy from below' (Dinerstein

et al. 2010), organizing communitarian solutions related to social needs, in particular related to the acceleration of the process of pauperization of the inhabitants of Buenos Aires (see Ozarow, 2014): popular dining rooms, art workshops, popular education for the illiterate, charity, collaboration with workers in recovered factories, implementation of survival strategies and micro endeavours) (Hauser, 2003c). There are new forms of autonomous learning such as the *bachilleratos populares* (popular secondary schools) which function as secondary schools for adults financially supported by the state and autonomously run by the asambleas (Solana, 2011: 49).

Reconstructive justice: the escrache

In 1995, the children and young relatives of those made 'disappeared' by the dictatorship from 1976 to 1982 created a new movement. They named it Children for Identity and Justice, against Forgetting and Silence (*Hijos por la Identidad y la Justicia contra el Olvido y el Silencio*, HIJOS). Most of the perpetrators of those disappearances have never been brought to justice. In 1995, now in their mid-twenties, they decided to act collectively on the institutional violence and injustice perpetuated against them, their families and Argentine society.[3]

Although they are unique, HIJOS followed the path paved by the Mothers of the Plaza de Mayo (*Madres de Plaza de Mayo*, from now onwards Madres). In 1977, Madres fought for human rights, together with other human rights movements, in the shadows of the dictatorship. Madres was formed originally by 14 women who had met in the corridors of police stations, hospitals, ministries, consulates, embassies, churches, official and military dependencies, political parties and morgues in search of their 'disappeared children', who decided to hold a demonstration in the Plaza de Mayo on a Thursday. Once they were there, they were forced to walk and stay mobile, for the regime prohibited the gathering of more than three people in the streets. So they began to circulate around the main monument of the Plaza de Mayo. Later on, they brought banners with photographs and names of their children and put white scarves on their heads. They were brave women. Some of them were made disappeared as well. But they explained that 'to dream alone is only a dream, but to dream with others is revolutionary' (Mothers of Plaza de Mayo, in Guzmán Bouvard, 1994: 189). The gendered meaning of [their] activism (Molyneux, 2001: 179) led them to be labelled 'mad old women' by the dictators and 'mothers of terrorists' by the democrats, but they demanded and still demand *'aparición con vida'* ('bring back alive') their children. *Abuelas de Plaza de Mayo* (Grandmothers) was formed soon after under the motto 'Identity, Family and Freedom', and they actively searched for their grandchildren who were kidnapped from the womb of mothers in captivity. Both movements travelled and denounced. With legal and medical help, they organised their own justice system to search for their children, this including DNA searches.

What triggered HIJOS's search for another form of justice was not just the assassination or disappearance of their parents and relatives, but the legalisation of the crimes against humanity. In the 1980s, the crimes were both condemned and condoned. The Alfonsín administration brought the military to trial, transforming Argentina into the only Latin American country that had her 'Nuremberg' after abolishing the self-amnesty law no. 22.924, sanctioned by the military regime in March 1983, and passed another law no. 23.040 on 22 December 1983. The latter empowered the national prosecutor to bring the military to trial. The government chartered the National Commission for the Disappearance of People (*Comisión Nacional sobre la Desaparición de Personas,* CONADEP) to investigate the fate of the thousands of 'disappeared' people. During the first four years of democratic rule, the victims of abduction and torture, their relatives and Argentine society as a whole went through a painful process of awareness and sharing of the experience of terror. The CONADEP (1986) was a shocking summary comprises 50,000 pages of documentation, which condensed the most horrific stories of abduction, torture, rape and executions, which provide the required information for the trials. But two new bills, the Full Stop (*Punto Final*) and Due Obedience (*Obediencia debida*),[4] brought shadows to the process of justice in as much as they limited the punishment of *only* the military *juntas* and not their collaborators and constrained the trials to a certain period of time. This was a disappointing turning point for the euphoria created by the transition to democracy: with President Alfonsín, democracy was considered 'consolidated' and the chapter was closed: 'the house', he said, 'is in order'.

But during the 1990s, President Menem not only endorsed the injustice perpetuated by these two bills, but issued a presidential pardon to the heads of the military *juntas* the only ones that had been condemned under Alfonsín. In order to solve the military problem that had tormented the Alfonsín's cabinet, the resolution of which had been criticised for closing the process down, President Menem swept the dirt under the carpet by using the political pardon or *indulto*, which allows the president to free political prisoners in extreme or exceptional circumstances. Thus, president Menem freed those members of the military *juntas* who had been jailed after the public trial of April 1985. For instance, General Videla, head of the first of four military *juntas* who ran Argentina from 1976 to 1982, was found 'guilty of 66 counts of homicide, 306 counts of false arrest aggravated by threats and violence, 93 counts of torture, 4 counts of torture followed by death and 26 counts of robbery' (Guzmán Bouvard, 1994 160), together with 11 other members of the *juntas*, walked free.

HIJOS did not expect the state to fulfill their dreams of justice. Their concrete utopia was about another form of justice, a 'reparatory' social justice that could free them from their pain: 'We must recover the joy of doing and thinking collectively and the capacity to celebrate life, which has been stolen from us. We need to exorcise our sadness at the rhythm of the drums and the warmness of a mate's hug. That's is the only lifejacket that can save us from the shipwreck' (HIJOS, *HIJOS*, no 12, 2002: 1).

HIJOS's justice was named *escrache*. In the slang of Buenos Aires *escrachar* means to put someone under the public scrutiny of others, to reveal in public, to make apparent the persons who want to hide their actions.[5] For HIJOS, this was not a form of protest among many but 'a practical procedure for the production of justice' (HIJOS in Colectivo Situaciones, 2002b: 40). HIJOS's *escraches* were acts of public condemnation at the doorsteps of the repressor's home (or the accomplice of the military regime who walked free as a result of the application of the 'democratic law'). They enact a different type of justice that is communitarian, territorial, direct, autonomous, a dignifying justice. HIJOS confronted the repressors, one by one, at the doors of their own homes. The *escrache* entails an appropriation of public space for the purpose of disclosing the truth and exercising public justice. Consensus with the community is essential for organising the escrache and this means a direct involvement of the neighbours in the several stages of the process leading to the *escrache*. Horizontality and consensus are key in the work with the community where perpetrators lived. Work with the community includes the production of banners and pamphlets, and holding *asambleas* and talks with students, unions, neighbours, at social centres and with other local organisations.

In order to identify the domicile of the repressor and his/her relatives, HIJOS investigated the databases constructed by the CONADEP, as well as consulted with human rights movements and political journalists. Once the person is identified, red tint is used to paint the name of repressors on the doorstep of their houses, and outline of a body as a weapon to indicate the social death of the person in question. The *escrache* is noisy, local and networked, and moves the protest to the neighbourhood where the subject to popular justice lives. The rationale behind this is to denounce and expose the offenders in front of their own communities, in order to achieve the 'civil death' of the person. Rather than being silent, the *escrache* is preceded by a performance with screams, dancing and other artistic expressions reminiscent of a carnival or circus, or even football championships celebrations (HIJOS interviewed in Colectivo Situaciones, 2002b: 3). HIJOS networks with other movements and organisations (e.g., art groups, student unions, trade unions, artists, human rights activists, cultural centres) of every neighbourhood to articulate action and increase participation and support in the *escraches*.

HIJOS' *escrache* is a significant form of organising hope. It is not directed to demand justice to the 'state', but it is concrete utopia. The *escrache* does not ask for anything, does not expect anything, (although it has been used by other movements as a form of calling attention to the media or put pressure on the state). It is an act of civil condemnation that disregards the injustice of the judiciary system, and empowers civil society to exercise the right to condemn the guilty (HIJOS, in Colectivo Situaciones, 2002b: 53). As Seidel suggests with HIJOS 'in Argentina, the impossible has turned into a lived reality' (Seidel, 2011: 311). The *escrache* is not an act of revenge, as it has been accused of (Seidel, 2011), but a utopian act of hope and social reparation:

> The escrache is on the side of justice ... true justice will not happen spontaneously. When crime is organised by and within the state [as in state terrorism], it is society which ought to identify the criminals, judge them, prosecute them and condemn them. We are for a popular justice which does not forget and does not forgive state terrorism ... despite that some people believe that one day they will wake up and society will be reconciled with its hangmen. (HIJOS, *escrache* against Frimon Weber, in Colectivo Situaciones, 2002b: 21–23)

The Kirchner administration (2003) showed sympathy for human rights organisations including HIJOS, for they mobilise in pursuit of a solution to the unresolved problem of physical disappearance and the uncertainty with regards to the trials to the perpetrators of crimes against humanity from 1976 to 1982. In July 2003 the magistrate Baltasar Garzón demanded Argentina to extradite 45 Argentine officers for their trial (Campbell and Goñi, *The Guardian* 18.8.03, 9). President Kirchner responded positively to the judge's demand. Furthermore, founding his decision on a UN international treaty from 1995, which confirms the inexhaustible durability of such crimes, he reversed in the Full Stop and Due Obedience Bills passed during

Alfonsin's period in office, and the pardons issued by President Menem, the imprisonment of criminals began with the incarceration of 45 military involved by magistrate Canícoba Corral. The long-expected cleansing of the Supreme Court, particularly the trial of its President Julio Nazareno, who was accused of several acts of corruption during the Menem administration also became true.

Imagining dignified work

Between 20 and 26 June 1996, more than 5,000 people – many of them public sector and unemployed workers – besieged the towns of Cutral Có and Plaza Huincul (small towns of the Neuquén province, Patagonia) to make themselves visible to the authorities. The privatisation of Argentine state-owned oil company *Yacimientos Petrolíferos Fiscales* (YPF), which was the main resource of economic development and a historical provider of energy, oil, gas and electricity in Neuquén, led to the closure of the plants, leaving thousands jobless. In absence of universal welfare provision, the dismantling of the quasi-welfare state developed around the company, caused the community to collapse. During 1997, social protest in Neuquén expanded in new forms. In May 1997, this time in the northwest province of Jujuy, a *roadblock* of motorway 34 was decided by the Multisectorial of the small town Libertador General San Martín, as the economic crisis worsened and discontent stemmed from the lack of response to people's demands from either Ledesma (main sugar company) or the government.

The young Piqueter@s –as they were called by a journalist were brutally repressed at the roadblocks they organized to protest, but the roadblocks expanded and continued expanding right up until December 2001. When they were asked the reasons for resisting and risking their lives the unemployed answered that recovering dignity and a meaning for their lives was the most important thing: 'We, young people, joined the struggle because there is no possibility of employment unless one migrates somewhere else. Our life does not make sense at all. I fought against repression; I helped to repel the gas bombs' (Young, unemployed, male participant at the roadblock, 22 August 1997). 'I was not scared ... It wasn't fear but nuisance; hatred ... the Mayor supported the military police. The newspapers published that' (Young, unemployed, male participant at the roadblock, 22 August 1997).

The Piqueter@s' utopia of dignified work began to take shape at the motorways behind the smoke of burning tires, in the battlegrounds. The roadblocks built up on previous social and local trade union protests surrounding oil policy in the north and south of the country during the 1980s (Benclowicz, 2011). As unemployment became mass unemployment the roadblocks became the new sites for resistance and hope. Progressively, new organising processes began to demarcate new territories for the development of communal projects and collective activities that addressed the needs of their families, and practiced democratic decision-making processes in the neighbourhoods where the power of Peronist *'punteros'*, that is, front-line workers who make political use of social programmes and maintain the clientelistic system among the poor, making them dependent on political party favours in order to have policy access (Auyero, 2000).

The neoliberal transformation of the state and labour deconstructed the imaginary integration of the proletariat into the state-form that had been built in the 1940s and 1950s in the context of import-substitution strategies of industrialisation and the consolidation of a national working class. While the integration of the proletariat into the state clearly hides the reality of domination and exploitation (Colombo, 1993: 182) it *does* make working-class struggles a part of the economic development, thus 'empowering' workers and their trade unions in specific forms. The Peronist 'dignified worker' (see Sitrin, 2012) associated dignity with a strong, productivist work ethic and a state-sponsored labour movement conceived as the vertebral spine of the political project. To be sure, attempts at deconstructing the strong connection between the state and workers' identity and organisation in Argentina began with the coup d'état against President Perón by General Aramburu in 1955, and marked the history of Argentine politics. The last dictatorship (1976) gave the final stroke, whereby the target was to 'disappear' mainly Peronist political activists union leaders and workers. Yet, the celebration and legalisation of such obliteration was done under the democratically elected neoliberal Peronist populist government of President Menem. While holding a close relation with union bureaucracy, president Menem's attack on labour transformed and restructured the social organisation of work, rescinded labour and social rights, and repressed the grass-roots labour movement: 'We are [doing] bad but going well' (*'Estamos mal pero vamos bien!'*), the president's message to the working people, alluded to the importance of *their sacrifice* for the attainment of economic growth, stability and competitiveness of the country.

Unemployed workers organisations (*Organizaciones de Trabajador@s Desocupad@s*, UWOs) and the Piqueteros' identity of resistance was formed at the roadblocks against the violence of stability, where the unemployed attained visibility and UWOs put forward a variety of demands to the state that included job creation, investment in the local areas now devastated by privatisation, welfare provision and employment programmes. The roadblock became the site for the struggle for resources that were to be used in the neighbourhood to attend both everyday requirements of the common and long-term issues related to housing, education and environmental protection (Dinerstein, 2010: 360). Long is the list of communal activities and cooperative projects within the framework of the social and solidarity economy, devised and developed by the UWOs, depending on the area where they worked: housing, nurseries, food banks, community wardrobes, community farms, housing and water cooperatives, sport activities, training and education, alphabetisation, promotion of health and prevention, cleansing of brooks and small rivers, recycling, refurbishing public buildings and houses, maintaining and repairing hospital emergency rooms and schools.

The sources of funding of these projects have been a controversial matter among UWOs when it comes to their views on autonomy. Following the trajectory of grass-roots resistance, the UWOs fought for the re-appropriation of state-focused social programmes for collective purposes (Svampa and Pereyra, 2003) by benefiting from specific features of the policy such as the lack of universality, the low supply of benefits, the absence of clear criteria for beneficiary selection (Garay, 2007: 306) and mainly the possibility that beneficiaries of social programmes could work in a community project as a form of workfare. They demanded the management of these programmes. So the state allowed for the participation of the UWOs in the administration and distribution of employment programmes, which otherwise would have been assigned to individual beneficiaries by local authorities (Dinerstein, 2010). This appropriation of resources and its use in their own cooperative projects (related to the needs of the commons) made their demand of employment programs much more complex than just a demand to be included 'into the system' (i.e., to get a job). To be sure, the request for job creation was top in the list of demands produced by all UWOs. But the UWOs were not just for 'inclusion'. Autonomous organising challenged the sociological premise that the sphere of production is the home for the attainment of a shared experience, collective purpose and a sense of identity achieved among workers (Cole, 2007: 1134). These accounts make the work experience absolutely dependent on paid work. They reify and naturalise the work ethic in abstraction of the exploitative nature of capitalism. The UWOs questioned the assumption that located them 'outside' in practice. This does not mean that *all* UWOS rejected the inclusion into the labour market in favour of anti/non-capitalist work. As argued elsewhere (Dinerstein, 2014b), the UWOs' concrete utopia of dignified work asserted itself in a plurality of meanings, and what is usually called 'movement' is, in fact, a heterogeneous and fragmented number of relatively small UWOs that emerged at different points between 1996 and 2000 (and continue emerging out of splits within current organisations or as new ones). This plurality of UWOs held different ideological affiliations and political alliances that comprise different projects that range from counter-power to socialism to social movement unionism alone, with trade unions and parties of the left.

The General Mosconi Unemployed Workers Union (*Union de Trabajadores Desocupados de General Mosconi*, UTD) was created by highly skilled, former YPF workers in the province of Salta. The UTD recreated the culture of work and work ethics in the small town by means of a range of community and cooperatives that tackle communal needs as well as socio-economic and environmental long-term problems. They regard dignified work as cooperative, genuine and stable. The Federation for Land, Housing and Habitat (*Federación Tierra, Vivienda y Hábitat de La Matanza*, FTV), a member of the executive committee of the Argentine Workers Central (*Central de Trabajadores Argentinos*, CTA) and pioneer in the organisation of workers' housing cooperatives in La Matanza, Greater Buenos Aires, defended for decent and genuine work for all (in the form of job creation, welfare provision and a fairer income distribution). On the other extreme, closely related to the political left and left-wing parties, the National Piquetero Block (*Bloque Piquetero Nacional*, BPN),[6] defined dignified work as anti-capitalist: dignified work would only be possible with the arrival of a new (socialist) mode of production achieved by taking the power of the state. A fourth meaning of 'dignified work' came from the CTDAV, which proposed that human realisation cannot be attained by means of improving the management of capitalism and the distribution of wealth.

The CTDAV has attracted the attention of scholars and activists for their utopian engagement with work. These UWOs such as MTD Solano, for example, defined dignified work as non-capitalist, while simultaneously rejecting traditional revolutionary strategies of taking control of state power. Social reform or future revolution would not lead to dignified work. Dignified work is the result of a praxis at the grass roots, that is projected into the future and therefore is able to anticipate an alternative reality – the reality of dignity (MTD Solano and Colectivo Situaciones, 2002).

The utopia of dignified work must not be confused with the ILO's concept of and campaign for decent work[7] (see also UN-NGLS, 2010; see Munck, 2013). While decent work introduces elements of solidarity and changes in the type and scope of growth, it neither challenges the market economy (Coraggio, 2008) nor 'the concept of economic growth *per se*' (Santos and Rodríguez Garavito, 2006: xxxix-xl).

Dignified work responds to a non-capitalist ethic that cannot be achieved through the improvement of a system of exploitation (MTD, 2002). Despite the CTDAV was barely significant numerically and branches only existed in a few of Greater Buenos Aires' neighbourhoods, their courage to dare to dream collectively of an anti-capitalist world paid too high a price: on the 26 of June 2002 Maximiliano Kosteki and Darío Santillán were killed by the police at the CTDAV's roadblock to Avellaneda bridgem, while hundreds were injured. The media and movements characterised the event as a manhunt. The masacre produced political tensions among UWOs. The FTV leader D'Elia stood against autonomous groupings when, the day after the massacre of June 2002, he subscribed to the widespread opinion that the Piqueteros of the CTDAV had provoked the reaction of the police and had 'crossed the threshold' by organising their own security at the roadblock with covered faces and the use of sticks for self-defence. The FTV leader told me the morning after the repression (on the 27 June 2002), 'we were aware of the government's repressive plans, I have been told about the government decision to repress the roadblock ... this is why we did not participate. The CTDAV is responsible for the lives of their members'.

The massacre also the call for national elections by the Duhalde administration and intensified the debate on what form of class action was appropriate to pursue the spirit of the popular insurrection within and among the UWOs. Divisions among UWOs intensified, parting the water between those who wanted power and those who advocated the construction of a counter-power (Dinerstein, 2003a). While the FTV campaigned and participated in the national elections, the CTDAV took a cautious attitude. But their project of counter-power began to weaken with the political recomposition of the state 'led by President Kirchner, whose progressive policies towards the attainment of decent work via the support or creation of new cooperatives, and the financial support to the UWOs' projects came with co-optation and de radicalisation. In September 2003, the MTD Solano and the MTD Kosteki from Guernica (a county of the province of Buenos Aires), followed by the MTD Allen and MTD Cipolletti, Rio Negro, left the network. Their decision was based on their discontent with the development of factions or blocks within the network, which was reproducing the logic of bureaucratic organisations and unequal power relations, and weakening the *asamblea* as the site of decision making and construction of new social values. Furthermore, in 2006, the MTD Allen and Cipolletti renamed their organisations, as Discovering Social Movement (*Movimiento Social Descubrir*) and Dignity Social Movement (*Movimiento Social Dignidad*) respectively. They were afraid of fading away as a result of Kirchner's policy of co-optation and financial help to the Piqueteros and decided to forge 'new radicalities'. They no longer regard themselves as 'the unemployed' and focus on the 'resistance to the Kirchnerista's wave that is coming to get us!'[8] Other UWOs also renamed their organisations as networks of a variety of movements: the MTD Teresa Rodríguez changed to Teresa Rodríguez Movement. The emergence of the Popular Front Darío Santillán (*Frente Popular Darío Santillán,* FPDS) (Solana, 2011: 49)[9] with many activists that participated in the CTDAV is another indicator of the tendency to reorganise hope and reinvent utopian demand of dignified work beyond the politisation of unemployment that characterised the 1990s.

The factories and the workers: hope and self-management

The process of factory occupations and recovery by their workers that began in the late 1990s and expanded during and after the 2001 crisis revitalised the socialist utopia of *autogestión* (self-management) and put working-class autonomy into the agenda of the urban rebellion. Unlike other Latin American experiences where the formation of workers cooperatives is encouraged by the state (like in Venezuela and Bolivia) the Argentine one was the true result of autonomous organising for survival. During the late 1990s, many companies staged fraudulent bankruptcies (*quiebras*) and drained factories of a variety of resources. A new bankruptcy legislation Law No. 24,522 was passed under the Menem presidency to regulate the conditions of continuity of the contract in those enterprises that went bankrupt. Very few bankruptcies occur normally as a consequence of the impact of the crisis on business. Most of the bankruptcies were forged after emptying the company by seemingly accumulating debt with fictitious creditors, non-declaration of assets and asset stripping, and destruction of inventory by bribing functionaries in charge of accounting control (Fajn, 2003: 34–35), all of which was achievable in the climate of impunity in which entrepreneurs operated during the 1990s (Dinerstein, 2007).

During the 1970s, factory occupations had been a tool for demonstrating the bargaining power of industrial workers gathered in the General Workers Confederation (*Confederación General del Trabajo,* CGT), the state-sponsored Peronist Labour Confederation in demand of wage increases and better working conditions. The new factory occupations were patchily organised by either workers alone, or with their shop-floor representatives –not necessarily supported by their official unions, but mainly by outsider activists, movements and left-wing militants – most in small enterprises with obsolete machinery and technology in an atmosphere of political excitement.

This time, the union bureaucracy was not involved in the factory occupations. During the 1990s, the co-optation of the CGT by the Menem government in a kind of compromise where the unions were to accept and contribute to the labour reform in return to their financial stability (the management of the union-led health-care system of *Obras Sociales*) and their bargaining power (against the IMF's demand for the decentralisation of collective bargaining). The CGT unions negotiated their survival by detaching themselves from their *raison d'être* and by exchanging workers' rights for the government's or capitalists' financial or political privileges for the CGT unions to make business out of privatisation and deregulation. This perversion of the trade unions meant that the financial stability of the unions was attained by means of the legalisation of the instability of workers' lives in a moment in which these policies were being imposed. By so doing, they sustained their organisations financially but lost membership and legitimacy. The super-structural recreation of the power of the CGT by the Menem administration did not account for the reality at the grassroot. Neither the CGT nor the government could control the emergence of grass-roots anti-bureaucratic union resistance and the expansion and politicisation of labour conflict in new forms. The period also witnessed both the decline of the Metallurgical Workers Union (*Unión Obrera Metalúrgica*, UOM) as a paradigm of trade unionism in Argentina and the reappearance of movimientista trade unionism led by the CTA created in 1992. The new central organised fragmented labour resistances that emerged against the labour reform and its implications (i.e., casualisation of jobs, unemployment, crime and poverty) under new premises (Dinerstein, 2013).

CTA supported the factory occupations for it constituted a new current of union opposition at the workplace, as well as at the political level, by challenging corporate unionism and hierarchical forms of union organisation and organising fragmented struggles against unemployment and for welfare provision.

The process of factory occupation and the creation of the WRC (Workers recovered companies) opened a debate about workers' democracy (Meyer and Chaves, 2008), self-management, autonomy, the state and the law. There is extensive literature on WRCs. The attention of the authors has focused on workers' experience of management, control of the labour process and new forms of industrial relations within the factories (Aiziczon, 2009; Deledicque and Moser, 2006); politics and experiences of resistance and mobilisation strategies (Picchetti, 2002; Fajn, 2003; Meyer and Chaves, 2008); workers' subjectivity (Fajn, 2003; Shukaitis, 2010); legalities and politicalities (Carpintero et al., 2002; Martínez and Vocos, 2002; Echaide, 2006; Vietta and Ruggieri, 2009), the relation between WRCs and the market (Atzeni and Ghigliani, 2007); and WRCs and the state policy (Dinerstein, 2007; Upchurch et al., 2014; Ozarow and Croucher, 2014).

Workers of WRCs defied the 'unavoidability' of bankruptcy and unemployment and were driven by the intuitive impulse to self-determination:

> Taking over the business, the factory, was really powerful. It was a huge decision that included all the *compañeros*. At first we didn't know what to do, but when we realised that they were going to come and take the machines, well, then we had to make a decision. We took over the workplace. That step was reflexive, instinctive. (Worker from Chilavert, cited in Sitrin, 2006: 69)

Workers at the Brukman garment factory workers, who decided to stay in the factory overnight after the decision was taken in a spontaneous workers' assembly on 18 December, on the run-up to the popular insurrection of December 2001, confirm this experience: 'we were not involved in politics, we did not have any intention to occupy the factory as part of a political strategy ... we stayed indoors for fear of losing our jobs and because we had no money to return home! It just happened' (Brukman worker, author's interview, 14 June 2002).

Can such an spontaneous and somehow defensive attitude based on 'fear' be the foundation of concrete utopia? The answer to this question lies in seeing *autogestión* as a concrete tool to fulfil a real necessity which, in turn, facilitates the transition from fear to hope, and moves onto the unknown. In the first case of occupations and recovery, the events forced workers to act quickly. In others, the occupation and recovery became a logical direction to take, drawing from the experience of previous occupations (see Ozarow and Croucher, 2014).

Concrete utopia is not predetermined or planned: self-management worked through the openness of the reality of bankruptcy and potential unemployment. The autonomous organising of WRCs involved *simultaneous* processes of self-organising within the workplace, resisting ejection, the legal battle for ownership and formation of new cooperatives, the companies' reinsertion in the market, and the relation with the state and its financial and technical assistance that was offered ot the factories in 2003 and 2004. WRCs became both a territory for workers' resistance and nodes of social networks. Repression and ejection (like the military occupation of the Brukman factory by hundreds of gendarmes on 2 April 2003) were the initial obstacles to overcome, particularly under the Duhalde presidency.

The workers' struggled to find the right legal form to mediate their pursuit of self-management. There were two legal options: the formation of a cooperative, and workers' control with statisation of the company (see Echaide, 2006). Both represented different political views on the utopia of self-management vis-à-vis the state. Both allowed the workers to organise autonomously at the work place. In both cases the occupation became a process of 'recovering' of the factory or enterprise, and the attainment of cooperation, organisational democracy and equal distribution of gains. The rationale behind the cooperative strategy was to achieve a legal status that would facilitate access to credit and institutional support, in order to become profitable and competitive enterprises (Ghigliani, 2003). An example of the cooperative strategy is the Metallurgical and Plastic Industry of Argentina (*Industrias Metalúrgicas y Plásticas Argentinas*, IMPA). This factory was occupied in May 1998 some time after the managers declared bankruptcy before the judiciary and closed the factory doors in 1997. Workers engaged in a four-month struggle to maintain their jobs, supported by neighbours and social organisations. They took over and reorganised production democratically, improved marketing and increased the number of employees from 60 to 130. IMPA compensated its technological backwardness by utilising 100 per cent of recycling aluminium systems developed by its own workers, thus breaking the monopoly of leading firms. IMPA's commercial success is also due to the elimination of capitalist profit and 90 per cent of the managerial-hierarchical (unproductive) staff (Martínez and Voscos, 2002).

The second form, i.e. workers' control over production with demands for statisation of the company was embraced by the poltical left and factory occupations that consider the takes as contributing to a wider process of political emancipation. In this case, the state frees the cooperative from the burden of the company's debt, with the workers focusing on 'the implementation of a 'non-reformist reform' whose success depends on the generalisation and expansion of the process of self-control to other social forces' (Lucita, 2003: 43). While in the former case the cooperative is an end in itself, in the latter the factory takeover becomes a key element of a wider struggle for socialism.

A good example of the 'state-centred' strategy and of the political radicalisation of factory occupation is Zanón Ceramics (*Cerámicas Zanón*). Located in the province of Neuquén, the site of the popular upheavals of Cutral Có and Plaza Huincul of 1996 and 1997, Zanon's workers' struggles, led (exceptionally) by left-union activists, produced, in the recent past, 20 per cent of the national production of exported ceramics to 30 countries. In October 2001, Zanón was recovered by its workers, after a process of 'emptying' the factory by its owners in connivance with the union bureaucracy and after a long period of resistance and negotiations it became FaSinPat (*Fábrica sin patrón*, or factory without bosses).

Following Ghigliani while the shortcoming of the cooperative model is that the enterprise cannot escape the logic of the capitalist system for production and must be subordinated to the demands of the market – and this means that wages, production pace and working conditions are always at stake, the deficiency of the workers' control with statisation is that the possibility of real control depends on the elimination of the capitalist-social relations of production altogether, and this ultimately requires to take the power of the state. The capitalist character of the state is, according to critics of the cooperative model, a barrier for the development of workers' self-management and autonomy (Ghigliani, 2003).

With the exception of a few, most of the occupied factories resumed their production under the form of workers' cooperatives, beneath the umbrella provided by the National Movement of Recovered Enterprises (*Movimiento Nacional de Empresas Recuperadas*, MNER), with its motto 'Occupy, Resist, Produce!', supported by the CTA and some sectors of the Catholic Church. The explanation for this is both political and practical. Led by MNER the concept of 'take' or 'factory occupation' was transformed into 'workers' recovered enterprises'. The MNER was well connected with the Kirchner administration and was able to offer legal support as well as lobbying capacity with the government to get help in the process of dealing with company debt, create the cooperative out of a bankrupt company and resists and survive financially the incessant evacuations of workers out of the factory by the police during the process of legalization of the occupations. The cooperative concrete utopia was accompanied by micro ventures with the neighbourhood *asambleas* and the UWOs directed at the creation of a new, solidarity economy. Practically, this legal form was directly encouraged by the new legislation on bankruptcy (i.e. *Ley de Concursos y Quiebras*, no. 24,522, article 190), which establishes that magistrates can allow workers to continue with the production of goods and services of the enterprise at stake until the legal declaration of bankruptcy and on condition that workers presented a project and organisational plan under the form of workers' cooperatives.

At some point in the process of resistance, the expropriation of the factory from the owner was *legalised* in specific circumstances: of fraudulent bankruptcies and draining of a variety of resources: emptying of the company by seemingly accumulating debt with fictitious creditors, non-declaration of assets and asset stripping, destroying of the inventory by bribing functionaries in charge of accounting control (Fajn, 2003: 34–35). In this case, the magistrates ruled in favour of workers' cooperatives, and expropriated the companies' furniture, machinery and installations by declaring them and their assets 'public goods.' In 2009, Zanón was expropriated and the cooperative FaSinPat was legalised as workers' control with the statisation of the factory. Statisation was equated to the peoples' ownership: 'Zanón is the people's factory!'

New policies like the 2004 Programme for Self-Managed Work agreed upon between the Department of Employment and the MNER. provided financial and technical support to recovered companies. Six-month monthly support of 150 pesos (£30) for workers in the course of resisting ejection (between the states of employment and unemployment referred to as 'workers in standby' (MTEySS, Programme coordinator, Interview June 2005) and allocated 500 pesos per worker (maximum of 50,000 pesos) to the 'productive unit' for technical assistance and training; the purchase of raw material, inputs, tools, equipment, repairing or putting in motion old machinery; and support for the expansion of the WRCs and their consolidation in the market. In order to enjoy the benefits of the programme, the F/Es needed to be included in a register of Productive Units Managed by Workers (see MTEySS, n.d., 2005a, 2005b). Registration in the Register of NGO for Local Development and Social Economy allowed WRCs to be tax-exempt for a two-year period to help low-income workers in vulnerable situations (MTEySS, Coordinator Area of Technical Evaluation and Assessment, *Plan Manos a la Obra*, Interview 18 August 2005, Buenos Aires). The programme effectively helped workers to reorganise production and the labour force, prepare business plans, repair inadequate old machinery and refurbish buildings in order to meet legal requirements, increase production levels and commercialisation of products, improve quality and reduce costs by purchasing new equipment, and diversify production to reinvest in capital assets such as equipment to improve safety at work and environmental conditions within the factory (Dinerstein, 2007).

More recent evaluations of the universe of WRCs up until 2008 suggest that occupations and recovering continued expanding after 2001 and, as

Palamino et al. suggest, as 'extended backwards into the past, since actors that might not have considered themselves WRCs in the early days of the phenomenon might now take the identifying mark of a "recovered" factory' (Palomino et al., 2010: 254). According to Palomino et al., 'it is the movement's current protagonists – in their imaginaries and memories – that make these first "anticipatory" or "prefigurative" experiences with workspace recoveries and conversations still exist as such' (Palomino et al., 2010: 254).[10] These views on the factory occupation emphasise the experience of self-management as the ultimate experience of solidarity and the creation of new values.

Workers' experience of occupations is unique as a learning process of self-management full of uncertainties and surprises. According to a recent report by *Facultad Abierta* (Open Faculty, Faculty of Philosophy, University of Buenos Aires), trade unions are becoming more involved in the process of recovering enterprises as a dimension of industrial conflict: while only 44 per cent of WRCs were supported by unions in 2010, at present this is the case for 64 per cent of the WRCs (Magnani, 2014).

Critics argue that the WRCs are at risk of getting into self-exploitation, that is, that the WRCs can become 'little more than the self-organisation and management of one's own misery and exploitation' (Shukaitis, 2010: 66) with the risk of self-surveillance, subordination to market conditions and political co-optation, with a democratic management always being constrained by the urgencies and demands of the market (Atzeni and Ghigliani, 2007: 657 and 661; Deledicque et al., 2005; Ozarow and Croucher, 2014). The lack of available cheap credit and the problems that arise from the precarious legal situation due to the inefficiency of the application of the bankruptcy law led to a precarious consolidation of the process (Magnani, 2014).

Can self-management move workers from the demand of 'the dignity of work' (Shukaitis, 2010: 73) to dignified work and self-determination as part of a broader process of emancipation? As Hudis explains, Marx's answer to this question, related to the possibility of transition from an old to a new society (Hudis, 2012: 179), is both positive and negative. According to Marx,

> The cooperative factories run by workers themselves are, within the old form, the first examples of the emergence of a new form, even though they naturally reproduce in all cases, in their present organization, all the defects of the existing system, and must reproduce them. But the opposition between capital and labour is abolished here, even if at first only in the form that the workers in association

become their own capitalist, i.e., they use the means of production to valorize their own labour. These factories show how, at a certain stage of development of the material forces of production, and of the social forms of production corresponding to them, a new mode of production develops and is formed naturally out of the old. Without the factory system that arises from the capitalist mode of production, cooperative factories could not develop. (*Capital*, vol. 3: 571)

Despite the differences in the approach to the role of the factory occupation and recovering in a future process of radical transformation, the WREs became a symbol of the art of organising hope. *Autogestión* was understood, as Lefebvre suggests, not as a model but as a strategy of dis-alienation of an urban society (see Charnock, 2010: 1295) that must be 'extend[ed to] to all levels and sectors. To Lefebvre, this perpetual struggle for *autogestión* 'is the class struggle' (Lefebvre (2001/1979: 780). The occupied factory opens multiple sites of hope in the autonomous landscape. Raúl Godoy, the Secretary General of *Sindicato Obreros y Empleados Cerámicos de Neuquén* (Ceramic Workers Union of Neuquén, SOECN) during the period 2000–2005, and organiser of the occupation and recovery of FaSinPat prefers to leave the issue open:

Look, this [process of factory occupation and recovery] is big, because what one has read in the books many times, what one has regarded as a utopia, has become now necessary and possible ... Let's say, if we could take this – and we will do it, that is the goal, to a regional, country, world, level, there would be nothing else to say, I don't know, we would be talking of another world, I don't know ... . (cited in Aiziczon, 2009: 12)

Concluding Remarks: Essentials of urban concrete utopia and the ritual of inversion

What are the fundamentals elements of concrete utopia in Argentina 2002? First and foremost, it must be said that the experience of autonomous organising entailed an emotional journey. This is referred to as *política afectiva* (affective politics) by participants in the movements and activist-scholars (Sitrin, 2006; Motta, 2013; Colectivo Situaciones, 2001). *Política afectiva* is an embodied form of politics that relies on the human capacity to understand, listen and cooperate. It defies the separation between the being and the social (Dinerstein 2005b) to engage with what Bloch refers to as a 'collaboration of feelings' (Bloch, 1971: 19). In *política afectiva* there is an 'empowering ethics of commitment'

(Critchley, 2008: 39) that does not respond to the Kantian external moral obligation to be 'in solidarity' with others but emanates from the collective experience of organising hope. In *política afectiva* solidarity is not driven by Kant's categorical imperative that maintains externality between my autonomy and the heteronomous character of the social but by what Jean-Luc Nancy refers to as 'being in common' or 'Being singular plural: in a single stroke, without punctuation, without a mark of equivalence, implication, or consequence. A single, continuous – discontinuous mark tracing out the entirety of the ontological domain' (Nancy, 2000: 37).

With *política afectiva*, the Cartesian split between mind and body is also disallowed. When, in the second of his *Meditations on First Philosophy* (1641), Descartes asks 'what then am I?' he answers 'A thing that thinks' and 'What is that? A thing that doubts, understands, affirms, denies, is willing, and also imagines and has sensory perceptions' (cited by Bakhurst and Sypnowich, 1995: 2). The Cartesian self is, in its very nature, *disembodied* and it is 'a profoundly *asocial* phenomenon' (Bakhurst and Sypnowich, 1995: 3, emphasis added). Conversely, Spinoza considers a human being 'as a mode of extension, a body, or as a mode of thought, a mind' (cited by Bakhurst and Sypnowich, 1995: 14): 'If there is only one order of nature, it seems inadmissible to speak of the body and mind as two different orders' (Morris, 1991: 24). The relationship between mind and body in Spinoza's account 'is not one of causal interaction but one of identity' (Rosenthal, 1971: 7). The implication of this for *política afectiva* is that an *adequately understood* emotion (affect) makes a person an agent of self-knowledge. Knowledge is important because 'to be free is ... to cause things to happen according to our understanding of the way things are and ought to be' (Rosenthal, 1971: 16). Freedom is a form of self-determinism and virtue is power as the capacity to act. This is freedom not as free choice but as necessity (Dinerstein, 1997).

To Bloch, the dialectic between passion and reason is mediated by what he refers to as *docta spes* or educated hope. Concrete utopia is an act of collective learning *in practice*: 'it is a question of learning hope' (Bloch, 1959/1996: 3). In short, *política afectiva* is a way of transforming the world by connecting with our own emotions about what is wrong, and fight against the rationalisation of political action that distance ourselves from our humanity and dignity. Affective politics is informed by a particular form of love that, as Hardt suggests, is based on the power in each other, camaraderie in Whitman terms, rather than an abstract feature of our humanity; 'a common experience and a common power that we can create' (Hardt, 2006: 38). This love for the other is not an externally compulsory moral imperative of solidarity with the neighbour. It is 'internally compelling ... an empowering ethics of commitment' (Critchley, 2008: 39).

Second, the identities that emerged from *política afectiva* are selves of resistance involved in individual and collective acts of self-determination and hope, rather than fear and hopelessness. Hence, disillusioned and apprehensive citizens became politically active and *solidarios* neighbours, 'the unemployed' became Piqueteros and unemployed workers, workers on the verge of losing their jobs became self-managed – *autogestionados* – workers of their own factories, the families of the victims of the 'disappeared' or 'terrorists' became architects of their self-realising a reparatory justice and the children of radical dreamers. All these contravened state classifications as well as roles assigned by the traditional left and the workers' movement. These are *not yet* subjectivities in motion, rather than descriptors of class, race, or gender. Their actuality indicates *the presence of an absence* in the social field, like, for example, true democracy, and therefore they anticipate what that does not yet exist.

Third, concrete utopias are about the reappropriation of the commons and the demarcation of non-state public spaces (Ouviña, 2008) where other forms of sociability and solidarity, caring practices, good relations and emancipatory horizons were sculpted. The factory, the streets, the neighbourhood, or parts of it, are 'heterotopic places' (Lefebvre, 1991/1974: 292). As Harvey suggests Lefebvre's notion of heterotopic place 'delineates liminal spaces of possibility where "something different" is not only possible, but foundational for the defining of revolutionary trajectories. This "something different" does not necessarily arise out of a conscious plane, but more simply out of what people do, feel, sense, and come to articulate as they seek meaning in their daily lives' (Harvey, 2012: xviii).

Territories of hope are 'contradictory spaces' (Lefebvre, 1991: 164 and 293), embedded in the reality of their production and, therefore, they are in tension with 'isotopias', that is, with the 'accomplished and rationalized spatial order of capitalism and the state' (Harvey, 2012: xviii). In these territories, there are 'clashes of spacialisations' (Hesketh, 2013) (i.e., disputes over territory of the space of capital versus the space for hope to occur).

Fourth, concrete utopia stands against, abstract representational democracy. Democratic democracy means 'democracy in its most essential form' (Esteva, 1999: 155). *Vecin@s*, wokers in WRCs, Piqueter@s, HIJOS, and the multiple instances of encounter among them, used the *asamblea* as the main organ for horizontal decision-making. Democracy is, not, a 'procedure' but a joyful passion. To Spinoza, while sad passions 'lead us to selfish rivalry, abjection, and the worst of the miseries ... [i.e.] the world of sadness (let us remember this) is the world of the powerful ... that is, the territory of hatred', joyful passions 'are in tune with the very effort for the perseverance of the being, the essential force of men [and women]' (Kaminsky on Spinoza in Kaminsky, 1998: 327–328).

Fifth, the collective enterprise of defeating fear and learning hope required a new emancipatory grammar and new common notions came to occupy a central place in the *lucha por el sentido* (i.e., the struggle over the meaning of both the crisis and the rebellion). The defence of dignity became for many of these projects the engine of their political struggle: 'We put dignity at the center of our work. And dignity was precisely that work against humiliation and conformism. And then we started to block roads for dignity' (MTD Solano in MTD Solano and Colectivo Situaciones, 2002: 248).

Sixth, these concrete utopias were not a product of the mobilisation of civil society, but a product of 'the critique of civil society', for ultimately the existence of a 'civil society' presupposes the depoliticisation of the social field and the confinement of the political within the institutional space, (i.e., the state) (Brissette, 2013). This means a 'fracturing of subjectivity' (Brissette, 2013: 219): 'it is this doubling – living as a communal being in the state and a private individual in society – that would seem to be the locus of our unfreedom, and this is what makes the state's claim to universality and community illusory.' As Holloway and Picciotto highlight: 'The autonomisation of the state is, like all forms of fetishism, both reality and illusion, the reality depending ultimately on the successful struggle of the ruling class to maintain the complex of social relations on which the illusion rests' (Holloway and Picciotto, 1977: 80). The separation between the state and civil society is key to the success of capital (Holloway and Picciotto, 1977: 80). Although imperfect and criss-crossed by contradictions, concrete utopias represent the temporary overcoming of this 'fracturing' by a clear attempt not to revitalise civil society but to 'transform civil society into a subject' (Tischler, 2001: 178) – a subject that empowers itself 'in rising up' and activates 'the power it already has' (Esteva, 1999: 159).

In 2003, the public perception of QSVT and the movements' 'radical action' was reinterpreted and rephrased. Both the government and some of the QSVT movements concur in the construction of Kirchner's populist neo-desarrolista project. The rephrasing of autonomous organising by the state was achieved through an implicit pact materialised out of a political ritual. Political rituals have two interlocking functions: to provide a symbolic unity among participants of the ritual as members of a determinate community and to exclude those who are not participating or associated with that community (Plotkin, 1995: 175). December 2001 produced what Matta calls a *ritual of inversion*, that is, a ritual wherein people occupy a social space from which they were excluded in the past or what Rancière refers to as a moment of disagreement. But the arrival in power of President Kirchner transformed the original event into a *ritual of reinforcement*, that is, a ritual that reinforces the social classification of subjects by making clear each one's position (Matta quoted by Plotkin, 1995: 215). New policies legalised and legitimised the 'takes', the Piqueter@s commons, HIJOS struggle for justice. Financial support for the improvement and expansion as workers' self-managed business, and overt recognition for their substantial contribution in preventing unemployment rates from further increasing, enable the State's appropriation and translation of QSVT action into an aspect of governability (Dinerstein, 2007).

For good reasons, Marx was reluctant to engage in a 'speculative discussion of the future' (Hudis, 2012: 85). The projection of concrete utopia depends on the material conditions and energies that are present at the time when the impulse and need of organising hope arises. QSVT, argues Zibechi (2010), 'is still happening' for those engaged in the concrete utopias do not give in to new forms of repression, discrimination and state violence. The forms of organising hope that emerged during that particular conjuncture of Argentine politics in 2001 have survived as new tools for organising around the expansion of the new forms of social interaction or issues that are emerging as a result of the new political conjuncture.

The fact that both crisis and social mobilisation in Argentina 2001 found, at the end of the road, a recomposition of the elites in power, and the integration of concrete utopia into the state agenda brought about, once again, the question of where the possibility of political change resides. This was, of course, an interrogation that lied at the heart of the autonomy debate but in 2003 it became diluted amidst new concerns about President Kirchner's project. As a result of this, some have argued that I had been too optimistic about QSVT and the subsequent creation of concrete utopias (Grigera, 2006), that there was no political reinvention in Argentina 2001 (Iñigo Carrera, 2006). My response to this criticism at the time (Dinerstein, 2008a) was, and still is, that the political significance of a specific form of insubordination cannot be fully grasped by disregarding the political, social and economic forms of the

capitalist transformations and the crises which preceded and contextu-
alised insubordination. There is an inner connection between the form
of capitalist development (and crisis) and the forms of insubordination
produced at its heart. I still maintain that QSVT cannot be judged from
an abstract model of revolutionary –abstract- utopia. Nothing 'went
wrong' with revolution in Argentina 2001 as many left activists asked
themselves at party meetings. December 2001 was a moment of de-mediation that placed autonomous organising at the centre of politics in
a country with a high degree of institutionalisation of politics. QSVT
transformed autonomous organising into the art of organising hope, i.e.
a tool to construct experience concrete utopia.

QSVT's demands could not and cannot be easily fulfilled. Written in
the subjunctive tense, QSVT is a 'utopian demand' (Weeks, 2011), that
is: 'a political demand that takes the form not of a narrowly pragmatic
reform but a more substantial transformation of the present configuration of social relations' (Weeks, 2011: 176). This is a demand that contains
the *not yet* within it, according to the concrete and material conditions
provided by the context and relations that produce the utopian demand.
Concrete social utopias cannot remain intact as abstract utopias do, for
they belong to the material world and are constantly reshaped by struggles. The facts show that power has been recomposed in the hands of
the Peronist centre-left, but this is not a good enough reason to object to
utopia. QSVT exists beyond the facts. And, according to Bloch, 'As long
as the reality has not become a completely determined one, as long as it
possesses still unclosed possibilities ... then no absolute objection can be
raised by merely factual reality' (Bloch, 1959/1986: 197).

As argued elsewhere, 'although many of the demands put forward
during the December 2001 events were diluted, and then, incorporated
into the state agenda (though not before a period of disarray and repression)', both 'disagreement and hope remain the hidden transcripts
of the political recovery of Argentina post-crisis' (Dinerstein, 2014b).
Above all, despite setbacks, the QSVT concrete utopias exposed 'another
politics' (Denis, 2012), a passionate politics that organise true encounters (see Hardt, 1994). This is an experience of what Rancière calls 'politics to be':

> In order to maintain its democratic institution of the social this way
> for politics to be rises upon incessantly against the State. It affirms in
> actu the possibility of annihilating the division between governors
> and governed, or of reducing it to almost nothing, inventing public
> space and a political space under the banner of isonomy. In short,

this way for politics to be is a transformation of the power in potential to act in concert: it signifies the passage from power over human beings to power with and between human beings, the between being the place where the possibility of a common world is won (Abensour, 2011: 96–97).

6
Contesting Translation: Indigenous-Popular Movements (Bolivia)

Introduction: indigenous-popular movements and the state

In this chapter, I discuss the third mode of autonomous organising (i.e., contradiction) by looking at the struggles of indigenous-popular movements in present Bolivia. Autonomy (self-determination and self-government) is an ancestral practice among indigenous people in Latin America, but it became a new 'paradigm of resistance' (Burguete Cal y Mayor, 2010) relatively recently. As a 'discourse, a practice and a legality', autonomy became a 'new political paradigm' (Patzi Paco, 2004: 187) that positioned them vis-à-vis other paradigms (Burguete Cal y Mayor, 2010: 66).

The emergence of autonomy as a new form of indigenous movements' resistance is an outcome of political and legal transformations that occurred since the 1970s when indigenous people firmly rejected their legal definition as 'minorities'. Since they inhabited the lands that they are reclaiming collectively before the formation of the nation-states, they demanded to be considered as 'nations' and 'peoples' (*pueblos originarios*) (Burguete Cal y Mayor, 2010: 72). At different points during the period between the 1930s and 1970s, significant changes in citizenship regimes in Latin America reshaped institutions and had a significant impact on the relationship between indigenous peoples and the state, and the forms of organisation and mobilisation of indigenous peoples (Yashar, 2005: 60). These new institutions integrated (*translated*) indigenous identities into peasant identities. As Yashar explains,

> a corporatist citizenship regime recognised Indians' freedom from elite control, recatalogued Indians as peasants, and as such, granted them rights and access previously denied to them. The state and union

organizations imposed a peasant identity on Indians as the ticket for political incorporation and access to resources. (Yashar, 2005: 60)

The erosion of these corporatist regimes led to emergence of ethnic-based organisations, which explains the '*indigenous* character of the contemporary movements' (Yashar, 2005: 66 and 68, italics in the original). Since then, indigenous communities required to be recognised *as such*, rather than as part of the peasant community, and negotiated their autonomy with the state.

In the late 1980s, Special Rapporteur Martínez Cobo, on the UN Sub-Commission for the Prevention of Discrimination and Protection of Minorities, articulated an operational definition that used the term 'indigenous people' to replace 'minorities'. In his study titled 'The Problem of Discrimination against Indigenous Populations', he stated:

> Indigenous communities, peoples and nations are those which, having a historical continuity with pre-invasion and pre-colonial societies that developed on their territories, consider themselves distinct from other sectors of the societies now prevailing in those territories, or parts of them. (Martínez-Cobo, 1987)[1]

With this working definition, Martínez-Cobo was producing a momentous change in the way indigenous people were perceived up until that point. He opened a new period for the indigenous struggle for autonomy, for it gave the *pueblos originarios* an entity, and put their struggle for the recognition of their right to self-determination in the international agenda in the 1980s. The right to self-determination for indigenous people was finally recognised in the United Nations Declaration on the Rights of Indigenous People, in September 2007. With this, 'the UN took a foremost step forward in the advancement and protection of indigenous and tribal peoples' rights throughout the world'. This general principle enables indigenous peoples to choose the kind of political organisation they prefer (Sánchez, 2010). The UN declaration that recognizes the fundamental right to self-determination is supported by ILO:

> Promoting full application of ILO standards, in particular the Indigenous and Tribal Peoples Convention, 1989 (No. 169), and efforts to secure decent work for indigenous peoples, in line with their rights and aspirations, are the ILO's main strategies in this regard.[2]

During the continental campaign '500 Years of Indigenous, Afro-Descendant, Peasant and Popular Resistance' that took place in 1992 against official celebrations of the 500 years since the 'discovery' of the Americas, it became apparent that indigenous people positioned themselves at the front of their own demands instead of being an appendix of *campesino* movements, and denounced internal colonialism (López Bárcenas, 2011: 81–82). The campaign, which resulted in the creation of the Latin American Coordination of Rural Organisations (*Coordinadora Latinamericana de Organizaciones el Campo*, CLOC), gathered indigenous people supported by rural and other non indigenous movement organisations, all unified behind an identity based on resistance, self-determination and the reinforcement of their cultural, social, moral and political struggle to exercise their rights (Martínez-Torres and Rosset, 2008: 310).

Hence, to speak of the 'emergence' of indigenous people as protagonists of anti-capitalist struggles is misleading. This would be better referred to as a new expression of a long-standing demand for the recognition of indigenous people's rights to self-determination that, this time, stands against 'accumulation by dispossession' (Harvey, 2005) and multiculturalism as a policy of integration (see De la Cadena and Starn, 2007).

In order to understand why indigenous peoples had become political actors in the era of neoliberal globalisation, it is important to examine both the transformations that constitute the bases for the existence of indigenous people including ideologies and state-indigenous peoples' relationship, and changes to the non-indigenous conception of the indigenous 'problem' by dominant elites as well as at the level of national international public opinion (Stavenhagens [1997] in Ströbele-Gregor, 2001). Indigenous resistance is not simply another instance of the multiplicity of struggles that are taking place in the world but offer a *different* experience and understanding of capitalism, coloniality, power and resistance.

I have purposely selected the case of Bolivia to discuss the 'contradicting' mode of autonomy for three reasons. First, indigenous-popular movements in Bolivia are recognised as the most 'radical and powerful movements in the Americas' (Kohl and Farthing, 2006: 154). Second, Bolivia is the first country with a democratically elected president to come from an indigenous background (Aymara) and an experience as a union leader of the *cocaleros*. Third, while in Ecuador the state recognises the indigenous people as 'people', Bolivia has created the plurinational state: a unique form of the state that abandoned the monoculture and universal representation of all inhabitants of Bolivian territory as 'Bolivians', to allow the coexistence of many nations (e.g., Aymara, Quechua) within the Bolivian 'plurinational' state. The case of Bolivia enables me to discuss first the *distinctiveness* of the indigenous form of autonomous organising, and the main contradictions that inhabit such form, which are relevant to an understanding of autonomy in general; and second, since autonomous organising is embedded in and shaped by its context of production and development, it is inevitably criss-crossed by the tensions and contradictions that inhabit capitalist-social relations. I explore the struggles –and their open and/or hidden contradictions – through which the meaning notion of 'autonomy' was and is fought over in Bolivia.

The military-peasant pact of 1952 led to the settlement of a corporatist citizenship regime that *translated* indigenous identity into the form of 'peasant identity' which implied the formation of union-like peasant organisations able to be integrated into the corporatist state. The above-mentioned erosion of the corporatist citizenship regime led to the formation of new movements set out to defend autonomy vis-à-vis the end of the state-led citizenship regime, with regional variations between the Bolivian Andes and the Amazon (Yashar, 2005). These differences in the form of defending autonomy 'occurred against distinct regional patterns of state formation' (Yashar, 2005: 153). The demise of the above-mentioned military-rural workers pact of 1952 that occurred in the late 1970s also led to the creation of the Unified Syndical Confederation of Rural Workers in Bolivia (*Confederación Sindical Única de Trabajadores Campesinos de Bolivia*, CSUTCB). The CSUTCB came to represent a new vigorous actor: the rural Aymara, Quechua and Castilian indigenous speakers thus replacing the hegemonic position of the Bolivian working class and the Bolivian Union Central (*Central Obrera Boliviana*, COB) (Regalsky, 2006).

While the state's translations threaten autonomy with deradicalisation, they also encourage resistance. Due to their internal contradictions, any translation is prone to enter into crisis and produce moments of de-mediation (Bonefeld, 1987; Gunn, 1987a; Dinerstein, 2005b). At a specific moment of crisis, insubordination becomes an untranslatable force. At those moments of de-fetishisation of the state, money and the law, the space for autonomy opens up and, for an instant avoids appropriation, and the subsequent possibility of the immanent expression of hope as in the *not yet*.

In what follows, I examine four moments of the struggle over the meaning of autonomy in Bolivia. The first is the struggle over the Law of Popular Participation (*Ley de Participación Popular*, LPP, 1994) by the Federation of Neighbourhood Councils (*Federación de Juntas Vecinales*, FEJUVE) of El Alto. This is the moment of *neoliberal* translation, when autonomy was transformed into a tool for neoliberal decentralised governance by the law. The second is the indigenous-popular water and oil wars against the privatisation of natural resources. This is a moment of crisis of the neoliberal translation that revealed the limits of capital and the state. The third is the moment of formation of the plurinational state, that is, a moment of re-mediation and re-appropriations of autonomy by a new form of the state. Finally, by looking at the conflict in and against 'development' between indigenous people and the plurinational state around the Isiboro Secure National Park and Indigenous Territory (*Territorio Indígena y Parque Nacional Isiboro Secure*, TIPNIS) (i.e. the TIPNIS conflict), I expose the contradiction that inhabits the plurinational form of the capitalist state. The TIPNIS marked moment of fissure of the plurinational translation that begins to call into question the viability of the *plurinational-capitalist* state.

The neighbourhood councils of El Alto: with and against neoliberal translation

El Alto has not been labelled 'rebel city' (Lazar, 2008) for nothing. It is characterised by a culture of political participation of a multiplicity of grass-roots movements that permanently deliberate and act upon everyday life communal concerns and means of survival. Almost every inhabitant of El Alto *participates* in neighbourhood councils (*Juntas Vecinales*, JV). Yet, 'to participate' does not mean to join a movement or do community work but to fulfil a civic duty of managing the everyday affairs of the common on the basis of the tradition of the *ayllu*. The *ayllu* is a communitarian institution originated in the Andes, which 'in the 1990s returned as a form of organisation' (Puente and Longa, 2007: 105). The organisation of communal life by the exercise of traditional techniques of deliberation, justice and politics embodies the 'original territoriality' (*territorialidad originaria*) (Yépez Mariaca, 2010: 102) and articulates the recuperation of its historical memory with the production of new collective imaginaries that confront new oppressions and survives at the margins of the state structures.

At the JVs, the *vecinos* of El Alto discuss collectively plausible solutions to their communal problems. Ongoing protests, marches and roadblocks are the tools by which the *vecinos* request their inclusion in decision-making processes related to their urban life. The JVs' *asambleismo*, enjoys the massive participation of neighbours at different levels of organisation (council, district, assembly, and at *cabildo*, or meetings). The JVs are 'semi-legal' for they dispute the legitimacy of the state in El Alto.

El Alto is plural and heterogeneous in terms of social identity: it is plagued with a variety of traditions, customs, practices and knowledges (Puente and Longa, 2007: 99). The city has been referred to as the 'condensation and embodiment of the history of the Bolivian nation' (Prada Alcoreza, 2003: 41 and 42). The high level of civic participation in El Alto occurs in a context of structural poverty and racism. In this strategic place where, as Arbona (2007: 132) suggests, Bolivia connects with the global economy, there coexist 'the promises of urban living and the failures of the neoliberal project': urban poverty and unsatisfied vital needs such as drinkable water, education, housing, electricity and security prevail. Since the 1950s, the population of El Alto grew at a fast pace mainly due to two migratory processes (Puente and Longa, 2007) caused by both the agrarian reform of 1953, which reduced the size of the land of family units and forced new members of the families to migrate (Deledicque and Contartese, 2008), and the neoliberal reforms implemented since 1985, which forced miners to migrate to El Alto. El Alto concentrates a significant percentage of the Aymara population of Bolivia – more than 80 per cent self-identified as indigenous people (Mamani Ramírez, 2003: 16) – and has become notoriously a symbol of racial discrimination and exclusion (Arbona, 2005).

The JVs emerged in the 1950s as the organisational tool to deal routinely with the above-mentioned urban problems created by unplanned urbanisation and the constant housing construction demanded by incomers vis-à-vis institutional passivity (Mamani Ramírez, 2005). Gathered in the FEJUVE, the JVs became an institutional reference for the neighbourhoods. At present, the JVs function as *micro governments* (Mamani Ramírez, 2005) and routinely deal with the 'politics of vital needs' (Cabezas, 2007). They challenge the framework of 'need' created by development institutions (see Escobar, 1992) and offer alternative approaches and practices for the management of everyday life. In the politically and socially multicoloured El Alto, the JVs coexist with multiple social-organisational experiences like trade unions, small enterprises, women organisations, sport groups, cultural groups, and students, and articulate an *indigenous-popular* field (Deledicque and Contartese, 2008).

In El Alto the interaction between the indigenous and the popular constitutes a political, ideological cultural and territorial field:

> The indigenous as the great civilizational matrix with its population, linguistic, cultural and territorial dimensions; the popular, made up of indigenous people in the urban sectors who no longer feel indigenous, plus workers, intellectuals, and other sectors that do not belong to the elite. Here, the indigenous appears as the orienting matrix of

the project, whereas the popular constitutes the ideological matrix of the new political articulation. (Mamani Ramírez, 2008: 23)

The *ayllu*, the law and the NGO

The JVs and other popular organisations in El Alto were formally recognised by the law for the first time in 1994. The LPP created the legal figure of Grassroots Territorial Organisations (*Organizaciones Territoriales de Base*, OTB) by which almost 15,000 organisations enrolled in an official register between 1994 and 1997. This admission into the state's records offered them the responsibility for developing local plans and 'mobilising community labour for public works' (Kohl and Farthing, 2006: 132). The legislation decentralised 20 per cent of the national budget to over 300 municipalities so that local social organizations could now take part in decisions about the use and distribution of resources for public work and offer their own candidates for local elections (Chaplin, 2010: 350).

Although at first sight this might look like a good policy, the JVs and other indigenous-popular movements experienced the participatory rhetoric of the LLP as an attack on their autonomy, that is, as a tool to rebuild the municipal level of the state and keeping the parallel state run by indigenous urban organisations under control (see Pérez, 2006). Consequently, *ayllu*-like grass-roots organisations rejected the LPP as 'the alledge organisational means by which governments channel resources down to local level and citizens channel their demands up' (Lazar, 2006: 187). The governmental attempt to obliterate the JVs' autonomy marked the beginning of a new struggle over the meaning of autonomy, which asserted itself as a struggle over the law. This transpired in many ways. Above all, like in the Zapatista's case, the state designed the specific form of participation (actors, functions, timing and administrative requirements) that should be used in the process of decentralisation. These invalidated the traditional forms of collectivist social participation in El Alto.

The participatory tone of the LPP concealed President Sánchez de Lozada's intention to control indigenous-popular autonomous organising, and in particular, the self-government of these communities. Regalsky (2006) suggests that this was a condition to activate a functional land market and make changes in the agrarian law. Neoliberal decentralisation attempted to 'localize the collateral damage or defer contradictions' which 'demanded the deployment and sustainability of a discourse of prosperity as the only alternative to promote development' (Arbona, 2007: 130). While the LPP was argued to be a tool to engage distant communities and encourage participation (Goudsmit, 2006: 201), these 'damn laws' (*leyes malditas*), as rural indigenous organisations named them (the other 'damn law' being about educa-tion reform), created the conditions to fragment big, rural, indigenous organisations via the incorporation of the leaders of the CSUTCB, in the municipal administration (Regalsky, 2006).

Before going any further, it is important to establish the difference between neoliberal decentralisation and indigenous-popular autono-mous organising. Unlike the decentralisation promoted by neoliberal governments and international development organisations aimed at controlling over autonomous organising by using 'folkloric, culturist and developmentalist' discourses encouraged by the state (López Bárcenas, 2011: 98), indigenous-popular autonomy is about exercising self-deter-mination with the intention to 'disperse power' (López Bárcenas, 2011: 97). The autonomous praxis that organises everyday life of indigenous people existed before the nation-states were built so it does not have a 'countervailing power to the State: it makes it superfluous' (Esteva, 2011: 126). In other words,

> self-determination is not negotiable ... [They] consider themselves as the last colonised people that still exist and assert that the failure to comply to their request represents a form of racism and discrimination by the international community'. (Daes, cited in López Bárcenas, 2011: 83)

Following López y Rivas (2011: 109), 'indigenous autonomies are not given but conquered'. On this respect, the construction of autonomy is an arduous, complex and contradictory process with, against and beyond neoliberal decentralisation.

While the JVs rejected the LPP in defence of their autonomy, they also observed the law in order to achieve representation in the local state for their purposes with the help of NGOs. The state's recognition came at too high a price, as money penetrated the *ayllu* and damaged its integrity. In this sense, the law did not simply enact neoliberal govern-ance by redefining the mechanisms of citizens' participation, but altered the established system of communal self-government and control of the processes of election of authorities and rotation of posts at municipal levels.

First, the LLP dismantled the traditional system of communal represen-tation where occupying political posts was not a symbol of progress or enrichment. The introduction of political competition and of the logic of money in the indigenous environment fostered a new elite that was ready to participate in liberal politics, thus replacing the idea of service with the liberal logic of political and financial profit (Patzi Paco, 2006).

Second, as the JVs were compelled to conform to the law require-ments that gave them the required legal status to receive resources and undertake their public work in their area, the law imposed a bureau-cratic rationality on the life of the urban communities. The logic of the 'expert' transformed the function of the president of the JVs, who suddenly became a mediator between the JVs and the state (Contartese and Deledicque, 2013) and was now exposed to 'decentralised corrup-tion' (Booth et al. in Kohl and Farthing, 2006: 142).

Third, NGOs and government officials expanded their dominion over the communities. The NGO-isation of Latin American societies is explained by a shift in international development policy for which NGOs became an organisational tool for 'governing the movements' (Zibechi, 2007: 252). This involved the consideration of 'social capital' as a key concept for the new development agenda since the 1990s (Molyneux, 2002). Barrientos et al. (2008: 772) argue: 'it is striking to note that social policy has become a highly visible and contested issue in the region. It is at the centre of political developments and it is directly linked to economic policy'. A shift from poverty reduction to rethinking social policy in general took place. Many NGOs cooperated more closely with popular movements thus facilitating policy changes (Esteves et al., 2009: 2).

While communities are not passive recipients of NGO intervention, the NGO-isation from above deradicalised autonomous movements (Cornwall and Brock, 2005). Focused programmes run by NGOs always translate innovative practices into components of policy that usually depoliti-cise them and/or mobilise them for political purposes other than those actors involved in these practices (see Reygadas et al., 2009). In the case of indigenous movements, the expansion of NGOs reinforced colonial and dependency practices (Esteves et al., 2009: 7). Development projects have tended to de-structure and damage indigenous organisations.

The LPP fits into the alternative development strategy that encourages community engagement and participation from below. Moving from poverty alleviation to the promotion of development (Coraggio, 1999: 82), WB funded community-driven development programmes focused on 'people-centred development' (Pieterse, 1998) and supported 'partici-patory decision-making, local capacity building, and community control of resources'. Some of these projects, based on new associative forms of production and cooperation, are said to lead to sustainable development and obtain funding for the marginalised to obtain land and housing, women to be empowered by micro credit, etc. (Santos and Rodríguez Garavito, 2006). The approach recognises the importance of civil society in local development – acknowledgement that authorises Civil Society

Organisations (CSO), mainly NGOs, to receive institutional, financial and technical help to pursue their projects.

But 'integration' and 'participative' policies transform autonomy into a tool for neoliberal governance promoted by international development. Cornwall and Brock (2005: 4) highlight how new policy 'buzzwords' such as 'participation', 'empowerment' and 'poverty reduction' are used for the reframing of WB policy discourse as 'feel-good terms'. The new vocabulary possesses a 'moral tone' (Cornwall and Brock, 2005: 8) that 'speak[s] to the laudable aim of enabling poor people to have voice and choice ... In the texts of mainstream development agencies, this triad of "good things" is used to purvey a storyline that situates them as guardians of rightness and champions of progress' (Cornwall and Brock, 2005: 15). While catchwords are associated to ownership, accountability, governance and partnership that correspond to the neoliberal governance, they exclude another association with 'dissident meanings' such as the exclusion of 'social justice', 'redistribution' and 'solidarity' (Cornwall and Brock, 2005: 18). The policy rhetoric demarcates the limits of what 'participation' and 'empowerment' mean. In so far as it excludes dissident meanings, this rhetoric is inevitably realised through political processes that include co-optation, coercion and, on many occasions, direct state violence that is imposed to those who do not purchase such a storyline.

This leaves little scope for differentiating current from alternative forms of development, and led some authors to claim that the 'alternative' in 'alternative development' has no more meaning than 'new' in 'advertising' (Pieterse, 1998: 346–349).

Fourth, the state co-opted indigenous leadership into the 'democratic distribution of resources' and triggered two kinds of dispute (Regalsky, 2006): on the one hand, the competition among organised communities such as unions, *ayllus* associations and JVs, which struggled to get legal recognition within geographical limits at the expense of other organisations; on the other hand, a dispute to obtain approval for municipal public work among those organisations, which belong to the same municipal jurisdiction (Regalsky, 2006). In short, municipalisation and electoralisation of communal systems fissured communitarian autonomy (Deledicque and Contartese, 2008).

Despite being trapped in the decentralisation/participation game, the JVs and the FEJUVE continued resisting the law and the state. They were key protagonists of the water, tax and gas wars that took place between 2000 and 2005 (see next section). Evo Morales took power and the JVs in El Alto resisted the process of translation of their autonomy into the logic of the state (i.e., the reinforcement of hierarchies and the subordination of indigenous organising to the state time and political dynamic) (Viaña and Orozco, 2007).

Water, coca, tax and gas 'wars': natural resources, state crisis and de-mediation

In the previous section, I explored how, during the neoliberal period, the state and the law engaged with the *ayllu*-like autonomous organising and practices, and intended to translate them into the grammar of neoliberal decentralised governance. This was resisted, but in any case it unleashed a series of predicaments among the JVs in El Alto.

In this section, I address the intense sequence of 'wars' between indigenous-popular movements and the state, capital and the law, during the period 2000–2005. I contend that this period that culminated with the downfall of Sánchez de Losada's administration built up as a process of de-mediation that led to the crisis of the state. Moments of de-mediation (Gunn, 1987a; Bonefeld, 1987) are moments of collective frenzy when, as Bloch suggests, utopia cannot go any further, and metaphorically, the distance between the subject and the object almost disappears. Autonomy simply *is*.

The intensification of the exploitation of natural resources by transnational conglomerates is by no means a specific feature of Bolivia's economy. The formation of new 'sacrificial zones' (Di Risio et al., 2012) for exploitation of natural resources that subordinates indigenous and rural workers livelihoods to the rules of transnational corporations (TNCs) in the extractive and agribusiness industries is a common feature of the pink tide's political economy. During the neoliberal period, the privatisation of strategic state-owned companies throughout the 1990s impoverished the state finances and challenged the national sovereignty of natural resources. Most governments of the pink tide have nationalised their countries' natural resources (e.g., oil), but the GDP growth of these economies relies heavily – to a greater or lesser degree depending on the country, on the income revenue generated from the exploitation of natural resources by global capital, a policy that –ironically- goes against the communal life of many of those who made the pink tide revolution a dream come true. Governments justify their alliance with transnational conglomerates by arguing that this economic strategy allows for economic growth at a fast pace, which in turn *will* facilitate further (revolutionary) changes in the economic and social structures of society in the future.

The opposition to the privatisation of the distribution of water and gas in Bolivia has an additional component that many analyses of struggles against privatisation have ignored: privatisation not only means that global capital's appropriation of 'national resources' for profit making. More importantly, privatisation destroys the Aymara way of management and distribution of natural resources that is in place. Gutiérrez Aguilar (2008: 104) highlights how Aymara communities which coexist in peace with nature at 4,000 metres over the sea level, have their own system of production with an effective irrigation system, and a system of obligation in the participation and rotation in the posts through which almost nobody is outside the public duties. They have a fair distribution of land and collective property in place, as well as a system of exchange that is not subordinated to the market commodity, the *ayni*.

Since indigenous and peasant families are subsumed into the market economy by exclusion or semi-exclusion and they practice non-capitalist relations within their communities, based on the 'logic of reciprocity': 'neighbours helping neighbours' and 'production of subsistence' (Martínez-Torres and Rosset, 2008: 310). This refers to the fundamental difference between indigenous and non-indigenous autonomous struggles vis-à-vis the state and capital discussed in Chapter 2: the indigenous movements' anti-capitalist struggle (against appropriation of resources and privatisation) is an anti-colonial struggle, i.e. in this case against the destruction of their management of water, which is connected to indigenous cosmologies and politics. As Webber explains, during the water and gas wars,

> The protesters sought to defend indigenous *usos y costumbres* [customs and habits] in the communal management of water and land – under threat from privatisation – laws. They sought to assert Aymara indigenous pride in the face of racist state-repression that led to several civilian deaths. These were struggles for indigenous liberation. They were also anticapitalist, as peasants sought to defend communal customs against the blood and fire processes of capitalist expansion (Webber, 2011a: 172).

The popular-indigenous struggle against privatisation of water began on 9 April 2000 when a multitude of neighbours of south Cochabamba occupied the headquarters of the water company *Aguas del Tunari* and ended the contract that transferred the control and administration of the provision of water in the region to private hands (Gutiérrez Aguilar, 2008: 57–58). Their slogan of the Network for the Defense of Water and Life was '*El agua es nuestra, carajo!* (Water is ours, damn it!)'. The following narrative –based on Ceceña's presentation of events (Ceceña, 2005: 36–37) captures the essence of the war. All begins in September 1999, when the government signs a contract with *Aguas del Tunari* giving the company the monopoly for the distribution of water in Cochabamba and its surroundings which was ratified by Law 2029 (Service of Drinkable Water and Sewerage). As soon as the law was passed the *regantes* [the peasants who look after natural sources of water such as lakes, rivers and wells and distribute the water in the bases of an Andean tradition in order to plant and harvest different crops [see Ceceña, 2005: 64)] began a series of road blockages. There were two days of combat in the first battle of the *regantes* against the State (Solon, 2003: 19). Ceceña's chronology shows the intensity of this 'war':

In November of 1999 neighbours, factory workers, professional associations, peasants, *regantes* organisations, professional associations and water commissions who campaigned against the privatisation of water created the Network for the Defence of Water and Life (*Coordinadora de Defensa del Agua y la Vida*, CDAYV). In December 1999, the price of the service increased in some cases by 100 per cent, so the CDAYV calls for a demonstration against the contract with *Aguas del Tunari* and the law 2029. In January 2000, the government promises to revise the contract and modify the legislation. But in February, the Coordinadora rejects the government proposal and occupies Cochabamba. This led to the militarization of the city and repression of demonstrations, battles between the multitude and the police. The roadblocks continue, the city main square is occupied and as a result of this, the price returns to where it previously was. The CDAYV calls for a public consultation in which 50,000 people participated and demands the modification of the law, and the end of the contract with *Aguas del Tunari*. Since the government declares the consultation illegal, the Coordinadora calls for more roadblocks to defend the public distribution of water. After three days of civic strike, negotiations resume but as negotiations where taking place the government arrests the representative of the Coordinadora accusing them of sedition and damage to private property. The church supports the Coordinadora and a multitude gathers in the main city square. Despite the end of the contract is publicly announced by the city prefect, the government does not fulfil the promise and declares state of siege. The homes of many activists are raided in Cochabamba and La Paz. 22 leaders of the Coordinadora and the peasants' movements from the Highlands (*Altiplano*) were captured. 'The Coordinadora continues with its demands but the government colludes by accusing them of being part of the drug cartels to weaken their power. A final massive march led to the cancellation of the contract'. But in April 11 'as the parliament is passing the changed to the contested Law, the body of Juan Carlos Rodrigues (23 years old) active participant in the water war who was responsible to alert of the arrival or the police by ringing the bells of the Cathedral, appears hung in the bell tower of the Cathedral' (Ceceña, 2005: 37).

A second Aymara uprising against privatisation of water began on 9 April 2000, when the *campesinos* from the highlands (*Altiplano*) blocked the highways to Copacabana. Soon the roadblocks expanded to other indigenous communities: to Chuquisaca, Cochabamba and Santa Cruz (Gutiérrez Aguilar, 2008: 99–100; Webber, 2011a). Led by Felipe Quispe, the rural Aymara communities rose up in defence of their communal form of sociability and everyday administration of natural resources. In this case, the roadblocks initiated by the CSUTCB rejected a bill that, like the previous case, was going to privatise the access to water in the region. Aymara people made clear that their struggle against accumulation by dispossession (privatisation) was inextricably interlocked with their struggle to defend a paradigm of life. They demanded the government to pass this legislation for it violated communal indigenous understandings of water: 'in the logic of the ayllus, water cannot be bought or sold, or subjected to market logic because water is a vital part of life: it is the blood of the *pachamama* … Mother earth, pachamama, would die if it [water] became a commodity with market value' (Mamani Ramírez, 2004: 81). Aymara insurgents also demanded the cancellation of the 1996 Law of the National Agrarian-Reform Institute (*Instituto Nacional de Reforma Agraria*, INRA), which threatened the 'traditional *ayllu*-systems of land-governance in the *Altiplano*, especially as the INRA process increasingly emphasised land-titling and individual property-rights, a response to pressures from the World Bank and large-landholding lobbyists' (Webber, 2011a: 169). What followed were confrontations, the imprisonment of the leaders of the upheaval (including Felipe Quispe) and the assassination of Ramiro Quispe Chambi and Hugo Aruquipa. The state used extreme violence against Aymara insurgents who destroyed public buildings and liberated their political prisoners (see Quispe, 2006).

During October 2000, the roadblockades organised by the CSUTCB expanded extraordinarily: 'over 50,000 assembled in Achacachi from provinces throughout the department of La Paz to decide on further actions. Talks of an Aymara nation, civil war, and a march to La Paz were in the air' resonating the 'revolutionary specter of 1781' (Webber, 2011a: 170–171). The struggle in defence of *usos y costumbres* continued over 2001, with violent episodes of police repression in June and July 2001.

In February 2003, the government issued a tax increase (*impuestazo*), suggested by the IMF, that included a 12.5 per cent income tax to those whose incomes were two minimum wages. This *impuestazo* was directed to reduce fiscal deficit, although the IMF knew that it was a mission impossible, like when it forced Argentina to the 'Zero Deficit' plan in 2001. Like in Argentina, the *impuestazo* led to unrest, protest and uprising. But in

Bolivia, this included a police strike. The tax war (or tax riots) began with a confrontation between the police and the military, when the latter was sent to control the police's unrest, and escalated into a general commotion with the result of 29 people dead and hundreds wounded (Kohl and Farthing, 2006: 172). The struggle led to the annulation of the tax increase. But the events of February were only the tip of the iceberg of an old problem (Espinoza and Gonzálvez, 2003: 31) that led to the gas war. Many movements believed that the law of gas and oil privatisation of 1997 to be reversed because gas and oil represented a good source of income. Proof of this were figures in the government's reports that showed that corporations operating in Bolivia, such as British BP and Spanish Repsol, had one of the lowest operating and exploration costs in Bolivia and anticipated a profit of ten to one (Kohl and Farthing, 2006: 173).

The gas war – which would take many lives – began in July 2002 when an unlikely coalition of 'military leaders, local anti-globalization activists, JVs, octogenarian pensioners and veterans, union representatives, highland campesinos and coca growers' (Kohl and Farthing, 2006: 174) initiated a campaign to 'recover gas for Bolivians'. During September and the first days of October, there were marches and civic strikes, days of protest and assemblies, with the participation of COB, CDAYV, FEJUVE, and the *cocaleros*. El Alto uprised on 8 October when movements demanded the annulment of the project to export gas to Chile and changes in the hydrocarbons law, and showed opposition to Bolivia's entry to the Free Trade Agreement of the Americas (FTAA).

They also demanded the resignation of President Sánchez de Losada and the nationalisation of oil. The mass urban movement fenced La Paz, reviving the popular imaginary of the epic of Túpac Katari (leader of the resistance against colonial powers in the late 1700s) (Contartese and Deledicque, 2013). Under the Aymara enclosure of the city, civic strike organised by FEJUVE and COB went ahead, paralysing the city.

The government's reticence to negotiate betrayed the Andean thinking of complementarity of opposites (dual complementarity), which makes indigenous people engage in permanent negotiations and renegotiations about what is just and balanced (see Gutiérrez Aguilar, 2008: 103–110). During the indigenous-popular uprising, people governed themselves. Every corner of El Alto was organised with roadblocks, vigils in the street corners, barricades, independent radios, popular guards to avoid looting of shops, assemblies in the streets, churches and unions (Gilly, 2004). There were no visible leaders.

On 12 and 13 October there was a carnage. Brutal state repression did not weaken mobilisation but 'in the countryside of the department of La

Paz and the cities of El Alto and La Paz actually intensified the spiral of political, racial and class-based polarisation in the country and solidified new solidarities within those sectors at the receiving end of the state's coercion' (Webber, 2011a: 34–35). A multitude of mobilised indigenous-popular movements finally brought down the government of Sánchez de Losada.

During these wars, two realities were demarcated: the reality of power and the reality of autonomous organising. October 2013 was an *instant* when, paraphrasing Bloch, the subject became the 'predicate', and autonomy 'came home' where it belongs. As the state entered into a crisis (de-mediation) people encountered themselves as self-empowered beings. For a moment, the state turned out to be surperfluous. This can be called a moment of *immanence* for the state's time (i.e., the time of duration) (Holloway, 2010a) was now subordinated to that Benjamin calls 'now time' (*jetztzeit*), a flash, or 'the time of insubordination' (Tischler, 2005). The moment of de-mediation revealed the fragility of the 'objective' reality projected by the state. During the wars, the nation-state could not sustain the separation between political and economic spheres of social relations, for a majority felt, acted and resisted the state autonomously. The separation betweem indigenous and non-indigenous was also momentarily erased. This was a moment of plurality.

Yet, the period 2000–2005 did not culminate with the obliteration of the state. Rather, a new struggle *over the form of* autonomous organising emerged – in this case, with and against the new plurinational state. The formation of the plurinational state was the immediate outcome of the period 2000–2005 when a process of recomposition of mediation, or remediation began. The plurinational state and legislation will address both the anti-colonial and anti-capitalist spirit of October, leading to new predicaments and conflicts among the movements that supported Evo's revolution.

The 'plurinational' translation and the contradictions of Aymara politics

The creation of the plurinational state signals the beginning of a new period in Bolivian and Latin American history. After the intense crisis, the state recomposed itself as a mediator of the translation of indigenous autonomous organising into the new parameters of legibility. It recomposed what I called elsewhere the 'guardians of the distance' (Dinerstein, 2005) between society and itself were created and new rules for the process of integration of indigenous demands into the state this time, the plurinational form of the state were recomposed.

Indigenous-popular movements have been crucial for the emergence of the political centre-left in Latin America and the political reconfiguration of the region. In Bolivia, the process of resistance culminated with the election of Evo Morales in 2005. More than a traditional party, the Movement for Socialism – Political Instrument for the Sovereignty of the Peoples (*Movimiento al Socialismo –Instrumento político por la Soberanía de los Pueblos*, MAS-IPSP) is a movement that favours the direct participation of social organisations in the political arena (Do Alto, 2010). In 1999, the MAS-IPSP expanded its influence. It won elections in nine municipalities. The 'coca war' in November 2001, when coca producers from the Chapare region, supported by the CDAYV and the CSUTCB, mobilised against the Supreme Decree No. 26415 that prohibited the production, transport and sale of the coca leaf that is planted in zones designated as illegal, put Evo Morales at the centre of Bolivian politics. Despite efforts of national authorities to deteriorate his public image -e.g. the government, the right-wing congressional people and the media accused Morales of being the intellectual creator and instigator of the assassination of four policemen in Sacaba (Gutiérrez Aguilar, 2008), the MAS-IPSP came second after Sánchez de Losada in the 2002 elections.

But the support of indigenous people to Evo Morales is a complex matter that deserves further attention (see Tapia, 2007). Indigenous-popular movements were actively involved in the *Pacto Unidad* (Unity Pact, PU) and a common programme was going to be discussed in 2004 in order to plan the Bolivian Constituent Assembly ahead of time. The 2006 plan proposed the creation of the plurinational state with a new territorial ordering based on the recognition of indigenous peoples' autonomies. At the local level, indigenous municipalities would follow their communal habits, uses and customs (i.e., self-government). The PU advocated juridical pluralism (coexistence of indigenous-peasant legality and western legality). In 2006, the MAS-IPSP obtained more than 50 per cent of the vote at national level, with variation in the regions.

On 6 December 2009 the formula Morales-García Linera won national elections with 64 per cent of the vote, expanding influence in the half-moon region (Tarija, Beni, Pando and Santa Cruz de la Sierra) but losing support in El Alto. Evo Morales organised a movement that did not have a 'party apparatus' (Do Alto, 2010) and whose leadership addressed the movements' demands from the movements (Contartese and Deledicque, 2013). The elections' results disclosed the fact that the government had won more supporters among middle classes as a result of a policy of recruitment of professional cadres for the MAS-IPSP. The party offered membership to some sectors of the middle class (something that was not possible before). These new 'invited members' began to occupy parliamentary positions, which indicated a step away from the initial government's direct identification with indigenous-popular movements (Contartese and Deledicque, 2013). In addition to this, tensions within the MAS-ISP increased as a result of a new rule that established that indigenous-popular movements could not participate in the MAS-IPSP as movements, but they were required to attain representation within the Constituent Assembly through the MAS-IPSP. Indigenous movements encouraged and supported the formation of the MAS-IPSP because it was a movement and not a traditional political party. This rule forced autonomous movements to be *represented by* the party and this was experienced as a form of controlled integration of indigenous-popular movements into the dynamics of the Constituent Assembly, and the transformation of the latter into a quasi parliament that put away the movements' dream for the creation of a new genuine political forum with their direct participation (Chávez and Mokrani, 2007).

The dilemma of indigenous politics

Aymara people demand both autonomy from, and inclusion into, the (new) state. This is not a paradox of 'autonomy'. In general, as Sánchez (2010) highlights, the majority of the indigenous organisations in Latin America advocate free determination through self-government *within* the countries where they are inserted so that they do not prefer the constitution of their own state but to developed their paradigm of life within existent states. The problem, argues Sánchez, is that 'the majority of states are not willing to recognise effectively either the right to self-determination of indigenous people or, consequently, the concrete forms of its exercise. This is why indigenous people continue struggling in their respective countries' (Sánchez, 2010: 261). This points to a distinctive relation between indigenous people and the nation-state, founded on a dilemma of indigenous politics: the demand for both autonomy and inclusion (with autonomy already being exercised in the communities). Gutiérrez Aguilar calls this 'dual intentionality' i.e. 'a simultaneous demand to be left alone (autonomy) and to be included (the state attends to their needs), is at the base of the ancestral notion of "pact" and the two most important political ideas of the Aymara world: the *pachakuti* and the *tinku*, respectively, the alternity of contraries and the encounter of opposites' (Gutiérrez Aguilar, 2008: 113). The realisation of this dual intentionality requires a fundamental transformation of the state and politics.

The main problem that arises from the legal recognition of autonomy is that the liberal law is based on a (liberal, Western capitalist) worldview of society that is not compatible with the practice to self-determination (Sánchez, 2010: 281). Indigenous people self-determination is based on the rights of 'collectivities' (people that enables them) to maintain their forms of thought and understanding of the world and, above all, a different relationship between the individual and society. The state recognition of self-determination requires the design of an 'autonomy regime' that can give indigenous people the faculties required for the exercise of their autonomy (Sánchez, 2010: 73). This means that indigenous autonomy cannot truly exist without the recognition of autonomy from a different state that moves away from multicultural pluralism, that is, the tolerance of the difference within a hierarchical system wherein the universal – liberal-prevails to the peoples' pluralism (the rights of the peoples). A new regime should consist of definitions of self-government, territory, competencies, participation and representation in national political life (Sánchez, 2010: 262). Indigenous peoples' demand is not for 'more nationalism and more state but above all another state' (Quijano, 2006: 20). The MAS-IPSP was committed to assure the legal, juridical and political changes that would lead to the recognition of indigenous' rights to autonomy (self-government) and their constitution as political collectivities (Sánchez, 2010: 259 and 263).

The plurinational state

The new political constitution of the plurinational state, promulgated on 9 February 2009 in El Alto by President Evo Morales after a referendum that validated this decision with 62 per cent of the electorate, is unprecedented in Latin America (and the world) and addressed the demand for the recognition of the right to self-determination of indigenous people. The formation of the new plurinational state revokes the principle of universal citizenship on which the liberal state is based. Unlike the liberal state that universalises abstractly the condition of citizenship to all inhabitants in Bolivia, transforming them into 'Bolivian citizens' – thus subordinating other nationalities that inhabit Bolivian territory to the 'Bolivian' citizenship – the new plurinational state represents different 'nation' in the Bolivian territory and responds to the Aymara system of political organisation. To Vice President García Linera (2003: 53–54), the plurinational state accepts and embraces polycentrism as a principle of authority to respond to an overwhelming (*desbordante*) society. The Bolivian National Constitution also incorporated the indigenous cosmology of *buen vivir*. The new political constitution of the state (*Constitución Política del Estado*) involves the widening of political, and social, individual and collective, rights of indigenous people.

Conflicting views on the plurinational state and the political economy of Bolivia unfolded within the MAS-IPSP, related to the tension that the revolutionary experience brought about, in particular this clashes between political achievements and economic developments. On the one hand, the appreciation of the new plurinational state is based on the unprecedented representation of indigenous people in the state, which tackles the problem of internal colonialism. García Linera (2006: 26) describes *Evismo* as 'a form of political-State "self-representation" of the plebeian society'. Similarly, Stefanoni (2007: 50) regards the MAS-IPSP as a 'new plebeian nationalism that drives a neo-developmentalist model within which traditional power articulations are crisscrossed by *a ethnification* of politics'. *La Comuna* scholars argue that this is the first time that indigenous peoples are represented by an inclusive state and that the state of exclusion that prevailed in Bolivia, by which everything related to the indigenous was considered pre-social and therefore there was a 'perpetual prevention of *lo indio* in the public ordering' (García Linera, 2008: 136), has come to an end: 'the nation-state has died, the Plurinational, communitarian and autonomous State is born' (Prada Alcoreza, 2010: 89). The new state – argues Prada Alcoreza – is plurinational in a non-liberal way, communitarian, participatory, 'auto-nomic pluralism' (Prada Alcoreza, 2010: 92); that is, a 'territorial model that conceives different forms of autonomy but in particular indigenous autonomy in equal conditions that the rest, it promotes gender equality' (Prada Alcoreza, 2010). Others moderately understand the formation of the new state as a work in progress. Kohl (2010: 108) highlights the difficulties that the Morales government confronts: pressures from national oligarchies, inadequate state capacity, embedded corruption, constant popular resistance to marginalization and exploitation and influence of transnational actors. Kohl (2010: 155) also suggests that the government is trying to maintain the support of grass-roots movements by implementing a series of mechanisms that enable them to directly participate in the political processes at national level.

On the other hand, the Andean-Amazonian capitalism offers a form of capitalism that gives the state a significant role in economic development under the 'development paradigm' that indigenous peoples reject. The state, argues García Linera,

is the only thing that can unify society, it represents the synthesis of general will and plans the strategic framework and the first wagon of the economic locomotive. The second is the Bolivian private investment; the third is foreign direct investment; the fourth is micro enterprising, the fifth is the peasant economy; and the sixth indigenous economy.

This is the strategic order in which the country's economy needs to be structured. (García Linera, 2007 cited by Stefanoni (2007: 209)[3]

According to those in office, the goal of the MAS-IPSP in power is, therefore, to develop the national industry and improve income distribution through the modernisation of the industrial, the urban artisan micro-entrepreneurial and the rural-communal sectors. Like this the state can attend one of the modes of the dual intentionality: integration and welfare provision. As Escobar highlights, it is believed that. 'Andean-Amazonian capitalism' 'articulates capitalist and non-capitalist forms and which, through virtuous state action, can generate the surplus needed to support a transition to a post-capitalist order' (Escobar, 2010: 29). But critics argue that the MAS-IPSP economic and development policy is betraying the Bolivian revolution that Morales had initiated, leading to the 'bureaucratic stagnation' of the revolutionary process (Webber, 2012). The government is regarded not only as reformist but also committed to a continuation of neoliberalism, which is being praised by the IMF and WB for its achievements (see Gutiérrez Aguilar, 2011; Moldiz Mercado, 2012). Vice President García Linera interprets these antagonisms as 'creative tensions' in the construction of the plurinational state (Dausá, 2012). In the next section, I discuss this 'tension' at the heart of the Bolivian revolution through a brief analysis of a recent 'war' between indigenous people and the Morales-García Linera administration: the TIPNIS conflict.

The TIPNIS conflict: Predicaments of the 'decolonial/capitalist' state

The 2009 constitution promised two conflicting things: to assure that the government would access natural-resources wealth to benefit the majority of its citizens' development and to address indigenous peoples' demands for self-determination and territory' (Regalsky, 2010). These opposing goals clashed during the dispute for and against the construction of a highway, which would connect Cochabamba and Beni by passing through the TIPNIS indigenous reserve. The TIPNIS conflict was a critical moment for the Morales administration for it embodied the impossible task to create a *decolonial/capitalist state*. TIPNIS became an Indigenous Territory at the beginning of the 1990s as an outcome of the March for Territory and Dignity led by the Indigenous Confederation of the Bolivian East, Chaco and Amazon (*Confederación Indígena del Oriente, Chaco y Amazonia*, CIDOB). In 2008, facing the need to improve road infrastructure and internal communication, the government proposed constructing a highway to connect San Ignacio de Moxos (Beni) and Villa Tunari (Cochabamba). The indigenous communities and their supporters organised a march to oppose the plan for the construction of the highway between August and October 2011. The conflict, which included the shameful repression of indigenous protest, ended with a Short Bill (*Ley Corta*) that declared TIPNIS an *untouchable* territory.

On the one hand, following Rossell Arce (2012: 4–5), this conflict shows the predicaments that *Evismo* as a political force must face for representing a rainbow of social forces: First, it represents coca producers, miners and peasants, who have never exercised full citizenship and lived at the back of the state, organising themselves in what the United Nations Programme for Social Development refers to as the cavities (*huecos*) of the state, between legality and illegality. Second, *Evismo* represents indigenous peoples whose background is the subordination to colonial paradigms. The MAS-IPSP's indigenous mandate of 'governing by obeying' proved to be very difficult to achieve (Fuentes, 2012b).

On the other hand, TIPNIS conflict revealed the 'Janus face' of the plurinational state: the developmental of the capitalist face and the plurinational indigenous face. While the latter sets the basis for the recognition of different 'nations' within the same territory, the former carries the functions of development in the hands of the capitalist state. The conflict was also reflected in differentiated attitudes from indigenous people and rural workers towards the state's contradiction during the conflict: while indigenous people opposed the government's plans for the reasons already mentioned, the *campesinos* (descendants of Quechua and Aymara) supported it. The latter are organised in agrarian trade unions and are in favour of improvements in infrastructure, and demand access to arable land, an economic source (Rossell Arce, 2012: 13).

As we have seen, economic policy in Bolivia and other countries of the pink tide like Ecuador have frequently contravened not only the duty of defending natural resources and protecting the environment, but the principles of the cosmology of *buen vivir* that they claim to defend. As it is now, driven by accumulation by dispossession supported by IMF's and WB's advice, economic 'development' requires new displacements and exclusions of indigenous people from their lands and the exploitation of natural resources such as gas, water and oil usually by transnational conglomerates. The conflict at the heart of Evo's revolution could not be more pronounced: While indigenous people are allowed to exercise their political self-determination as different nations within the Bolivian territory, they are simultaneously subordinated to the 'national' and 'international' logic of capitalist development. In this regard, Webber highlights

> one of the ways the MAS sought ideologically to overcome the apparent contradiction of promoting simultaneously democratic indigenous revolution and neoliberal continuities in various polit- ical and economic power structures, was to separate the anticolonial indigenous revolution against racist oppression from the socialist revolution to end class exploitation (Webber, 2011b: 190).

But can this two be separated? Quijano posed the following question: 'Can the multicultural and/or multinational distribution of the control of the state take place separately from the redistribution of the control of labour, its resources and products, and without changes equally deep in other spheres of the pattern of power?' (Quijano, 2006: 18). This question can be answered with another question: *Can the plurinational regime eliminate the contradictions that exist in the capitalist form of the state?* A simple but spot-on answer was provided (retrospectively) by an indigenous person from Colombia at the International Symposium on Autonomy (Nicaragua in 2005), when she referred to 'the difficulties for the construction of autonomy for indigenous people "within a capitalist system" (cited in Sánchez, 2010: 271–272).

The discontent with the MAS-IPSP policy at the 2 June 2010 Annual Congress of FEJUVE, the official candidates of the MAS-IPSP were displaced and more than 2,500 delegates to the congress appointed, instead, a woman, Fanny Nina, to the presidency for the first time in history. During the governmental crisis provoked by the increase in the price of petrol in December 2010 (*Gazolinazo*), the FEJUVE mobilised actively against the government. Movements from El Alto 'ordered' the government 48 hours to annul Supreme Decree 748, or they would increase their protests in January. A series of protests, the declaration of the president as *persona non grata,* several civil strikes that paralysed the transport system and the mobilisation of teachers, factory workers, students, merchants and inhabitants of El Alto supported the demand until 31 December, when the president annulled the decree that he had issued a few days earlier (Contartese and Deledicque, 2013). In June 2012, the 3,000 delegates representing 729 out of 920 JVs of El Alto defined the government as 'colonial and oligarchic' and called Vice President García Linera an enemy of indigenous and *campesino* people.

In their 'Manifesto' of the Ordinary Congress of the FEJUVE of El Alto. They claim:

> Nowadays, it continues to maintain the capitalist system and the neoliberal political system, and nothing has changed at all for the impoverished people who are still politically dominated, economically exploited by the capitalist system, and racially and culturally marginalised by the *criolla* oligarchy (Manifesto of the FEJUVE Ordinary Congress, El Alto).

A reflection on the nature of the State

My argument has been that from 2000 to 2005, intense struggles in indigenous-popular movements in Bolivia did not *only* challenge the government/state but contested the objectivity of the demarcation of reality by the state. During this period, the state became a 'field of struggle' (*campo de lucha*) (García Linera et al., 2010). In order to explore in what ways the state is vulnerable to the struggles of civil society, I offered a materialist view that explains the state as 'political form' of the social relations of capital (Holloway and Picciotto, 1977; Clarke, 1991). This means that the state is a 'mediation', it is a particular 'form' of capitalist social relations. The starting point to analyse the state is not the state struggle but the capital social relations organised by the state. In order to understand the state, the state must be dissolved as a category (Holloway, 1994). The explanation for the crisis of the state cannot be found in the state itself but in the struggle that emerged at the social level, which is embodied in the state form. In the materialist critique of the state, the specificities of the political and the economic are explained as the political and economic forms through which class struggle asserts itself at specific historical moments of capitalist development. Clarke argues that

> the class struggle does not simply take place within these forms. The forms of capitalist domination [in this case the state] are themselves the object of class struggle, as capital and the working class confront them as barriers to their own reproduction ... their development is the outcome of a history of struggle in and against the institutional forms of the capitalist mode of production (Clarke (1988: 16).

He highlights that

> we have to look behind the institutional separation between economics, law and politics to see money, law and the state as

complementary economic, legal and political forms of the power of capital ... the three aspects being united in capitalist property, money representing the most abstract form of capital, whose power is institutionalised in the law and enforced by the state. (Clarke, 1988: 15)

The state is not a state in a capitalist society but a *capitalist state*. The TIPNIS conflict shows the continuation of internal colonialism and the difficulties for the new plurinational state to translate autonomous organising as self-determination, in light of the contradictions imposed by capitalist form of the plurinational state.

The plurinational state assumed the task of *demarcating of a new reality* that integrated the dual demand of the Aymara people: autonomy and inclusion. While the plurinational state and the law give recognition and legitimacy to the right to self-determination of indigenous people, such right is permanently threated by development policy required to strengthen Andean-Amazonian capitalism, of which the plurinational state is the political form. This disharmony between the political and economic forms of social relations in not unique to the plurinational state. The liberal state maintains a separation between the political citizenship and economic exploitation that sustains the capitalist system. In the specific case of the 'plurinational' state the contradiction is that while the plurinational state is based on a plurality of citizenships including those of indigenous peoples (e.g., Aymara, Quechua) – who are now considered 'nations' living together with Bolivians in Bolivian territory, free to decide how they want to live, including forms of political participation and production and the use and management of natural resources – the political economy of Andean-Amazonian capitalism requires, ultimately, the subordination of 'all nations' to the logic of Bolivia's economic development. The TIPNIS conflict has had a happy ending. Yet, it constitutes the epitome of an insurmountable contradiction in the political and economic form of capital coexisting within the plurinational-developmentalist *form* of the state.

A final reflection

At intense moments of struggle, like October 2003 in La Paz, it seems that 'utopia cannot go any further' (Bloch, 1959/1986: 315–316). If 'antagonism opens into subversion' as Negri argues (Negri, 1991: 139), mediation becomes 'de-mediated'. In García Linera words, with insurgency, 'the community becomes possibility of an overflowing of the state regime' (García Linera, 2008: 208). He argues that

Unlike the quiet time when the subaltern past projected itself as a subalternised present, now is the accumulation of insubordinate past distillates in the present to defeat the past meekness ... the *porvenir* (future) appears in the end as the unusual invention of a common will that blatantly flees from all the pre-written routes, recognizing itself in this audacity as the sovereign self-constructor. (García Linera, 2008: 206)

But, continuing with Bloch, moments of Becomeness are *unreachable* and only lie 'in the intention towards it, in the intention which is never demolished' (Bloch, 1959/1986: 315). 'Moments of subjectivity' (Dinerstein, 2002a) are followed by moments of disappointment, appropriation and translation. When the intensity of the event is flattened, 'the inertia of the normal time of the state [becomes] one of the biggest obstacles for emancipation' (Gutiérrez Aguilar, 2008: 49). The openness and contradictory character of social processes requires that hope must be disappointable.

However, the engagement of the indigenous-popular field with the *not yet* is apparent not only at moments of de mediation but also –and more importantly -in the way that everyday courses of action of many movements follow a concealed agenda. This agenda as Regalsky highlights, is not purposely hidden because it is also obscure to them (Regalsky, 2003). This not yet/other itinerary is followed as a path that contains decisions made in the past and that also look into the future. This is not surprising.

Too often, other forms of understanding and relating to the world remain invisible (and untranslatable): 'what is erased belongs to the temporalities and the spatialities of other social realities' (Vázquez, 2011: 37). Interestingly, Bloch contends that 'not all people exist in the same time Now ... they do so only externally, through the fact that they can be seen today. But they are thereby not yet living at the same time with the others' (Bloch, 1962/1991: 97). Beyond moments of insubordination, indigenous peoples routinely enact the *kairós*, another 'subjective time that can be stored, enlarged and even immobilised by [people] ... a time inhabited by adventure, nostalgia, hope ... ' (Valencia García, 2007: 63), like the Aymara '*manqhapacha*' (inner space-time).

In this 'non contemporaneity' that Bloch refers to in a very different context, or this 'diachronic concomitance' in the words of Prada Alcoreza (2003: 46), new interstices that engage with the *not yet* are opened and Becomeness can be rehearsed. This not yet reality outflows the imprisonment of a reality and time demarcated by our analysis of events and by the plurinational-developmentalist state, and require the development of a prefigurative critique of political economy. If we are to discuss truly the prefigurative power of autonomous organising, we need to account for both the predicaments that underpin the art of organising hope and the process of formation of the untranslatable dimension of the latter, *beyond* the struggle with and against the state. There is –I argue- a fourth mode of autonomous organising that engages with the non-factual reality of the *not yet*. I turn now to examine how the MST's dreams of agrarian reform venture beyond capitalist reality in Brazil.

7

Venturing beyond the Wire: The *Sem Terra's* Dream (Brazil)

Introduction: the MST, from landlessness to groundbreaking vision

At the start of the new millennium we find the rural world everywhere to be in a state of crisis. The historical origins of this crisis, in
the nations of the South, can be found in colonial land grabs and the
displacement of farming peoples from fertile lands with adequate rain-
fall, toward steep, rocky slopes, desert margins, and infertile rainforest
soils, and the progressive incorporation of these displaced peoples into
poorly paid seasonal labor forces for export agriculture. As a result of
this legacy, only slightly modified in the post colonial period, the landless and near landless have long made up the poorest of the poor.

This statement made by the international peasant movement *La Vía
Campesina* (VC) in a joint paper with the International NGO/CSO
Planning Committee for Food Sovereignty (IPC) at the International
Conference on Agrarian Reform and Rural Development (ICARRD) in
January 2006 (VC and IPC, 2006: 6), tells us about an ongoing state of
affairs: the problem of landlessness and the conflicts over the land are
pervasive features of the new millennium.

The predominance of the neoliberal paradigm of land reform of the
past two decades – they argue – has made things worse (VC and IPC,
2006: 6). The neoliberal approach measures policy success in terms of
'economic growth' (i.e., in terms of profit making for those who are
seen as the actors driving economic growth) and not in terms of social
justice, dignity and food sovereignty. Under the spell of the WB, IMF
and the World Trade Organisation (WTO), nation-states determine the

171

form and content of the agrarian reform within the 'parameters of a depoliticized (market oriented) project' (Rosset et al., 2006: 7). Hence, agrarian reforms are based on patchy land distribution, privatisation of public/communal lands, of property rights, promotion of land rental markets and land sale (Borras Jr, 2006: 99). These policies constitute key components of 'accumulation by dispossession' (Harvey, 2005).

Rural workers and families played a significant role in the struggle for the land and agrarian reform against neoliberal structural adjustments. Latin American peasants are now aware of the exploitation they have suffered for centuries and are determined to end it (Arruda Sampaio, 2005: 19). The politicisation of peasant movements began in the 1930s. When their revolts against landowners and local authorities were sporadic, diffuse and inorganic. Today we see a proliferation of much more formal organisations (Quijano, 2000a: 173 and 177). The increase and expansion of land conflict led to 'more concerted form of rural social mobilization' (Bebbington, 2007: 807). A new wave of peasant-based but also peasant-led struggles organised action with indigenous communities for 'land, territorial autonomy, freedom and democracy' (Veltmeyer, 2007: 124).

In Brazil, the emergence of the struggle for agrarian reform as an axiom for rural workers' movements as well as the formation of the *campesino* identity, began to take shape in the late 1940s and 1950s under the influence of the Brazilian Communist Party (PCdoB) and in the 1950s and during the 1960s with the Peasant Leagues (*Ligas Camponesas*, LC) in Northeast Brazil and the Landless Farmers' Movement (*Movimento dos Agricultores Sem Terra*, MASTER).

The political influence of the struggles for agrarian reform led by the LC and later by the National Confederation of Rural Workers (*Confederação Nacional de Trabalhadores na Agricultura*, CONTAG), constituted significant factors leading to the military coup against President Goulart in 1964 (Días Martins, 2006). President Goulart's Basic Reforms Plan, which was supported by trade unions and the political left, included an agrarian reform, a tax reform and tight controls over foreign companies.

The deep restructuring of the countryside known as 'conservative modernisation' or 'painful modernisation' (Silva, 1982) undertaken by the dictatorship of 1964, led to the expansion of landlessness. The process accelerated technological modernisation of some sectors of the agro industry by offering credit and subsidies to landowners, and expropriating and expelling 30 million farmers and rural workers, who emigrated to the cities or other areas of Brazil (Mançano Fernandes, 2000b: 49). The 'Brazilian miracle', with its pauperisation, unemployment and expropriation of small producers particularly in the southern area of the country, provided the context for the production of another miracle: the emergence of the MST.

The CONTAG and the radical wing of the Catholic Church influenced the 'symbolic and identitarian construction of rural workers' at national level (Porto-Gonçalves, 2005: 22). While the CONTAG managed trade union networks in several geographical points of the country it was not proactively defending the landless rural workers' rights to the land. Instead, with their historical influence on Brazilian society, LT priests mobilised peasants, denounced social injustice and facilitated the organisation of encounters, meetings and training workshops (Deledicque et al., 2008). The priests questioned the absolute character of private property and emphasised the significance of the social use of the land, and rural workers' right to it. In addition, the Land Pastoral Commission (*Comissao Pastoral da Terra*, CPT) encouraged and helped rural families with land occupations in the late 1970s, such as the large estates of Macali and Brilhante, and Encruzilhada Natalino camp in Rio Grande Do Sul. One of the rural workers who occupied the Macali estate at the time explains:

> Father Arnildo called us to a meeting. He asked us what we wanted to do. Were we prepared to struggle to get a plot of land? João Pedro Stédile was there. It was the first time I met him. He told us that there was unregistered land in the region and, if we organised ourselves, we could conquer it. So that's how we organised the first occupation – of Macali, on 7 September 1978. The following year we occupied Brilhante (cited in Branford and Rocha, 2002: 8).

The CPT encouraged the formation of a national movement that could become a political actor (Harnecker, 2002: 27) within the context of a politicised general atmosphere in Brazil due to the process of transition to democracy. As Stédile (2009) narrates, in 1984 the working class and the parties of the left were mobilising, exiles had returned, the Workers Party (*Partido dos Trabalhadores*, PT), the Central Workers (*Central Única dos Trabalhadores*, CUT) and the National Congress of the Working Class (*Conferência Nacional das Classes Trabalhadoras*, CONCLAT) were already formed and the LT church continued generating consciousness in defence of the poor:

> Between 1979 and 1984 dozens of land occupations took place across the country. The urban working class and farmers in rural areas were on the offensive, organising. They wanted to fight. As a result of all

that, the leaders of landless struggles from sixteen Brazilian states met in Cascavel, in January 1984, encouraged by the work of the CPT, and right there, after five days of debates, discussions, collective reflections, we founded the MST. (Stédile, 2009)

The participants to that first meeting defined the movement as a mass movement that would engage in a mass struggle, autonomous in nature. Their aims were to fight for the agrarian reform, for a free and just society, to end capitalism, to enlarge the category of *sem terra* rural worker towards other sectors such as smallholders, and to guarantee the use of the land to those who work and live in it (Branford and Rocha, 2002: 23).

To be sure, the lack of an agrarian reform is still one the most significant problems of Brazil's economy. Brazil is the largest country in the world 'in terms of arable land'[1] with 'one of the most perverse and highly concentrated landholding structures, with a Gini-coefficient near 0.9 –nearly total concentration of ownership in few hands – as a result of its *latifundio*-style (large estates-based) agriculture and land tenure system' (Sauer, 2006: 177–178). Large estates occupy 153 million of hectares, almost half of the area occupied by all rural properties (Pinassi, 2008: 99). The market-assisted land reform (titling and commodification that encouraged peasants to buy land and use land banks) (Veltmeyer, 2007: 118) promoted by the WB as part of the neoliberal retreat of the state, which is endorsed by the Rural Democratic Union (*Uniao Democratica Ruralista*, UDR), offers no solution to rural workers and the need for land and agrarian reforms. Throughout the 1980s, the MST's utopian proposal continued to be supported by the CPT, as well as the CUT and the PT (Días Martins, 2006: 265).

The MST consolidated as a mass movement and expanded throughout the north and northeast, beyond the colonial areas of the southern provinces of Brazil where had originated. Gradually, the movement forged an identity that sheltered a multiplicity of paths, traditions and experiences of resistance: communist and reformist, catholic, labour, rural and urban (Zibechi, 1998; Coletti, 2003). The MST is at present the most combative and influential movement in Brazilian history fighting for land and agrarian reform. The movement is territorially organised through encampments and settlements at municipal, state and national levels. It is financially autonomous and works independently from party politics and religious organisations, but it has jointly work with the CPT, the CUT and the VC. While the PT and the MST share an experience of resistance, which have put the need for agrarian reform at the heart of the Brazilian public agenda in the 1980s, the relation of the MST with the PT in the government has been most contentious. The MST has forged a new revolutionary identity and project that draws on unorthodox Marxism and LT. The MST is not a 'sectoral agrarian reform social movement' but 'a political movement with a national political agenda' (Petras, 1998: 124). This mass movement puts in practice an agrarian reform *de facto* at encampments and settlements, after having 'illegally' occupied carefully selected, unused, productive lands, the titles of which are negotiated according to the law after the occupation of the land.

The MST became the voice of the struggle for land and agrarian reform in Brazil, thus displacing the centrality of CUT in this role. The MST's tactics seek to mobilise support and strengthen the demands of the landless workers by moving beyond 'land distribution' and relating it to the broader issues such as right to food, job creation, environmental sustainability, reduction of urban violence and against market-driven reforms that only benefit transnational corporations to the detriment of rural families. Massive public demonstrations politicise and connect the struggle against landlessness with wider sections of Brazilian society. For example, the National March for Employment, Justice and Agrarian Reform, where activists joined the MST march at different points and arrived together in the capital city of Brasília on 17 April 1997 on the anniversary of the Eldorado dos Carajás massacre. Another example is the fourth National Congress also held in Brasília, where 11,000 landless Brazilians participated in August 2000: 'these events are still in the minds of the Brazilian people, in a time when agrarian reform is associated with the false promises of the federal government' (MST website).[2]

The MST seeks a type of agrarian reform that opposes the WB market-oriented reform. The *sem terra* dream and work for an equalitarian and just society in the present. This utopia is built every day as a concrete praxis in the settlements, where rural workers not only plant seeds and produce crops and material goods, but also cultivate a new life of the common, inspired in the values of cooperation, dignity, collective property, democracy, gender equality, education and environmental sustainability.

The socialisation of the land, based on a sustainable socio-economic model that includes education and cooperation are central to the MST's political proposal. It is about 'social appropriation' based on 'cooperative relations among settlers and alternative patterns of land appropriation and use' (Días Martins, 2006: 267–268). The MST's 'imagined community' (Wolford, 2003b) undermines the existing order and 'proposes the democratisation of the polity, of technology and knowledge, and of the economy via grass-root co-operativism' (Robles, 2001: 148–149).

The MST's peasant agricultural model of agrarian reform MST offers an alternative definition of 'property rights' that are 'socially oriented and controlled forms of rural property' (Meszaros, 2000: 518). To the MST, an 'efficient' agrarian reform can be measured by the capacity of the Brazilian people to decide over the property and use of the land, but this is inextricably connected to a social and economic transformation. Indicators of success are environmental protection democracy, cooperation, education, gender equality and solidarity. The MST is a 'social formation' (Meszaros, 2000) and represents the working class (Wolford, 2003) from a *movimientista* and revolutionary perspective (Pinassi, 2008: 107). With VC, the MST has transformed the land question into a demand of a plural 'democratic process in which a range of people not only "participate", that is play a central role in setting the agenda, but also shape and dictate the contours of agrarian policy' (Rosset et al., 2006: 12) towards food sovereignty.

Despite its originality, the MST is a movement of its time and shares many features with other new rural movements which represent a new *campesinado* in Latin America, but also in Asia and Africa. Following Moyo and Yeros (2008b: 57), this new *campesinado* is characterised by a mixture of rural-urban small farmers and proletariat, including some urban unemployed; they are led by intellectual *campesinos* and use tactics of direct action. Their strategy is 'anti-political', and is defined by the autonomy from political parties and the state, but seeks alliances with political parties, unions and other social movements. Ideologically, these new movements tend to fuse the language of Marxism with the ethnic/racial political grammars, and are responsive to gender and ecological issues. They are cosmopolitan, that is, they hold an internationalist view and participate in international alliances.

The MST is inspired in a non-dogmatic Marxism. As Löwy (1988) reminds us, Marxism in Latin America is always confronted with a social and ethnic plurality in historical context, such as the past 500 years of injustice (Zibechi, 1998; Wolford, 2003a, 2003b) and the influence of LT. While some have criticised the movement's strong leadership, for it overshadows the autonomous dream of social emancipation of the landless (Navarro, 2006: 170), others have emphasised how, by facilitating the awareness and organisation of the subaltern class, the MST is contributing to a process of wider emancipation (Martins de Carvalho, 2006: 183).

A desalambrar!

Over its 30 years of existence, the MST had many achievements and went through setbacks and disappointments too. To account for the whole of this complex and inspiring experience of autonomous resistance is beyond the scope of this chapter (see Branford and Rocha, 2002). My aim is to elaborate on the idea that the MST has not only defied the power of the Brazilian state and landowners of *latifundios*, transnational agribusiness, and given voice and facilitation to the self-organisation of the landless, but it has confronted, disputed and transcended the *parameters of legibility* of the capitalist demarcation of reality. The difference is crucial to my argument that autonomy is the art of organising hope (a tool for prefiguration): while with the former, the MST fight for land reform can be located within the capitalist reality, the latter allows us to appreciate the many ways in which movement is demarcating non-capitalist possibilities beyond the line demarcated by power. My account of the MST autonomous struggles focuses on the production of an untranslatable 'excess' that informs the fourth mode of autonomy proposed in this book.

I interpret the MST's act of *cutting the wire* (*desalambrar*) (i.e., the ritual of trespassing that initiates all the movement's land occupations) as a metaphor for the thousand and one actions of *venturing beyond* the reality demarcated by the 'wire'. I expose three ways in which the MST ventures beyond the wire. First, the MST ventures beyond the wire 'literally' by *occupying* the land. They organise negation. When the landless families gather together to trespass into the fertile, arable yet unused land of a powerful *terrateniente*, after overcoming fears and anxieties, they reject the capitalist coding of their own fate. Once they have trespassed, they initiate a journey into the exciting (unknown) possibility of an alternative life. The second form in which the MST ventures beyond the wire is by territorialising the struggle for the land by means of the creation of 'territories of hope' or concrete utopias (settlements) where the MST's agrarian dream is concretely fashioned at the settlements. The MST agrarian reform *de facto*, where the settlers delineate a new space for an emotional, social, political and pedagogical daily journey into cooperative work, democracy, self-respect, tolerance, comradeship, solidarity and self-reflection. The third form of venturing beyond the wire is by steering through the contradictions brought about by the relationship with the state, which includes joint action, negotiation, cooperation, confrontation and antagonism. In what follows, I explore these three forms of venturing beyond the wire with which the MST contributes to the process of prefiguration of an alternative reality to hunger and landlessness.

Occupying the land: hunger, liberation theology and the radical use of the law

The CPT's anticipatory illumination and the far-sighted vision of the six key founders of the MST found its roots on the revolutionary ideas of LT. As Branford and Rocha highlight, 'João Pedro Stédile, Jaime Amorim,

Edgar Jorge Collink, Ademar Bogo, Adelar Pizetta and Neuri Rossito all trained for the priesthood within the Catholic Church – four of them in the same class in a seminary in Santa Catarina – but gave up their studies, because they wanted to be involved directly in the political struggle for revolutionary change' (Branford and Rocha, 2002: 240). They had helped to organise the first land occupations in the late 1970s and beginning of the 1980s with the CPT. Stédile was working for the State Department of Agriculture as an economist and secretly advised the landless families to occupy the land (Branford and Rocha, 2002). Their plan was not simply to occupy unused land and defend the occupation as it had been occurring, but to occupy *in order to* both negotiate the rights and titles to the land and create the space from where to anticipate their dream of communal life and political conscientisation for radical change.

As argued in Chapter 3, the significance of LT for Latin American radical politics cannot be overemphasised. LT produces a synthesis between Marxism and 'religion' that is embodied in the MST's praxis. To Stédile, LT is an 'interesting socio-political-religious phenomenon' that offers a synthesis between Marxism and the popular culture and religiosity that is expressed in Latin America's observance to Christianity.[3]

The courage demonstrated by the landless rural families during the first occupations of the 1970s showed that they were ready to move beyond the wire. Theirs was not a 'fantasy' but a *possibility* deeply rooted in the material world. For landless rural workers in Brazil *land occupation* connects with the most central human need: hunger. When there is hunger the given reality is not only 'unjust' but inhuman. As Martínez Andrade (2009) argues, hunger must be addressed from a counter-perspective against reformist or neo-institutionalist positions of the hegemonic system. Bloch points to hunger as the driving force that mobilises subjects. Hunger is a 'basic drive [of] self-preservation ... to preserve one's being, that is and remains, according to Spinoza's unerring definition, the "appetitus" of all beings' (Bloch, 1959/1986: 67).

Hunger connects danger and hope. Without celebrating it, Bloch reflects on the significance of hunger for mobilisation:

> Hunger cannot help continually renewing itself. But if it increases uninterrupted, satisfied by no certain bread, it suddenly changes. The body-ego then becomes rebellious, does not go out in search of food merely within the old framework. It seeks to change the situation

which has caused its empty stomach ... The No to bad situations which exist, the Yes to the better life that hovers ahead, is incorporated by the deprived into revolutionary interest. (Bloch, 1959/1986: 75)

In Brazil, when the landless act upon their needs they confront brutal repression. The state and terratenientes use ruthless force against the hungry, landless families. This happened not only during the dictatorship and the neoliberal administrations of Presidents Fernando Henrique Cardoso (FHC) and Fernando Collor de Melho –with the massacres of Corumbiara, Rondónia and Eldorado dos Carajás in mid-1995 and 1996, respectively, but also under the MST-friendly PT government of Lula da Silva. The latter could not extricate the strong alliance between powerful landowners, agribusiness and the Brazilian judicial power that jointly acted against the MST's activists (Stédile, 2013). Marx's and Engels's critique of private property in the *Communist Manifesto* of 1848 illuminate the irrationality behind latifundio:

You are horrified at our intending to do away with private property. But in your existing society, private property is already done away with nine-tenths of the population ... You reproach us, therefore, with intending to do away with a form of property the necessary condition for whose existence is the non-existence of the immense majority of society. (Marx and Engels, 1848: 98)

The occupation of the land is a journey of hardship and danger that nonetheless makes the landless indignant dignified people. For rural landless families, it is also an act of self-respect and survival – a rejection of a 'fate', a escape from deprivation, illness and immense poverty: it is an act of hope. The association between hunger and hope rejects the cynical rationalisation of hunger that promotes 'the commodification of subsistence' (Clayes, 2012: 845), contests anti-human WB-led food and agrarian policy that benefits transnational agribusiness in detriment of the *life* of rural families, and engages with an alternative reality that the rural landless are dreaming of.

Land occupation is a key component of the MST's method of resistance and has been a matter of tension between the MST and rural unions due to the former's characterisation of the occupations as 'illegal'. However, for the MST the occupation is not illegal. The MST makes a radical use of the law, showing 'contemporary significance of the realm of legality in the construction and reproduction of social struggles' (Meszaros, 2000: 517; on this see also Santos and Rodríguez Garavito, 2005). The tactic of land occupation uses the agrarian legislation established in the 1960s, which allowed expropriation of lands that were considered unproductive. The state is empowered by the law to expropriate these lands and re-distribute them (Veltmeyer, 2007: 125).

The Brazilian National Constitution of 1988 lays down the principle that the government undertakes land reform without affecting the properties that are productive. The constitution classifies as unproductive farms those landholdings which 'do not achieve the percentage of the use of tillable land, or whose yields are below 100 per cent of the average per-hectare productivity rates' (Sauer, 2006: 179).

The MST's strategy has been to occupy 'illegally' (but legitimately) and then, while families wait in the encampments, to negotiates and to force the implementation of 'the law' and legal titling of the land following legal procedures based on the measurement of the productivity of the land. The MST's 'occupation as strategy' (Días Martins, 2006: 269) is based on the movement's interpretation of the law:

> Regarding the legal protection given to property, the federal Constitution determines that only those properties, which are fulfilling their social function will receive legal protection ... unproductive lands must be appropriated. In not being appropriated by virtue of the inertia of the Public Power, the occupations are legitimate and necessary (MST).[4]

The law is used to demand expropriation of the property that has no social use. The legal expropriation and the compensation process is undertaken by the National Institute for Colonisation and Agrarian Reform (*Instituto Nacional de Colonização e Reforma Agrária*, INCRA) and the Ministry of Agrarian Development (*Ministério do Desenvolvimento Agrário*, MDA) (Sauer, 2006).

'Step one' of the MST's strategy, a key step before the actual occupation (Rosset, 2006a: 223) is, then, to move families into rural camps where settlers are disciplined and socialised against the use of drugs and alcohol, and domestic violence, and learn to cooperate among each other. The camps are installed near the field that the rural workers wish to occupy. This step can last for years. Families are located in barrack tents, in clusters of 15 families, who organise the means of survival. As soon as the land is occupied, in 'step two', the new settlers plant crops and organise communal kitchens, schools and health-care clinics (Rosset, 2006a: 223), and prepare for both resistance against frequently brutal evictions and terms of the negotiation with the state. The key to the MST's success is that the occupation of the land serves two purposes: it accelerates the negotiation for it creates conflict and aids the beginning of the practice of agrarian reform *de facto* in the settlements, which shows that an alternative form of agrarian reform can be rehearsed in the present.

We see that, as Bloch (1959/1996: 4) suggests, venturing beyond does not mean merely visualising abstractions but to grasp the new 'as something that is mediated in what exists and is in motion'. The landless engage with their own reality of landlessness and hunger, and shape their concrete collective dream. But the journey is uncertain: 'We did not have the faintest idea of whether this was possible' or how long it was going to take, Stédile explains (Stédile, 2009). It does not matter, for, as Lear states, 'radical hope anticipates a good for which those who have the hope as yet lack the appropriate concepts with which to understand it' (Lear, 2006: 103). The landless find plausible answers to their questions 'as they walk', by self-reflecting collectively on the meaning of their own actions – at the MST encampments and settlements, resisting police brutality, and interacting at marches and commemorations, meetings, and joyful celebrations, and at the arduous negotiations with other movements (e.g., CUT) and the governments.

Territories of hope: producing, learning and connecting

The second form of venturing beyond the wire is territorialising the struggle for the land. The movement's alternative agrarian reform is materialised within the territories delineated as encampments and settlements. These territories of hope are sites for both resistance and survival and shaping a new democratic, agrarian way. The MST envisions and realises new conquests such as education, health, housing, democracy and cooperative work, through praxis. To Bloch, concrete utopia 'by no means coincides with abstract utopia dreaminess, nor is directed by the immaturity of merely abstract utopian socialism' (Bloch, 1959/1986: 146).

The occupation, argues Mançano Fernandes (2008: 337), is a form of access to the land, but also 'introduces questions...and reveals new situations...it modifies reality, increases the flux of social relations'. Since organising the occupation is connected to the need for survival and is a product of a consciousness constructed within the lived reality, the occupation is a learning process (*aprendizaje*). The occupation means both the 'spatialisation' of the struggle for the land and a site for conscientisation (Harnecker, 2002: 13). Every settlement has its own features, dynamics, forms of political socialisation and temporalities, which depend on negotiations, political circumstances, praxis and local developments

(Mançano Fernandes, 2008: 338). As we have seen with the other movements, these territories of hope are always in danger of being appropriated by the state via policy and the law for they are embedded in and criss-crossed by capitalist-social relations. Stédile highlights that these 'territories' are not free, liberated zones but sites of resistance: 'we must use these spaces where we have more control over, to generate a new culture, new social relations. This is an ongoing work the outcomes of which will be seen in the long term'.[5]

The MST's territorial activity of organising hope comprises three forms: the organising of agricultural production by means of creating small cooperatives and small agribusiness; the pedagogical experience that organises the social and everyday life of the landless family in the settlements; and the political project with a proposal of an alternative agrarian reform to the one promoted by the WB, landowners and agribusiness. The MST *mística* is an essential component of all three.

Production, cooperation and love

The initial MST's motto 'Occupy and Resist' became 'Occupy, Resist and Produce' at the end of the 1980s, when the MST began to promote new forms of collective production and commercialisation by setting settlers' cooperatives. The settlements created opportunities for agricultural and non-agricultural work for a variety of rural people: those who chose to work on the land to make as a living and would have little chance of entering the formal labour market, those who sought temporary shelters for the homeless, and the landless. The implementation of the cooperative projects, in general, allowed for a population that previously lived an unstable and precarious insertion in the world of work, centralisation of family reproduction strategies in the lot itself, in most cases using other sources of income and work of the same (small businesses, construction, domestic work, etc.). The family income is the result of a complex combination of different contributions, with the activities from the most important of the lot most of the time.

The settlements developed into anticipations of potential land reform. The establishment of settlements impacts on power relations within and outside the territory. On the one hand, it gives settlers the power and confidence to speak for themselves and, consequently, to be heard and legitimised as members of their common. On the other hand, the settlements alter local power relations, especially in smaller municipalities, where settlers reach greater relative political importance and where the economic crisis has damaged local communities. The MST seeks not only to ensure the economic survival of the settlements but also to gain social legitimacy through cooperative production. In this sense, cooperatives are stimulated by establishing rules of conduct into the settlements. Political education is prioritized as much as formal education with special attention to children and the youth. The cooperatives create their own brand names to sell their products, and mobilised rural workers to put forward other demands related to production and life in the settlement, such as access to credit, schools, health for the settlers, public transport and electricity, that could improve the quality of life of the settler families (Mançano Fernandes, 2000a: 36).

Cooperative production is enriched by a multiplicity of life and work experiences and family life of the settlers. The latter are workers who owned and lost their land, rural workers, dispossessed, self-employed, or workers who have been inactive for a while. They seek a place in the settlements, not only to return to farming but to feel safe and have a place to live. The decision of joining in the occupation of land is not made by atomised individuals nor determined by political consciousness. It is a family decision, with the consideration of friendship networks, kinship, religion and previous political experiences. Since the occupation of the land brings together a multiplicity of experiences and situations, the MST organisational and capacity is tested daily at the settlement. Seven values are emphasised: solidarity, beauty, valorisation of life, the love for symbols, the love for being the people, the defence of work and of study, and the capacity to become indignant (Bogo, 1998: 6 cited by Martins de Carvalho, 2006: 193). In the settlements, argues Stédile 'people know that their fate is in their hands' (Stédile, 2004: 39), and democracy is an everyday practice. The MST's *not yet* land reform involves the 'democratisation of land ownership, access to education at all levels and the development and application of new agricultural techniques' (Stédile, 2004: 39). An MST leader explains their participatory system in the settlement:

> Each core is constituted by 15–20 families who discus together all actions taken, and participate in decision-making processes about finance for self-sufficiency, gender issues, education, the form adopted by the settlement, health, etc. The settlement has a coordinator and each group nominates two (one female and one male) representatives who help with the general coordination of the settlement coordination. Each settlement also selects equal numbers of men and women to represent them in a brigade of several settlements. The annual congress gathered all settlers to reach consensus on issues already discussed in each settlement. (MST in Durston, 2008.)

Docta spes: *the pedagogical experience of the MST*

The pedagogical is central to new forms of emancipatory politics in Latin America (Motta, 2014; Motta and Cole, 2013). Pedagogical experiences are an essential components of autonomous organising at individual, organisational and political levels. They facilitate the attainment of dignity, the capacity to negate and create alternative political projects and experiences, and to develop the strength to confront and move beyond capital, based on an understanding of the situations and conditions within which the struggle develops. Bloch argues that 'educated hope' (*docta spes*) guides praxis. We find this idea also in Spinoza to whom an adequately understood emotion makes people agents of self-knowledge. Knowledge is a creating process is a process of 'learning hope'.

The MST praxis is inspired in Paolo Freire's 'language of hope and utopian vision' (Giroux and MacLaren, 1997: 147) in harmony with LT (and Bloch's philosophy). As Giroux and MacLaren highlight, Freire's critical utopianism offers a kind of education to which radical change 'must always speak to the "annunciation of a new reality", [this] which becomes not only a temporary "concrete reality" but a "permanent cultural revolution"' (Giroux and MacLaren, 1997: 149). This Blochian reading of Paolo Freire illuminates the connection between Bloch's philosophy and Freire's pedagogy of the oppressed. In Freire's critical pedagogy,

> real, radical democracy [is] understood…as something latent in the present something immanently future bearing that can be grasped in the flickering moment of anticipatory consciousness. The utopian imagination for both thinkers drives forward the multiple levels of human desire while at the same time it is the result of an unconscious ontological pulling from the "not yet" of the still inarticulate future'. (Giroux and MacLaren, 1997: 147–148)

The attainment of self-respect and feeling dignified are essential for the struggle of the landless because, as Freire suggests, 'during the initial stage of the struggle, the oppressed, instead of striving for liberation, tend themselves to become oppressors or sub oppressors. The very structure of their thought has been conditioned by the contradictions of the concrete, existential situation by which they were shaped' (Freire, 1970/1996: 28). 'Self-depreciation' argues Freire is another characteristic of the oppressed which derives from their internalization the opinion of the oppressor holds of them. So often do they hear that they are good for nothing, know nothing and are incapable of learning anything – that they are sick, lazy and unproductive – that in the end they become convinced of their own unfitness (Freire, 1970/1996: 45).

The MST's pedagogical experience is both formal and informal. The MST runs schools for children and adults, and for the children of the settlers in the encampments and settlements. It provides training to promote the values of dignity and self-valorisation, love for oneself and solidarity. The MST forms teachers and cadres. The guiding principles of the MST's education programme are the link between practice and theory, education for work, to take reality as the basis of knowledge, provide useful contents, produce an organic link between educational processes and economic and political processes, undertake the democratic management and self-organisation of students, train teachers, combine individual and collective learning processes and encourage a predisposition to investigate reality (Chassot, 2000: 45).

The content of education is deeply connected to rural work and the formation of cadres is the fundamental pillar of the movement. Both are connected for the MST regards the school as a social and political institution and education as a life-long pedagogical experience that includes everyday cultural practices (Stubrin, 2008: 20). The end of illiteracy (which is common among rural workers) is also a significant goal the MST education *policy*. The *Escola Nacional Florestan Fernandez* (ENFF) National School Florestan Fernandez) – one of the most important MST schools – was opened in January 2005 to 'think, plan, organise and develop the political and ideological formation of the militants and cadres of the MST' (Pizetta, 2007: 246). The political formation of cadres facilitates democratic discussions, training, organising, helping the landless families to fight fear and make the decision to occupy the land, negotiating with local authorities and working at all of the MST organisation events. Education seeks to improve praxis. Education is a learning process of responsible production in harmony with the environment, which means politicisation. Finally, the school also connects rural workers with other movements in Latin America and the Caribbean to jointly repudiate imperialism and construct sisterhood (Deledicque et al., 2008).

The production and reproduction of knowledge does not seek only to appreciate reality but also to transform it. The settlements are 'schools of life' (Branford and Rocha, 2002: 125). The school adopts the Marxist method of historical materialism in order to prioritise an understanding of the present capitalist contradictions and serve the organisation of the working class against the dominant class and imperialism (Pizetta, 2007: 247). The ENFF encourages activities that enable the development of a militant consciousness, uses knowledge for the organising process, produces analysis of the situation and compiles the experience of resistance to exchange experiences and share *vivencias* with other movements (Deledicque et al., 2008). In short, as Pizetta vividly describes it, the MST's approach to learning is 'an on going pedagogical experience of politicisation: learning takes place in infinite and continuous processes of reflection on practice, practice... involves the permanent production and socialisation of new knowledge that emerges out of the concrete experience reality, out of the contradictions of that reality' (Pizetta, 2007: 243).

Mística: *mobilising hope, creating identity*

So far, I have pointed to two elements of the MST: cooperative work and pedagogy. In this section, I explore the third component of the MST's concrete utopia: *mística*. While the term has no English equivalent (Issa, 2007: 126), it can be translated as a form of *política afectiva* (affective politics) (see Chapter 5) that facilitates an emotional experience of the collective, an understanding of the struggle and the mobilisation of feeling of love, friendship, solidarity and, above all, the belief in the possibility of change (Issa, 2007). In Chapter 5, I contended that *política afectiva* is an embodied form of politics that relies on the human capacity to 'being singular plural' (Nancy, 2000). Although emotions are central to the process of mobilisation and further engagement with the social struggle, they have been neglected in the study of social movements (see Aminazade and McAdam, 2011) and Marxist analyses alike.

The MST's *mística* is a central element of the MST's life. It is the glue that keeps the movement's fabric composed without closing up its pores and fibres. *Mística* mobilises feelings of happiness, joy, engagement, dignity, love and comradely work, and enables the MST to function as a vast network social-movement organisation. *Mística* defies the separation between the individual being and the collective. *Mística* appeals to (paraphrasing Spinoza) the joyful passions, which unlike 'sad passions' – the realm of power and misery – 'are in tune with the very effort for the perseverance of the being, the essential force of men [and women]' (Kaminsky on Spinoza in Kaminsky, 1998: 327–328). *Mística* possesses a transformative effect on individual self-esteem and collective self-determination and has an adverse effect on power. While it builds up confidence in the struggle among MST members, it simultaneously projects a different picture of the landless to the powerful: it rejects the image of fragmented, miserable and subordinated 'landless people' to portray, instead, dignified rural workers who are organising hope against inhuman conditions and cynical policy.

The *mística* is 'a pedagogy of empowerment' that 'narrates history and experience, reviving the collective memory of the Brazilian peasantry and ultimately contributing to the formation of a collective Sem terra identity' (Issa, 2007: 125).

The *mística* gives the movement a great moral force and faith in victory that transpire and infect you with joy and confidence in the future (Harnecker, 2002: 15). *Mística* is used in the schools with music and poetry, songs, dance flags, hymns, images, narratives in national marches and internal and network meetings, and in the ritual of cutting the wire and moving beyond ... . MST's militants explain: 'without mística there cannot be militants. We get nourished from this ... How do you face fear and stay away from your family? One of the legacies of the movement is militancy based on, mística and love for the cause' (Clarice, MST militant, cited in Issa, 2007: 129). Peloso (MST) regards *mística* as a vital and mysterious projection of hope. It is:

> the determination that springs from our indignation against injustice and from our belief in the very real possibility of building a new society. ... It is an injection of vitality, which gives us determination and daring so that we can overcome pessimism and push ahead with our project for including the excluded in the liberation of the Brazilian people. (Peloso, 1997, translated by Branford and Rocha, 2002: 29–30)

In the same way that Bloch rejects the idea of hope as a naïve belief in a better and an abstract utopia, Peloso argues that the *mística* 'is the "soul of the left" that generates the necessary "claws" to fight injustices and the disposition to engage in the historical concretion of our dreams'.

The MST with and against and beyond state, development and agribusiness

So far, I have discussed two forms in which the MST ventures beyond the wire: by occupying the land (negation) and by articulating a concrete utopia at the settlements (creation). In the next section, I discuss the third form of venturing beyond the wire: how the MST navigates the contradictions brought about by the relationship with the state, landowners and agribusiness. I examine the MST's proposal of a new type of agrarian reform (the peasant agricultural model), the contentious relationship with both the neoliberal and the pink tide governments, against and beyond the market-led and policy leading to the commodification of the settlements. Is the MST producing a surplus possibility that is untranslatable in the grammar of the state, capital and the law?

Present neoliberal agrarian policies in Brazil were shaped under FHC's government (Sauer, 2006: 179). During his first period in office, FHC implemented an active land distribution policy (Mançano Fernandes, 2003). But during his second period in office, he was ideologically trans- formed. He adhered to a market-driven agrarian reform that criminalised the struggle of the landless (Mançano Fernandes, 2003: 34).[6] Criminali- sation of the struggles of the landless became the policy that punished those rural families who participated in occupations by excluding them from the state-led process of settling families legally in the occupied land.

The WB 'New Rural World' programme launched in 1998 was based on three issues: the use of land reform to alleviate rural poverty instead of using the democratisation of the land as a tool to develop the economy; 'decentralisation of all landholding actions', that is, the delegation of power from the federal government to local authorities – which does not mean democratisation but the predominance of the will of powerful landowners over the landless and Brazilian society; and the 'commodi- fication of landless farmworkers' historic demands', that is, the 'market- oriented land reform' (Sauer, 2006: 179).

The government's tight focus on controlling rural workers' strug- gles intensified the conflict in the countryside. In 2000, the MST was involved in 80 trials and ten of its cadres were assassinated (Mançano Fernandes, 2008: 355). FHC attacked the MST's wave of occupations and massive marches against his neoliberal policy by stating that the move- ment had 'crossed the line', that is, 'overstepped the limits of democ- racy' (Branford and Rocha, 2002: 204).

During the late 1990s, state policy intended to transform the settle- ments into a tool for business and decentralised governance by means of the competitive insertion of settlements in the market, inducing farmers to embrace corporate behaviour and by passing onto the settlement administrative tasks that were previously realised by the federal govern- ment (like the construction of roads). The government's intention was to 'emancipate' the settlements from the MST's rule and, in two years' time, transform them into 'family farms' (Servolo Medeiros, 2000: 43). As in the other cases, decentralisation – the backbone of neoliberal govern- ance – disputed the meaning of autonomy and used them as a tool for the implementation of a policy that was adverse to those living in these territories. It is true that this policy increased the participation of repre- sentatives of rural workers organisations in the State Rural Development Councils, Regional Councils and Municipal Development Councils. However, the decentralisation of management atomised rural workers and weakened rural workers movements, making them more dependent on local governments (Servolo Medeiros, 2000), and therefore on the power of landowners who had influence on the local governments.

The arrival of the PT to power (which counted on the active militant support of the MST) brought about high expectations about the possibility of implementing the MST's encompassing proposal of agrarian reform, but the PT betrayed its promise. While as a presidential candidate during his election campaign 'Lula' Da Silva had claimed that 'with one flourish of my pen I'm going to give you so much land that you won't be able to occupy it all' (Branford, 2005: 56), as president of Brazil, he abandoned the idea of the agrarian reform altogether. In order to arrive in power, the PT had formed an alliance with forces that range from the left (MST, CUT) to the right (*ruralistas*). While the MST and other agrarian movements could participate in the election of representatives and technicians who run the INCRA and wrote the National Plan for the agrarian reform, the pressure from the right put a limit to the possibility of attaining the MST's dream through the state, following the two proposal designed by professor Plínio de Arruda Sampaio, which were rejected by the PT government.

The PT's neoliberal approach to agrarian reform led to another escalation of social conflict and violence. In 2004, the MST launched its 'Red April' that consisted of 80 occupations throughout Brazil. In 2003, there had been 73 murders of landless workers, and 68 murders in 2004 in the state of Mato Grosso alone (Deledicque et al., 2008). In June 2003, MST's activists undertook their third action against Monsanto by occupying a 307-hectare farm in the central state of Goiás: 'There is torrid debate in Brazil over whether genetically modified (GM) crops should be let in amid mounting pressure on the government from the multinationals' (BBC News, 3 June 2003). MST leader, Luiz Arantes, argued that Monsanto Goiás is an 'illegal centre' that produces GM. The MST worried about the legalisation of GM which will force small farmers out of business' (BBC News, 3 June 2003).[7] The MST also continued working for public support:

> From 1 May until 17 May 2005, thousands of Brazil's rural workers [began] their 180 mile journey in the "National March for Land Reform". They march[ed] from Goiânia and converge[d] on the capital of Brazil to deliver a message to the public and the governing Workers Party: land reform is the critical path to Brazil's development of social equality, food security and a vibrant civil society. Your contribution to this effort is crucial to the success of this march. (Porto-Gonçalves, 2005)

The MST also demanded the punishment of the murderers of rural workers, the demarcation of indigenous lands and peoples of African descent, the democratization of the media, the requirement of consultation processes, the rejection of GM products in the laboratories, water and preservation soil and biodiversity and crop (Porto-Gonçalves, 2005).

Let us note that in 2008, Brazil scored as the global champion in the consumption of toxic agrichemicals, many of them forbidden in other countries, according to the UN. Frei Betto (2012) highlights that 50 per cent of these chemical products are applied in the cultivation of soya, which is exported for animal fodder:

> Toxic agrichemicals do not only contaminate food. They also degrade the soil and prejudice biodiversity. They affect the quality of the air, of water and of the land. And all this because they have been granted a green light by three ministries, in which they are analyzed before coming to market: Health, Agriculture and Environment. (Frei Betto, 2012)

The PT's paradigm of agrarian capitalism believes that a solution to the agrarian question can be found in the *integration* of rural workers' communitarian production into the capitalist market. The role of the state is, then, to provide credit to impoverished sectors and encourage the buying of the land through the Land Bank (*Banco de la Tierra*) with support of the WB. As already mentioned, this 'agrarian reform' translates the MST settlements into 'family farms' and reflects the pink tide's obedience to the new international development approach towards the appropriation of some forms of autonomous organising at the grassroots and their translation into tools of 'alternative development'. The implementation of this new policy approach in Brazil necessitated the creation of new peasant movements related to the CUT and the PT, such as the Federation of Family Agriculture Movement of the South region (*Federação dos Trabalhadores na Agricultura Familiar da Região Sul*, FETRAF-SUL). The policy is presented as an innovation in agrarian policy. The reason given is that it prevents rural workers from falling deeper into poverty. Yet, it is far from presenting a 'new' development model (Servolo Medeiros, 2000).

Moreover, the patchy allocation of land that was initially supported by the MST with the promotion of 'family agriculture' constitutes a perverse policy, for it empowers the agribusiness sector by transforming the MST's settlements into the means for profit making: rural workers and farmers must purchase technology, machinery, pesticides, seeds and fertilizers from the transnational conglomerates. WB development economists belief that the 'redistribution of land to small farmers would lead to *greater overall productivity and economic dynamism*' (Courville and Patel, 2006: 7).

The Economist Intelligence Unit 2010 report on Brazilian agribusiness emphasises the high performance of companies that operate in Brazil:

> Brazil is in a unique position to lead the global agricultural sector in the medium to the long term. With an abundant supply of natural resources – water, land and a favourable climate – it has the opportunity to be the largest agribusiness superpower, supplying the world market while also providing affordable food for its own population. (Economist Intelligence Unit, 2010: 2–3)[8]

In short, the perversion of this policy does not only rely on the fact that Brazilian agribusiness industry and transnational conglomerates are blooming, but that their success *depends on* the misery of rural workers, either because they are whose farming is made absolutely dependent on transnational conglomerates like Monsanto or because they are still waiting for a piece of land and struggling for food.

With President Dilma Rousseff (who took office in 2011), the power of transnational agribusiness was strengthened. The agribusiness sector has become hegemonic within the government, so that rural workers' achievements at the MST's settlements are at a stalemate with regards to making improvements in production. The MST considers this a temporary defeat in their struggle for the agrarian reform vis-a-vis the state. In a long-awaited meeting with the president on 23 February 2014, the MST leaders expressed these concerns and presented their proposal once again. Atiliana Brunetto, leader of the movement, brought with her a basket full of products from the MST settlements. As she was handing the basket to her president, Brunetto said: 'Here it is what we consider life, represented in our food, seeds and crafts and our symbols' (cited by Albuquerque, 2014b).

Sitting around an oval table, the MST's leaders explained that the provisional measure for the agrarian reform recently launched that allows the settlers to sell their land, is a regressive measure for it would lead to a reconcentration of lands in few hands, providing that agribusiness are into land-grabbing and offer significant amounts of money for these lands. The MST also complained about the conservative stand of INCRA, and suggested creating an inter-ministerial level of administration in order to coordinate action because the institute is managed in a conservative way that does not correspond to the reality of the rural workers. They also discussed the need to solve the problem of more than 100,000 families who are still waiting for their land, 60 per cent of which are located in the northeast of Brazil (MST website, Albuquerque, 2014a).

Let me summarize the MST's Popular Agrarian Reform programme:

(i)   To produce food for the Brazilian people and not for export;
(ii)   To change the technological matrix for food production, by implementing agro ecology (i.e., the production of healthy food without the use of toxic agrochemicals in harmony with the environment, preservation of biodiversity, without destroying local vegetation or contaminating soil, water, rivers and subterranean water;
(iii) To develop agroindustry in the countryside to add value to the products and generate income for farmers, for those incomes to remain in the hands of farmers – and not in the hands of big transnational corporations – towards job creation in the countryside; and
(iv)   To organise cultural and recreational activities and education in the countryside.

This proposal aims to eradicate poverty in rural areas; fight against social inequality and the degradation of nature, which is derived from the structure of property; guarantee better life conditions for all people and job opportunities, income, education, culture and leisure, encouraging their permanency in rural areas, particularly the youth; guarantee gender equality in the countryside; and preserve vegetation and animal biodiversity (MST website).[9]

Venturing beyond: food sovereignty

As I was writing this chapter between 10 to 14 February 2014, more than 16,000 delegates from 23 estates and the federal district gathered at the VI (Sixth) MST Congress in Brasília, titled 'Fighting to Create a Popular Agrarian Reform' ('¡Luchar, Construir Reforma Agraria Popular!'). At the Congress, the MST celebrated its thirtieth birthday with a debate about how to tackle the imposition of a model of agro production that responds to transnational capital. The MST characterised the current situation as intolerable, deeming 2013 as the worst year for the agrarian reform. It is surely not only a struggle against traditional *latifundio* but against transnational agribusiness and financial capital. The industry bought 30 million of hectares of land in the last 20 years. The prevalence of an agro-export model based on *monocultivo* affects food production. While food production was reduced from 35 to 20 per cent, the sugar cane industry (for ethanol) soared to 122 per cent (MST, Houtart, 2014). Following Houtart, the other significant problem discussed by the MST at the annual congress was transgenics: Mato Grosso, the great producer of transgenic soya, imports 90 per cent of food from other states, yet six million people were displaced from their lands. The movement denounced that Brazil has the higher proportion of use of toxics in the world (five kilograms per inhabitant). According to the MST, in 2013 the country imported six million tons of fertilizers and exported 18 million tons of corn to the USA.

Brazil, highlights Houtart (2014) 'has never had classic agrarian reform promoted by industrial bourgeoisie but went directly from *latifundio* to agribusiness. This caused environmental destruction (particularly Amazonia), job destruction and rural migration. The new government's coalition with conservative parties is suffering the pressure of the ruralistas who have the media support. Agribusiness prevails in agrarian policy. In these circumstances, how to define a strategy? This is the MST's challenge' (Houtart, 2014).

In 2004, the MST shifted its strategy and embraced agrarian reform with a new emphasis on *food sovereignty*. By so doing, the MST moved forward to articulate a demand that *escapes translation*. The VC coined the term 'food sovereignty' in 1996, in order to emphasise that no agrarian reform can be successful without the right of the peoples of the world to decide democratically on the production and consumption of food. Jointly with the VC, the MST has been advocating and campaigning for 'a new type of agrarian reform that is not limited to the distribution of land...we must build our own agro cooperatives...We must democratise education...we must develop an appropriate new environment...we must prioritize the reorganisation of agriculture to produce food and work for people' (Stédile, 2004: 33). The MST and the VC created the Social Movements Network (SMN) in order to coordinate action in the struggle for food sovereignty with a focus on unemployment.

It is important to point to the fundamental difference between both food security and food sovereignty. Food security is a term used by the UN Food and Agriculture Organisation (FAO) to describe a 'condition' that exists when 'all people, at all times, have physical, social and economic access to sufficient, safe and nutritious food which meets their dietary needs and food preferences for an active and healthy life'.[10] Food security does not ask where food comes from, 'or the conditions under which it is produced and distributed. National food security targets are often met by sourcing food produced under environmentally destructive and exploitative conditions, and supported by subsidies and policies that destroy local food producers but benefit agribusiness corporations' (Declaration of Nyéléni, International Forum on Food Sovereignty, Mali, 2007). Instead, food sovereignty

> emphasizes ecologically appropriate production, distribution and consumption, social-economic justice and local food systems 'as ways to tackle hunger and poverty and guarantee sustainable food security for all peoples. It advocates trade and investment that serve the collective aspirations of society. It promotes community control of productive resources; agrarian reform and tenure security for small-scale producers; agro-ecology; biodiversity; local knowledge; the rights of peasants, women, indigenous peoples and workers; social protection and climate justice. (Declaration of Nyéléni, International Forum on Food Sovereignty, Mali, 2007)

While food security can provide a patchy and temporary solution to the problem of hunger, *food sovereignty* confronts agribusiness with the hope for a democratic and autonomous agrarian project: 'Food sovereignty challenges the market-led agrarian reform in favour of agribusiness and at the expense of peasants' lives. ... Food sovereignty then alludes to an inalienable right to food and requires a radical and more comprehensive process than "securing" food to eliminate hunger in the world' (Nyéléni Newsletter, 2013: 1).[11]

The final declaration of the World Forum on Food Sovereignty, held in Havana, Cuba, on 7 September 2001 (Civil society preparatory meeting for World Food Summit + 5), states that

> Food sovereignty implies the implementation of a radical process of comprehensive agrarian reform adapted to the conditions of each country and region, which will provide peasants and indigenous farmers – with equal opportunities for women – with equitable access to productive resources, primarily land, water and forests, as well as the means of production, financing, training and capacity building for management and interlocution. (Rosset, 2006b: 301)

The VC did not just use existing rights to defend the right to food. With the concept of food sovereignty, the global peasant movement has *created* a new right, thus 'institutionalizing subversion' (Clayes, 2012). By developing an alternative food paradigm to market economy of food security and by 2), the VC and the MST 'contribute to shaping a cosmopolitan, multicultural, and anti-hegemonic conception o human rights'.

In 2002, Jean Ziegler, Special Rapporteur of the UN Commission on Human Rights from the Right to Food Programme, described 'the right to food is a human right that is protected by international law' (cited in Rosset, 2006b: 301). This means a right to have 'regular, permanent and unobstructed access either direct or by means of financial purchases, to quantitatively and qualitatively adequate and sufficient food corresponding to cultural traditions of the people to which the consumer belong, and ensuring a physical and mental, individual and collective, fulfilling and dignified life free from anxiety. Governments have a legal [and not only political or moral] obligation to respect, protect and fulfill the right to food' (cited in Rosset, 2006b: 301).

In this vein, the MST proposes to replace the existing agro-business model with a 'peasant agricultural model' which embraces food sovereignty as a right and exists in the settlements, which are templates of a new practice here and now (Sampaio, 2005). This 'model' prioritises family needs, as well as preservation, of the quality of the land. It attaches great importance to the use of non-aggressive techniques for the environment. As Arruda Sampaio highlights, 'the basic assumption of the model is its integration into a non-capitalist development of the economy, based on the universalisation of decent standards of consumption for the entire population in order to not only eliminate poverty, but also to eliminate social inequality that exist in the countries of the continent' (Arruda Sampaio, 2005: 20–21).

The integration of the demand for food sovereignty to the proposal of agrarian reform in Brazil reformulates the movement's approach against the government's commodification of the settlements. This reform has become serviceable to agribusiness for the latter monopolises both the input and the output moments of the commodity chain, subordinating small farmers to transnational conglomerates like Monsanto. Food sovereignty, instead, implies much more than a patchy agrarian reform: it requires a radical social, political and economic transformation of the Brazilian countryside by means of a global struggle to the agrarian reform *with* food sovereignty, and this escapes the possibility of translation into the logic of the state and capital (Dinerstein and Ferrero, 2012). Food sovereignty is an essential component of a democratic agrarian reform (World Development Movement, 2013)[12] that opposes 'the policies and programmes for the commercialization of land promoted by the World Bank instead of true agrarian reforms by governments' (Rosset, 2006b: 301; VC and IPC, 2006).

But to the MST, the attainment of a true agrarian reform in Brazil depends on the peoples' self-organising capacity. The MST, Porto-Gonçalves (2005: 22) suggests, has tried to maintain a delicate balance between institutionalisation and autonomy. Instead of visualising how to take power, the MST has undertaken the mundane and contradictory task of creating spaces for autonomy in the occupations, encampments, settlements and schools. The MST sees the state as a mediation of the struggle and the need to cover immediate needs, but not as a final goal.

Conclusion: untranslatability

In the previous sections, I explored three ways in which the MST 'ventures beyond the wire', thus contributing to both the process of transcending the demarcated reality of landlessness and the construction of an alternative reality. By exploring the process of occupying the land, shaping concrete utopia and navigating contradictions vis-à-vis the state, I pointed to the creation of a concrete utopia in the settlements and the intricate and contested relation between the MST and the state, the predicaments that the MST navigates permanently and through which it encounters moments of disappointment.

I contend that the demand of agrarian reform with food sovereignty is 'excessive', i.e. creates an untranslatable excess. Like democracy, self-management, dignified work and indigenous autonomy, food sovereignty is a 'utopian demand' (Weeks, 2011: 176). As argued in Chapter 5, it goes beyond a pragmatic reform and embraces a more encompassing transformation of social relations (Weeks, 2011: 176) (i.e., capitalist, patriarchal and colonial). This is a demand that engages with the reality of the *not yet*, in accordance to the material conditions provided by the context. This project is untranslatable into the logic of the state and capital but, as we have seen, it can be anticipated through autonomous organising.

The MST's 'pedagogy of the oppressed' and the *mística* enable the *conscientização* (i.e., the transformation of the *not yet* consciousness into knowledge) of the conditions and dynamics that led to landlessness and the potential to create an alternative to it.

The MST greatest achievement has been, perhaps, that their struggle for another demarcation of the land meant also a struggle for another demarcation of the reality of 'landlessness'. This required courage, hope and a learning process that the MST undertakes at every instance of the movement activities.

When he won the elections in 2003, President Lula da Silva announced that the aim of his government could be considered fulfilled '*if* all Brazilians could have breakfast, lunch and dinner every day'. We can hear now the silence of this well-intentioned but failed promise. Commenting on his theatrical play titled *The Chairs*, the founder and genius of the theatre of the absurd, Eugène Ionesco once said: 'to give unreality to reality one must give reality to the unreal, until the point is reached – inadmissible, unacceptable to the reasoning mind – when the unreal elements speak and move...and the nothingness can be heard, is made concrete' (cited in Eslin, 1991: 152). The MST has done both: it has made hunger *unreal* and has transformed the vague *possibility* of an agrarian social reform that can serve the purpose of the realisation of millions of Brazilian landless rural workers into one of the most compelling *realities* of Brazilian political economy and a rural world in crisis. In the next chapter, I further explore the nature of the excess produced by the art of organising hope.

Part III
Rethinking Autonomy

8
Confronting Value with Hope: Towards a Prefigurative Critique of Political Economy

Introduction: defying theoretical boundaries

In my review of the four modes of autonomy and their conversion into the key of hope (Chapters 2 and 3), I posed the question of whether autonomous organising is a praxis that fluctuates eternally between rebellion and integration or whether there is anything else to autonomy that can informs its political virtues to produce radical change? I suggested that when the Zapatistas, the QSVT movements, the Network for the Defence of Water and Life and the MST cross boundaries and venture beyond 'the wire', they create a surplus possibility or excess that escapes translation. By excess I mean an untranslatable aspect of the autonomous praxis that constitutes both a threat to capital and a source of inspiration for the movements. In this chapter, I discuss the nature of excess and offer a *prefigurative critique of political economy*. This method reads Marx's critique of political economy in the key of hope. This does not mean that I will engage directly with Marx's views on alternatives to capitalism (see Hudis, 2012) but emphasise Marx's critique of political economy as a prefigurative method and epistemology. As argued in Chapter 3, Bloch reads Marx as a not yet theory, as a philosophy of the future, as a method that takes us in the right direction, puts us in motion, in contact with our inner self and with hope, the expectant emotion that strives for radical thinking and equips us with the capacity to organise hope collectively.

As we have seen in Chapter 2, the Puebla School theorises 'excess' by engaging with Adorno's negative dialectics. Adorno overrules the resolution of the dialectic contradiction in a positive synthesis. To Tischler (2009: 103), the particularity – a critical category – 'expresses the surplus of the existing confronted with what is dominant, or the system, a surplus or excess created by social antagonism'. Autonomy is explained as the refutation of any homogenisation and identity. The latter, claims Holloway, 'is the standpoint of traditional Marxism' (Holloway, 2010a: 205). By theorising the totality, communism becomes 'an alternative social synthesis' rather than the 'breaking of the social synthesis'. The capitalist social synthesis, highlights Holloway, is maintained with the continual subordination of human practice (doing) to the value-creation process as the latter self-expands (Dinerstein, 2012), but this does not mean 'total' subordination. Total subordination is impossible (Holloway, 2010a: 173). There is excess and excess is a mismatch produced by the impossibility of complete transformation of human practice (doing) into abstract labour (value and money): 'concrete doing is not, and cannot be, totally subordinated to abstract labour. There is a non-identity between them: doing does not fit into abstract labour without a reminder. There is always a surplus, an overflowing. There is always a pushing in different directions' (Holloway, 2010a: 173).

The 'cracks' occur at the interstices of capitalism. The cracks, argues Holloway, 'clash with the rule of value' (Holloway, 2010a: 65). While we can intuitively accept that the method of the crack constantly interrupts the fluidity of the 'capitalist synthesis' (Holloway, 2010), or what Negri calls 'the fabric of capitalism' (1991: 115), this is not self-evident.

Let's us bring back Bloch's notion of the not yet discussed in Chapter 3. The *not yet* is a category that is central to human action, a category that, as Mittleman highlights, Bloch makes an 'attractive force…, a nothing that acts as something' (Mittleman, 2009: 188). The not yet, argues Bloch, is what renders reality its quality of Real:

> Real possibility … it is the specific regional character of reality itself, on the Front of its occurrence. How else could we explain the future-laden properties of matter? There is no true realism without the true dimension of this openness. (Bloch, 1959/1986: 237–238)

The *not yet* challenges objectivity and facticity. Facts do not explain 'real' issues such as landlessness, unemployment or poverty. To Bloch, facts are 'simply processes', i.e. 'dynamic relationships in which the Become has not completely triumphed' (Bloch, 1959/1986: 196–197). For example, 'the fact of unemployment' depends on a particular form of work, i.e. capitalist work and the subsequent type of society it creates, i.e. capitalist society. Both the reality and the concept of unemployment hide the possibility of not being unemployed, not by finding a job in the labour market but by conceiving work in alternative ways. The possibility of not being unemployed does not rest in the solution to the problem of 'unemployment' via state policy, but in the possibility to demarcate a reality beyond unemployment as a 'fact'. Each fact contains its negation within it. Each fact is incomplete, for it conceals the possibility of an alternative to it. Bloch proposes that

> the world as it exists is not true. There exists a second concept of truth, which is not positivistic, which is not founded on a declaration of facticity, on 'verification' through the 'facts' but which is instead loaded with value (*wertgeladen*) – as, for example, in the concept of 'true friend', ... the kind of storm one finds in a book, a poetic storm, the kind that reality has never witnessed, a storm carried to the extreme, a radical storm and therefore a *true* storm ... And if that doesn't correspond to the facts – and for us Marxists, facts are only reified moments of a process – in that case, *too bad for the facts* (*um so schlimmer für die Tatsachen*), as Hegel said in his late period. (Bloch and Löwy, 1976: 37–38, italics in the original)

A key question of this chapter is whether autonomous organising in Latin America has opened a dimension of the real that does not 'correspond to the facts' (Dinerstein, 2014a). If so, how can we unveil and grasp this non-factual dimension of autonomous organising? To be sure, at this point, we are required to reflect on the nature of our enquiry, and move from the question of *translation* – and the subsequent concern with the dangers of the appropriation of autonomy by the state – which emphasises the weakness of autonomy and the power of the state and capital, to the question of *untranslatability,* and the beauty of prefiguration. Following Vázquez: 'What is that which remains untranslatable, outside the scope of translation? What is excluded from its movement of incorporation?' (Vázquez, 2011: 36). The question of untranslatability requires, as Bonefeld argues, that we 'think out of things' in order to 'discover their social constitution' (Bonefeld, 2009: 128). The task of critical theory is to reveal the struggle that underpins the 'naturalised' world of capital. As I have shown in Part II of the book, this cannot be done abstractly. While thinking means venturing beyond, we must venture beyond

> in such a way that what *already exists is not kept under or skated over* ... real venturing beyond never goes into the mere vacuum of an In-Front-of-Us, merely fanatically, merely visualizing abstractions. Instead, it grasps the New as something that is mediated in what

> exists and is in motion, although to be revealed the New demands
> the most extreme effort of will. (Bloch, 1959/1996: 4, my italics)

Marx's critique of political economy in the key of hope, or, as I have
called this method, the prefigurative critique of political economy
enables us to uncover the second concept of true that Bloch refers to, the
truth that exists beyond facticity. The prefigurative critique of political
economy is itself a process of theoretical prefiguration that follows the
movement of autonomous organising, the forms of which depend on
the movements' struggles. The critique acknowledges the uncertainty
and ambivalence in the practice of theorising (Gibson-Graham, 2006:
xxxi). By linking hope, the *not yet* and the value form, I substantiate the
claim that autonomy is politically relevant as the art of organising hope
because the politics of autonomy confront value with hope.

Autonomy: a *real* abstraction

Political economy treats social *forms* (labour, money) as naturally given
features of society. Marx did not offer an alternative political economy
or an economic critique but a critique of political economy, that is a
critique that challenges the categories of political economy. Marx's
method reveals the social, political, economic, legal, cultural, identitarian, *forms* through which capitalism is naturalised. In this way, Marx
did not seek to criticise just bourgeois political economy, 'but the notion
of political economy as such' (Bonefeld et al., 1992a: xiii). He revealed
how the categories of political economy are formal abstractions, that
is concepts that are abstracted from the reality of struggle and therefore delineate a reality that can exist in detachment from the reality
of struggle, as if the struggle belongs to a separate domain of life and
hence of study. This displacement of categories from the reality of their
own production (Dinerstein and Neary, 2002a), i.e. class, becomes a
descriptor and allows political economy to present the capitalist world
as 'it is', as *the* world.

I claim that autonomy or the art of organising hope is about prefiguring alternative realities by transcending the demarcations of the capitalist, patriarchal and colonial ones. Hence, a prefigurative critique of
political economy relies on *real* abstractions. What is the difference?
Formal abstractions (categories) describe a world as it is presented
before our eyes, and as we experience it, they seem to be simple tools
to understand 'reality'. In the famous paragraphs of the introduction
to *Grundrisse* –'a fundamental work of demystification' (Negri, 1991:
155) – Marx discusses the (political) *problem* of formal abstractions of

the method of political economy: 'It seems to be correct to begin with the real and the concrete, with the real precondition, thus to begin in economics with e.g. the population, which is the foundation and the subject of the entire act of production. However, on closer examination, this proves false' (Marx, 1993: 100). Why? Marx argues that, for example, 'the population is an abstraction if I leave out, for example, the classes of which it is composed. These classes in turn are an empty phrase if I am not familiar with the elements on which they rest. E.g. wage labour, capital, etc.' Marx describes his method (concrete-abstract-concrete):

> the concrete is concrete because it is the concentration of many determinations, hence unity in the diverse. It appears in the process thinking, therefore, as a process of concentration, as a result, not as a point of departure, even though it is the point of departure in reality and hence also the point of departure for observation. (Marx, 1993: 101)

The implication of this is that the concrete is not just what it is, but a real abstraction, that is, it is what it is and it is what is not, because the struggle that underpins the constitution of the category itself is challenged by its 'no form'. That is, the concrete, i.e. poverty, is abstraction *in* reality rather than 'abstractions *of* reality', that is an abstraction *in the social relations which produce them* (Gunn, 1992, emphasis added). With formal abstractions, political economy – and social sciences in general – describes a *reality* without accounting for the fact that such reality and the concepts that explain reality are subjects of class struggle. The formal abstractions of political economy, argues Clarke,

> deny the social character of its fundamental categories and therefore makes these categories into eternal truths that can be distorted by unwise political intervention, but can never be suppressed. In turning its fundamental categories into eternal truths political economy makes the society to which these categories correspond itself an eternal truth. (Clarke, 1991: 85)

With some exceptions, social scientists remain formidably unaware of the fact that the categories they use, say, poverty, do not describe an unfair condition suffered by millions, but a category that emerged out of the dynamic of class struggle. The continuous use of the terms 'poverty and the poor' contribute to the naturalisation and therefore the perpetuation of the society that produce those conditions. The poor, poverty, the population, class, gender, civil society all hide the struggle that inhabits them, and therefore the possibility for the second concept of truth to emerge. They naturalise capitalism as the only possible society against which everything else is measured. However, as Clarke clearly indicates, 'denaturalising' formal abstractions entails a political task, that is inextricably interlocked with denaturalising capitalist society (Clarke, 1992: 140). Formal abstractions, argues Clarke, are not 'ideological devices' to be revealed (i.e. false consciousness), but reflect the fetishised world of capital as we experience it:

> the mystification of political economy does not simply represent an ideological inversion of reality, but the ideological expression of that inversion. This is why the critique of political economy is not simply a critique of a mystificatory ideology, but of the alienated forms of social life which political economy describes but cannot explain. (Clarke, 1992: 140)

Gunn highlights that 'Marx ... places his theorisation at the mercy of his world of determinate abstractions, counting upon their movement. Nothing in the world subsequent to Marx suggests that the contradictions he signalled have ceased to move' (Gunn, 1994: 57–58). Moreover, 'that movement was his object of analysis' (Gunn, 1994: 57–58). In Part II of the book I put the notion of autonomy at the mercy of the movement of struggle that underpins the movements' collective actions.

My analysis is informed by autonomy as a real abstraction. Understood as a real abstraction, autonomy becomes a category and practice that is necessarily embedded within the struggles in and against the value form. Autonomy does not simply describe social movement 'practices' (formal abstraction), but 'determinate social processes' (Clarke, 1992: 141). The critique of formal abstractions enables the investigation of veiled material processes of struggle which foster historical social forms that mediate the production of both order and insubordination. 'Real' includes contradiction and potential possibility within it. As Gunn illuminates: 'Marx was the first and only social theorist to make "abstraction in" (otherwise: determinate or substantive abstraction) the sole coin of his own theoretical work' (Gunn, 1994: 56). To be sure, as Elson highlights, Marx's method, cannot provide with a 'Cartesian Absolute Knowledge of the world, its status as true knowledge validated by some epistemological principle' (Elson, 1979: 143) because the knowledge is about an 'object' whose existence as well as the forms achieved by it, depend on human praxis. The method of determinate abstractions reveals the historical movement of constitution and transformation of both social relations and the concepts created to understand them. In Marx's words (Marx, 1995: 119, italics in the original),

> The same men who establish their social relations in conformity with the material productivity, produce also principles, ideas, and categories, in conformity with their social relations. Thus the ideas, these categories, are as little eternal as the relations they express. They are *historical and transitory products*. There is a continual movement of growth in productive forces, of destruction in social relations, of formation in ideas; the only immutable thing is the abstraction of movement – *mors immortalis*.

Value and hope as unrealised materialities

Marx's critique of political economy reveals the mystery that underpins capitalism: the value form, which, I contend, is the key to grasp the process of prefiguration and the nature of the excess produced by the politics of autonomy. In this section, I speak of the non-facticity of both value and hope. But first, let me briefly reflect on the significance of abstract labour to my proposal that autonomy is the art of organising hope. According to Marx, the self-expansion of capital is the expansion of indifference 'toward any specific kind of labour'. Indifference, argues Cleaver,

> is not that of the workers, who may have very distinct preferences, but is that of capital ... It is this social dimension of work that is designated, at least in a part, by what Marx calls the 'substance of value' or 'abstract labour', is measured by socially necessary labour time and has the form of exchange. Thus value is the conceptual tool for analysing human activities incorporated into capital as work. (Cleaver, 2002: 14)

Indeed to Marx, (1990: 138) 'commodities possess an objective character as values only in so far as they are all expressions of an identical social substance, human labour, that their objective character as values is therefore purely social'. To Marx 'human labour power in its fluid state, or human labour, creates value, but it is not itself value. It becomes value in its coagulated state, in objective form' (Marx, 1990: 142). Abstract labour is not related to the natural property of the commodity but is about homogenised human labour time that acts as equivalence between commodities. Concrete labour is mediated by and becomes socially realised through its opposite – abstract labour – regardless of the concrete form of exploitation of labour. Abstract labour is the specific form of existence of human practice in capitalist society. As argued elsewhere, 'there is a real ground to labour, but the ground to labour is not material: the ground is a social relation. In such a situation, labour is not recognised, validated or rendered equivalent as a result of any intrinsic capacity or social need, but only to the extent that it forms a part of this social generality' (Dinerstein and Neary, 2002b: 234).

As Holloway highlights, the capitalist synthesis is attained by subordinating doing (my concrete capacity to work and create) *into* abstract labour (a measurement and a form of existence of work, and the substance of value). What constitutes the substance of value is not, then, *concrete* labour, my flesh and human energy, but abstract labour – abstracted from concrete labour, something that is immaterial 'which has nothing corporeal about it' (Marx, 1993: 309).

Despite its un-substantiality, value in motion dominates the social, expands across the whole existential condition (Lilley and Papadopoulos, 2014). As Negri (1991: 148) put it, value is 'pure and simple command, the pure and simple form of politics'. But value is invisible:

> Marx not only speaks of a 'phantom-like objectivity' ... or 'purely fantastic objectivity' ... but also says that value is 'invisible' ... in commodities. Or as Bellofiore [2009: 185] put it, strictly speaking, value 'is a *ghost*', which achieves materiality in the form of money. (Bonefeld, 2010: 266)

While the term 'self-expansion' indicates that capital is self-driven this does *not* mean that capital moves 'regardless' concrete work. Abstract labour cannot be separated from concrete labour. Labour is concrete and remains *concrete* (Chibber, 2013; Bonefeld, 2010). Capital ultimately depends on it. Capital is labour but in capital labour exists in a 'form of being denied' (Gunn, 1992: 23). While capital's indifference toward specific kinds of work do not matter in terms of the expansion of capital as form of production and reproduction of human society, as Negri argues 'capital *constitutes* society' (1991: 114, my italics), the deployment of 'concrete labour' and its forms of organisation and resistance matter politically. I will return to this point later on when I discuss real subsumption and hope.

The main point I want to make now is that not only value dominates the social, despite it possesses no substance, but that value is an unrealised social reality, is a not yet reality. Value does not exist in the present but has to be realised in the future through money, which anticipates it in the present. As Bonefeld states:

> Labour time as the measure of the magnitude of value is not fixed and given. The labour time that 'was yesterday undoubtedly socially necessary for the production of a yard of linen, ceases to be so today' [*Capital*]. Whether the concrete expenditure of time is valid as socially labour time can only be established *post festum*. The expenditure of concrete labour is thus done 'in the hope, rather that the assurance, that [it] will out to be socially required' [T. Smith]. (Bonefeld, 2014: 135)

We have established that value does not exist as such, it is an unre-alised social reality. Let us look at Bloch's concept of hope again. As argued in Chapter 3, hope possesses a utopian function that enables us to engage with the reality of the *not yet*. Hope expresses a possibility to 'realize something which is not yet anywhere' (Bronner, 1997: 177) but it cannot be ruled out a priori. Hope is a 'dawn forwards ... The singular characteristics are not yet because the sun which radiates its light on everything has not yet rise; it is still dawn, but no longer dark ... hope is not merely a projection of reason, a 'mental crea-tion' of human thought, but an expression of what is really possible' (Bronner, 1997: 177).

Both, then, value and hope, are unrealised materialities. They are not mental creations but material dynamics that are not yet. Both, value and hope, are expansive forces of a totally different kind, but both exist beyond the parameters of legibility of the demarcated reality, and therefore, both require an effort to be conceptualised. They are both mysterious. Value requires to be socially validated and attains concreteness only through the form of money. Hope is an emotion of the cognitive kind that guides action and is material-ised in concrete utopia, which in the case of social utopias remains in constant motion and contradiction. As they are, they cannot be captured by the formal abstractions of political economy, for formal abstractions displace value and hope onto 'descriptors' such as the economy, sociology of emotions, politics. The latter have become scientific, as Holloway highlights, 'by virtue of [their] exclusion of the scream' (Holloway, 1995: 155); that is, by virtue of the exclusion of the struggle that underpins 'economics' and 'politics', as formal abstractions that eliminate the process of struggle within them and the reality they are intending to grasp.

Disputing the content of the not yet: Value and anti-value in motion

As unrealised and invisible forces in motion, value, the emotion of the ghost, and hope, the human emotion, are antagonistic and incompatible. They move in/towards opposite directions. They are antagonistic: capital self-expands as value in motion; hope is 'anti-value in motion' (Dinerstein and Neary, 2002a). Capital subordinates human doing (work, leisure, education, art) to profit making. It does so by including or excluding labour, by integrating or oppressing resistance. Hope drives us in a direction of the unknown, the alternative that is beyond the 'wire'. It pushes us into dangerous waters and exciting experiences in the streets, in uprisings and occupations, that anticipate the future in the present.

The antagonism between value and hope is the antagonism between the possibility of constructing a reality of hopelessness or a reality of hope. Landlessness is hopelessness: a form of subjugation that deprives peasants from their means of survival and/or incorporates them precariously into the labour market for the benefit of transnational conglomerates. The MST's settlements are translated into 'family farms' to suit market-led agrarian reform and agribusiness. But landlessness can also be the pursuit of the land, for dignity, self-respect and food sovereignty. Continuing with the example, the prefigurative critique of political economy enables us to grasp the excess produced by the MST's struggle: while the landless – organised *politically* and autonomously in the MST – confront the government, the landowners, challenge the law and transnational agribusiness conglomerates, at the settlements, the MST's members experience an alternative practice and values that create the possibility for another agrarian reform (i.e., a concrete utopia that contests the WB-led reforms that aim to transform settlements into family farms to suit Monsanto).

In the key of hope, the MST's collective action can be said to be a struggle that *confronts value with hope*. While the former can be observed empirically – and this is where the focus of autonomy vis-à-vis the state usually is on – the latter reveals an *alternative demarcation of reality* that cannot be empirically graspable by the formal abstractions of political economy but that, nonetheless, produces radical change. When hope is organised, the process of valorisation of capital is contested.

If we accept that both value and hope are unrealised in the present, the utopian function of hope not only disrupts the process of valorisation of capital and upsets the 'capitalist synthesis' (Holloway, 2010) but, as anti-value in motion, *disputes the content of the not yet.* To Bloch (1971: 41), the Real 'is that which does not yet exist, which is in quest of itself in the core of things and which is awaiting its genesis in the trend latency of the process.' The not yet is not something that will happen in the future as it is expected or predicted. *The not yet is an unresolved form of the present,* the content of which cannot be decided a priori, for it is marked by class struggle.

As we have seen, the four movements explored in this book ventured beyond what it is and oriented themselves towards something unknown – even when the unknown existed in an oppressed and invisible manner, like in the case of indigenous cosmologies. The possibility to realise concrete utopias is not 'objective' but depends on human praxis. What is at stake when QSVT, the Zapatistas, indigenous-popular movements in Bolivia and the MST ventured beyond the wire is the meaning of the *unrealised materiality: value or hope.*

The contention between value and hope over the content of the not yet is non-factual. It asserts itself as *a struggle over the form of its mediations*; that is, it attains *factuality* as a struggle over democracy, the land and the agrarian reform, justice, workers' self-management, dignified work, indigenous autonomy. The factuality of the struggle over the (im)possibility of autonomy takes differ *political* forms. The analysis of the political struggle between the MST, the state and agribusiness over the agrarian reform, or Aymara insurgency against the privatisation of water do not fully account for the significance of the MST's Aymara insurgency, respectively. In order to account for the excess that emerges out of the art of organising hope, we must translate the struggle between state, agribusiness and the landless into a process through which value is confronted by hope. Hope voices a 'lack' that value expands indifferently. And it is this 'lack' that, once it is acknowledged and mobilised, can move mountains.

Hope imposes a limit to the expansion of value. The politics of autonomy confront the unfettered expansion of an abstraction at the expense of human realisation. In this way the Zapatistas' ¡Ya Basta! was a scream of hope. As anti-value in motion, hope enables movements to generate a surplus or excess that is untranslatable into the grammar of the state, capital and the law. The real radical change brought about by the art of organising hope is invisible to the parameters of the struggle over mediations of the capital relation. It is only when autonomy is regarded as a real abstraction that we can detect the invisible struggle that underpins the value form. Hope confronts value with a second concept of truth that ventures beyond the given.

Subsumption by exclusion: The not yet as indigenous cosmologies

What is the nature of the excess produced by indigenous peoples' art of organising hope? In this section, I explore this question by returning to the issue of *difference* between indigenous and non-indigenous autonomy discussed in Chapter 2. I proposed that we should consider issues of identity as resistance and the meaning of the collective, treat the past as memory, and account for the historical position of indigenous people vis-à-vis capital and the state for an understanding of indigenous people struggles. I suggested that, despite the roots of their oppression, indigenous people are not excluded from, but subsumed, in capital in a specific form which I named 'subsumption by exclusion'. By 'real subsumption by exclusion' I designated a particular case of real subsumption of labour and society in capital that while being part of the process valorisation of capital, it attains the phenomenological form of 'exclusion'. In what follows, I expand on this idea and point to the significance of real subsumption by exclusion for an understanding of the production of excess in the indigenous peoples' art of organising hope. My argument is that the notion of 'real subsumption by exclusion' enables us to do both highlight the significance of indigenous cosmologies as a threat internal to the universalising force of capital, on the one hand, and to recognise particular trajectories of experience of power, oppression and domination and, therefore, of prefiguration, within falling either into Eurocentric or Third World fundamentalisms (Grosfoguel, 2008; 2009), on the other hand.

Post colonial theory, coloniality, race and pluriversality

The 'decolonial turn' (Maldonado-Torres, 2011) in postcolonial theory, produced as a result of a split by a Latin American group within Subaltern Studies,[1] offers a critique of both postcolonial studies and Marxist World-System theory as they emphasise either cultural or structural factors, leading to binary oppositions: discourse/economy and subject/structure. Decolonial scholars criticise postcolonial studies' understanding of global capitalism for they do not analyse how racial discourses organise world populations in an international division of labour that has direct economic effects (Castro-Gómez and Grosfoguel, 2007). Their main point is the role of racial oppression or the invention of racial oppression in the process of class formation in Latin America. The category of 'indio' was invented by the invaders during the colonisation process, with the purpose of dominating indigenous populations by making a clear distinction between European civilisation and progress, and the other (López Bárcenas, 2011: 76). 'Indio' emerged as a social category that was not related to any particular quality of the persons involved but arbitrarily designated 'inferiority'. 'Indio' is, according to Bonfil Batalla (1987), a 'supra-ethnic category' that does not denote any specific content of the groups that it comprises but rather entails the condition of being colonised. 'Internal colonialism' is intrinsic to the process of nation building for it *required* the destruction of indigenous peoples' rights to their communal lands and self-government, and this included the physical elimination of the 'unruly'. This destruction inhabits the postcolonial period and the indigenous struggles for self-determination. In this vein, Grosfoguel (2008) proposes an alternative conceptualisation of race as an 'organizing principle of the international division of labour and of the global patriarchal system'.

The classification of indigenous people as 'inferior races' or as 'different' oppressed the paradigms of life that existed before colonisation. Indigenous cosmologies were invisibilised or, in the best-case scenario, labelled as 'cultural traditions' and lately incorporated via multiculturalism. Decolonial scholars argue that coloniality, (not colonialism), persists in the present. The process of independence in Latin America was *not* a process of real democratisation that dismantled the structures and dynamics of coloniality but meant 'a re-articulation of the coloniality of power over new bases' (Quijano, 2008: 214). 'The mythology of the "decolonization of the world"', argues Grosfoguel (2008), obscures the continuities between the colonial past and current global colonial/ racial hierarchies and contributes to the invisibility of 'coloniality' today. This is not, of course, a Latin American exclusive phenomenon, but a worldwide one. The 'trauma of colonialism permeates all levels of social subjectivity' (Fanon, cited by Moraña et al., 2008: 3).

Quijano (2008: 184) concurs that the formation of the international division of labour in the Spanish-dominated region under the reign of Castilla and Aragon contained a racial division of labour within it. The end of slavery for the Indians (to preclude their complete extermination) led to their serfdom. This social classification and the racial hierarchies of the control over labour continued to expand, providing a specific role to the Indians. Therefore, 'from the beginning of the colonization of America, Europeans associated non-paid or non-waged labour with the dominated races because they were "inferior" races' (Quijano, 2008: 186), or 'savage people in many places of America' (a term used by Hobbes to represent his violent hypothetical 'state of nature') (Santos, 2007b: 3). This has also permeated critical thought and the left's treatment of the issue of 'race'. The example of Argentina is paradigmatic in this respect.

General Roca's infamous military 'conquest of the desert' in Argentine Patagonia in 1879 as a strategic action towards the formation of the modern nation-state illustrates this point. Roca's genocide obliterated indigenous people who were considered a fetter to the civilisation (*civilizatorio*) process led by the liberal 'Generation of the 80s'. Once indigenous people were physically obliterated from the extensive territory of Patagonia and, as the provincial *caudillos* were being defeated by the liberal elite of Buenos Aires, a new labour force – among which there were many anarchist, socialist and syndicalist workers – was brought from Europe. These workers were the protagonists of the struggle in Rebel Patagonia, where 3,000 rural workers, who were on strike in Río Gallegos, Santa Cruz, were slaughtered by means of a military operation to 'clear Patagonia of red anarchists' ordered by Hipólito Irigoyen, the first democratically elected president of Argentina(!). This 'anarchist moment' and *not* the struggle of indigenous people against the military under General Roca's command is taken as the starting point of any analysis of resistance in twentieth-century. This example shows both that racial discrimination is *entangled* in a hierarchical manner with working-class formation, and that this hierarchy was confirmed and reproduced by the European anarchist and syndicalist workers.

Coloniality and the left

Authors of the decolonial school question the lack of epistemological consciousness in the left. When worldwide resistances are examined, argues Grosfoguel (2008, 2009), the discussions are rarely accompanied by an epistemological reflection of the application of categories that belong to Eurocentric modern thought to all struggles. Grosfoguel argues that in the valid attempt to find commonalities differences tend to be neglected making analysis superficial. The imposition of categories on the analysis of resistance in the south reproduce the coloniality of power that movements are struggling against. When difference is addressed, the left is unaware that the idea of 'multiplicity of resistance' or 'diversity' *a la* Chantal Mouffe[2] is a political derivative of 'multiculturalism', a policy that adapts diversity to epistemic coloniality. Decolonial authors contend that the world is 'pluriversal' (Conway and Singh, 2011: 702): 'a truly universal decolonial perspective cannot be based on an abstract universal (one particular that promotes itself as universal global design), but would have to be the result of critical dialogue between diverse critical epistemic/ethical/political projects towards a pluriversal as opposed to a universal world'. (Grosfoguel, 2009) The term *pluriversity* coined by Mignolo (2000) indicates the inclusion of all the epistemic particularities towards a 'transmodern decolonial socialization of power' (Grosfoguel, 2009). In Mignolo's words, 'pluriversality is not cultural relativism, but entanglement of several cosmologies connected today in a power differential. That power differential is the logic of coloniality covered up by the rhetorical narrative of modernity. Modernity is a fiction that carries in it the seed of Western pretence to universality' (Mignolo, 2013).[3]

Boaventura de Sousa Santos argues for the incongruous existence of two paradigms of life sheltered by capitalist societies and the subordination of one by another was, and continues to be in the present, as a result of 'abyssal thinking' (Santos, 2007b). Abyssal thinking is a mode of thinking that relies on the tracing of an invisible line that leaves aside other forms of thinking and universalises the particular form of thinking it contains. By bringing Bonfil Batalla's distinction between 'imaginary' and 'deep' Mexico to light, Esteva (2011) concurs the most important divide in Mexican society is not between rich and poor, or about ideological or political divisions. It is rather 'the presence of two civilizations, two different horizons of intelligibility, in the same society' (Esteva, 2011).

Subaltern studies: why do they get it wrong?

In his devastating critique of postcolonial theory, more precisely SS, Chibber (2013) argues that SS show a poor understanding of how 'capital, power and agency actually work' (Chibber, 2013: 285). I concur, and want to bring to light two of Chibber's thought-provoking ideas to enrich my discussion of autonomy, value and hope. First, he notes that SS make a crucial mistake in coupling 'universalisation' of capital with 'homogenisation of power relations' (p. 150), with the exception of Chakrabarty, who claims that capitalism has failed in its universalising mission (p. 133). In both cases, the east is seen as forced into relations of power that do not belong to their psychologies or their politics. But is the universalisation of capital the same as the homogenisation of power relations? What does capitalism universalise? Chibber contends that 'what capitalism universalises ... is a particular strategy of economic reproduction' (Chibber, 2013: 111) and indicates that if universalisation of capital and homogenisation of power relations in the west and east are decoupled, we can easily realise that capital's universalisation not only allows differences to exist but – more importantly – it promotes them for they are beneficial for the expansion of capital. In this vein, specific form of politics, power and class relations, etc. co-exist with the self-expansion of global capital as a universal project.

Although the nature of my enquiry and critique is different from Chibber's there is a second point in Chibber's argument that is also relevant to my discussion of the confrontation of value by hope in the case of indigenous resistance: SS – and more specifically Chakrabarty offer a mistaken treatment of *the concept of abstract labour* that misleads them towards the conflation between universalisation and homogenisation and, consequently, the possibility to discern the importance of abstract labour to understand both difference and universalisation is obscured. SS's mistreatment of abstract labour is apparent in the argument that 'abstract categories are incapable of explaining the genesis of historical diversity' (Chibber, 2013: 131) and the belief that historical diversity is, first of all, concrete. In this vein, SS confuse abstract labour with homogeneous labour. SS do not grasp the dual nature of work in capitalism: concrete and abstract. This unawareness directs them to focus on what they regard as the concrete, i.e. the historical diversity, rejecting the *abstract aspects* of the social relation of capital. I have two concerns. First, SS's rejection of the abstract aspects of the capital relation constitutes the basics for mistaken interpretation that indigenous people are positioned outside the real subsumption of labour and 'society in capital' (Negri, 1991: 114). Grosfoguel (2009) argues that 'these exterior spaces are not pure or absolute. They have been affected and produced by European modernity, but never fully subsumed nor instrumentalized. It is from the geopolitics of knowledge of this relative exteriority, or margins, that "critical border thinking" emerges as a critique of modernity towards a pluriversal [Mignolo, 2000] transmodern world of multiple and diverse ethico-political projects in which a real horizontal dialogue and communication could exist between all peoples of the world'. Second, the decolonial school misunderstand of Marxism and equates Marx's critique of political economy with 'political economy' (see Grosfoguel, 2009). They have also overlooked recent Marxist emphasis on the need to read Marx's as an open theory, as open Marxism (Bonefeld et al., 1992a, 1992b, 1995, Gunn, 1992), i.e. as a theory of struggle (Holloway, 1993a, 1993b).

How is this relevant to my argument about autonomy and excess? Let me briefly reflect on two chief characteristics of capitalism. The first and most important feature of capitalism is *not* the incorporation into, or exclusion of workers from, the production process. A significant feature of capitalism is the constant subordination of concrete labour into abstract labour. This is a compulsion to subsume the needs of human beings to the whims of an abstract measurement that has no concrete existence until it reaches the form of money. As we have discussed, what matters to capital is socially necessary labour time, labour abstracted from the concrete work that is performed by specific workers for specific capitalists in specific branches of industries: it is abstract labour that constitutes the substance of value. Unemployment, for example, is a *form of* capitalist work by which workers are subsumed in capital in a more intensive way than those workers who work for total subordination of human activity under the rule of money and value becomes apparent in the impossibility of reproduction of human life (excluding state policy intervention). Unemployment affects concrete labour, but not abstract labour (Dinerstein, 2002a).

The second feature of capitalism is *real* subsumption. Under the *formal* subsumption of labour, concrete labour was directly subordinated to capital (Marx, 1990: 1034) and the latter, argues Marx, 'ha[d] not yet succeeded in becoming the dominant force, capable of determining the form of society as a whole' (Marx, 1990: 1023). However, the transition *from formal to real subsumption* that came with industrialisation, and expanded with global capital, means that, at that point, 'the entire development of socialized labour ... in the immediate process of production, takes the form of the productive power of capital' (Marx, 1990: 1024). As Negri argues, 'capital progressively subsumes all the elements and materials of the process of circulation (money and exchange in the first place, as functions of mediation) and, thereafter, all those pertaining to the process of production, so that herein lies the foundation for the passage from manufacture to big industry to social factory' (Negri, 1991: 114). The main point is that with the 'real subsumption of labour and society by capital' (Negri, 1991: 114), labour subjectivity is no longer externally subjected by capital but integrated into it in a way that 'capital becomes the subject' (Bonefeld, 1996). By labour I do not mean workers but human activity or 'doing' (Holloway, 2002). '*Capital*', argues Negri, 'does not appear simply as a unified process, but as itself a *subject* [as Marx argues] "Value appears as subject" [*Grundrisse*, p. 311; 218] (Negri, 1991: 76). '*Valorization*' continues Negri, *is a continuous and totalitarian process* ... In the process of valorization capital conquers a totalitarian subjectivity of command' (Negri, 1991: 76). With a caveat: self-expansion of capital is not *total* but a totali*sing* force. Capital valorisation is expressed in the present continuous tense (motion) allowing the possibility of not expanding: value is, I claim, an unrealised materiality.

Are indigenous people outside the universalising and totalising force of global capital? If we accept that the most important feature of capitalism is the transformation of doing into abstract labour rather than the incorporation of workers into the labour process or the circuits of consumption the answer is negative. While the persistence of colonialism in the form of 'coloniality of power' (Quijano, 2000b) and the socioeconomic, political and cultural differences between the west and the east and the north and the south persist, the discussion about indigenous people's autonomy and their forms of prefiguring alternative societies requires to be coupled with another enquiry about the ways in which *real subsumption* has transformed indigenous people's position in the global world of capital, particularly since the 1970s. The question is: How is real subsumption under present forms of accumulation 'by dispossession' (Harvey, 2005) *reorganising* the subordination of indigenous people? What kind of subsumption subordinates indigenous people? Land grabbing and the commodification of indigenous lands have put indigenous demands and struggles at the centre of the struggle against capitalism. Why are indigenous struggles for autonomy a 'fetter' for the TNCs involved in the commodification of the land and extractivism? Why did the Zapatistas' uprising provoke panic among global businesses, governments and international institutions in 1994? While the self-expansion of capital through the ongoing subordination of doing (concrete labour) into abstract labour (Holloway, 2010) contains the expansion of indifference 'toward any specific kind of labour' concrete labour articulates diverse forms of resistance against capital's indifference and for self- affirmation and autonomy. Forms of resistance are shaped by historical, geographical, political, economic and social forms that mediate the art of organising hope in each case. The state and the law translate autonomy into the grammar of power in specific contexts. This means that the process of valorisation of capital as the expansion of indifference-universalisation comprises a *political* process of classification, control, regulation of the art of organising hope. While the struggle against indifference creates, recreates and reinvents concrete utopia against dehumanisation, commodification, oppression and invisibility, the struggle against classification engages with the more universal quality of distinct resistance: the unity in the diverse a unity that does not suffocates difference, a pluriversality. Since concrete and abstract labour are inseparable, these two dynamics interact within every form of resistance to capital and beyond capital. *The art of organising hope negates and creates, contradicts and produces excess; it is concrete and abstract. It is particular and universal.* Exclusion is a phenomenological – political – expression of an experience of subsumption of labour in capital, where the latter *appears in* the *form of* the former. Real subsumption by exclusion means subsumption into the global-social relation of capital in specific forms

– real illusions, that oppress and render invisible indigenous cosmologies, insofar as they are incompatible with the development paradigm and capitalist, patriarchal and colonial societies, but also translates them into the grammar of the state and capital in a deradicalised fashion, via 'alternative development' and 'multiculturalism' policies, and, more contradictorily, into the national constitutions and the plurinational state. My final question is how does indigenous people's art of organising hope disputes the content of the not yet from a position of subsumption by exclusion and how is this different from non-indigenous forms of organising hope?

Indigenous cosmologies as the art of organising hope

The argument of this book is that the art of organising hope (prefiguration) comprises four interlocked modes: negating the given, creating concrete utopia, navigating contradictions and producing overflows of human activity beyond demarcation. While both non-indigenous and indigenous autonomous organising confronts value with hope by disputing the content of the *not yet* reality, indigenous movements' hope is rooted in practices, knowledges and cosmologies that have been cherished and preserved for a long time and had remained oppressed and invisibilised. Aymara insurgency against privatisation in defence of the management of water in Bolivia shows how indigenous struggles defend and mobilise ancestral practices with political imagination. As argued in Chapter 6, autonomy emerged as a new form of indigenous movements' resistance as an outcome of political and legal transformations that occurred since the 1970s when indigenous people firmly rejected their legal definition as 'minorities'. They demanded to be considered as 'nations' and 'peoples' (*pueblos originarios*) (Burguete Cal y Mayor, 2010: 72). Unlike non-indigenous forms of autonomy, indigenous' autonomy is guided by specific forms of politics, ideas and social relations that have not been destroyed by the force of capital. Having said that I also showed the corrosive impact of the penetration of the rule of money and power in the ayllus of El Alto. Yet, neither participatory neoliberal governance nor the plurinational form of the state can translate into the grammar of capital, the *kairós*, which is a different time, 'subjective time', which, as Valencia García explains, is one 'that can be stored, enlarged and even immobilised by [people and it is] a time inhabited by adventure, nostalgia, hope' (Valencia García, 2007: 63).

Indigenous cosmologies like *buen vivir* naturally outflow and overwhelm the imprisonment of a reality demarcated by the capitalist, colonial and patriarchal powers, including that of the plurinational-developmentalist state. The indigenous-popular movements' struggles over the content of the not yet do not constitute 'projects' but manifest themselves in every day courses of action through which the movements follow a hidden agenda, an agenda that will be revealed to them as they go. *'Preguntando caminamos'* delineates an unknown path that enacts decisions that have been made in the past, with *miras al futuro* (Regalsky, 2003). While in both cases the not yet belongs to another social reality, the indigenous' art of organising hope confronts value with experiences that already exist, related to other conceptions and experiences of nature, time, space, relations between people and nature, conceptualisation of the world, alternative knowledges, and politics.

What oppresses me? Some final remarks

Why, despite being different, indigenous peoples' art of organising hope is inspirational for the non-indigenous world? A tentative answer to this question could be that accumulation by dispossession (Harvey, 2005) *subsumes by 'excluding'*. As opposed to other moments in capitalist development where the 'integration' of labour into the state and institutionalisation of class conflict were vital to the process of accumulation, subsumption by 'exclusion' relies on expropriation, displacement, invisibilisation, expulsion, and the constant classification and translation of autonomy into tools for the democratisation of sustained misery a misery, that constitutes the everyday reality of both indigenous *as well as* non-indigenous, rural, urban workers' people, alike. Accumulation by dispossession is creating common grounds for new forms of struggles that are beginning to find the unity in the diverse. This is not just theory. We can find it in the Zapatistas' characterisation of neoliberal globalisation as a war against *humanity* and their proposal that we should all ask ourselves *what is it that oppresses me*? In order to create 'a world with the many world that the world needs' (Ponce de León, 2001: 114–115) one has to account for the existence of different forms of oppression and resistance, which, I argue, mobilise hope against the self-expanding force of capital as an 'impossible form of humanity' (Dinerstein and Neary, 2002a).

The art of organising hope is about transcending the parameters of legibility of the capitalist, patriarchal and colonial reality delineated and informed by the formal abstractions of political economy. In order to grasp *excess* we are required to locate autonomy *in* the reality of the valorisation of capital. A prefigurative critique of political economy can grasp the struggle over the content of the not yet that underpins autonomy for both indigenous and non-indigenous: 'the fleeting, fugitive quality of the value form, internally related and radically unfixed 'signals its openness to a future' (Gunn, 1992: 32), a future that is temporarily captured, organised and anticipated by the prefigurative force of the politics of autonomy.

Ernst Bloch and Walter Benjamin agreed that the temporality of moments of hope could not be actually apprehended. The way both philosophers succeed in capturing the temporality of hope is 'by reproducing another hopeful moment, the moment of hope in their own writing' (Miyasaki, 2004: 23). This means that the only way to grasp hope is by creating other hopeful moments, as I have envisioned to do with this book. Should we be concerned about facts? Richter notes that 'the relation between factual and hope is constantly in flux because it is in hope that what could in the future be considered a fact has not yet shucked the traces of its own contingency ... Hope, then will have been the name for the centrifugal movement of forces that will not let a "fact" simply come into its own as a form of self-identity' (Richter, 2006: 53). The politics of autonomy do not allow value as a 'fact' to come into its own identity.

9
Living in Blochian Times: Opening Remarks

Hope is an essential component of any process of resistance against power. Nothing new. No hope, no change. Yet, my argument has been that we must see the present condition as 'living in Blochian times', a time when utopia can be no longer objected. But this is of course a different kind of 'utopia'. Bloch highlights that 'Once [s]he has grasped [her]self and that which is [hers], without alienation and based in real democracy, so there will arise in the world something that shines into everyone's childhood, but where no one has yet been: *Heimat* [Home]' (cited from Thompson, 2009: xix). This utopia, or the art of organising hope, is a ceaseless search for 'home' for at home, paraphrasing Bloch, the subject becomes the predicate.

Over the past thirty years, the idea that 'there is no alternative' (TINA) expanded worldwide and became the global dominant discourse. The demise of the USSR in 1989 made capitalism a triumphant global phenomenon, despite that it brings misery to the world. Since then, academics, intellectuals and activists have tried to understand in a variety of ways how capitalism survives its own inadequacies, and what are the problems of radical resistance to defeat it. Political economists have taught us how global capitalism works, described and explained the malaises brought about the dynamics that govern neoliberal globalisation, and why and how the 'system' enters recurrently into crisis. Political scientists have explained the worrisome political apathy and the current motivational deficit that affects citizen's participation in institutional politics, and the challenges of non-institutionalised mobilisation. Sociologists have addressed the devastating social impacts that unemployment, poverty, social exclusion, illegal immigration, child labour, human trafficking, drug addiction, and youth crime are having on communal life. Yet, such analyses have tended to perceive the mobilisation by those resisting neoliberal globalisation as 'external' to the process of accumulation, thus regarded as a 'response' to the sinister effects of the global accumulation by dispossession.

The politics of autonomy in Latin America reposition the interrogation of subjectivity for radical politics. Movements convey, in a variety of ways, a critique of the rule of money capital over human life and rehearse diverse forms in which a dignified way of life could be attained. These struggles challenge the foundations of bourgeois social sciences and enable us to rediscover the world's diversity of epistemologies and practices. More importantly, since new mobilisations are producing own theorising profusely (Cox and Nielsen, 2007; Cox, 2013; 2014; Motta, 2011; 2014), the possibility of understanding them without engaging with their ideas, theories and imaginaries faces a dead end.

While I exposed the rich and diverse experience of the *prefigurative struggle* of movements in search for alternatives, I also emphasised the need to rethink our methods, and sharpen our critique in a way that they can match the emancipatory energy that emerged in Latin America around two decades ago. Autonomous organising created new collectivities and demarcated new territories of hope that disputed the given horizons. These spaces are not, however, 'liberated zones' but deeply embedded in the capitalist/colonial/patriarchal power relations. It is precisely because they are embedded that they can confront value with hope, thus producing radical change.

The movements' journey inspired me to venture beyond my own theoretical limitations and explore an alternative way of understanding autonomy. This alternative proposal entailed a mission impossible: to show that autonomous organising mobilises something that does *not yet* exist but, nevertheless, occupies a central place in the movements' autonomous politics. I offered a prefigurative critique of political economy by emphasising the significance of Marx's method for discovering the potential of autonomy to produce radical change, that is to create an excess that is untranslatable into the grammar of capital. Bloch's philosophy enabled me explore the politics of autonomy in the key of hope. I conceptualised autonomy as determinate abstraction and followed the movement that prefigures new realities.

I argued that autonomy is a tool for prefiguration, but also that this is not a simple process. Both narrow definitions of autonomy as a self-contained process of creative organising without consideration of the material struggles with, against and beyond state, capital and the law, and analyses of autonomy that do not deal with the dual nature of labour in capitalist societies and the significance of the 'abstract' aspects of the capital relation that concretely affect individual and social lives, fail to inform the politics of autonomy. As I have shown here, prefiguring is a complex process of *struggle* that includes the negation of the given reality; the articulation of concrete utopia; the struggle (predicaments) with, against and beyond the state, the law and capital, which can lead to disappointment; and the production of excess, that is, practices that are beyond demarcation.

The art of organising hope offers not only a political tool to resist and reject capital as a form of society, but to anticipate alternative social relations, sociabilities and practices and, by so doing dispute the content of the *not yet* that dwells in both value and hope. That is, autonomy disputes the form of the future in the present. Capital is not a given. Value has to be realised. Hope is a *political* problem for capital, for it drives people outwards, forwards, in the opposite direction, towards an encounter with their own humanity against hopelessness, hunger and fear.

I put the autonomy debate on its head. My question was not whether autonomous organising can produce radical change without taking the power of the state, but how do the state and capital 'cope' (mediate) with the radical prefigurative power of autonomous organising. How does the state translate concrete utopia into governance tools through the law and policy? What are the limits of the appropriation and institutionalisation of autonomy by the state? What is the scope for untranslatability? How is excess produced? What is it about?

I use four concepts from Bloch's philosophy to put autonomy in the key of hope and thus to inform the complexity of the politics of autonomy in Latin America. The first one, *the real is process*, designates the movement of *organising negation* (as both practical negativity and identity as resistance) i.e. negating the given reality and explore is another reality that lives in 'the darkness of the present'. In Chapter 4, I suggested that a key feature of neoliberalism in the region was the construction of hopelessness via the uprooting of revolutionary dreams and repression, indebtedness, 'democracy', the dismantling of the world of work, poverty, the commodification of indigenous land, the expulsion of rural workers from their land, and the use of brutal violence as the means for policy implementation. The Zapatistas' uprising (1994), initiated a process of organising negation, thus restating hope in the region and the galaxy.

The second concept, *concrete utopia*, describes the process of *shaping absences* and elaborating alternatives, which in the case of indigenous people is related to enacting memories and traditions in new creative forms. In Chapter 5, I exposed the QSVT's capacity to create concrete utopias related to democracy, work and justice by the autonomous organising that irrupted and expanded during and after the Argentine crisis of December 2001. All concrete utopias explored in this book are democratic, territorial, plural, cooperative, inventive and dignifying. They shared the importance of *política afectiva*, the appropriation of the public space, the territorialisation of resistance and the demarcation of new territories of hope, the use of the *asamblea* and horizontalism as a form of political interaction and decision making, the defence of dignity, an engagement in cooperatives and diverse form of the social and solidarity economy, a experience of temporality and the use of a new grammar of hope. Autonomy is indeed a collective practice within territorial and/or imagined 'transformative spaces' for the development of practical critique. By delineating new 'heterotopic spaces' (Lefebvre, 1974/1991) (i.e., areas of urban neighbourhood, rural settlement or indigenous snails), the movements articulated a critique of abstract democracy, civil society, policy, coloniality and development.

As the art of organising hope, autonomy is also a *contradictory* enterprise, full of predicaments. I engaged with a third idea of Bloch's philosophy: that hope is surrounded by *danger* so that there is a necessity for *disappointment*. This idea informs the struggle over the meaning of autonomy, the danger of appropriation and translation by the state, the law and capital, and the setback and disillusions that can occur. Autonomous movements navigate through the contradictions brought about by the relationship with the state, which includes joint action, negotiation, cooperation, confrontation and antagonism. Autonomy, therefore, endures the tension that can only be temporarily resolved, between rebellion (resistance and change towards a new world(s) and institutionalisation – that is, the incorporation of their project into state programmes and legislation which also officially advocate economic, social, cultural and political change) (Böhm et al., 2010).

In Chapter 6, I investigated four moments of the struggle over the meaning of autonomy in Bolivia during the period of 2000–2005. By exposing the struggle over the Law of Popular Participation (LPP) of 1994 by the Federation of Neighbours' Councils (FEJUVE) of El Alto I argued that this was a moment of *neoliberal* translation when autonomy was transformed into a tool for neoliberal decentralised governance by the law. Following this, the water and oil wars against the privatisation

of natural sources, marked a moment of crisis of the neoliberal translation that asserted as a process of *de-mediation*. Finally, the formation of
the plurinational state marks a moment of re-mediation and re-appropriation of autonomy by a new form of the state. I discussed the new
contradiction that inhabits the plurinational form of the capitalist state
by exploring the TIPNIS conflict as a moment of fissure of the plurinational translation that began to call into question the viability of the
plurinational-capitalist state.

I argued that the struggle over the meaning of autonomy not only
leads to appropriation but also creates a surplus that resists translation
(untranslatability). Bloch's concept of the *not yet* informs the surplus
created by the movements' praxis that transcends the parameters of
legibility of the capitalist reality and anticipates another reality that
does *not yet* exist by venturing beyond demarcation. Untranslatability
is a dimension of all the movements explored here. In Chapter 7, I
argued that the MST does not only defy the power of the Brazilian
state, landowners of *latifundios* and transnational agribusiness, and
give voice and facilitate the self-organisation of the landless, but also
it confrontes, disputes and *ventures beyond the wire*, by *occupying* the
land, *territorialising* its struggles and by creating 'territories of hope'
or concrete utopia (settlements) where the MST's agrarian dream is
concretely fashioned. Finally the MST challenges demarcations, by
confronting the WB-led agrarian reform with a project of peasant-led
agrarian reform with food sovereignty that exceeds the possibility of
realisation via state policy.

In Chapter 8, I problematised 'factual reality' and exposed the material basis for untranslatability. I established the inner connection between
the value form, hope and the *not yet*. Both, value and hope operate in a
non-factual reality (i.e., they are both *unrealised* materiality). Autonomous
organising confronts value with hope, thus disputing the meaning of the
not yet. In fact, what is at stake when value is confronted by hope is the
content of the not yet. When value is confronted by hope, hope opens
up the possibility of dignified work, popular justice, true democracy,
indigenous autonomy, workers' self-management and peasant-led agrarian
reform with food sovereignty.

I have also exposed the importance of grasping the difference
between real and formal subsumption of labour in capital for an
understanding of the political significance of indigenous autonomy
and suggested that present forms of capital accumulation are fostering
common grounds between indigenous and non-indigenous resistance.

Table 9.1 offers a summary of the politics of autonomy by the four movements.

In Blochian times, Marx's critique of political economy becomes naturally a *prefigurative* critique of political economy. I just activated this dimension by reading Marx's critique in the key of hope and placing the unnamed, the unrealised, the silenced, the imageless and the invisibilised dimension that is mobilised by Latin American movements' mundane-yet-extraordinary collective actions at the core of the 'autonomy' debate. This invisible and unspoken dimension is at odds with the capitalist, patriarchal and colonial realities and the classificatory character of academia, and it is absent in many of the analyses of autonomy that confuse Marxism with economics or political economy.

The prefigurartive critique of political economy shows that movements' anticipatory consciousness of the *not yet* that emerges from a praxis towards real possibility escapes regulation, institutionalisation, integration, translation and classification. Autonomy can only be partially incorporated into the hegemonic canon of new international development discourse, institutional dynamics and policy if radical hope is left out of the equation. Appropriation by deradicalisation incorporates only those aspects of movements' collective actions that fit into a regulatory framework of an improved system of fairer exploitation.

The art of organising hope does not enquire 'what could we be that we are not', but 'what could we be that we are not *yet*'. It is the word 'yet' that, makes autonomy prefigurative. If we take the word *yet* out of the sentence and simply pronounce: 'It is something that we could be, but we are not', there is no hope. If, instead, we say, 'It is something that we could be, but we are not *yet*', it means that the collective dream is *really* possible (Icaza and Vazquez 2013). The possibility that autonomous movements are disappointed at some point is, however, a necessity in the art of organising hope, for hope is about uncertainty; it is 'surrounded by dangers'.

Autonomy and the open veins of capital

Autonomy does not offer 'dreams of perfect communion' (Rothenberg, 2010: 28), or produce 'the eros effect' that evolves out of the experience of opposition and solidarity (Katsiaficas, 2006: 15). Autonomous organising is not about avoiding the state or capital or succumbing to the state

Table 9.1 Summary of autonomous organising in Latin America

	Zapatistas (Mexico)	QSVT (Argentina)	Indigenous-popular movement (Bolivia)	MST (Brazil)
Negating: the real is process	*¡Ya Basta* (Enough is enough!) Indigenous uprising, war to the Mexican State	*¡Que se vayan tod@s! Que no quede ni un@ sol@!* (All of them out! No one should stay!) Popular uprising	*¡El agua es nuestra carajo!* (Water is ours, dammit!). Oil and water wars against privatisation	*¡A desalambrar!* Land occupation against landlessness
Creating: Shaping concrete utopia	JBGs; autonomy *de facto*	Cooperative work in the neighbourhoods, community projects, self-management, popular justice, radical democracy	Indigenous self-management of water systems (Aymara); self-government in El Alto (JVs) and ayllu organisations	Settlements, alternative agrarian reform, production, cooperation, solidarity, pedagogic experience, mística
Contradiction: translation and disappointment	Neoliberal translation of indigenous demand for autonomy into free municipality as a tool for decentralised governance Negotiation with the state until up to 2003 (disappointment) demand for recognition of indigenous' rights to self-determination and self-government	Populist translation and appropriation of the radical ethos of QSVT via policy. Movements' use of state resources to attain their goals of autonomy through the use of financial incentives to cooperatives and communal projects, NGO-isation of autonomous movements	Revolutionary appropriation of indigenous autonomy by the plurinational state. Popular indigenous movements' demand for 'inclusion'	Neoliberal translation 'settlements' into 'family farms' via WB-led policy MST's negotiations (disappointment) with the government over the agrarian reform Food security
Excess: the not yet	Indigenous autonomy and cosmologies	Dignified work	Indigenous autonomy/ cosmologies	Peasant-led agrarian reform, food sovereignty

and capital. As the political form of the capital relation, the state mediates and shapes the form of autonomy. Autonomy organises the utopian impulse but it does not know where it goes exactly. As Raúl Gatica, an indigenous community activist in Oaxaca put it, 'autonomy is not a theory but a practice in development' (Notes from Nowhere, 2003), and theory, argues Holloway (2010a: 215), is 'the uncovering of that which is hidden ... theory is critique, critique of the forms that conceal, and yet are generated by, human activity'.

Recently, I presented a paper at an international symposium on the Potentials and Limits of the Social and Solidarity Economy, convened by the United Nations Research Institute for Social Development (UNRISD) (sponsored by the International Labour Organisation in Geneva on 7 June 2013). Having the argument of this book in mind, I problematised the issue of *translation* of social movements' collective actions into policy. I referred to the imperative need to deconstruct capitalist realism in order to engage with what I called the 'beyond zone' of movements' action, i.e. the place *where* they articulate new realities that unfortunately are invisibilised by existing parameters of legibility, and the approaches and theorisations which suits them. Puzzled by my approach, the chair of my panel expressed his bewilderment by jokingly arguing that, after listening to me, he felt that he was in the *Twilight Zone*. He was referring to the American television series created by Rod Serling in the 1950s, which used fantasy and fiction as the means to introduce critical ideas to an American audience. We all laughed at this crazy idea of the 'hidden' reality of capitalism and the possibility of moving onto a 'beyond zone'!

In Blochian times, however, we *are* demarcating another reality where there is a real (not objective) possibility of no longer being hungry, poor, jobless or landless, or oppressed. The politics of autonomy navigates in the open veins of capital. From the 'beyond zone' of the *not yet*, we can predict the true *Twilight Zone* of this century is, indisputably, capitalism. I cannot prove it with facts. As Marcos would say, it is an *intuition*. It is, overall, 'a question of *learning* hope ... the work of this emotion' highlights Bloch, 'requires people who throw themselves actively into what is becoming to which they themselves belong' (Bloch, 1959/1986: 3).

The 'Closing Remarks to the First Intercontinental Encounter for Humanity and against Neoliberalism' by the Chiapas' rebels that took place almost 20 years ago condense the essence of this book:

> As to what happened in these days, much will be written later. Today we can say that we are certain of at least one thing: a dream that is

dreamed in the five continents can realize itself in La Realidad. Now, who will be able to tell us that dreaming is lovely but futile? Now, who will be able to argue that dreams, however many the dreamers, cannot become reality? (Zapatistas, 1996: 115)

Not me ...

Notes

1 *Embracing the Other Side*: An Introduction

1. See Chibber's critique of post colonial theory (Subaltern Studies), particularly with reference to the latter's equation of universal with homogeneous. Against this, Chibber argues that 'as capitalism spreads across the globe, it does not inevitably turn every culture into a replica of what has been observed in the West' (Chibber, 2013: 150).

2 *Meanings of Autonomy*: Trajectories, Modes, Differences

1. On the common and community see debates in *Community Development Journal*, Supplement 1, 2014, and *Rethinking Marxism* 22(3), 2010.

3 *Autonomy in the Key of Hope*: Understanding Prefiguration

1. I am borrowing the term 'mode of being denied' from Richard Gunn (1987a; 1987b) who coined this term to characterise the form of existence of labour in capitalist society. See also Bonefeld 1994; 1995.
2. I have the opportunity to discuss and clarify the difference between concrete and real utopia with Professor Eric O. Wright during the XVIII ISA World Congress of Sociology, 13–19 of July 2014, in Yokohama, Japan, at a session on counter hegemonic politics, convened by the Future Research Group (R07) where I presented and discussed Zapatismo. He used the term 'erosion of capitalism' that I am citing during his address on Real Utopias at one of the plenaries, at this World Congress.

5 *Shaping Concrete Utopia*: Urban Experiments (Argentina)

1. I am using the term 'left' as a generic, which includes several organisations such as Workers Party (*Partido Obrero*, PO), the Socialist Workers Movement (*Movimiento Socialista de los Trabajadores*, MSTA) and the Communist Party (*Partido Comunista*, PC), among others. There are significant differences among them, which deserve to be considered in detail, but this is beyond the scope of this chapter. For a history of these organisations see Argentina: Historical and Political Background Notes, Political Parties and the Left at http://leftparty.org/docARGnotes.html. For similar developments between indigenous and popular movement and the left in Bolivia, see Garcia Linera (2008: 297).

2. Kirchner went to the second round after having obtained only 22 per cent of the vote, almost the same as his opponent, Menem. It was clear that the anti-Menemist votes for López Murphy, Carrió and Rodríguez Saá during the first round would be directed to Kirchner in the second round. But the second round never took place. President Menem resigned from the presidential race before the second round, which would have spelled a clear defeat for him. Hence, Kirchner won the elections by default.

3. In Castilian (the Spanish language spoken in Latin America), the term 'hijos' means 'sons' and it is used as a generic for sons and daughters (i.e., offspring).

4. The 'Due Obedience' bill differentiated three levels of responsibility in the violations of human rights, with the degree of punishment differing for those who planned and supervised, those who committed 'excesses' and those who obeyed orders (Tedesco, 1999: 65). Thanks to the use of this criterion, those who participated directly in state terrorism (e.g., those working in the task groups in more than 300 torture camps) walked free.

5. Zibechi (2003a) highlights that the roots of the *escrache* is *serenata* (rough music) and the *charivari*. 'Rough music' is defined in the *Oxford Dictionary* of 1708 as 'the harmony of the pot pans and saucepans'. He draws on E.P. Thompson's and Charles Tilly's accounts of the methods used between 1650 and 1850 in England that entailed a noisy congregation that ritualised and satirised the protest using metal tools and musical instruments. The *charivari* was a small carnival or street theatre that publicised the scandal in question. Being between mocking and protesting, the role of the community was key for the success of the *charivari*.

6. For example, the Unemployed Workers Section of the Workers Party (*Polo Obrero*), the Unemployed Workers Front (*Frente Unico de Trabajadores Desocupados*), close to the Workers' Party (*Partido Obrero*), and the Liberation Territorial Movement (*Movimiento Territorial de Liberación*, MTL) from the Communist Party.

7. ILO, *Decent work agenda*, http://www.ilo.org/global/about-the-ilo/decent-work-agenda/lang – es/index.htm, last accessed 7 March 2014.

8. '¿Qué significa, hoy, ser Piquetero? (Dos ex MTD frente al espejo)', laVaca. org, 14 June 2006 http://argentina.indymedia.org/news/2006/06/416442_comment.php.

9. See Interview with Pablo Solana on the FPDS by W.L. Fuentes Sánchez (2011), http://rcci.net/globalizacion/2011/fg1163.htm.

10. Palomino et al. (2010)'s database is guided by self-reported definitions provided by workers. In 2008, there were 221 factories. Their analysis included 170 ... three-quarters of which were recovered during the 2000–2004 period. The *Facultad Abierta* (Faculty of Philosophy, University of Buenos Aires) reports that there are 311 WREs employing 13,462 workers in 2013 (E. Magnani, *Página/12*, 20 April 2014).

6 *Contesting Translation*: Indigenous-Popular Movements (Bolivia)

1. Icelandic Human Rights Centre: http://www.humanrights.is/the-human-rights-project/humanrightscasesandmaterials/humanrightsconceptsideasandfora/Undirflokkur/indigenouspeoples/.

2. 'ILO standards and the UN Declaration on the Rights of Indigenous Peoples' at http://www.ilo.org/wcmsp5/groups/public/ – -ed_norm/ – -normes/documents/publication/wcms_100792.pdf.
3. Citation from *El Deber*, 22 January 2007, Santa Cruz de la Sierra.

7 *Venturing beyond the Wire*: The *Sem Terra's* Dream (Brazil)

1. See http://www.eiu.com/default.aspx and http://www.economistinsights.com/sites/default/files/Accenture_Agribusiness_ENGLISH.pdf.
2. See http://www.mstbrazil.org/about-mst/history.
3. Interview with João Pedro Stédile by Kostas Athanassiou, www.elartefacto.com.ar.
4. MST, *A Lei e as Ocupaçcões de Terras*, 1998, at 3 cited in English by Meszaros (2000: 531, italics in the original).
5. Interview with João Pedro Stédile by Kostas Athanassiou (n.d.) www.elartefacto.com.ar.
6. The former president is the co-author of the book Cardoso and Faletto, 1971/1979 *Dependency and Development in Latin America*, Berkley-Los Angeles-London: University of California Press, which constitutes a landmark in dependency theory.
7. See http://news.bbc.co.uk/1/hi/world/americas/2961284.stm. See *La Vía Campesina*'s campaign against Monsanto: Zacune, J. (with contributions from activists from the world), 'Lucha contra Monsanto: Resistencia de los movimientos de base al poder empresarial del agronegocio en la era de la 'economía verde' y un clima cambiante' http://www.viacampesina.org/downloads/pdf/sp/Monsanto-Publication-ES-Final-Version.pdf.
8. See http://www.eiu.com/default.aspx and http://www.economistinsights.com/sites/default/files/Accenture_Agribusiness_ENGLISH.pdf.
9. MST proposal (in Spanish) http://www.movimientos.org/es/content/programa-agrario-del-mst-%C2%A1luchar-%C2%A1construir-reforma-agraria-popular. More information about the VI Conference: http://www.movimientos.org/es/etiquetas/mst-vi-congreso and http://www.mst.org.br.
10. See http://www.fao.org/economic/ess/ess-fs/en/.
11. Nyéléni is the newsletter of a broader Food Sovereignty Movement that considers the Nyéléni 2007 declaration as its political platform. The Nyéléni Newsletter aims to be the voice of this international movement. The organizations involved are Development Fund, ETC Group, FIAN, Focus on the Global South, Food First, Friends of the Earth International, GRAIN, Grassroots International, IPC for food sovereignty, La Vía Campesina, Marcha Mundial de las Mujeres, Oxfam Solidarity, Real World Radio, Roppa, The World Forum Of Fish Harvesters and Fish Workers, and VSF–Justicia Alimentaria Global.
12. See https://wdm.org.uk/food-sovereignty.

8 *Confronting Value with Hope*: Towards a Prefigurative Critique of Political Economy

1. Grosfoguel (2009) explains that one of the reasons for the split of the Latin American Sublatern Studies Group was that some of the members produced 'a

Eurocentric critique of Eurocentrism' and other disputed this and engaged in a 'decolonial critque', i.e. 'a critique of Eurocentrism from subalternized and silenced knowledges' (Grosfoguel, 2009).

2. i.e. 'pluralism within each regime is restricted to a hegemonically contained "conflictual consensus" on its constitutional principles, and among regimes is restricted to a similar consensus on the hegemonic and ostensibly unquestionable values of a now-globalised modernity' (Conway and Singh, 2011: 696).

3. From Walter Mignolo's web site: http://waltermignolo.com/on-pluriversality/.

Bibliography

Abensour, M. (2011) *Democracy against the State. Marx and the Machiavellian Moment* (Cambridge: Polity Press).

Acosta, A. and Martínez, E. (eds) (2009) *El buen vivir. Una vía para el desarrollo* (Quito: AbyaYala).

Adamovsky, E. et al (2011) *Pensar las Autonomías. Alternativas de emancipación al capital y el Estado* (México, DF: Bajo Tierra and SISIFO).

Adler Hellman, J. (1992) 'The Study of New Social Movements in Latin America and the Question of Autonomy'. In Escobar, A. and Alvarez, S., *The Making of Social Movements in Latin America* (San Francisco and Oxford: Westview Press, Boulder), pp. 52–61.

Adler Hellman, J. (2000) 'Real and Virtual Chiapas: Magic Realism and the Left', *Socialist Register* 36, pp. 161–186.

Adorno, T.W. (1995) *Negative Dialectics* (New York: Continuum).

Agamben, G. (2005) *State of Exception* (Chicago and London: University of Chicago Press).

Agnoli, J. (2000) 'The Market, the State and the End of History'. In Bonefeld, W. and Psychopedis, K. (eds) *The Politics of Change: Globalization, Ideology and Critique* (Houndmills and New York: Palgrave Macmillan), pp. 196–207.

Aiziczon, F. (2009) *Zanón. Una experiencia de lucha obrera* (Buenos Aires and Neuquén: Herramienta).

Albertani, C. (2009a) 'El principio de autonomía'. In Albertani, C., Rovira Sancho, G., and Modonesi, M. (eds) *La Autonomía Posible, reinvención política y emancipación* (México, DF: UAM), pp.17–23.

Albertani, C. (2009b) 'La rebelión Zapatista en hilo del tiempo'. In Albertani, C., Rovira Sancho, G., and Modonesi, M. (eds) *La Autonomía Posible, reinvención política y emancipación* (México, DF: UAM), pp. 501–518.

Albertani, C. (2011) '¿Qué es una sociedad autónoma?', *Transversales*, 22, pp. 19–36.

Albuquerque, L. (2014a) 'MST vuelve a poner el tema de la Reforma Agraria en el Gobierno', *América Latina en Movimiento*, http://alainet.org/active/71332, last accessed 18 May 2014.

Albuquerque, L. (2014b) 'The MST meets Dilma Rousseff: Landless Movement again Raises the Question of Agrarian Reform', *América Latina en Movimiento*, 18 February 2014, last accessed 1 Septempber 2014, http://alainet.org/active/71409.

Almeyra, G. and Thibaut, E. (2006) *Zapatistas: un nuevo mundo en construcción* (Buenos Aires: Maipue).

Altamira, J. (2002) *El Argentinazo. El presente como historia* (Buenos Aires: Rumbos).

Alvarez Béjar, A. (2001) 'El plan Puebla Panamá: ¿desarrollo regional o enclave tansnacional?', *OSAL*, 4, pp. 127–133.

Aminazade, R. and D. McAdam (2001) 'Emotions and contentious politics'. In Aminazade, R. et al (eds) *Silence and Voice in the Study of Contentious Poltics*, (Cambridge UK – New York: Cambridge University Press), pp. 14–50.

Arbona, J.M. (2005) 'Los límites de los márgenes. Organizaciones políticas locales y las Jornadas de Octubre de 2003 en El Alto, Bolivia', *Nueva Sociedad*, 2, pp. 6–15.

Arbona, J.M. (2007) 'Neo-liberal Ruptures: Local Political Entities and Neighbourhood Networks in El Alto, Bolivia', *Geoforum*, 38, pp. 127–137.

Arditi, B. (2007) 'Post-hegemony: Politics Outside the Usual Post-Marxist Paradigm', *Contemporary Politics*, 13(3), pp. 205–226.

Arditi, B. (2008) *Politics on the Edges of Liberalism: Difference, Populism, Revolution, Agitation* (Edinburgh: Edinburgh University Press).

Arditi, B. (2011) 'Agitado y revuelto: del "arte de lo possible" a la política emancipatoria'. In Adamovsky, E. et al., *Pensar las Autonomías. Op. cit.* pp. 289–316.

Arruda Sampaio, P. de (2005) 'La reforma agraria en América Latina: una revolución frustrada', *OSAL*, 16, pp. 15–22.

Arruda Sampaio, P. de et al. (2009) 'Manifesto in Defense of the MST, Revista América Latina en Movimiento', 23 September 2009, http://alainet.org/active/33230&lang=es, last accessed 8 May 2014.

Atzeni, M. and Ghigliani, P. (2007) 'Labour Process and Decision Making in Factories under Workers' Self-Management: Empirical Evidence from Argentina', *Work, Employment and Society*, 21(4), pp. 653–671.

Aubry, A. (2003) 'Autonomy in the San Andrés Accords: Expression and Fulfilment of a New Federal Pact'. In Rus, J., Hernandez Castillo, R., and Mattiace, S. (eds) *Mayan Lives, Mayan Utopias: The Indigenous Peoples of Chiapas and the Zapatista Rebellion* (Oxford: Rowman & Littlefield), pp. 219–242.

Auyero, J. (2000) *Poor People's Politics* (Durham, NC and London: Duke University Press).

Bagguley, P. (1991) *From Protest to Acquiescence? Political Movements of the Unemployed* (London: Palgrave Macmillan).

Bachurst, D. and Sypnowich, C. (eds) (1995) *The Social Self* (London: Sage).

Barrientos, A., Gideon, J. and Molyneux, M. (2008) 'New Developments in Latin America's Social Policy', *Development and Change* 39(5), pp. 759–774.

Basualdo, E. and Azpiazu, D. (2002) *El proceso de privatización en Argentina* (Buenos Aires: Universidad Nacional de Quilmes-IDEP).

Basualdo, E. and Kulfas, M. (2002) 'Fuga de capitales y endeudamiento externo en la Argentina', *Realidad Económica*, 173, pp. 76–103.

Bebbington, A. (2007) 'Social Movement and the Politicization of Chronic Poverty', *Development & Change*, 38(5), pp. 793–818.

Bebbington, A., Bury, J., Humphreys Bebbington, D., Lingan, J. et al. (2008) 'Mining and Social Movements: Struggles over Livelihood and Rural Territorial Development in the Andes', Brooks World Poverty Institute, Working Paper No. 33, University of Manchester.

Bellofiore, R. (2009) 'A Ghost Turning into a Vampire'. In Bellofiore R. and Fenischi, R. (eds) *Re-Reading Marx* (London: Palgrave Macmillan).

Benclowicz, J. (2011) 'Repensando los orígenes del Movimiento Piquetero', *Latin American Research Review* 46(2), pp. 79–103.

Betto, F. (2012) 'Rumbo a la reforma agraria', *América Latina en Movimiento*, http://alainet.org/active/53460, last accessed 9 March 2012.

Beverley, J. (2001) 'The Im/possibility of Politics: Subalternity, Modernity and Hegemony'. In Rodríguez, I. (ed.) *The Latin American Subaltern Studies Reader* (Durham, NC and London: Duke University Press).

Beverungen, A., Murtola, A.M., and Schwartz, G. (2013) 'The Communism of Capital?', *Ephemera*, 13(3), pp. 483–495, http://www.ephemerajournal.org/issue/communism-capital, last accessed 14 May 2014.

Bey, H. (2011) *TAZ: The Temporary Autonomous Zone, Ontological Anarchy, Poetic Terrorism* (New York: Autonomedia).

Biekart, K. (2005) 'Seven Theses on Latin American Social Movements and Political Change: A Tribute to André Gunder Frank (1929–2005)', *European Review of Latin American and Caribbean Studies*, 79, pp. 85–94.

Bielsa, R. et al. (2002) *¿Qué son las Asambleas Populares?* (Buenos Aires: Peña Lillo–Continente).

Blanchard, D. (2009) 'La idea de autonomía. Socialismo o Barbarie y el mundo actual'. In Albertani, C., Rovira Sancho, G., and Modonesi, M. (eds) *La Autonomía Posible, reinvención política y emancipación* (México, DF: UAM), pp. 152–163.

Bloch, E. (1918/2000) *The Spirit of Utopia* (Stanford, CA: Standford University Press).

Bloch, E. (1959/1986) *The Principle of Hope* (Cambridge, MA: The MIT Press).

Bloch, E. (1962/1991) *Heritage of Our Times* (Cambridge: Polity Press).

Bloch, E. (1970) *A Philosophy of the Future* (New York: Herder and Herder), Internet Archive 2010, Lyrasis Members and Sloan Foundation, http://www.archive.org/details/philosophyoffutu00bloc. Original edition: *Tubinger Einleitung in die Philosophie*, Vol. I. (1963) (Frankfurt am Main: Suhrkamp Verlag).

Bloch, E. (1971) *On Karl Marx* (New York: Herder and Herder).

Bloch, E. (1972/2009) *Atheism in Christianity* (London and New York: Verso).

Bloch, E. (1976) 'Dialectics of Hope', *New German Critique*, 9, pp. 3–10.

Bloch, E. (1977) *Kann Hoffnung enttaüscht warden?*, Literarische Aufsattze, Gesamtausgabe, Vol. 9 (Frankfurt am Main: Suhrkamp).

Bloch, E. (ed.) (1988) *The Utopian Function of Art and Literature: Selected Essays*, trans. by Zipes, J. and Mecklenburg, F. (London: MIT Press).

Bloch, E. (1998) 'Can Hope Be Disappointed?'. In *Literary Essays* (Stanford, CA: Stanford University Press), pp. 339–345.

Bloch, E. and Löwy, M. (1976) 'Interview with Ernst Bloch', trans. by Williams Hill, V., *New German Critique*, 9, pp. 35–45.

Böhm, S., Dinerstein, A.C., and Spicer, A. (2010) 'The (Im)possibilities of Autonomy. Social Movements in, against and beyond the State, Capital and Development', *Social Movement Studies*, 1(9), pp. 17–32.

Boltanski, L. and Chiapello, E. (2006) *The New Spirit of Capitalism* (London: Verso).

Bonefeld, W. (1987) 'Marxism and the Concept of Mediation', *Common Sense*, 2, pp. 67–72. Out of print, available at http://commonsensejournal.org.uk/issue-2/.

Bonefeld, W. (1994) 'Human Practice and Perversion: Beyond Autonomy and Structure', *Common Sense* 15, pp. 43–52. Out of print, available at http://commonsensejournal.org.uk/issue-15/.

Bonefeld, W. (1995) 'Capital as Subject and the Existence of Labour'. In Bonefeld, W. et al., *Open Marxism* Vol. 3, (London: Pluto Press), pp. 182–212.

Bonefeld, W. (1996) 'Money, Equality and Exploitation: An Interpretation of Marx's Treatment of Money'. In Bonefeld, W. and Holloway, J. (eds) *Global Capital, Nation States and the Politics of Money* (London: Palgrave Macmillan), pp. 178–209.

Bonefeld, W. (2002) 'State, Revolution and Self-Determination'. In Bonefeld, W. and Tischler, S. (eds) *What Is to Be Done? Leninism, Anti-Leninist Marxism and the Question of Revolution Today* (Aldershot: Ashgate), pp. 128–150.

Bonefeld, W. (2004) 'The Principle of Hope in Human Emancipation: On Holloway', *Herramienta*, 25, pp. 197–208.

Bonefeld, W. (2005) 'Uncertainty and Social Autonomy', *Libcom.org*, http://libcom.org/library/uncertainty-and-social-autonomy-bonefeld, last accessed 14 March 2014.

Bonefeld, W. (2008) 'The permanence of primitive accumulation: commodity fetishism and social constitution'. In Bonefeld, W. (ed.) *Subverting the Present, Imagining the Future* (New York: Autonomedia), pp. 51–66.

Bonefeld, W. (2009) 'Emancipatory Praxis and Conceptuality in Adorno'. In Holloway, J., Matamoros, F., and Tischler, S. (eds) *Negativity and Revolution: Adorno and Politics* (London: Pluto Press), pp. 122–148.

Bonefeld, W. (2010) 'Abstract Labour: Against Its Nature and on Its Time', *Capital & Class*, 34(2), pp. 257–276.

Bonefeld, W. (2014) *Critical Theory and the Critique of Political Economy: On Subversion and Negative Reason* (New York, London, New Delhi and Sydney: Bloomsbury).

Bonefeld, W., Gunn, R., and Psychopedis, K. (1992a) (eds) *Open Marxism: Theory and Practice*, Vol. 1 (London: Pluto Press).

Bonefeld, W., Gunn, R., and Psychopedis, K. (1992b) (eds) *Open Marxism: Theory and Practice*, Vol. 2 (London: Pluto Press).

Bonefeld, W., Gunn, R., Holloway, J., and Psychopedis, K. (1995) (eds) *Open Marxism*, Vol. 3 (London: Pluto Press).

Bonefeld, W. and Holloway, J. (1996) 'Introduction: The Politics of Money'. In Bonefeld, W. and Holloway, J. (eds) *Global Capital, Nation States and the Politics of Money* (London: Palgrave Macmillan), pp. 1–6.

Bonefeld, W. and Psychopedis, K. (2005) *Human Dignity. Social autonomy and the critique of capitalism*, (Aldershot: Ashgate).

Bonfil Batalla, G. (1987) *Mexico Profundo: Una Civilización Negada* (México, DF: SEP/CIESAS).

Bonnet, A. (2002) 'The Command of Money-Capital and the Latin American Crises'. In Bonefeld, W. and Tischler, S. (eds) *What Is to Be Done? Leninism, Anti-Leninist Marxism and the Question of Revolution Today* (Aldershot: Ashgate), pp. 101–127.

Boron, A. (1993) 'El experimento neoliberal de Carlos Saúl Menem', *El Cielo por Asalto*, 6, pp. 59–80.

Boron, A. (1995) 'Estamos mal pero vamos bien', *Doxa*, 13/14, pp. 1–10.

Boron, A. (2001) 'La selva y la Polis. Reflexiones en torno a la teoría política del zapatismo', *OSAL* no 4, pp. 177–186.

Boron, A. (2003) 'La sociedad civil después del diluvio neoliberal'. In Sader, E. and Gentili, P. (eds) *La trama del neoliberalismo. Mercado, crisis y exclusión social* (Buenos Aires: CLACSO, EUDEBA), pp. 51–92.

Boron, A. (2005) 'Holloway on Power and the "State Illusion"', *Capital & Class*, 84, pp. 35–38.

Boron, A. (2012) 'Argentina: Dilemas de la izquierda marxista', *América Latina en Movimiento*, 475, http://alainet.org/publica/alai475w.pdf, last accessed 14 May 2014.

Boron, A., Gambina, J., and Minsburg, N. (eds) (1999) *Tiempos Violentos. Neoliberalismo, globalización y desigualdad en América Latina* (Buenos Aires: CLACSO–EUDEBA).

Borras, S. (Jr) (2006) 'The underlying assumptions, theory and practice of neoliberal land policies'. In Rosset, P., Patel, R. and Courville, M. (eds) *Promised Land.*

Competing versions of agrarian reform, (Oakland – California: Food First Books), pp. 99–176.

Bourdieu, P. (1998) *Acts of Resistance. Against the new myths of our time* (Cambridge: Polity Press).

Bowman, P. and Stamp, R. (20110 (eds) *Reading Rancière* (London and New York: Continuum).

Branford, S. (2005) 'The Lula government and the agrarian reform'. In Wainwright, H. and S. Branford (eds) *In the Eye of the Storm Left-wing activists discuss the political crisis in Brazil*, Online Dossier, Transnational Institute, http://www.tni.org/sites/www.tni.org/files/download/brazildossier.pdf.

Branford, S. (2009) 'Brazil: Has the Dream Ended'?. In Lievesley, G. and Ludlam, S. (eds) *Reclaiming Latin America: Experiments in Radical Social Democracy* (London and New York: Zed Books), pp. 153–169.

Branford, S. and Rocha, J. (2002) *Cutting the Wire: The Story of the Landless Movement in Brazil* (London: Latin America Bureau).

Breines, W. (1989) *Community and Organization in the New Left, 1962–1968: The Great Refusal* (New Brunswick, NJ: Rutgers University Press).

Bricker, K. (2013) '"Practice First, Then Theory:" The Zapatista Little School Shares Lessons Learned During 19 Years of Self-Governance', *Americas programme*, 5 September 2013, http://www.cipamericas.org/archives/10606, last accessed 14 May 2014.

Brissette, E. (2013) 'Prefiguring the Realm of Freedom at Occupy Oakland', *Rethinking Marxism,* Vol. 25(2), pp. 218–227.

Bronner, S. (1997) 'Utopian Projections: In Memory of Ernst Bloch'. In Daniel, J.O. and Moylan, T. *Not Yet: Reconsidering Ernst Bloch (*London and New York: Verso), pp. 165–174.

Burch, S. (2012) 'Ecuador: pelear en la correlación de fuerzas', *América Latina en Movimiento*, 475, pp. 25–27.

Burch, S. and Tamayo, G. (2011) 'Crisis civilizatoria e indignación generalizada', *América Latina en Movimiento*, 471, pp. 5–8.

Burdick, P., Oxhorn, P., and Roberts, K. (eds) (2009) *Beyond Neoliberalism in Latin America: Societies and Politics at the Crossroads* (New York: Palgrave Macmillan).

Burguete Cal y Mayor, A. (2003) 'The de facto Autonomous Process'. In Rus, J., Hernández Castillo, R., and Mattiace, S. (eds) *Mayan Lives, Mayan Utopias: The Indigenous Peoples of Chiapas and the Zapatista Rebellion* (Oxford: Rowman & Littlefield), pp. 191–218.

Burguete Cal y Mayor, A. (2004) 'Chiapas: nuevos municipios para espantar municipios autónomos'. In Hernández, R., Paz, S., and Sierra, M.T. (eds) *El Estado y los indígenas en tiempos del PAN* (México: Porrúa, CIESAS, Cámara de Diputados LIX Legislatura).

Burguete Cal y Mayor, A. (2010) 'Autonomía: la emergencia de un nuevo paradigma en las luchas por la descolonización en América Latina'. In González, M., Burguete Cal y Mayor, A., and Ortiz, P. (eds) *La Autonomía a debate* (Quito: FLACSO, GTZ, IWGIA, CIESAS, UNICH), pp. 63–94.

Cabezas, M. (2007) 'Caracterización del ciclo rebelde 2000–2005'. In Turrión, I.P. and Espasandin López, J. (eds) *Bolivia en movimiento. Acción colectiva y poder político* (Madrid: Ediciones de Intervención Cultural/El Viejo Topo).

Calcagno, A. (2001) 'Ajuste structural y modalidades de desarrollo en América Latina'. In Sader, E. (2001) (ed.) *El ajuste estructural en América Latina. Costos sociales y alternativas,* Buenos Aires: CLACSO, ASDI) pp. 75–98.

Calderón, F. (1986) (ed.) *Los movimientos sociales ante la crisis*. Buenos Aires: CLACSO/Universidad de las Naciones Unidas.

Campbell, D. and Goñi, U. (2003) 'Argentina begins healing process by reopening wounds of the Dirty War', *The Guardian*, 18 August 2003, last accessed 30 August 2014, http://www.theguardian.com/world/2003/aug/18/argentina. duncancampbell.

Canitrot, A. (1994) 'Crisis and Transformation of the Argentine State (1978–1992)'. In Smith, W., Acuña, C. and Gamarra, E. (eds) (1994a) *Democracy, Markets and Structural Reform in Latin America: Argentina, Bolivia, Brazil, Chile, and Mexico*, (Miami: University of Miami), pp.75–102.

Carlsen, L. (2006) 'An Uprising against the Inevitable', *Americas programme*, http://www.cipamericas.org/archives/1315, last accessed on 14 August 2013.

Carlsen, L. (2014) 'Zapatistas at Twenty', *Americas programme*, 14 January 2014 http://www.cipamericas.org/archives/11287.

Carlsson, C. and Manning, F. (2010) 'Nowtopia: Strategic Exodus?', *Antipode*, 42(4), pp. 924–953.

Carpintero, E., Hernández, M., and Petras, J.F. (eds) (2002) *Produciendo realidad: las empresas comunitarias* (Buenos Aires: Topia Editorial en colaboración con La Maza).

Castoriadis, C. (1975/2005) *The Imaginary Institution of Society* (Cambridge: Polity Press).

Castoriadis, C. (1991) *Philosophy, Politics, Autonomy: Essays in Political Philosophy* (Oxford: Oxford University Press).

Ceceña, A.E. (2001a) 'Modernización neoliberal en México. Nueva valorización del territorio y sus recursos'. In Sader, E. (ed.) *El ajuste estructural en América Latina: Costos sociales y alternativas* (Buenos Aires: CLACSO, ASDI), pp. 51–73.

Ceceña, A.E. (2001b) 'La marcha de la dignidad indígena', *OSAL*, 4, 9–14.

Ceceña, A.E. (2005) *La guerra por el agua y por la vida. Cochabamba: una experiencia de construcción comunitaria frente al neoliberalismo y al Banco Mundial* (Cochabamba: Coordinadora de Defensa del Agua y de la Vida).

Ceceña, A. and Barreda, A. (1998) 'Chiapas and the Global Restructuring of Capital'. In Holloway, J. and Peláez, E. (eds) *Zapatista! Reinventing Revolution in Mexico* (London: Pluto Press), pp. 39–63.

Cerda García, A. (2011) *Imaginando Zapatismo. Multiculturalidad y autonomía Indígena en Chiapas desde un Municipio Autónomo* (Mexico, DF: Universidad Autónoma Metropolitana).

Chalieu, P. (C. Castoriadis) (1955) 'Sur le contenu du socialisme', *Socialism ou Barbarie*, 17 (July), last accessed 14 May 2014, https://collectiflieuxcommuns. fr/spip/spip.php?article64.

Chaplin, A. (2010) 'Social Movements in Bolivia: From Strength to Power', *Community Development Journal*, 45(3), pp. 346–355.

Charnock, G. (2010) 'Challenging New State Spatialities? The Open Marxism of Henri Lefebvre', *Antipode*, 42(5), pp. 1279–1303.

Chassot, A. (2000) 'Sem terra (ainda), mas com muita educaçao', *OSAL*, 2, pp. 45–48.

Chatterton, P. (2005) 'Making autonomous geographies: Argentina's popular uprising and the "Movimiento de Trabajadores Desocupados" (Unemployed Workers Movement)', *Geoforum*, 36, pp. 545–556.

Chatterton, P. (2010) 'Introduction to the Symposium Autonomy: the struggle for survival, management and the common', *Antipode* 42(4), pp. 897–908.

Chávez, P. and Mokrani, D. (2007) 'Los movimientos sociales en la Asamblea Constituyente. Hacia la reconfiguración de la política', *OSAL*, 22, pp. 107–117.

Chibber, V. (2013) *Postcolonial Theory and the Specter of Capital* (London – New York: Verso).

Choudry, A., Majavu, M., and Wood, L. (2013) 'Struggles, Strategies and Analysis of Anticolonial and Postcolonial Social Movements', *Interface*, 5(1), pp. 1–10 http://www.interaltamirafacejournal.net.

Clarke, S. (1988) *Keynesianism, Monetarism and the Crisis of the State* (Aldershot: Edward Elgar).

Clarke, S. (ed.) (1991) *The State Debate* (London: Palgrave Macmillan).

Clarke, S. (1992) *Marx, Marginalism & Modern Sociology: From Adam Smith to Max Weber* (London: Palgrave Macmillan).

Clayes, P. (2012) 'The Creation of New Rights by the Food Sovereignty Movement: The Challenge of Institutionalizing Subversion', *Sociology*, 46(5), pp. 844–860.

CLDHCN (2001) 'Informe Preliminar sobre Lavado de Dinero en la Argentina', MP E. Carrió, Cámara de Diputados de la Nación, August 2001, last accessed 20 August 2014, http://www1.hcdn.gov.ar/dependencias/ari/Principal/principal.htm.

CLDHCN (2002) 'A un año del preinforme de la Comisión de Lavado de Dinero', *Cámara de Diputados de la Nación*, last accessed 20 August 2014, http://www1. hcdn.gov.ar/dependencias/ari/Principal/principal.htm.

Cleaver, H. (1992) 'The Inversion of Class Perspective in Marxian Theory: From Valorisation to Self–Valorisation'. In Bonefeld, W. et al. (eds) *Open Marxism*, Vol. II (London: Pluto Press), pp. 106–44.

Cleaver, H. (1993) 'Marxian Categories, the Crisis of Capital and the Constitution of Social Subjectivity Today', *Common Sense*, 14, pp. 32–55. Out of print, available at http://commonsensejournal.org.uk/issue-14/.

Cleaver, H. (1996) 'The Subversion of Money-as-Command in the Current Crisis'. In Bonefeld, W. and Holloway, J. (eds) *Global Capital, Nation States and the Politics of Money* (London: Palgrave Macmillan), pp. 141–177.

Cleaver, H. (2002) 'Work is Still the Central Issue!'. In Dinerstein, A. and Neary, M. (eds) *The Labour Debate: An Investigation into the Theory and Reality of Capitalist Work* (Aldershot: Ashgate), 135–148.

Cleaver, H. (2009) 'Trayectorias de Autonomía'. In Albertani, C., Rovira Sancho, G., and Modonesi, M. (eds) *La Autonomía Posible, reinvención política y emancipación* (Mexico, DF: UAM), pp. 152–163.

Cleaver, H. (2011) 'Work Refusal and Self-Organisation'. In Nelson, A. and Timmerman, F. (eds) *Life Without Money: Building Fair and Sustainable Economies* (London: Pluto Press).

Cleaver, H. and De Angelis, M. (1993) 'An Interview with Harry Cleaver', University of Texas, last accessed 14 May 2014, http://la.utexas.edu/users/hcleaver/InterviewwithHarryCleaver.html.

Cole, D. (2000) *Negativity in Politics: Dionysus and Dialectics from Kant to Poststructuralism* (London and New York: Routledge).

Cole, M. (2007) 'Re-thinking Unemployment: A Challenge to the Legacy of Jahoda et al', *Sociology*, 41(6), pp. 1133–1149.

Colectivo Situaciones (2001) *MTD Solano* (Buenos Aires: Ediciones de Mano en Mano).

Colectivo Situaciones (2002a) *19 y 20 Apuntes para el nuevo protagonismo social* (Buenos Aires: Ediciones de Mano en Mano).

Colectivo Situaciones (2002b) *Genocida en el Barrio. Mesa del Escrache Popular* (Buenos Aires: Ediciones de Mano en Mano).

Colectivo Situaciones (2005) *Bienvenidos a la Selva; Diálogos a partir de la Sexta Delaración del EZLN* (Buenos Aires: Tinta Limón).

Colectivo Situaciones (2012) 'Closures and Openings in the Impasse', *South Atlantic Quarterly*, 111(1), pp. 133–144.

Coletti, C. (2003) 'Avanços e impasses do MST e da luta pela terra no Brasil nos anos recentes'. In Seoane, J. (ed.) *Movimientos sociales y conflicto social en América Latina* (Buenos Aires: CLACSO).

Colombo, E. (1993) 'La integración imaginaria del proletariado'. In Colombo, E. (ed.) *El imaginario social* (Montevideo: Altamira), pp. 173–212.

CONADEP (National Commission on Disappeared People) (1986) *Never Again* (London and Boston, MA: Faber and Faber).

Contartese, D. and Deledicque, M. (2013) '¿Participación ciudadana o auto organización popular? Movilización y resistencia en las Juntas Vecinales de El Alto, Bolivia'. In Dinerstein, A.C. et al. (eds) *¿Movimientos sociales y autonomía colectiva. La política de la esperanza en América Latina* (Buenos Aires: Capital Intelectual), pp. 41–68.

Conway, J. and Singh, J. (2011) 'Radical Democracy in Global Perspective: Notes from the Pluriverse', *Third World Quarterly*, 32(4), pp. 689–706.

Coraggio, J.L. (1999) *La Política social y la economía del trabajo* (Madrid: Miño y Dávila).

Coraggio, J.L. (2008) 'Crítica de la political social neoliberal: las nuevas tendencias'. In Ponce Jarrín, J. (ed.) *¿Es posible pensar una nueva política social para América Latina?* (Quito: FLACSO Ecuador and Ministerio de Cultura del Ecuador), pp. 81–93.

Cornell, A. (2012) 'Consensus: What It Is, What It Isn't, Where It Comes From and Where It Must Go'. In Khatib, K., Killjoy, M., and McGuire, M. (eds) *We Are Many: Reflections on Movement Strategy from Occupation to Liberation* (Oakland, CA: AK Press).

Cornwall, A. and Brock, K. (2005) 'Beyond Buzzwords: "Poverty reduction", "Participation" and "Empowerment" in Development Policy', Overarching Concerns Programme, Paper 10 (Geneva: UNRISD).

Coronil, F. (2000) 'Naturaleza del postcolonialismo: del eurocentrismo and globocentrismo'. In Lander, E. (ed.) *La colonialidad del saber: Eurocentrismo y ciencias sociales. Perspectivas latinamericanas* (Buenos Aires: CLACSO), pp. 87–112.

Cortez Ruíz, C. (2004) 'Social Strategies and Public Policies in an Indigenous Zone in Chiapas, Mexico', *IDS Bulletin*, 35(2), pp. 76–83.

Courville, M. and Patel, R. (2006) 'The Resurgence of Agrarian Reform in the Twenty-First Century'. In Rosset, P., Patel, R., and Courville, M. (eds) *Promised Land: Competing Versions of Agrarian Reform* (Oakland, CA: Food First Books), pp. 3–22.

Cox, L. and Nilsen, A. (2007) 'Social movements and the "Movement of Movements": studying resistance to neoliberal globalisation', *Sociology Compass*, 1(2), pp. 424–442.

Cox, L. (2013) 'Eppur si muove'. In Barker, C., Cox, L., Krinsky, J. and Nilsen, A. (eds) *Marxism and Social Movements* (Leiden: Brill), pp. 125–146.

Cox, L. (2014) 'Movements Making Knowledge: A New Wave of Inspiration for Sociology?' *Sociology*, 48(5), pp. 954–971.

Crabtree, J. (2009) 'Bolivia: Playing by New Rules'. In Lievesley, G. and Ludlam, S. *Reclaiming Latin America: Experiments in Radical Social Democracy* (London and New York: Zed Books), pp. 91–108.

Crass, C. (2013) *Towards Collective Liberation: Anti-Racist Organising, Feminist Praxis, and Movement Building Strategy* (Oakland, CA: PM Press).

Critchley, S. (2008) *Infinitely Demanding. Ethics of Commitment, Politics of Resistance* (London – NY: Verso).

Cuninghame, P. (2010) 'Autonomism as a Global Social Movements', *Journal of Labour and Society*, 13, pp. 451–464.

Cuninghame, P. and Ballesteros Corona, C. (1998) 'A Rainbow at Midnight: Zapatistas and Autonomy', *Capital & Class*, 66, pp. 12–21.

Daly, F. (2013) 'The Zero Point: Encountering the Dark Emptiness of Nothingness'. In Thompson, P. and Žižek, S. *The Privatization of Hope: Ernst Bloch and the Future of Utopia* (Durham, NC: Duke University Press), pp. 164–202.

Dausá, A. (2012) 'Bolivia: Novena Marcha', *América Latina en Movimiento*, 26 April, last accessed 14 May 2014, http://alainet.org/active/54361&lang=es.

Davis, D. (1999) 'The Power of Distance: Theorising Social Movement in Latin America', *Theory and Society*, 28(4), pp. 585–638.

Day, R.J.F. (2004) 'From Hegemony to Affinity', *Cultural Studies*, 18(5), pp. 716–748.

De Almeida, L. and Ruiz Sánchez, F. (2000) 'The Landless Workers' Movement and Social Struggles Against Neoliberalism', *Latin American Perspectives*, 27(5), pp. 11–32.

De Angelis, M. (1995) 'Beyond the Technological and the Social Paradigms: A Political Reading of Abstract Labour as the Substance of Value', *Capital & Class*, 57, pp. 107–134.

De Angelis, M. (1998) '2nd Encounter for Humanity & Against Neoliberalism', *Capital & Class*, 65, pp. 135–142.

De Angelis, M. (2000) 'Globalization, New Internationalism and the Zapatistas', *Capital & Class*, 70, pp. 9–36.

De Angelis, M. (2004) 'Building a New World, Bottom Up'. In Chandra, P., Ghosh, A., and Kumar, R. (eds) *The Politics of Imperialism and Counterstrategies* (New Delhi: Aakar), pp. 330–360.

De Angelis, M. (2007) *The Beginning of History: Value Struggles and Global Capital* (London: Pluto).

De Angelis, M. (2008) 'Marx and primitive accumulation: the continuous character of capital's enclosures'. In Bonefeld, W (ed.) *Subverting the Present, Imagining the Future* (New York: Autonomedia), pp. 27–50.

De Angelis, M. (2010) 'The Production of Commons and the "Explosion" of the Middle Class', *Antipode*, 42(4), pp. 954–977.

Deere, C. and Royce, F. (eds) (2009) *Rural Social Movements in Latin America* (Gainesville, FL: University Press of Florida).

De la Cadena, M. (2010) 'Indigenous Cosmopolitics in the Andes: Conceptual Reflections beyond "Politics"', *Cultural Anthropology*, 25(2), pp. 334–370.

De la Cadena, M. and Starn, O. (eds) (2007) *Indigenous Experience Today* (Oxford and New York: Berg).

De la Fuente, M. (2000) 'La guerra por el agua en Cochabamba. Crónica de una dolorosa victoria', *Documentos de reflexión académica*, No. 15 (Cochabamba: Universidad Mayor de San Simón).

De la Garza Toledo, E. (ed.) (2005) *Sindicatos y nuevos movimientos sociales en América Latina* (Buenos Aires: CLACSO, ASDI).

Deledicque, M. and Contartese, D. (2008) 'The Juntas Vecinales de El Alto, Bolivia', Final Case Study Research Report. ESRC NGPA – Dinerstein RES-155-25-0007.

Deledicque, M., Ghiotto, L., Pascual, R., and Contartese, D. (2008) 'The Movement of Rural Landless Workers (MST) in Brazil', Final Case Study Research Report. ESRC NGPA – Dinerstein RES-155-25-0007.

Deledicque, L. and Moser, J. (2006) 'El proceso de trabajo en empresas recuperadas. La Unión Papelera Platense: Un estudio de caso', *LabourAgain*, date accessed 10 May 2013, http://www.iisg.nl/labouragain/documents/melina_moser.pdf.

Deledicque, M., Moser, J. and Féliz, M. (2005) 'Recuperación de empresas por sus trabajadores y autogestión obrera. Un estudio de caso de una empresa en Argentina', *Revista de economía Pública, social y cooperativa*, CIRIEC España,Vol.1 (51), pp. 51–76.

Deleuze, G. and Guattari, F. (1999) *A Thousand Plateaus: Capitalism & Schizophrenia* (London: Athlone Press).

Denis, R. (2012) 'The Birth of an "Other Politics" in Venezuela', *South Atlantic Quarterly*, 111(1), pp. 81–93.

De Oliveira, F. (2004) '¿Hay vías abiertas para América Latina?'. In Boron, A. (ed.) *Nueva hegemonía mundial. Alternativas de cambio y movimientos sociales* (Buenos Aires: CLACSO), pp. 111–118.

Días Martins, M. (2006) 'Learning to Participate: The MST Experience in Brazil'. In Rosset, P., Patel, R., and Courville, M. (eds) *Promised Land: Competing Versions of Agrarian Reform* (Oakland, CA: Food First Books), pp. 265–276.

Díaz-Polanco, H. 1996. "La autonomía de los pueblos indios en el diálogo entre el EZLN y el gobierno federal", *Revista del Senado de la República*, 2, n. 2 (January–March), pp.104–15.

Díaz-Polanco, H. and Gorman, S. (1982) 'Indigenismo, Populism, and Marxism', *Latin American Perspectives*, 9(2), pp. 42–61.

Dikeç, M. (2010) 'Colonial Minds, Postcolonial Places', *Antipode*, 42(4), pp. 801–805.

Dinerstein, A.C. (1997) 'Marxism and Subjectivity: Searching for the Marvellous. (Prelude to a Marxist Notion of Action)', *Common Sense*, 22, pp. 83–96. Out of print, available at http://commonsensejournal.org.uk/issue-22/.

Dinerstein, A.C. (1999) 'The Violence of Stability: Argentina in the 1990s'. In Neary, M. (ed.) *Global Humanisation: Studies in the Manufacture of Labour* (London and New York: Mansell), pp. 46–75.

Dinerstein, A.C. (2001) 'Roadblocks in Argentina', *Capital & Class*, 74, pp. 1–7.

Dinerstein, A.C. (2002a) 'Regaining Materiality: Unemployment and the Invisible Subjectivity of Labour'. In Dinerstein, A. and Neary, M. (eds) *The Labour Debate. An Investigation into the Theory and Reality of Capitalist Work* (Aldershot: Ashgate), pp. 203–225.

Dinerstein, A.C. (2002b) 'The Battle of Buenos Aires: Crisis, Insurrection and the Reinvention of Politics in Argentina', *Historical Materialism*, 10(4), pp. 5–38.

Dinerstein, A.C. (2003a) 'Power or Counter Power? The Dilemma of the Piquetero Movement in Argentina Post-Crisis', *Capital & Class*, 81, pp. 1–7.

Dinerstein, A.C. (2003b) '¡Que se vayan todos! Popular insurrection and *Asambleas Barriales* in Argentina', *Bulletin of Latin American Research*, Vol. 22 (2), pp. 187–200.

Dinerstein, A.C. (2005a) 'A Call for Emancipatory Reflection: Introduction to the Forum', *Capital & Class*, 84, pp. 12–42.

Dinerstein, A.C. (2005b) 'Entre el éxtasis y el desencuentro. Los desafíos de la rebelión'. In Bonet, A., Holloway, J. and Tischler, S. (eds) *Marxismo Abierto. Una visión Europea y Latinoamericana,* Vol. I (Buenos Aires: Herramienta Ediciones), pp. 147–186.

Dinerstein, A.C. (2007) '"Workers" Factory Takeovers and New State Programmes: Towards the "Institutionalisation" of Non–Governmental Public Action in Argentina', *Policy and Politics* 35 (3), pp. 527–548.

Dinerstein, A.C. (2008a) 'Here Is the Rose, Dance Here! A Riposte to the Debate on the Argentinean Crisis', *Historical Materialism,* 16(1), pp. 101–114.

Dinerstein, A.C. (2008b) 'Lessons from a Journey: The Piquetero Movement in Argentina'. In Bonefeld, W. (ed.) *Subverting the Present–Imagining the Future: Insurrection, Movement, Commons* (New York: Autonomedia), pp. 231–246.

Dinerstein, A.C. (2010) 'Autonomy in Latin America: Between Resistance and Integration. Echoes from the Piqueteros experience', *Community Development Journal,* 45(3), pp. 356–366.

Dinerstein, A.C. (2012) 'Interstitial Revolution: On the Explosive Fusion of Negativity and Hope', *Capital & Class,* 36(3), pp. 521–540.

Dinerstein, A.C. (2013) 'From Corporatist to Autonomous: Unemployed Workers Organisations and the Remaking of Labour Subjectivity in Argentina'. In Howell, J. (ed.) *Non-Governmental Public Action and Social Justice,* Vol. 2, (Houndmills and New York: Palgrave Macmillan), pp. 36–59.

Dinerstein, A.C. (2014a) 'Too Bad for the Facts, Confronting Value with Hope', *South Atlantic Quarterly,* 113(2), pp. 367–440.

Dinerstein, A.C. (2014b) 'Disagreement and Hope: The Hidden Transcripts in the Grammar of Political Recovery in Post-Crisis Argentina'. In Levey, C., Ozarow, D., and Wylde, C. (eds) *Argentina Since the 2001 Crisis: Recovering the Past, Reclaiming the Future* (Houndmills and New York: Palgrave Macmillan), pp. 115–133.

Dinerstein, A.C. (2014c) 'The Dream of Dignified Work: On Good and Bad Utopias', *Development & Change* 45(5), pp. 1–22.

Dinerstein, A.C., Contartese, D., and Deledicque, M. (2010) *La ruta de los Piqueteros. Luchas y Legados,* (Buenos Aires: Capital Intelectual).

Dinerstein, A.C. and Deneulin, S. (2012) 'Hope Movements: Naming Mobilization in a Post-Development World', *Development and Change,* 43(2), pp. 585–602.

Dinerstein, A.C. and Ferrero, J.P. (2012) 'The Limits of Participatory Democracy in South America', *Bath Papers in International Development,* 16 (Bath, UK: Centre for Development Studies, University of Bath), http://www.bath.ac.uk/cds/publications/.

Dinerstein, A.C., Contartese, D., Deledicque, M. Ferrero, J.P., Ghiotto, L. and R. Pascual (2013) *¿Movimientos sociales y autonomía colectiva. La Política de la Esperanza en América Latina,* Capital Intelectual: Buenos Aires.

Dinerstein, A.C. and Neary, M. (2002a) 'From Here to Utopia: Finding Inspiration for the Labour Debate'. In Dinerstein, A.C. and Neary, M. (eds) *The Labour Debate: An Investigation into the Theory and Reality of Capitalist Work* (Aldershot: Ashgate), pp. 1–26.

Dinerstein, A. C. and Neary, M. (2002b) 'Anti-Value-in-Motion: Labour, Real Subsumption and the Struggles against Capitalism'. In Dinerstein, A.C. and Neary, M. (eds) *The Labour Debate: An Investigation into the Theory and Reality of Capitalist Work* (Aldershot: Ashgate), pp. 225–238.

Di Risio, D., Gavaldà, M., Pérez Roig, D. and Scandizzo, H. (20 12) *Zonas de sacrificio. Impactos de la industria hidrocarburífera en Salta y Norpatagonia* (Neuquén: Observatorio Petrolero del Sur -America Libre).

Do Alto, H. (2010) 'La "revolución" de Evo Morales o los caminos sinuosos de la refundación de Bolivia'. In Gaudichaud, F. (ed.) *El volcán latino–americano. Izquierdas, movimientos sociales y neoliberalismo al sur del Río Bravo*. Electronic version of the first edition (Paris: Edición Textuel) 2008, http://www.rebelion. org/docs/115701.pdf.

Drimer, R. (1990) *La deuda externa. Propuesta para la República Argentina*, Biblioteca Política Argentina, Vol. 284 (Buenos Aires: Centro Editor de América Latina).

Dunkerley, J. (2007) 'Evo Morales, the "Two Bolivias" and the Third Bolivian Revolution', *Journal of Latin American Studies*, 39, pp. 133–166.

Durston, J. (2008) 'Los Movimientos Sociales de Pobres Rurales y sus aportes a la democratización'. In Domike, A. (ed.) *Sociedad Civil y Movimientos sociales. Construyendo democracias sostenibles en América Latina* (New York and Washington, DC: BID), pp. 145–182.

Dussel, E. (2013) *Ethics of Liberation: In the Age of Globalisation and Exclusion* (Durham, NC and London: Duke University Press).

Earle, D. and Simonelli, J. (2005) *Uprising of Hope. Sharing the Zapatista Journey to Alternative Development* (Walnut, Lanham, New York, Toronto and Oxford: Altamira Press, Rowman & Littlefield).

Echaide, J. (2006) *Debate sobre las empresas recuperadas. Un aporte desde lo legal, lo jurídico y lo político* (Buenos Aires: Monte Ávila Editores Latinoamericana).

Ellner, S. (2012) 'The Distinguishing Features of Latin America's New Left in Power', *Venezuelanalysis.com,* 17 January, last accessed 30 March 2013, http://venezuelanalysis.com/analysis/6754.

Elson, D. (1979) 'The Value Theory of Labour'. In Elson, D. (ed.) *Value: The Representation of Labour in Capitalism*, CSE Books (London: Humanities Press), pp. 115–180.

Escobar, A. (1992) 'Imagining a Post-development Era? Critical Thought, Development and Social Movements', *Social Text*, 31/32, pp. 20–56.

Escobar, A. (2010) 'Latin America at a Crossroad: Alternative Modernizations, Postliberalism, or Postdevelopment?', *Cultural Studies*, 24(1), pp. 1–65.

Escobar, A. and Alvarez, S. (1992) *The Making of Social Movements in Latin America: Identity, Strategy and Democracy* (Boulder, San Francisco and Oxford: Westview Press), pp. 1–18.

Eslin, M. (1991) *The Theatre of the Absurd* (London: Penguin).

Espinoza, C. and Gonzálvez, G. (2003) 'Bolivia arrinconada en la azotea de su historia', *OSAL*, 10, pp. 29–36.

Esteva, G. (1999) 'The Zapatistas and People's Power', *Capital & Class*, 68, pp.153–182.

Esteva, G. (2003) 'The Meaning and Scope of the Struggle for Autonomy'. In Rus, J., Hernández Castillo, R., and Mattiace, S. (eds) *Mayan Lives, Mayan Utopias: The Indigenous Peoples of Chiapas and the Zapatista Rebellion* (Oxford: Rowman & Littlefield), pp. 243–270.

Esteva, G. (2005) *Celebración del Zapatismo* (México: Ediciones ¡Basta!).

Esteva, G. (2009) 'Mas allá del desarrollo: la Buena Vida', *América Latina en Movimiento* No 445, last accessed 30 August 2014, http://alainet.org/publica/445.phtml.

Esteva, G. (2011) 'Otra autonomía, otra democracia'. In Adamovsky et al. *Pensar las autonomías* (México: Bajo Tierra and Sisifo Ediciones), pp. 121–150.

Esteva, G. (2014) 'Commoning in the new society', *Community Development Journal*, Vol 49, Supplement 1, January 2014, pp. il44-il59, doi:10.1093/cdj/bsu016.

Esteva, G. and Prakash, M.S. (2008) *Grassroots Postmodernism: Remaking the Soil of Cultures* (London: Zed Books).

Esteva, G. and M. Prakash (1998) 'Beyond Development, What?', *Development in Practice* 8(3), pp. 280–296.

Esteva, G. and M. S. Prakash (1997) *Hope at the margins: beyond human rights and development* (New York: St. Martin's Press).

Esteves, A., Motta, S., and Cox, L. (2009) '"Civil Society" versus Social Movements', *Interface*, 1(2) (November), pp. 1–21, http://www.interfacejournal.net/2010/11/interface-issue-1-volume-2-civil-society-versus-social-movements/.

EZLN (1994/1995) *La Palabra de los Armados de Verdad y Fuego* (México, DF: Fuenteovejuna).

Fajn, G. (ed.) (2003) *Protesta Social, autogestión y rupturas en la subjetividad* (Buenos Aires: Centro Cultural de la Cooperación).

Fals Borda, O. (1992) 'Social Movements and Political Power in Latin America'. In Escobar, A. and Alvarez, S. (eds) *The Making of Social Movements in Latin America*, pp. 303–316.

Fanelli, J., Frenkel, R., and Rozenwurcel, G. (1994) 'Growth and Structural Reform in Latin America: Where We Stand'. In Smith, W.C., Acuña, C.H., and Gamarra, E.A. (eds) (1994b)) *Latin American Political Economy in the Age of Neoliberal Reform* (Boulder, CO: Lynne Reinner), pp. 101–125.

Fatheuer, T. (2011) 'Buen Vivir: A Brief Introduction to Latin America's New Concepts for the Good Life and the Rights of Nature', *Publication Series on Ecology*, 17 (Berlin: Heinrich Böll Foundation).

Feijóo, C. and Salas Oroño, L. (2002) 'Las asambleas y el movimiento social' in Bielsa, R. et al. (2002) *¿Qué son las Asambleas Populares?* (Buenos Aires: Peña Lillo – Continente), pp. 27–30.

Féliz, M. (2012) 'Neo-developmentalism: Beyond Neoliberalism? Capitalist Crisis and Argentina's Development Since the 1990s', *Historical Materialism*, 20(2), pp. 105–124.

Flesher Fominaya, C. (2010b) 'Collective Identity in Social Movements: Central Concepts and Debates', *Sociology Compass* 4/6, pp. 393–404.

Flórez-Flórez, J. (2007) 'Lectura no eurocéntrica de los movimientos sociales latinoamericanos'. In Castro-Gómez, S. and Grosfoguel, R. (eds) *El giro decolonial. Reflexiones para una diversidad epistémica más allá del capitalismo global* (Bogotá: Siglo del Hombre Editores), pp. 243–266.

Foweraker, J. (1995) *Theorizing social movements'* (London, Boulder, Colorado: Pluto Press).

Free Association (2011) *Moments of Excess: Movements, Protest and Everyday Life* (Oakland, CA: PM Press).

Frei Betto (2012) 'Brasil: Rumbo a la reforma agraria', *América Latina en Movimiento,* 21 March 2012, last accessed 13 May 2014, http://alainet.org/active/53548&lang=es.

Freire, P. (1970/1996) *Pedagogy of the Oppressed* (London: Penguin Books).

Frenkel, M., Fanelli, J.M., and Rozenwurcel, G. (1992) *Crítica al Consenso de Washington*, Working Paper 1 (Lima: FONDAD).

Fuchs, J. (1993) *Las Transnacionales en la Argentina,* Biblioteca Política Argentina, Vol. 410 and 411, (Buenos Aires: CEAL).

Fuchs, J. and Vélez, J.C. (2001) *Argentina de rodillas. Terrorismo Económico: de Martinez de Hoz a Cavallo* (Buenos Aires: Tribuna Latinoamericana).

Fuentes, F. (2012a) 'The Morales Government: Neoliberalism in Disguise?', *International Socialism*, 134, March, last accessed 1 May 2014, http://www.isj. org.uk/index.php4?id=803&issue=134.

Fuentes, F. (2012b) 'Bolivia: Challenges along Path of "Governing by Obeying the People"', *Bolivia Rising*, 12 February, last accessed 10 May 2014, http://bolivi-arising.blogspot.ca/2012/02/bolivia-challenges-along-path-of.html.

Galeano, E. (1971) *Open Veins of Latin America: Five Centuries of the Pillage of a Continent* (New York: Monthly Review Press).

Garay, C. (2007) 'Social Policy and Collective Action: Unemployed Workers, Community Associations and Protest in Argentina', *Politics and Society*, 35(2), pp. 301–328.

García Linera, Á. (2003) 'Crisis estatal y muchedumbre', *OSAL*, 10, pp. 53–60.

García Linera, A. (2006) 'El Evismo: lo nacional popular en acción' *OSAL*, 19, pp. 25–44.

García Linera, Á. (2008) *La potencia plebeya. Acción colectiva e identidades indígenas, obreras y populares en Bolivia* (Buenos Aires: CLACSO-Prometeo).

García Linera, Á. (2009) 'Comentario de Álvaro García Linera', *Cuadernos de pensamiento crítico latinoamericano*, 15 (Buenos Aires: CLACSO).

García Linera, Á. (2010) *Forma valor y forma comunidad. Aproximación teórico abstracta a los fundamentos civilizatorios que preceden al Ayllu Universal* (Buenos Aires: CLACSO – Prometeo).

García Linera, Á. (2011) *Las tensiones creativas de la Revolución. La quinta fase del Proceso de Cambio* (La Paz: Vice presidencia del Estado Plurinacional – Presidencia de la Asamblea Legislativa Plurinacional).

García Linera, Á., Prada Alcoreza, R., Tapia, L., and Vega Camacho, O. (2010) *El Estado, Campo de lucha* (La Paz: Comuna Muela del Diablo and CLACSO).

Gautney, H. (2010) *Protest and Organization in the Alternative Globalization Era: NGOs, Social Movements, and Political Parties* (Houndmill and New York: Palgrave Macmillan).

Geoghegan, V. (1996) *Ernst Bloch* (London and New York: Routledge).

Gerchunoff, P. (1993) (ed): *Las Privatizaciones en la Argentina. Primera Etapa* (Buenos Aires: Instituto Di Tella).

Ghigliani, P. (2003) 'Nuovo movimento operaio e l'occupazione delle fabbriche in Argentina', *Proteo*, No VII- 1, pp. 74–82, Last accesed 30 August 2014, http://www.proteo.rdbcub.it/article.php3?id_article=237.

Ghiotto, L. and Pascual, R. (2008) 'The Zapatistas Movement', Final Case Study Research Report, ESRC NGPA – Dinerstein RES-155–25–0007.

Ghiotto, L. and Pascual, R. (2010) 'Trabajo decente versus trabajo digno: acerca de una nueva concepción del trabajo', *Herramienta*, 44, pp. 113–120.

Gibson-Graham, J.K. (2005) 'Surplus possibilities: post development and community economies', *Journal of Tropical Geography*, 26(1), pp. 4–26.

Gibson-Graham, J.K. (2006) *Postcapitalist Politics* (Minneapolis and London: University of Minnesota Press).

Gibson-Graham, J.K, J. Cameron and S. Healey (2013) *Take Back the Economy. An Ethical Guide for Transforming Our Communities*, (Minenapolis-London: University of Minnesota Press).

Gilly, A. (2004) 'Bolivia: Una revolución del siglo XXI', *Cuadernos del Sur*, 37.

Giroux, H. and MacLaren, P. (1997) 'Paulo Freire, Postmodernism and the Utopian Imagination'. In Daniel, J.O. and Moylan, T. *Not Yet: Reconsidering Ernst Bloch* (London and New York: Verso), pp. 138–164.

Giroux, H. (2009) 'The Promise of an Educated Citizenry. The Audacity of Educated Hope, Counterpunch', January 23–25, http://www.counterpunch. org/2009/01/23/the-audacity-of-educated-hope/, accessed 30 June 2013.

González, M., Burguete Cal y Mayor, A., and Ortiz, P. (eds) *La Autonomía a debate* (Quito: FLACSO, GTZ, IWGIA, CIESAS, UNICH).

González Casanova, P. (2001) 'Los Zapatistas del Siglo XXI', *OSAL*, 4, pp. 5–14.

González Casanova, P. (2002) 'Democracia, liberación y socialismo: tres alternativas en una', *OSAL*, 8, pp. 175–180.

Gorz, A. (1982) *Farewell to the Working Class: An Essay on Post-industrial Socialism,* (London – Sydney: Pluto Press).

Gorz, A. (1999) *Reclaiming Work* (Cambridge: Polity Press).

Goudsmit, I. (2006) 'Praying for Government: Peasant Disengagement from the Bolivian State', *BLAR*, 25(2), pp. 200–219.

Graeber, D. (2004) 'Anarchism, or the Revolutionary Movement of the Twenty-First Century', *ZNET*, 6 January, last accessed 14 May 2014, http://www. zcommunications.org/anarchism–or–the–revolutionary–movement–of–the–twenty–first–century–by–david–graeber.html.

Graeber, D. (2013) 'A Practical Utopian's Guide to the Coming Collapse', *The Baffler* 22, http://thebaffler.com/past/practical_utopias_guide/print, accessed 28/01/2014.

Gramsci, A. (1968) 'Soviets in Italy (Writings from 1919 and 1920)', *New Left Review*, 51, pp. 28–58.

Grigera, J. (2006) 'Argentina: On Crisis and a Measure for Class Struggle', *Historical Materialism*, 14(1), pp. 185–220.

Grosfoguel, R. (2008) 'Transmodernity, Border Thinking and Global Coloniality. Decolonising Political Economy and Postcolonial Studies', *Eurozine*, 4 July, last accessed 14 May 2014, http://www.eurozine.com/articles/2008–07–04-grosfoguel-en.html.

Grosfoguel, R. (2009) 'A decolonial approach to political economy: transmodernity, border thinking and global coloniality', *Kult* 6, http://www.postkolonial. dk/KULT_Publications#udgivelse4.

Grosfoguel, R. (2012) 'Decolonizing Western Universalisms: Decolonial Pluriversalism from Aimé Césaire to the Zapatistas', *Transmodernity*, 1(3), last accessed 14 May 2014 http://escholarship.org/uc/search?entity=ssha_transmo dernity;volume=1;issue=3.

Grugel, J. and Riggirozzi, P. (2012) 'Post-neoliberalism in Latin America: Rebuilding and Reclaiming the State after Crisis', *Development & Change*, 43(1), pp. 1–21.

Gruppe Krisis (1999) *Manifesto against Labour*, last accessed 8 May 2014, http:// www.krisis.org/1999/manifesto-against-labour.

Gudynas, E. (2010) 'El día después del desarrollo', *América Latina en Movimiento*, 445, last accessed 14 May 2013, http://alainet.org/publica/445.phtml.

Gudynas, E. (2011) 'Debates sobre el desarrollo y sus alternativas en América Latina: Una breve guía heterodoxa'. In M. Lang and Mokrani, D. (eds) *Más allá del desarrollo* (Quito: Fundación Rosa Luxemburgo and AbyaYala).

Gudynas, E. (2012) 'El sueño de un capitalismo benévolo', *La Línea de Fuego*, 12, Quito.

Gudynas, E. (2013) 'Ecuador: Los derechos de la naturaleza después de la caída de la moratoria petrolera en la Amazonia', *América Latina en Movimiento*, 19 August, last accessed 14 May 2014, http://alainet.org/active/66547.

Gunn, R. (1987a) 'Marxism and mediation', *Common Sense* 2, pp. 57–66. Out of print, available at http://commonsensejournal.org.uk/issue-two/.

Gunn, R. (1987b) 'A Note on Class', *Common Sense* 2, pp. 15–25. Out of print, available at http://commonsensejournal.org.uk/issue-two/.

Gunn, R. (1992) 'Against Historical Materialism: Marxism as First-Order Discourse'. In Bonefeld, W., Gunn, R., and Psychopedis, K. (eds) *Open Marxism: Theory and Practice*, Vol. II (London: Pluto Press), pp. 1–45.

Gunn, R. (1994) 'Marxism and Contradiction', *Common Sense*, 15, pp. 53–59. Out of print. Available at http://commonsensejournal.org.uk/issue-15/.

Gutiérrez Aguilar, R. (2008) *Los ritmos del Pachakuti. Movilización popular y levantamiento indígena-popular en Bolivia* (Bueno Aires: Tinta Limón).

Gutiérrez Aguilar, R. (2011) 'Competing Political Visions and Bolivia's Unfinished Revolution: El conflicto de visiones políticas y la revolución inacabada de Bolivia', *Dialectical Anthropology*, 35, pp. 275–277.

Gutiérrez Aguilar, R. (2012) 'The Rhythms of the Pachakuti: Brief Reflections Regarding How We Have Come to Know Emancipatory Struggles and the Significance of the Term Social Emancipation', *South Atlantic Quarterly*, 111(1), pp. 51–64.

Guzman Bouvard, M. (1994) *Revolutionising Motherhood. The Mothers of the Plaza de Mayo* (Oxford: Rowman and Littlefield Publishers).

Hardt, M. (1994) 'Spinoza's Democracy: The Passions of Social Assemblages'. In Callari, A. (ed.) *Marxism in the Postmodern Age* (New York: Guilford).

Hardt, M. (2006) 'Bathing in the Multitude'. In Schnapp, J. and M. Tiews (eds) *Crowds*, Stanford – California: Stanford University Press), pp. 35–40.

Hardt, M. and Holloway, J. (2012) 'Creating Common Wealth and Cracking Capitalism: A Cross-Reading', *Herramienta*, 49, last accessed 14 May 2014, http://www.herramienta.com.ar/print/revista-herramienta-n-49/creating-common-wealth-and-cracking-capitalism-cross-reading.

Hardt, M. and Negri, A. (2004) *Multitude* (London: Penguin).

Hardt, M. and Negri, A. (2009) *Commonwealth* (Cambridge, MA: Belknap Press of Harvard University Press).

Harnecker, M. (2002) *Sin Tierra. Construyendo movimiento social* (Madrid: Siglo XXI de España).

Harvey, D. (2005) *The New Imperialism* (Oxford: Oxford University Press).

Harvey, D. (2007) *A Brief History of Neoliberalism* (Oxford: Oxford University Press).

Harvey, D. (2010a) *The Enigma of Capital and the Crises of Capitalism* (London: Profile).

Harvey, D. (2010b) 'Organizing for the Anti-Capitalist Transition', *Interface*, 2(1), pp. 243–261, last accessed 14 May 2014, http://www.interfacejournal.net.

Harvey, D. (2012) *Rebel Cities: From the Right to the City to the Urban Revolution* (London and New York: Verso).

Hauser, I. (2003a) 'Están construyendo un mundo nuevo', *Página/12*, 20 January, last accessed 4 February 2014, http://www.pagina12.com.ar/diario/elpais/1–15592–2003–01–20.html.

Hauser, I. (2003b) 'Las Asambleas mantienen el QSVT', *Página/12*, 24 March 2003, last accessed 4 February 2014, http://www.pagina12.com.ar/diario/elpais/1–17958–2003–03–24.html.

Hauser, I. (2003c) 'Haciendo economía solidaria' *Página/12*, 20 September 2003, last accessed 30 August 2014, http://www.pagina12.com.ar/diario/elpais/1–25712–2003–09–20.html.

Haworth, N. and Roddick, J. (1981) 'Labour and Monetarism in Chile 1975–80', *BLAR*, 1(1), pp. 49–62.

Henck, N. (2007) *Subcomander Marcos: The Man and the Mask* (Durham, NC and London: Duke University Press).

Hernández Navarro, L. (2006) 'The Breaking Wave. The Sixth Declaration and the Other Campaign'. In Subcomandante Marcos and the Zapatistas *The Other Campaign/La Otra Campaña* (San Francisco, CA: City Lights Books), pp. 7–59.

Hesketh, C. (2013) 'The Clash of Spatializations: Geopolitics and Class Struggles in Southern Mexico', *Latin American Perspectives*, Issue 191, 40(4), pp. 70–87.

Hidalgo Domínguez, O. (2006) *Tras los pasos de una guerra inconclusa: doce años de militarización en Chiapas* (San Cristobal de las Casas, México: CIEPAC).

Holloway, J. (1993) 'Open Marxism, History and Class Struggle', *Common Sense*, 13, pp. 76–86 out of print. Available at http://commonsensejournal.org.uk/issue-13/.

Holloway, J. (1994) 'Global Capital and the Nation State', *Capital & Class* 52, pp.23–49.

Holloway, J. (1995) 'From Scream of Refusal to Scream of Power: The Centrality of Work'. In Bonefeld, W., Gunn, R., Holloway, J., and Psychopedis, K. (eds) *Open Marxism*, Vol. III (London: Pluto Press), pp. 155–181.

Holloway, J. (2002a), *Change the World without Taking Power: The Meaning of Revolution Today* (London: Pluto Press).

Holloway, J. (2002b) 'Zapatismo and Social Sciences', *Capital & Class*, 78, pp. 153–160.

Holloway, J. (2002c) 'Class and Classification: Against, in and beyond Labour'. In Dinerstein, A.C. and Neary, M. (eds) *The Labour Debate: An Investigation into the Theory and Reality of Capitalist Work* (Aldershot: Ashgate), pp. 27–40.

Holloway, J. (2003) 'Conduce tu carro y tu arado sobre los huesos de los muertos', *Herramienta*, 24, last accessed 14 May 2014 http://www.herramienta.com.ar/debate-sobre-cambiar-el-mundo/conduce-tu-carro-y-tu-arado-sobre-los-huesos-de-los-muertos.

Holloway, J. (2009a) 'Why Adorno?'. In Holloway, J. Matamoros Ponce, F., and Tischler, S. (eds) *Negativity and Revolution: Adorno and Political Activism* (London: Pluto Press), pp. 12–17.

Holloway, J. (2009b) 'Negative and Positive Autonomism. Or Why Adorno? Part 2'. In Holloway, J. Matamoros Ponce, F., and Tischler, S. (eds) *Negativity and Revolution: Adorno and Political Activism* (London: Pluto Press), pp. 95–100.

Holloway, J. (2010a) *Crack Capitalism* (London: Pluto Press).

Holloway, J. (2010b) 'Crack and the Crisis of Abstract Labour', *Antipode*, 33(5), pp. 909–923.

Holloway, J. (2013) 'Communising'. In Brincat, S. (ed.) *Communism in the 21st Century* (Santa Barbara, CA: ABC-Clio).

Holloway, J., Matamoros Ponce, F., and Tischler, S. (eds) (2009) *Negativity and Revolution: Adorno and Political Activism* (London: Pluto Press).

Holloway, J. and Peláez, E. (eds) *Zapatista! Reinventing Revolution in Mexico* (London: Pluto Press).

Holloway, J. and Picciotto, S. (1977) 'Capital, Crisis and the State', *Capital & Class*, 2, pp. 76–101.

Honty, G. (2013) 'El Brasil petrolero: Entre la ilusión y la quiebra', *América Latina en Movimiento*, 11 April, last accessed 14 May 2014 http://alainet.org/active/68684.

Houtart, F. (2014) 'El 6° congreso del movimiento de los sin tierra en Brasilia: Una lucha contra la hegemonía creciente del agronegocio', *América Latina en Movimiento*, 26 February, last accessed 1 March 2014, http://alainet.org/active/71631.

Huanacuni Mamani, F. (2010) 'Buen vivir, vivir bien. Filosofía, estrategias y experiencias regionales andinas' (Lima, Peru: Coordinadora Andina de Organizaciones Indígenas – CAOI).

Huber, E. and Solt, F. (2004) 'Successes and Failures of Neoliberalism', *Latin American Research Review*, 39(3), pp. 150–164.

Hudis, P. (2012) *Marx's Concept of the Alternative to Capitalism* (Leiden and Boston: BRILL).

Hudis, P. and Anderson, K. (2002) 'Introduction'. In Dunayevskaya, R. *The Power of Negativity. Selected Writings on the Dialectic in Hegel and Marx* (Lanham, MD: Lexington Books).

Icaza, R. and Vázquez, R. (2013) 'Social Struggles as Epistemic Struggles', *Development and Change*, 44(3), pp. 683–704.

Ilel, K. (2011) 'Sustainable Rural Cities: A Nightmare Come True in Chiapas', last accessed 14 May 2014, http://upsidedownworld.org/main/mexico-archives-79/3023-sustainable-rural-cities-a-nightmare-come-true-in-chiapas.

Iñigo Carrera, J. (2006) 'The Reproduction of Capital Accumulation through Political Crisis', *Historical Materialism*, 14(1), pp. 221–248.

Issa, D. (2007) 'Praxis of Empowerment: *Mística* and Mobilization in Brazil's Landless Rural Workers' Movement', *Latin American Perspectives*, 34, pp. 124–137.

Jelin, E. (1985) *Los nuevos movimientos sociales*, Biblioteca Política Argentina, vol. 124, (Buenos Aires: CEAL).

Jelin, E. (1986) 'Otros silencios, otras voces: el tiempo de la democratización en Argentina'. In Calderón, F. *Los movimientos sociales ante la crisis* (Buenos Aires: CLACSO/Universidad de las Naciones Unidas).

Kaminsky, G. (1998) *Spinoza: la política de las pasiones* (Barcelona: Gedissa).

Katsiaficas, G. (2006) *The Subversion of Politics: European Autonomous Social Movements and the Decolonization of Everyday Life* (Oakland, CA and Edinburgh: AK Press).

Katsiaficas, G. (2009) 'El significado de los autónomos'. In Albertani, C., Rovira Sancho, G., and Modonesi, M. (eds) *La Autonomía posible, reinvención política y emancipación* (México, DF: UAM), pp. 131–150.

Katz, C. (2008) *La disyuntiva de la izquierda en América Latina* (Buenos Aires: Ediciones Luxemburg).

Kellner, D. (1997) 'Ernst Bloch, Utopia, and Ideology Critique'. In Daniel, J.O. and Moylan, T. *Not Yet: Reconsidering Ernst Bloch* (London and New York: Verso), pp. 80–95.

Khasnabish, A. (2008) *Zapatismo Beyond Borders: New Imaginations of Political Possibilities* (Toronto: University of Toronto Press).

Khasnabish, A. (2013) 'Tracing the Zapatista Rhizome, or the Ethnography of a Transnationalised Political Imagination'. In Juris and Kasnabish (eds)

Transnational Activism, Ethnography, and the Political (Durham, NC and London: Duke University Press).

Khasnabish, A. and Haiven, M. (2012) 'Convoking the Radical Imagination: Social Movements Research, Dialogic Methodologies, and Scholarly Vocations', *Cultural Studies Critical Methodologies*, 12(5), pp. 408–421.

Knoll, A. and Rivera Cusicanqui, S. (2007) 'Anarchism and Indigenous Resistance in Bolivia: Interview with Silvia Rivera Cusicanqui', *World War 4 Report*, 1 October, last accessed 14 August 2013, http://www.ww4report.com/node/450113.

Kohl, B. (2010) 'Bolivia under Morales: A Work in Progress', *Latin American Perspectives*, 37(3), pp. 107–122.

Kohl, B. and Farthing, L. (2006) *Impasse in Bolivia: Neoliberal Hegemony and Popular Resistance* (London and New York: Zed Books).

Laclau, E. and Mouffe, C. (1985) *Hegemony & Socialist Strategy: Towards a Radical Democratic Politics* (London: Verso).

Lander, E. (2010) 'Estamos viviendo una profunda crisis civilizatoria', *América Latina en Movimiento*, 452, last accessed 14 May 2014, http://www.alainet.org/publica/452.phtml.

Latouche, S. (1993) *In the Wake of the Affluent Society: An Exploration of Post-Development* (London: Zed Books).

La Via Campesina and the Planning Committee for Food Sovereignty (IPC) (2006) 'Agrarian Reform in the Context of Food Sovereignty, the Right to Food and Cultural Diversity', Civil Society Issue Paper No. 5, *International Conference on Agrarian Reform and Rural Development (ICARRD)*, January, Porto Alegre, Brazil.

La República Perdida II, Documentary Film, 1986, Buenos Aires: Orson Producciones SRL.

Lazar, S. (2006) 'El Alto, Ciudad Rebelde: Organisational Bases for Revolt', *BLAR*, 25(2) pp. 183–199.

Lazar, S. (2008) *El Alto, Rebel City: Self and Citizenship in Andean Bolivia* (Durham, NC: Duke University Press).

Lazar, S. and McNeish, J.A. (2006) 'The Millions Return? Democracy in Bolivia at the Start of the Twenty-First Century', *BLAR*, 25(2), pp. 157–162.

Lazzarato, M. (2012) *The Making of the Indebted Man: An Essay on the Neoliberal Condition* (Los Angeles, CA: Semiotext(e)).

Lear, J. (2006) *Radical Hope: Ethics in the Face of Cultural Devastation* (Cambridge, MA and London: Harvard University Press).

Lefebvre, H. (1991/1974) *The Production of Space* (Oxford: Blackwell).

Lefebvre, H. (2001/1979) 'Comments on a New State Form', *Antipode*, 33(5), pp. 769–781.

Levey, C., Ozarow, D., and Wylde, C. (eds) (2014) *Crisis, Response and Recovery: A Decade on from the Argentinazo 2001–11* (Basingstoke and New York: Palgrave Macmillan).

Levitas, R. (1990) *The Concept of Utopia* (Hempstead: Syracuse University Press).

Levitas, R. (1997) 'Educated Hope: Ernst Bloch on Abstract and Concrete Utopia'. In Daniel, J.O. and Moylan, T. *Not Yet: Reconsidering Ernst Bloch* (London and New York: Verso), pp. 65–79.

Levitas, R. (2001) 'Against Work: A Utopian Incursion into Social Policy', *Critical Social Policy* 21 (4), pp. 449–465.

Levitas, R. (2008) 'Pragmatism, Utopia and Anti-Utopia', *Critical Horizons*, 9(1), pp. 42–59.

Levitas, R. (2010) 'Back to the Future: Wells, Sociology, Utopia and Method', *The Sociological Review,* 58(4), pp. 531–546.

Levitas, R. (2013) *Utopia as Method: The Imaginary Reconstitution of Society* (Basingstoke and New York: Palgrave Macmillan).

Levy, Z. (1997) 'Utopia and Reality in the Philosophy of Ernst Bloch'. In Daniel, J.O. and Moylan, T. *Not Yet: Reconsidering Ernst Bloch* (London and New York: Verso), pp. 175–185.

Lievesley, G. (2009) 'Is Latin America Moving Leftwards? Problems and Prospects'. In Lievesley, G. and Ludlam, S. *Reclaiming Latin America: Experiments in Radical Social Democracy* (London and New York: Zed Books), pp. 21–36.

Lievesley, G. and Ludlam, S. (2009) 'Introduction: "A Pink Tide"?'. In Lievesley, G. and Ludlam, S. (eds) *Reclaiming Latin America: Experiments in Radical Social Democracy* (London and New York: Zed Books), pp. 1–18.

Lilley, S. and Papadopoulos, D. (2014) 'Material Returns: Cultures of Valuation, Biofinancialisation and the Autonomy of Politics', *Sociology,* 48(5), pp. 972–988.

Llorens, J. and Cafiero, P. (2002) '¿Qué se hicieron de las "cuantiosas" reservas del sistema financiero argentino? Reporte sobre el Vaciamiento del Sistema Financiero Argentino', *Cámara de Diputados de la Nación,* last accessed 20 August 2014, http://www1.hcdn.gov.ar/dependencias/ari/Principal/principal.htm.

Llorens, J. and Cafiero, M. (2001) '¿Por qué se quiere derogar la ley de subversión económica? Reporte sobre el Vaciamiento del Sistema Financiero Argentino', *Cámara de Diputados de la Nación,* last accessed 19 August 2014, http://www1. hcdn.gov.ar/dependencias/ari/Principal/principal.htm.

López Bárcenas, F. (2011) 'Las autonomías indígenas en América Latina'. In Adamovsky et al., *Pensar las autonomías. Alternativas de emancipación al capital y el estado* (México, DF: Bajo Tierra and SISIFO), pp. 53–70.

López Maya, M. (2003) 'The Venezuelan Caracazo of 1989: Popular Protest and Institutional Weakness', *Journal of Latin American Studies,* 35, pp. 117–137.

López Maya, M. and Lander, E. (2001) 'Ajustes, costos sociales y la agenda de los pobres en Venezuela: 1984–1998'. In Sader, E. (ed.) *El ajuste estructural en América Latina. Costos sociales y alternativas* (Buenos Aires: CLACSO, ASDI), pp. 231–254.

López y Rivas, G. (2011) 'Autonomías indígenas, poder y transformaciones sociales en Méjico'. In Adamovsky et al., *Pensar las autonomias. Alternativas de emancipacion al capital y el estado* (México, DF: Bajo Tierra and SISIFO), pp. 107–120.

Lorenzano, L. (1998) 'Zapatismo: Recomposition of Labour, Radical Democracy and Revolutionary Project'. In Holloway, J. and Peláez, E. (eds) *Zapatista! Reinventing Revolution in Mexico* (London: Pluto Press), pp. 126–158.

Löwy, M. (1988) *Marxism and Liberation Theology,* Note Books for Study and Research (Amsterdam: International Institute for Research and Education).

Löwy, M. (2007) *El marxismo en América Latina: antología, desde 1909 hasta nuestro días* (Santiago: LOM).

Lucita, E. (2003) 'Fábricas ocupadas y gestión obrera en Argentina. Ocupar, resistir, producir', *Cuadernos del Sur,* 34, Noviembre, Buenos Aires.

Lummis, D. (1996) *Radical Democracy* (Ithaca, London: Cornnell University Press).

Lynd, S. and Grubacic, A. (2008) *Wobblies and Zapatistas: Conversations on Anarchism, Marxism and Radical History* (Oakland, CA: PM Press).

Maeckelbergh, M. (2009) *The Will of the Many: How the Alterglobalisation Movement Is Changing the face of Democracy* (London: Pluto Press).

Maeckelbergh, M. (2011) 'Doing Is Believing: Prefiguration as Strategic Practice in the Alterglobalization Movement', *Social Movement Studies*, 10(1), pp. 1–20.

Maeckelbergh, M. (2012) 'Horizontal Democracy Now: From Alterglobalisation to Occupation', *Interface*, 4(1), pp. 207–234, http://www.interfacejournal.net.

Magnani, E. (2014) 'Para no perder el empleo' *Página/12*, 20 April 2014, last accessed 30 August 2014, http://www.pagina12.com.ar/diario/suplementos/cash/17-7607-2014-04-20.html.

Maiwaring, S. (1988) 'Political Parties and Democratization in Brazil and the Southern Cone', *Comparative Politics*, 21(1), pp. 91–120.

Maldonado-Torres, N. (2012) 'Decoloniality at Large: Towards a TransAmericas and Global Transmodern Paradigm', *Transmodernity*, 1(3), http://escholarship.org/uc/search?entity=ssha_transmodernity;volume=1;issue=3.

Mamani Ramírez, P. (2003) 'El rugir de la multitud: levantamiento de la ciudad Aymara de El Alto', *OSAL*, 12, pp. 15–26.

Mamani Ramírez, P. (2004) *El rugir de las multitudes: la fuerza de los levantamientos indígenas en Bolivia* (Qullasuyu: Ediciones Yachaywasi).

Mamani Ramírez, P. (2005) *Microgobiernos barriales en el levantamiento de la ciudad de El Alto* (El Alto, Bolivia: Centro Andino de Estudios Estratégicos – Instituto de Investigaciones Sociológicas de la Universidad Mayor de San Andrés).

Mamani Ramírez, P. (2008) 'Entrevista a Pablo Mamani', *Boletín Bolivia*, pp. 23–29.

Mançano Fernandes, B. (2000a) 'O MST e a luta pela reforma agrária no Brasil', *OSAL*, 2, pp. 29–36.

Mançano Fernandes, B. (2000b) *A formação do MST no Brasil* (São Paulo: Vozes).

Mançano Fernandes, B. (2003) 'O MST e os desafios para a realizaçâo da reforma agrária no governó Lula', *OSAL*, 11, pp. 31–40.

Mançano Fernandes, B. (2008) 'La ocupación como una forma de acceso a la tierra en Brasil: una construcción teórica y metodológica'. In Moyo, S. and Yeros, P. (eds) *Recuperando la tierra. El resurgimiento de movimientos rurales en África, Asia y América Latina* (Buenos Aires: CLACSO), pp. 335–357.

Mandel, E. (2002) 'Anticipation and Hope as Categories of Historical Materialism', *Historical Materialism*, 10(4), pp. 245–259.

Marazzi, C. (1996) 'Money in the World Crisis: The New Basis of Capitalist Power'. In Bonefeld, W. and Holloway, J. (eds) *Global Capital, National State and the Politics of Money* (Basingstoke and London: Palgrave Macmillan), pp. 69–91.

Martins de Carvalho, H. (2006) 'The Emancipation of the Landless Rural Workers within the Continental Movement of Social Emancipation'. In Santos B. de S. (ed.) (2006) *Another Production is Possible: Beyond the Capitalist Canon*, (London: Verso), pp. 179–201.

Martínez, J.H. (2008) 'Causas e interpretaciones del Caracazo', *Historia Actual Online (HAOL)*, 16, pp. 85–92.

Martínez, O. and Vocos, F. (2002) 'Las empresas recuperadas por los trabajadores y el movimiento obrero'. In Carpintero, E., Hernández, M., and Petras, J.F. (eds) *Produciendo realidad: las empresas comunitarias* (Buenos Aires: Topia Editorial en colaboración con La Maza), pp. 77–85.

Martínez Andrade, L. (2009) 'Consideraciones en torno al hambre y a la natura dominata. Pertinencia del Principio Esperanza', *Herramineta*, 42, http://www.herramienta.com.ar/revista-impresa/revista-herramienta-n-42.

Martínez-Cobo, J., (1987) *Study on the Problem of Discrimination against Indigenous Populations*, Doc. E/CN.4/Sub.2/1986/7 (Geneva: UN Commission on Human Rights).

Martínez-Torres, M. and P. Rosset (2008) 'La Via Campesina: Transnationalising Peasant Struggles and Hope'. In Stahler-Sholk, R. et al. (eds) *Latin American Social Movements in the Twenty-First Century* (Lanham, Boulder, New York, Toronto and Plymouth: Rowain & Littlefield), pp. 307–322.

Marx, K. (1871) 'The Paris Commune'. In *The Civil War in France*, http://www.marxists.org/archive/marx/works/1871/civil-war-france/ch05.htm.

Marx, K. (1981) *A Contribution to the Critique of Political Economy* (London: Lawrence & Wishart).

Marx, K. (1990) *Capital*, vol. 1 (London: Penguin).

Marx, K (1991) *Capital*, vol. 3 (London: Penguin).

Marx, K. (1992) 'Economic and Philosophical Manuscripts'. In *Early Writings* (London: Penguin), pp. 279–400.

Marx, K. (1993) *Grundrisse: Foundations of the Critique of Political Economy* (London: Penguin).

Marx, K (1995) *The Poverty of Philosophy* (New York: Prometheus Books).

Marx, K. and Engels, F. (1848/1985) *The Communist Manifesto* (London: Penguin).

Massumi, B. and Zournazi, M. (2002) '"Navigating Movements": A Conversation with Brian Massumi'. In Zournazi, M. (ed.) *Hope: New Philosophies for Change* (Annandale, NSW: Pluto Press Australia), pp. 210–242.

Matamoros Ponce, F. (2005) *Memoria y utopía en México. Imaginarios en la génesis del neozapatismo* (Xalapa, Veracruz, México: Universidad Veracruzana and Benemérita Universidad Autónoma de Puebla).

Matamoros Ponce, F. (2009) 'Solidarity with the Fall of Metaphysics: Negativity and Hope'. In Holloway, J., Matamoros, F., and Tischler, S. (eds) *Negativity and Revolution: Adorno and Politics* (London: Pluto Press), pp. 189–227.

Mattiace, S. (2003) 'Mayan Utopias: Rethinking the State'. In Rus, J., Hernández Castillo, R., and Mattiace, S. (eds) *Mayan Lives, Mayan Utopias: The Indigenous Peoples of Chiapas and the Zapatista Rebellion* (Oxford: Rowman & Littlefield), pp. 185–190.

Mattini, L. (2002) 'La hora de las comunas' in Bielsa, R. et al (2002) *¿Qué son las Asambleas Populares?* (Buenos Aires: Peña Lillo–Continente), pp. 44–55.

Melucci, A. (1988) 'Social Movements and the Democratization of Everyday Life'. In Keane, J. (ed.) *Civil Society and the State: New European Perspectives* (London: Verso), pp. 245–260.

Meszaros, G. (2000) 'Taking the Land into Their Hands: The Landless Workers' Movement and the Brazilian State', *Journal of Law and Society*, 27(4), pp. 517–541.

Mészaros, I. (1970) *Marx's Theory of Alienation* (London: Merlin Press).

Meyer, L. and Chaves, M. (2008) 'Aires de Libertad: Zanón bajo gestión obrera', *OSAL*, 24, pp. 115–142.

Mignolo, W. (2000) *Local Histories/Global Designs, Coloniality, Subaltern Knowledges, and Border Thinking* (Princeton, NJ: Princeton University Press).

Mignolo, W. (2011) *The Dark Side of Western Modernity* (Durham, NC and London: Duke University Press).

Minsburg, N. (1987) 'Capitales extranjeros y grupos dominantes argentinos/1–2 (Análisis histórico y contemporáneo)', *Biblioteca Política Argentina*, vols 196–197 (Buenos Aires: CEAL).

Mittleman, A. (2009) *Hope in a Democratic Age: Philosophy, Religion and Political Theory* (Oxford: Oxford University Press).

Mittleman, J. and Chin, C. (2000) 'Conceptualising Resistance to Globalisation'. In Mittleman, J. *The Globalisation Syndrome: Transformation and Resistance* (Princeton, NJ: Princeton University Press), pp. 165–178.

Miyazaki, H. (2004) *The Method of Hope: Anthropology, Philosophy, and Fijian Knowledge* (Stanford, CA: Stanford University Press).

Modonesi, M. (2009) 'Autonomía, antagonism y subalternidad: Notas para una aproximación conceptual'. In Albertani, C., Rovira Sancho, G., and Modonesi, M. (eds) *La Autonomía Posible: Reinvención política y emancipación* (México, DF: UAM), pp. 67–81.

Modonesi, M. (2010) *Subalternidad, anatagonismo, autonomía: Marxismo y subjetivación política* (Buenos Aires: CLACSO).

Modonesi, M. (2011) 'El concepto de autonomía en el Marxismo contemporáneo'. In Adamovsky, E. et al. *Pensar las autonomías. Alternativas de emancipación al capital y el estado* (México, DF: Bajo Tierra and SISIFO), pp. 23–52.

Moldiz Mercado, H. (2009) '¿Reforma o revolución en América Latina? El proceso boliviano'. In Regalado, R. (ed.) *América Latina hoy ¿Reforma o revolución?* (México: Ocean Sur), pp. 181–216.

Moldiz Mercado, H. (2012) 'Los problemas de la transición en Bolivia', *América Latina en Movimiento*, 475, pp. 18–20, http://alainet.org/publica/475.phtml.

Molyneux, M. (2001) *Women's Movements in International Perspective: Latin America and Beyond* (Basingstoke: Palgrave Macmillan).

Molyneux, M. (2002) 'Gender and the Silences of Social Capital: Lessons from Latin America', *Development and Change*, 33(2), pp. 167–188.

Mora, M. (2007) 'Zapatista Anticapitalist Politics and the "Other Campaign": Learning from the Struggle for Indigenous Rights and autonomy', *Latin American Perspectives*, 153, 34(2), pp. 64–77.

Mora, M. (2010) 'Las experiencias de la autonomía indígena zapatista frente al Estado neoliberal mexicano'. In González, M., Burguete Cal y Mayor, A., and Ortiz, P. (eds) *La Autonomía a debate* (Quito: GTZ, IWGIA, CIESAS, UNICH), pp. 291–315.

Morais, L. and Saad-Filho, A. (2005) 'Lula and the Continuity of Neoliberalism in Brazil: Strategic Choice, Economic Imperative or Political Schizophrenia?', *Historical Materialism*, 13(4), pp. 3–32.

Moraña, M., Dussel, E., and Jáuregui, C. (2008) 'Colonialism and Its Replicants'. In Moraña, M., Dussel, E., and Jáuregui, C. (eds) *Coloniality at Large: Latin America and the Postcolonial Debate* (Durham, NC and London: Duke University Press), pp. 1–22.

Morris, B. (1991) *Western Conceptions of the Individual* (New York –Oxford: Berg).

Motta, S.C. (2006) 'Utopias Re-imagined: A Reply to Panizza', *Political Studies*, 54, pp. 898–905.

Motta, S.C. (2009) 'Old Tools and New Movements in Latin America: Political Science as Gatekeeper or Intellectual Illuminator?', *Latin American Politics and Society*, 51(1), pp. 31–56.

Motta, S.C. (2011) 'Notes Towards Prefigurative Epistemologies'. In Motta, S.C. and Nilsen, A. (eds) *Social Movements in the Global South: Dispossession, Development and Resistance* (Basingstoke and New York: Palgrave Macmillan), pp. 178–199.

Motta S.C. (2013) 'On the Pedagogical Turn in Latin American Social Movements'. In Motta, S.C. and Cole, M. (eds) *Education and Social Change in Latin America* (New York and London: Palgrave Macmillan).

Motta, S.C. (2014) 'Epistemological Counter-Hegemonies from Below: Radical Educators in/and the MST and Solidarity Economy Movements'. In Motta, S.C. and Cole, M. (eds) *Constructing Twenty-First Century Socialism in Latin America: The Role of Radical Education* (Basingstoke and New York: Palgrave Macmillan).

Motta, S. and Cole, M. (eds) (2013) *Education and Social Change in Latin America* (Basingstoke and New York: Palgrave Macmillan).

Motta, S. and Nilsen, A. (2011b) 'Social Movements and/in the Post-colonial: Dispossession, Development and Resistance in the Global South'. In Motta, S. and Nilsen, A. (eds) *Social Movements in the Global South: Dispossession, Development and Resistance* (Basingstoke and New York: Palgrave Macmillan), pp. 1–31.

Moulaert, F. and Ailenei, O. (2005) 'Social Economy, Third Sector and Solidarity Relations: A Conceptual Synthesis from History to Present', *Urban Studies*, 42(11), pp. 2037–2053.

Moylan, T. (1997) 'Bloch against Bloch: The Theological Reception of *Das Prinzip Hoffnung* and the Liberation of the Utopia Function'. In Daniel, J.O. and Moylan, T. *Not Yet: Reconsidering Ernst Bloch* (London and New York: Verso), pp. 96–121.

Moyo, S. and Yeros, P. (eds) (2008a) *Recuperando la tierra. El resurgimiento de movimientos rurales en África, Asia y América Latina* (Buenos Aires: CLACSO).

Moyo, S. and Yeros, P. (eds) (2008b) 'El resurgiminto de los movimientos rurales bajo el neoliberalismo'. In Moyo, S. and Yeros, P. (eds) *Recuperando la tierra. El resurgimiento de movimientos rurales en África, Asia y América Latina* (Buenos Aires: CLACSO), pp. 19–78.

MTD (2002) 'El MTD y la construcción del poder popular', *Herramienta*, 21, pp. 137–144.

MTD Aníbal Verón (2003) *Darío y Maxi. Dignidad Piquetera. El gobierno de Duhalde y la planificación criminal de la masacre del 26 de Junio en Avellaneda* (Buenos Aires: Ediciones 26 de Junio).

MTD Solano and Colectivo Situaciones (2002) *Hipótesis 891* (Buenos Aires: Ediciones Mano en Mano).

MTEySS (n.d.) *Registro de Unidades productivas Autogestionadas por los Trabajadores, Plan Integral Mas y Mejor Trabajo* (Buenos Aires: MTEySS).

MTEySS (2005a) *Evaluación del Programa de Trabajo Autogestionado* (Buenos Aires: MTEySS).

MTEySS (2005b) *Guía 2005 de Empresas y Fabricas recuperadas Autogestionadas por sus trabajadores*, PTA (Buenos Aires: Secretaria de Empleo, MTEySS).

Munck, R. (1994) 'Workers, Structural Adjustment, and *Concertación Social* in Latin America', *Latin American Perspectives*, 21(3), pp. 90–103.

Munck, R. (2000) *Globalisation and Labour. The new great transformation* (London: ZED Books).

Munck, R. (2013) 'The Precariat: A View from the South', *Third World Quarterly*, 34(5), pp. 747–762.

Muñoz Ramírez, G. (2008) *The Fire and the Word: A History of the Zapatista Movement* (San Francisco, CA: City Lights Books).

Nancy, J.L. (2000) *Being Singular Plural* (Stanford, CA: Stanford University Press).

Navarro, Z. (2006) '"Mobilisation without Emancipation": The Social Struggles of the Landless in Brazil'. In Santos B. de S. (ed.) *Another Production Is Possible: Beyond the Capitalist Canon* (London: Verso), pp.146–178.

Negri, A. (1991) *Marx beyond Marx: Lessons on the Grundrisse* (New York: Autonomedia).

Negri, A. (1992) 'Interpretation of the Class Situation Today: Methodological Aspects'. In Bonefeld, W., Gunn, R., and Psychopedis, K. (eds) *Open Marxism*, Vol. II, (London: Pluto Press), pp. 69–105.

Nelson, A. and Timmerman, F. (eds) *Life Without Money: Building Fair and Sustainable Economies* (London: Pluto Press).

North, P. (2007) *Money and Liberation: The Micropolitics of Alternative Currency Movements,* (Minneapolis – London: University of Minnesota Press).

North, P. (2010) *Local Money: How to Make it Happen in Your Community (The Local Series), (*Devon: Transition Books).

Notes from Nowhere (2003) *We Are Everywhere: The Irresistible Rise of Global Anticapitalism* (London and New York: Verso).

Nyéléni Newsletter (International Movement for Food Sovereignty) (2013) *Newsletter* No 13, (last accessed 30 August 2014, http://www.nyeleni.org/DOWNLOADS/newsletters/NyeleniI_Newsletter_Num_13_EN.pdf.

O'Connell, A. (1988) 'La coordinación de los deudores latinoamericanos: el Consenso de Cartagena y el Grupo de los Ocho', *Estudios Internacionales*, No. 83 (July–September), pp. 373–385.

O'Donnell, G., Schmitter, P., and Whitehead, L. (eds) (1986) *Transitions from Authoritarian Rule: Prospects for Democracy* (Baltimore, MD: Johns Hopkins University Press).

Olesen, T. (2005) *International Zapatismo: The Construction of Solidarity in the Age of globalization* (London and New York: Zed Books).

Oliver, L. and Savoia, F. (2011) 'El 2010 en América Latina. La compleja y difícil lucha por una nueva hegemonía', *OSAL*, 29, pp. 13–24.

Ollier, M. (2003) 'Argentina: Up a Blind Alley Once Again', *BLAR*, 22(2), pp. 170–186.

Ortíz Quintero, L. (2009) 'Los indígenas y la autonomía'. In Albertani, C., Rovira Sancho, G., and Modonesi, M. (eds) *La Autonomía Posible, reinvención política y emancipación* (México, DF: UAM), pp. 449–447.

Otero, G. (2004) 'Contesting Neoliberal Globalism from Below: The EZLN, Indian Rights and Citizenship'. In Otero, G. (ed.) *Mexico in Transition: Neoliberal Globalism, the State and Civil Society* (London and New York: Fernwood Publishing & Zed Books), pp. 221–235.

Ouviña, H. (2004) 'Zapatistas, Piqueteros y Sin Tierra. Nuevas radicalidades políticas en América Latina', *Cuadernos del Sur*, 25, pp. 103–127.

Ouviña, H. (2008) 'Las asambleas barriales y la construcción de lo "público no estatal": La experiencia en la ciudad Autónoma de Buenos Aires'. In Levy, B. and Gianatelli, N. (eds) *La política en movimiento. Identidades y experiencias de organización en América Latina* (Buenos Aires: CLACSO), pp. 65–108.

Ouviña, H. (2009) 'La autonomía urbana en territorio argentino'. In Albertani, C., Rovira Sancho, G., and Modonesi, M. (eds) *La Autonomía Posible. Reinvención política y emancipación* (México, DF: UAM), pp. 245–284.

Ozarow, D. (2014) '"When All They Thought Was Solid Melted into Air: Resisting Pauperization in Argentina during the 2002 Crisis", *Latin American Research Review* 49 (1), pp. 178–202.

Ozarow, D. and Croucher, R. (2014) 'Worker Recovered Companies and the Sociology of Work', *Sociology* 48(5), pp. 989–1007.

Palomino, H., Bleynat, I., Garro, S., and Giacomuzzi, C. (2010) 'The Universe of Worker-Recovered Companies in Argentina (2002–2008): Continuity and Changes Inside the Movement', *Affinities: A Journal of Radical Theory, Culture, and Action*, 4(1), pp. 252–287.

Pascual, R., Ghiotto, L., and Dinerstein, A.C. (2013) 'Municipio libre o Comunidades rebeldes autónomas? Los Zapatistas y la construcción del nosotros revolucionario, Mexico'. In Dinerstein, A.C. et al. *¿Movimientos sociales y autonomía colectiva. La política de la esperanza en América Latina* (Buenos Aires: Capital Intelectual), pp. 117–146.

Patzi Paco, F. (2004) *Sistema Comunal. Una Propuesta Alternativa al Sistema Liberal* (La Paz: CEA).

Patzi Paco, F. (2006) 'Las tendencias en el movimiento indígena en Bolivia'. In Ezcarza, F. and Gutiérrez, R. (eds) *Movimiento indígena en América Latina: resistencia y proyecto alternativo* (La Paz: Gobierno Federal/Casa Juan Pablos, BUAP, UNAM y UACM).

Peloso, R. (1997) 'A força que anima os Militantes', MST publication, October 1997, last accessed 2 May 2014, http://www.panuelosenrebeldia.com.ar/content/view/188/245/.

Pérez, M. (2006) 'La Ley de Participación Popular en una perspectiva indígena'. In Grammont, H. (ed.) *La construcción de la democracia en el campo latinoamericano* (Buenos Aires: CLACSO).

Petras, J. (1998) 'The Political and Social Basis for Regional Variation in Land Occupations in Brazil', *Journal of Peasant Studies*, 25(4), pp. 124–133.

Petras, J. and Veltmeyer, H. (2005) *Social Movements and State Power: Argentina, Brazil, Bolivia, Ecuador* (London: Pluto Press).

Picchetti, V. (2002) 'Fábricas tomadas, fábricas de esperanzas. La experiencia de Zanón y de Brukman'. In Carpintero, E., Hernández, M., and Petras, J.F. (eds) *Produciendo realidad: las empresas comunitarias* (Buenos Aires: Topia Editorial en colaboración con La Maza), pp. 11–23.

Pickerill, J. and Chatterton, P. (2006) 'Notes Towards Autonomous Geographies: Creation, Resistance and Self-Management as Survival Tactics', *Progress in Human Geography*, 30, pp. 730–746.

Pieterse, J.N.(1998) 'My Paradigm or Yours? Alternative Development, Post-Development, Reflexive Development', *Development and Change*, 29, pp. 343–337.

Pinassi, M.O. (2008) 'El MST y la completa destructividad del capital', *Herramienta*, 37, pp. 97–110.

Pizetta, A. (2007) 'A formaçâo política no MST: um proceso em construçâo', *OSAL*, 22, pp. 241–250.

Plotkin, M. (1995) 'Rituales políticos, imágenes y carisma: la celebración del 17 de Octubre y el imaginario Peronista 1945–1951'. In Torre, J. C. (ed.) *El 17 de Octubre de 1945* (Buenos Aires: Ariel), pp. 171–218.

Ponce de León, J. (ed.) (2001) *Our Word Is Our Weapon. Selected Writings from Subcomandante Marcos* (New York: Seven Stories Press).

Porto-Gonçalves, C.W. (2005) 'A Nova Questão agrária e a reinvenção do campesinato: o caso do MST', *OSAL*, 16, pp. 23–34.

Porto-Gonçalves, C.W. (2009) 'Del desarrollo a la autonomía: La reinvención de los territorios', *América Latina en Movimiento*, 445, last accessed 14 May 2014, http://alainet.org/publica/445.phtml.

Postone, M. (1993) *Time, Labour and Social Domination: A Reinterpretation of Marx's Critical Theory* (New York: Cambridge University Press).

Prada Alcoreza, R. (2010) 'Umbrales y horizontes de la descolonización'. In García Linera, Á., Prada Alcoreza, R., Tapia, L., and Vega Camacho, O. *El Estado, Campo du lucha* (La Paz: Comuna Muela del Diablo and CLACSO), pp. 41–94.

Prada Alcoreza, R. (2003) 'Perfiles del movimiento contemporáneo. El conflicto social y político en Bolivia' *OSAL* vol.13, pp. 35–40.

Prevost, G. (2012) 'Conclusion: Future Trends in Latin American Politics'. In Prevost, G., Oliva Campos, C., and Vanden, H. *Social Movements and Leftist Governments in Latin America: Confrontation or Co-optation?* (London and New York: Zed Books), pp. 169–174.

Puente, F. and Longa, F. (2007) 'El Alto: los dilemas del indigenismo urbano. Entre la insurrección y el clientelismo'. In Svampa, M. and Stefanoni, P. (eds) *Bolivia: Memoria, insurgencia y movimientos sociales* (Buenos Aires: CLACSO-El Colectivo), pp. 97–124.

Quijano, A. (2000a) 'Los movimientos campesinos contemporáneos en América Latina', *OSAL*, 2, pp. 171–180.

Quijano, A., (2000b) 'Coloniality of Power, Eurocentrism, and Latin America', *Nepantla: Views from South*, 1(3), pp. 533–580.

Quijano, A. (2006) 'Estado-Nación y "movimientos indígenas" en la región Andina: cuestiones abiertas', *OSAL*, 19, pp. 15–24.

Quijano, A. (2008) 'Coloniality of Power, Eurocentrism, and Latin America'. In Moraña, M., Dussel, E., and Jáuregui, C. (eds) *Coloniality at Large: Latin America and the Postcolonial Debate* (Durham, NC and London: Duke University Press), pp. 182–224.

Quijano, A. (2009) 'Otro horizonte de sentido histórico', *América Latina en Movimiento*, 441, last accessed 14 May 2014, http://www.alainet.org/publica/441.phtml.

Quispe, F. (2006) 'La lucha de los Ayllus Kataristas hoy'. In Ezcarza, F. and Gutiérrez Aguilar, R. (eds) *Movimiento indígena en América Latina: resistencia y proyecto alternativo* (La Paz: Gobierno Federal/Casa Juan Pablos, BUAP, UNAM & UACM).

Ramírez Cuevas, J. (2009) 'El espíritu libertario de los movimientos sociales de México (La autonomía no es una utopía)'. In Albertani, C., Rovira Sancho, G., and Modonesi, M. (eds) *La Autonomía Posible, reinvención política y emancipación* (México, DF: UAM), pp. 391–411.

Rancière, J. (1999) *Disagreement: Politics and Philosophy* (Minnesota and London: University of Minnesota Press).

Rancière, J. (2006) *Hatred of Democracy* (London: Verso).

Rancière, J. (2011a) 'The Thinking of Dissensus: Politics and Aesthetics'. In Bowman, P. and Stamp, R. (eds) *Reading Rancière* (London and New York: Continuum), pp. 11–17.

Rancière, J. (2011b) 'Democracy against Democracy'. In Agamben, G. et al., *Democracy: In What State?* (New York: Columbia University Press), pp. 76–81.

Rancière, J. (2001) 'Ten Theses on Politics', *Theory & Event*, 5(3), http://muse.jhu.edu.ezp1.bath.ac.uk/journals/theory_and_Event/v005/5.3ranciere.html

Regalado, R. (ed.) (2009) *América Latina hoy ¿reforma o revolución?* (Mexico: Ocean Sur).

Regalado, R. (2012) 'Hacia dónde van los gobiernos de izquierda progresistas?', *América Latina en Movimiento*, 475, last accessed 1 May 2014, http://alainet.org/publica/475.phtml.

Regalsky, P. (2003) *Etnicidad y clase. El Estado boliviano y las estrategias andinas de manejo de su espacio* (La Paz: CEIDIS/CESU-UMSS/CENDA and Plural Editores).

Regalsky, P. (2006) 'Bolivia indígena y campesina. El gobierno de Evo Morales', *Herramienta*, 31, pp. 13–38.

Regalsky, P. (2010) 'Political Processes and the Reconfiguration of the State in Bolivia', *Latin American Perspectives*, 172, 37(3), pp. 35–50.

Reichelt, H. (2005) 'Social Reality as Appearance: Some Notes on Marx's Conception of Reality'. In Bonefeld, W. and Psychopedis, K. (eds) *Human Dignity: Social Autonomy and the Critique of Capitalism* (Aldershot: Ashgate), pp. 31–68.

Revilla Herrero, C., Arteaga Aguilar, W., and Espósito Guevara, C. (2008) 'Del repudio a la alternativa: procesos de revalorización y proyección de nociones de autoridad en la organización vecinal alteña', *VillaLibre. Cuadernos de estudios sociales urbanos*, No. 2 (La Paz: Centro de Documentación e Información Bolivia [CEDIB]), pp. 22–48.

Reyes, A. (2012) 'Revolutions in the Revolutions: A Post-counterhegemonic Moment for Latin America?', *South Atlantic Quarterly*, 111(1), pp. 1–27.

Reygadas, L., Ramos, T., and Montoya, G. (2009) 'Pandora Box: The Implications of Social Movements on Development', *Social Movement Studies*, 8(3), pp. 225–241.

Richards, D. (1997) 'The Political Economy of Neo-liberalism in Latin America: A Critical Appraisal', *Capital & Class*, No. 61, pp. 19–43.

Richter, G. (2006) 'Can Hope Be Disappointed? Contextualising a Blochian Question', *Symploke*, 14(1–2), pp. 42–54.

Rivera Cusicanqui, S. (2012) 'Ch'ixinakax utxiwa: A Reflection on the Practices and Discourses of Decolonization', *South Atlantic Quarterly*, 111(1), pp. 95–109.

Roberts, K. (2009) 'Beyond Neoliberalism: Popular Responses to Social Change in Latin America'. In Burdick, P., Oxhorn, P., and and Roberts, K. (eds) *Beyond Neoliberalism in Latin America: Societies and Politics at the Crossroads* (New York: Palgrave Macmillan), pp. 1–16.

Robles, W. (2001) 'The Landless Rural Workers', Movement (MST) in Brazil', *Journal of Peasant Studies*, 28(2), pp. 146–161.

Rodgers, D. (2010) 'Contingent Democratisation? The Rise and Fall of Participatory Budgeting in Buenos Aires', *Journal of Latin American Studies*, 42, pp. 1–27.

Rodríguez, I. (ed.) (2001) *The Latin American Subaltern Studies Reader* (Durham, NC and London: Duke University Press).

Rodríguez Garavito, C. and Barret, P. (2007b) '¿La utopía revivida?'. In Rodríguez Garavito, C., Barret, P. and Chavez, D. *La nueva izquierda en América Latina* (Bogotá, Barcelona, Buenos Aires: Grupo Editorial Norma), pp. 15–66.

Roggero, G. (2010) 'Five Theses on the Common', *Rethinking Marxism*, 22(3), pp. 357–373.

Rosenthal, D. (ed.) (1971) *Materialism and the Mind-Body Problem* (Upper Saddle River, NJ: Prentice-Hall).

Ross, J. (2006) *Zapatistas! Making Another World Possible: Chronicles of Resistance 2000–2006* (New York: Nation Books).

Rossell Arce, P. (2012) '2011: El parteaguas del evismo? Bolivia después del conflicto del TIPNIS', *Nueva Sociedad*, 237, pp. 4–16.

Rosset, P. (2005) 'Moving Forward: Agrarian Reform and Food Sovereignty'. Land Research Action Network (LRAN) and Centre for the Study of Rural Change in Mexico (CECCAM), Mexico & Global Campaign for Agrarian Reform (GCR), Via Campesina/FLAN/LRAN.

Rosset, P. (2006a) 'Alternatives: Between the State and the Movement Below'. In Rosset, P., Patel, R. and Courville, M. (eds) *Promised Land: Competing Versions of Agrarian Reform* (Oakland, CA: Food First Books), pp. 221–224.

Rosset, P. (2006b) 'Moving Forward: Agrarian Reform as a Part of Food Sovereignty'. In Rosset, P., Patel, R., and Courville, M. (eds) *Promised Land: Competing Versions of Agrarian Reform* (Oakland, CA: Food First Books), pp. 301–321.

Rosset, P., Patel, R. and Courville, M. (eds) (2006) *Promised Land: Competing Versions of Agrarian Reform* (Oakland, CA: Food First Books).

Rothenberg, M.A. (2010) *The Excessive Subject: A New Theory of Social Change* (Cambridge: Polity Press).

Sader, E. (2001) 'Una democracia sin alma social'. In Sader, E. (ed.) *El ajuste estructural en América Latina. Costos sociales y alternativas* (Buenos Aires: CLACSO, ASDI), pp. 137–140.

Sader, E. (ed.) (2001) *El ajuste estructural en América Latina. Costos sociales y alternativas* (Buenos Aires: CLACSO, ASDI).

Sader, E. (2008) 'The Weakest Link? Neoliberalism in Latin America', *New Left Review*, 52, July/August.

Sader, E. (2012) 'Posneoliberalismo en Brasil', *América Latina en Movimiento*, 475, last accessed 3 May 2014, http://alainet.org/publica/475.phtml.

Sader, E. and Gentili, P. (eds) (2003) *La trama del neoliberalismo. Mercado, crisis y exclusión social* (Buenos Aires: CLACSO, EUDEBA).

Salas, C. (2000) 'El modelo de acumulación y el empleo en América Latina'. In De la Garza Toledo, E. (ed.) *Reestructuración productiva, mercado de trabajo y sindicatos en América Latina* (Buenos Aires: CLACSO), pp. 181–198.

Sampaio, P. (2005) 'La reforma agraria en América Latina: una revolución frustrada', *OSAL*, 16, pp. 15–22.

Sánchez, C. (2010) 'Autonomía y Pluralismo. Estados plurinacionales y pluriétnicos'. In González, M., Burguete Cal y Mayor, A., and Ortiz, P. (eds) *La Autonomía a debate* (Quito: FLACSO, GTZ, IWGIA, CIESAS, UNICH), pp. 259–287.

Santos, B. de S. (2000) *Crítica de La Razón Indolente: Contra El Desperdicio De La Experiencia* (Bilbao: Desclee de Brouwer).

Santos, B. de S. (2004) 'The World Social Forum: Toward a counter-hegemonic globalisation (PART I)'. In Sen, J., A. Anand, A. Escobar and P. Waterman (eds) *The World Social Forum: Challenging Empires* (New Delhi: Viveka Foundation), pp. 235–245, available at http://www.choike.org/documentos/wsf_s318_sousa.pdf, last accessed 20 August 2014.

Santos, B. de S. (2005) 'The Future of the World Social Forum: The Work of Translation', *Development*, 48(2), pp. 15–22.

Santos B. de S. (ed.) (2006a) *Another Production is Possible: Beyond the Capitalist Canon* (London: Verso), pp. 179–201.

Santos, B de S. (2006b) *Renovar la Teoría Crítica, Reinventar la emancipación social* (Buenos Aires: CLACSO).

Santos, B. de S. (ed.) (2007a) 'Reinventing Social Emancipation: Towards New Manifestos'. In Santos, B. de S. (ed.) *Democratising Democracy: Beyond the Neoliberal Democratic Canon* (London: Verso), pp. xvii–xxxiii.

Santos, B. de S. (2007b) 'Beyond Abyssal Thinking: From Global Lines to Ecology of Knowledges', *Eurozine*, 29 June, last accessed 5 May 2014, http://www.eurozine.com/articles/2007–06–29-santos-en.html.

Santos, B. de S. (2008) (ed.). *Another Knowledge Is Possible: Beyond Northern Epistemologies* (London: Verso).

Santos, B. de S., Arriscado Nunes, J., and Meneses, M.P. (2008) 'Introduction: Opening Up the Canon of Knowledge and Recognition of Difference'. In Santos, B. de S. (ed.) *Another Knowledge Is Possible: Beyond Northern Epistemologies* (London: Verso), pp. xvix–lxii.

Santos, B. de S. and Avritzer, L. (2007) 'Introduction: Opening Up the Canon of Democracy'. In *Democratising Democracy: Beyond the Liberal Democratic Canon* (London: Verso), pp. xxxiv–lxxiv.

Santos, B. de S. and Rodríguez Garavito, C. (2005) *Law and Globalization from Below: Towards a Cosmopolitan Legality* (Cambridge, New York, Melbourne: Cambridge University Press).

Santos, B. de S. and Rodríguez Garavito, C. (2006) 'Introduction: Expanding the Economic Canon and Searching for Alternatives to Neoliberal Globalisation'. In Santos, B. de S. (ed.) *Another Production Is Possible: Beyond the Capitalist Canon* (London: Verso), pp. xvii–lxii.

Sauer, S. (2006) 'The World Bank's Market-Based Land Reform in Brazil'. In Rosset, P., Patel, R., and Courville, M. (eds) *Promised Land: Competing Versions of Agrarian Reform* (Oakland, CA: Food First Books), pp. 177–207.

Schatan, W.J. (1998) *El Saqueo de América Latina* (Santiago de Chile: Universidad Arcis, LOM Ediciones).

Schwartzböck, S. (2008) *Adorno y lo político* (Buenos Aires: Prometeo).

Scott, J. (1985) *Weapons of the Weak: Everyday Forms of Peasant Resistance* (New Haven, CT and London: Yale University Press).

Scott, J. (1990) *Domination and the Arts of Resistance* (New Haven, CT and London: Yale University).

Seidel, K. (2011) '"The Impossible Only Takes a Little Longer", or What May Be Learned from the Argentine Experience of Justice', *Social Anthropology/ Anthropologie Sociale*, 19(3), pp. 305–312.

Seoane, J., Taddei, E., and Algranati, C. (2009) 'Los movimientos sociales latinoa-mericanos', *Centre Tricontinental (CETRI)*, 10 February, last accessed 1 January 2014, www.cetri.be/spip.php?article1045&lang=es.

Seoane, J., Taddei, E., and Algranati, C. (2011) 'Las nuevas configuraciones de los movimientos populares en America Latina', *Realidad Económica*, last accessed 14 January 2014, http://www.iade.org.ar/modules/noticias/article.php?storyid=3411.

Servolo Medeiros, L. (2000) 'Conflictos sociales rurales en el Brasil contem-poráneo', *OSAL*, 2, pp. 37–48.

Shukaitis, S. (2010) 'Sisyphus and the Labour of Imagination: Autonomy, Cultural Production, and the Antinomies of Worker Self-Management', *Affinities: A Journal of Radical Theory, Culture, and Action*, 4(1), pp. 57–82.

Silva, J.G. (1982) *A modernização dolorosa* (Rio de Janeiro: Zahar Editora).

Singh, P. (2005) 'Indigenous Rights and the Quest for Participatory Democracy in Latin America', *International Studies*, 42(1), pp. 61–76.

Sitrin, M. (ed.) (2006) *Horizontalism: Voices of Popular Power in Argentina* (Oakland, CA and Edinburgh: AK Press).

Sitrin, M. (2012) *Everyday Revolutions: Horizontalism and Autonomy in Argentina* (London and New York: Zed Books).

Slater, D. (1985) 'Social Movements and a Recasting of the Political'. In Slater, D (ed.) *New Social Movements and the State in Latin America* (CEDLA), pp. 1–25.

Slater, D. (1994) 'Power and Social Movements in the Other Occident: Latin America in an International Context', *Latin American Perspectives*, 21(2), pp.11–37.

Smith, W.C. and C. Acuña (1994) 'Future Politico-Economic Scenarios for Latin America'. In Smith, W. C., Acuña, C. and E. Gamarra (eds) (1994a) *Democray, Markets and Structural Reform in Latin America: Argentina, Bolivia, Brazil, Chile, and Mexico, (*Miami: University of Miami), pp. 1–28.

Smith, W., Acuña, C. and Gamarra, E. (eds) (1994a) *Democracy, Markets and Structural Reform in Latin America: Argentina, Bolivia, Brazil, Chile, and Mexico,* (Miami: University of Miami).

Smith, W.C., Acuña, C.H., and Gamarra, E.A. (eds) (1994b) *Latin American Political Economy in the Age of Neoliberal Reform,* (Boulder, CO: Lynne Reinner).

Solana, P. (2011) '2001–2011: Las dimensiones de la rebelión al calor de la experiencia de los movimientos barriales y de trabajadoras desocupadas', *Herramienta,* 46, pp. 41–52.

Solón, P. (2003) 'Radiografía de un febrero', *OSAL,* 10, pp. 15–28.

Spinney, L. (2005) 'How Time Flies', *The Guardian,* 24 February, pp. 8–9.

Spivak, G. and Zournazi, M. (2002) '"The Rest of the World" A Conversation with Gayatari Spivak'. In Zournazi, M., *Hope: New Philosophies for Change* (Annandale, NSW: Pluto Press Australia), pp. 172–191.

Spronk, S., and Webber, J. (2007) 'Struggles against Accumulation by Dispossession in Bolivia: The Political Economy of Natural Resource Contention', *Latin American Perspectives,* 34(2), pp. 31–47.

Stahler-Sholk, R. (2007) 'Resisting Neoliberal Homogeneization: The Zapatista Autonomy Movement', *Latin American Perspectives,* 34, pp. 48–63.

Stahler-Sholk, R., Vanden, H., and Kuecker, G. (2007) 'Globalizing Resistance: The New Politics of Social Movements in Latin America', *Latin American Perspectives,* 34(2), pp. 5–16.

Stahler-Sholk, R., Vanden, H., and Kuecker, G. (eds) (2008a) *Latin American Social Movements in the Twenty-First Century: Resistance, Power, and Democracy* (London: Rowman & Littlefield).

Stahler-Sholk, R., Vanden, H., and Kuecker, G. (2008b) 'Introduction', *Latin American Social Movements in the Twenty-First Century: Resistance, Power, and Democracy* (London: Rowman & Littlefield), pp. 1–16.

Standing, G. (2011) *The Precariat: The New Dangerous Class* (London: Bloomsbury Academic).

Stavenhagens, R. (2006) 'Indigenous People: Land, Territory, Autonomy and Self-Determination'. In Rosset, P., Patel, R., and Courville, M. (eds) *Promised Land: Competing Versions of Agrarian Reform* (Oakland, CA: Food First Books), pp. 208–217.

Stavrakakis, Y. (2007) *The Lacanian Left: Essays on Psychoanalysis and Politics* (Albany, NY: SUNY Press).

Stédile, J.P. (2004) 'El MST y las disputas por las alternativas en Brasil', *OSAL,* 13, pp. 31–39.

Stédile, J.P. (2005) *A questão agrária no Brasil, Vol. III – Programas de reforma agrária: 1946–2003* (São Paulo: Ediciones Expressão Popular).

Stédile, J.P. (2007) 'El gobierno de Lula no tiene un proyecto popular', *América Latina en Movimiento,* 10 November, last accessed 1 May 2014, http://alainet. org/active/20154&lang=es.

Stédile, J.P. (2009) 'MST: 25 años de obstinación', *América Latina en Movimiento,* 1 August, last accessed 14 May 2014, http://alainet.org/active/28342.

Stédile, J.P. (2012) 'Balanço do ano velho e perspectivas para 2012', last accessed 5 May 2012, http://www.youtube.com/watch?v=GRKiEy6oY98&sns=fb2).

Stédile, J.P. (2013) 'Dilma, no entregue nuestro presal a empresas extranjeras', *América Latina en Movimiento*, 28 September, http://www.alainet.org/active/67716.

Stefanoni, P (2007) 'Siete preguntas y siete respuestas sobre la Bolivia de Evo Morales', *Revista Nueva Sociedad*, No. 209, pp. 46–65, last accessed 15 May 2014, http://www.nuso.org/upload/articulos/3429_1.pdf.

Stengers, I. and Zournazi, M. (2002) 'A "Cosmo-Politics" – Risk, Hope, Change: A Conversation with Isabelle Stengers'. In Zournazi, M., *Hope: New Philosophies for Change* (Annandale, NSW: Pluto Press Australia), pp. 244–272.

Ströbele-Gregor, J. (2001) 'De indio a actor político. Sobre los procesos de transformación de las organizaciones indígenas en los países andinos'. In Fahmel, B., Dresler, W., and Noack, C. (eds) *Identidades étnicas. Transformaciones en América Latina* (Mexico and Berlin: UNAM, IAI).

Stubrin, F. (2008) 'Movimiento de los Trabajadores Rurales Sin Tierra: Una experiencia alternativa de educación publica', *Ensayos e Investigaciones*, No. 28 (Buenos Aires: Laboratorio de Políticas Públicas).

Subcomandante Insurgente Marcos (SIM) (1996a) *First Declaration of La Realidad for Humanity and against Neoliberalism*, last accessed 20 March 2014, http://flag.blackened.net/revolt/mexico/ezln/ccrl_1st_dec_real.html.

Subcomandante Insurgente Marcos (1996b) 'Second Declaration of La Realidad for Humanity and Against Neoliberalism'. In Ponce de León, J. (ed.) (2001) *Our Word Is Our Weapon. Selected Writings from Subcomandante Marcos* (New York: Seven Stories Press), pp. 124–132.

Subcomandante Insurgente Marcos (1997) 'Why We Are Fighting: The Fourth World War Has Begun', *Le Monde diplomatique,* last accessed, 18 June 2013, http://mondediplo.com/1997/09/marcos.

Subcomandante Insurgente Marcos (2001) 'The Seven Loose Pieces of the Global Jigsaw Puzzle (Neoliberalism as a Puzzle: The Useless Global Unity Which Fragments and Destroys Nations)', *Chiapas Revealed*, No. 1, last accessed 14 May 2014, http://flag.blackened.net/revolt/mexico/ezln/1997/jigsaw.html.

Subcomandante Insurgente Marcos and the Zapatistas (2006) *The Other Campaign/ La Otra Campaña* (San Francisco, CA: City Lights Books).

Svampa, M. and Pereyra, S. (2003) *Entre la ruta y el barrio. La experiencia de las organizaciones Piqueteras* (Buenos Aires: Biblos).

Swords, A. (2007) 'Neo-Zapatista Network Politics: Transforming Democracy and Development', *Latin American Perspectives,* 34(2), pp. 78–93.

Tapia, L. (2007) 'Los movimientos sociales en la coyuntura del gobierno del MAS', *Wilka* No 1, CADES, La Paz (El Alto).

Taussig, M. and Zournazi, M. (2002) '"Carnival of the Sense". A conversation with Michael Taussig'. In Zournazi, M. *Hope: New Philosophies for Change* (Annandale, NSW: Pluto Press Australia), pp. 42–63.

Tavares Ribeiro Soares, L. (2001) 'Os custos socias do ajuste neoliberal no Brasil'. In Sader, E. (2001) (ed.) *El ajuste estructural en América Latina. Costos sociales y alternativas,* (Buenos Aires: CLACSO, ASDI, pp. 171–185.

Tavares, J. (2014) '"El capital está imponiendo el agronegocio como la única forma de producir" Interview with Pedro Stédile', 6 February, *América Latina en Movimiento,* last accessed 1 May 2014, http://www.alainet.org/active/71127&lang=es.

Tedesco, L. (1999) *Democracy in Argentina: Hope and Disillusion* (London: Frank Cass).

Teubal, M. (1986) *Crisis y Deuda Externa: América Latina en la Encrucijada* (Buenos Aires: IDES).

Teubal, M. (2000) 'Structural Adjustment and Social Disarticulation: The Case of Argentina', *Science and Society*, 64(4), pp. 460–488.

Thomas, P. (2009) *The Gramscian Moment: Philosophy, Hegemony and Marxism* (Leiden: Brill).

Thompson, P. (2009) 'Introduction'. In Bloch, E. *Atheism in Christianity* (London and New York: Verso) [Translated from *Das Prinzip Hoffnung*, Vol. 3, (Frankfurt am Main: Surhkamp), 1959 by J.T.Swann].

Thompson, P. and Žižek, S. (2013) *The Privatization of Hope: Ernst Bloch and the Future of Utopia* (Durham, NC and London: Duke University Press).

Thwaites Rey, M. (2001) *Alas rotas. La política de privatización y quiebra de Aerolíneas Argentinas* (Buenos Aires, Editorial Temas).

Thwaites Rey, M. (2003) La (des)ilusión privatista. *El experimento neoliberal en la Argentina* (Buenos Aires, EUDEBA).

Thwaites Rey, M. (2004) *La Autonomía como búsqueda y el Estado como contradicción* (Buenos Aires: Prometeo).

Tischler, S. (2001) 'La "sociedad Civil": ¿Fetiche? ¿Sujeto?', *Bajo el Volcán*, 3, pp. 169–181.

Tischler, S. (2005) 'Time of Reification and Time of Insubordination: Some Notes'. In Bonefeld, W. and Psychopedis, K. (eds) (2005) *Human Dignity: Social Autonomy and the Critique of Capitalism* (Aldershot: Ashgate), pp. 131–146.

Tischler, S. (2008) 'The Crisis of the Classical Cannon of the Class Form and Social Movements in Latin America'. In Bonefeld, W. (ed.) *Subverting the Present–Imagining the Future: Insurrection, Movement, Commons* (New York: Autonomedia), pp. 161–178.

Tischler, S. (2009) 'Adorno: The Conceptual Prison of the Subject, Political Fetishism and Class Struggle'. In Holloway, J., Matamoros, F., and Tischler, S. (eds) *Negativity and Revolution: Adorno and Politics* (London: Pluto Press), pp. 103–121.

United Nations-NGLS (2010) *Decent Work and Fair Globalization: A Guide to Policy Dialogue* (Geneva: United Nations) Hamish Jenkins.

Upchurch, M., Daguerre, A., and Ozarow, D. (2014) 'Spectrum, Trajectory and the Role of the State in Workers' Self-Management', *Labour History*, 55(1), pp. 47–66.

Valencia García, G. (2007) *Entre Cronos y Kairós. Las formas del tiempo sociohistórico* (México, DF: UNAM, Anthropos Editorial).

Vázquez, R. (2011) 'Translation as Erasure: Thoughts on Modernity's Epistemic Violence', *Journal of Historical Sociology* 24, pp. 27–44.

Vega Cantor, R. (2004) '¿Es posible conciliar la tradición con la revolución? A propósito de "Conduce tu carro y tu arado sobre los huesos de los muertos" de John Holloway', *Herramienta*, 25, pp. 185–196.

Vega Cantor, R. (2009) 'Crisis civilizatoria', *Herramienta*, 42, last accessed 14 May 2014, http://www.herramienta.com.ar/revista–herramienta–n–42/crisis–civilizatoria.

Veltmeyer, H. (2004) 'Globalization and Mobilisation: In Response to Susan Eckstein', *Labouragain*, last accessed 20 August 2014http://www.iisg.nl/labouragain/globalisation.php.

Veltmeyer, H. (2007) *On the Move: The Politics of Social Change in Latin America* (Ontario: Broadview Press).

Veltmeyer, H. (2008) 'La dinámica de las ocupaciones de tierras en América Latina'. In Moyo, S. and Yeros, P. (eds) *Recuperando la tierra. El resurgimiento de movimientos rurales en África, Asia y América Latina* (Buenos Aires: CLACSO), pp. 301–334.

Veltmeyer, H., Petras, J., and Vieux, S. (1997) *Neoliberalism and Class Conflict in Latin America* (Basingstoke and London: Palgrave Macmillan).

Viaña, J. and Orozco, S. (2007) 'El cierre de un ciclo y la compleja relación movimientos sociales-gobierno en Bolivia', *OSAL*, 22, pp. 119–129.

Vietta, M. And Ruggeri, A. (2009) 'The Worker-Recuperated Enterprises as Workers Cooperatives'. In McMurtry, J. and Reed, D. (eds) *Cooperatives in a Global Economy: The Challenges of Cooperation across Borders* (Newcastle: Cambridge Scholar Press), pp. 178–225.

Wallerstein, I. (1974) *The Modern World-System I: Capitalist Agriculture and the Origins of the European World-Economy in the Sixteenth Century* (New York: Academic Press).

Walsh, K. (2012) '"Other" Knowledges, "Other" Critiques: Reflections on the Politics and Practices of Philosophy and Decoloniality in the "Other" America', *Trasmodernity*, 1(3), pp. 11–27.

Warren, K. and Jackson, J.E. (eds) (2002) *Indigenous Movements, Self-Representation, and the State in Latin America* (Austin, TX: University of Texas Press).

Weber, K. (2013) 'Chiquitano and the Multiple Meanings of Being Indigenous', *BLAR*, 32(2), pp. 194–209.

Webber, J. (2011a) *Red October: Left-Indigenous Struggle in Modern Bolivia* (Leiden: Brill).

Webber, J. (2011b) *From Rebellion to Reform: Class Struggle, Indigenous Liberation and the Poltics of Evo Morales* (Chicago: Haymarket Books).

Webber, J. (2012) 'Revolution against "Progress"': The TIPNIS Struggle and Class Contradictions in Bolivia', *International Socialism*, 133, January, last accessed 1 May 2012, http://www.isj.org.uk/?id=780.

Weeks, K. (2011) *The Problem with Work: Feminism, Marxism, Antiwork Politics and Postwork Imaginaries* (Durham, NC and London: Duke University Press).

Weyland, K. (1996) 'Neopopulism and Neoliberalism in Latin America: Unexpected Affinities', *Studies in Comparative International Development*, 31(3), pp. 3–31.

Weyland, K. (2004) 'Assessing Latin American Neoliberalism: Introduction to the Debate', *Latin American Research Review*, 39(3): 143–149.

Wolford, W. (2003a) 'Families, Fields, and Fighting for Land: The Spatial Dynamics of Contention in Rural Brazil', *Mobilization*, 8(2), pp.157–172.

Wolford, W. (2003b) 'Producing Community: The MST and Land Reform Settlements in Brazil', *Journal of Agrarian Change*, 3(4), pp. 500–520.

Wright, E.O. (2010) *Envisioning Real Utopias* (London and New York: Verso).

Wright, E.O. (2013) 'Transforming Capitalism through Real Utopias', American Sociological Association, Presidential Address 2012, *American Sociological Review*, 78(1), pp. 1–25.

Wylde, C. (2011) 'State, Society and Markets in Argentina: The Political Economy of *Neodesarrollismo* under Néstor Kirchner 2003–2007', *BLAR*, 30(4), pp. 436–452.

Yashar, D. (2005) *Contesting Citizenship in Latin America: The Rise of Indigenous Movements in the Post-neoliberal Challenge* (New York: Cambridge University Press).

Yépez Mariaca, O. (2010) "El ayllu reterritorializado y su taypi, la ciudad de El Alto', *Villalibre, Cuadernos de estudios sociales urbanos*, 5, pp. 99–117.

Young, K. and Schwartz, M. (2012) 'Can Prefigurative Politics Prevail? The Implications for Movement Strategy in John Holloway's *Crack Capitalism*', *Journal of Classical Sociology*, 12(2), pp. 220–239.

Zapata, F. (2004) '¿Crisis del sindicalismo en América Latina?', *Labour Again*, last accessed 10 July 2013, http://www.iisg.nl/labouragain/crisis.php.

Zapatistas (2006) 'Tomorrow Begins Today (Closing Remarks at the First Intercontinental *Encuentro* for Humanity and against Neoliberalism)'. In Ponce de León, J. (ed.) *Our Word Is Our Weapon. Selected Writings from Subcomandante Marcos* (New York: Seven Stories Press), pp. 115–121.

Zibechi, R. (1998) 'El Movimiento Sin Tierra: una nueva vida en esta vida', *Viento Sur*, 39, pp. 7–16.

Zibechi, R. (2003a) *Genealogía de la revuelta. Argentina: la sociedad en movimiento* (La Plata – Montevideo: Letra Libre – Nordan-Comunidad).

Zibechi, R. (2003b) 'Los Movimientos sociales latinoamericanos: Tendencias y desafíos', *OSAL* 9, pp. 185–188.

Zibechi, R. (2007) *Autonomías y emancipaciones. América Latina en Movimiento* (Lima: Universidad Nacional Mayor de San Marcos, FEFCS).

Zibechi, R. (2010) 'Los días que parieron una década', *LaVaca*, 20 December, last accessed 7 March 2014, http://www.lavaca.org/notas/19–y–20–los–dias–que–parieron–una–decada/.

Zibechi, R. (2012) *Territories in Resistance: Cartography of Latin American Social Movements*. (Oakland, CA: AK Press).

Zipes, J. (1988) 'Introduction: Toward a Realization of Anticipatory Illumination'. In Bloch, E. (ed.) *The Utopian Function of Art and Literature: Selected Essays*, trans. by Zipes, J. and Mecklenburg, F. (London: MIT Press), pp. xi–xliii.

Žižek, S. (2000) *Looking Awry* (Cambridge,US: the MIT Press).

Žižek, S. (2008) *In Defence of Lost Causes* (London and New York: Verso).

Zournazi, M. (2002) *Hope: New Philosophies for Change* (Annandale, NSW: Pluto Press Australia).

Index

271

Made in the USA
San Bernardino, CA
16 April 2019